ORGANIZED OBSESSIONS

ORGANIZED OBSESSIONS

1,001 Offbeat Associations,

Fan Clubs, and

Microsocieties You Can Join

Deborah M. Burek
Martin Connors

with Christa Brelin

DETROIT   WASHINGTON, D.C.   LONDON

ORGANIZED OBSESSIONS

1,001 Offbeat Associations,

Fan Clubs, and

Microsocieties You Can Join

Published by **Visible Ink Press** ™
a division of Gale Research Inc.
835 Penobscot Building
Detroit, MI 48226–4094

ISBN 0–8103–9415–4

Art Director: Arthur Chartow
Design Supervisor: Cynthia Baldwin
Interior Design: Kathleen A. Hourdakis
Cover Design: Cynthia Baldwin
Cover Illustration by: Eric Hanson

Introduction

What do the Amalgamated Flying Saucer Clubs of America, the Annette Funicello Fan Club, Blue Blazes Irregulars, Children of the Green Earth, and the Dinosaur Society have in common? Well, for starters, in an alphabetic list they would all fall toward the front. More importantly, they represent that peculiar human impulse to further a cause or concern by organizing into a group. Divided we fall; united we can raise a much louder ruckus and collect the benefits of increased socialization (hanging out with our pals, bestowing awards, collecting dues).

Americans are joiners; while we value individuality highly enough to protect it by law, we like individuality even better when we can practice it with a group of people just like us. French scholar Alexis de Tocqueville made a note of this aspect of the national character some 160 years ago. "Americans of all ages, all conditions, and all dispositions are forever forming associations ... There are not only commercial and manufacturing companies ... but associations of a thousand other kinds – religious, moral, serious, futile, restricted." *Organized Obsessions* describes those associations that are somewhat off the beaten track, covering serious and not so serious groups advocating any number of just and sometimes scurrilous causes, including nudism, adventurism, environmentalism, and many other *isms* worth noting, as well as sugar-packet collecting. It's that kind of book.

According to statistics compiled by the editors of the *Encyclopedia of Associations*, more than 80 percent of Americans belong to some organization. At least 2,500 of us belong to the American Gourd Society, whose members are interested in making things out of gourds. The 3,000 members of Messies Anonymous are part of a self help group for the chronically disorganized. The 600 individuals in The One Shoe Crew take part in a shoe exchange for people with mismatched feet or who wear only one shoe (due to having only one foot). The 700 members of the Society for the Eradication of Television would like to make prime time a distant memory, advocating that we throw our television sets through the window and out of our lives. The 500 Bobs of Bobs International, the 15,000 Mikes of Mikes of America, and the 1,500 Jim Smiths of the Jim Smith Society celebrate the commonality of a name.

For groups charged with a political or commercial mission (such as the Better World Society, the Coalition to Stop Government Waste, the National Hemlock Society, or the Mushroom Caucus), mass is important for making the point and providing support. *Organized Obsessions* describes the growing men's movement (Male Liberation Foundation, National Organization for Changing Men) and the spectrum of groups pushing for further women's rights (one such is Emily's List, which supplies campaign seed money for female candidates). Some groups listed want to stop cosmetic and other testing on animals, while other associations are making a stand for a better environment. Senior citizen rights receive their due with such groups as Grandmothers for Peace, Grandparents Anonymous, and the Grey Panthers. And commercially oriented organizations such as the Loyal Order of Catfish Lovers (eat more catfish) and the Dairy Shrine (drink more milk) are also represented. And speaking of food, Lovers of the Stinking Rose promotes the use of garlic, an herb with mixed PR.

The group setting is perfect for collectors; we can show off our collection to an appreciative audience ("Let's have a nice round of applause for Mr. Darwimple, for sharing his sugar packet collection with us"), do some swapping, and pick up valuable information on collectibles. *Organized Obsessions* covers groups advocating the collection of animal licenses, spark plugs, pencils, locks, toothpicks, spoons, marbles, elephant memorabilia, barbed wire, Barbie dolls, bricks, hand fans, antique door knobs, cigarette packs, lighters, matches, cookie cutters, milk bottles, beer bottles, beer cans, pop cans, bottle caps, bottle openers, corkscrews, objects depicting frogs, fishing lures, wooden money, and many other items too numerous to mention, including sugar packets.

To function successfully, fan clubs also need people; although one fan can make a club, only the lonely need attend. Those who worship Elvis or Englebert or Cher or the Cowsills or the crew of the Starship *Enterprise* or various dead presidents or Mr. Ed find that devotion to the cause (obsessive admiration) is more fun and more socially acceptable when done in a group setting. One person doing his or her thing might be defined as an oddball, whereas 20 people is a consensus not to be messed with. And then you have those obsessed with a particular activity: kite flying, bicycle riding, ballooning, walking, hugging, laughing, sandcastle building, paintballing, sled dog racing, stiltwalking, and swimming in extremely cold water are among a few of the physical obsessions represented by an association.

Organized Obsessions also covers groups dedicated to the absurd: Ladies Against Women, the Committee for Immediate Nuclear War, the American Association of Aardvark Aficionados, the Church of Monday Night Football, the Free Territory of Ely – Chatelaine, the Institute of Totally Useless Skills, the International Brotherhood of Old Bastards, International Dull Folks Unlimited, the Ancient and Honourable Order of Small Castle Owners of Great Britain, the International Organization of Nerds, the National FRUMPS of America, and the International Stop Continental Drift Society are but a few of the tongue-somewhat-in-cheek associations covered. Add totally serious groups tracking Bigfoot, spotting UFOs, investigating the paranormal, promoting the New Age, advocating alternative sexual practices, or trying to reach Americans with the news that the world is flat, and you have an unusual stew of Americana, "Real People" style (with lots of gravy).

From the surreal to the serious to the strange, *Organized Obsessions* covers the downsizing of American culture by taking a look at 1,001 associations representing millions of individuals. *Organized Obsessions* is the perfect book for people looking for that special group to join, or for those who were unaware that others share their particular fascination or cause (for instance, sugar-packet collecting). Best of all, *Organized Obsessions* is a book for those who just like to browse and contemplate the unusual, the unlikely, and the occasionally underground micro-slices of everyday life.

People We Would Like To Thank   Thank you Christa Brelin for helping make the book; thank you Don Dillaman for expert information processing; thank you Mike Boyd (and ATLIS) for the usual exact and prompt typesetting; thank you Stephanie Sabra for making dozens of telephone calls; thank you Peggy Kneffel Daniels, Karen Troshynski, Jacqueline Barrett, and Holly Selden for research support; thank you Mary Beth Trimper and Evi Seoud for your efforts; and thank you to those associations who so enthusiastically provided us with information on their activities (or lack of them).

A Last Note   Research was based on groups found in Gale Research's *Encyclopedia of Associations,* the premier directory to associations, listing more than 20,000 in three massive volumes. Addresses and phone numbers for associations often change as the officers of the organizations change. Within *Organized Obsessions,* three or four bonus organizations are listed without addresses. Although we believe these organizations are still active, they have disappeared with no forwarding address. Anyone having information on these groups is invited to send it in to *Organized Obsessions,* care of Visible Ink Press. Anyone having really unusual sugar packets, pleased contact the Sugar Packet Collectors Club (page 243).

Abbott and Costello Fan Club
Absurd Special Interest Group
Abundantly Yours
Academy of Accounting Historians
Academy of Psychic Arts and Sciences
Academy of Science Fiction, Fantasy, and
    Horror Films
Accordion Federation of North America
ACT UP
Adult Video Association
Agatha Christie Appreciation Society
    Postern of Murder
Air Mail Pioneers
Aladdin Knights of the Mystic Light
Alan Thicke Fan Club
Alferd E. Packer Society
All American Association of Contest Judges
All Together
Alternative Resource Center
Alternative to the New York Times
    Committee
Always Causing Legal Unrest
Amalgamated Flying Saucer Clubs of
    America
American Accordion Musicological Society
American Accordionists' Association
American Alligator Farmers Association
American Alpine Club
American Armwrestling Association
American Association - Electronic Voice
    Phenomena
American Association for Parapsychology
American Association of Aardvark
    Aficionados
American Association of Handwriting
    Analysts
American Association of Meta-Science
American Atheists
American Banjo Fraternity
American Barefoot Club
American Bladesmith Society
American Breweriana Association
American Business Card Club
American Carousel Society
American Citizens Committee on Reducing
    Debt
American Coaster Enthusiasts
American Collectors of Infant Feeders
American Council of Spotted Asses

American Crime Fighters
American Divorce Association of Men
American Fancy Rat and Mouse Association
American Federation of Astrologers
American Go Association
American Gourd Society
American Guild of English Handbell Ringers
American Hair Loss Council
American Handwriting Analysis Foundation
American Hobbit Association
American Humor Studies Association
American International Checkers Society
American Kitefliers Association
American Lock Collectors Association
American Mead Association American Mensa
American Miniature Horse Association
American Miniature Horse Registry
American Name Society
American Ostrich Association
American Pain Society
American Pencil Collectors Society
American Physicians Poetry Association
American Poultry Historical Society
American Puffer Alliance
American Roque League
American Rubberband Duckpin Bowling
    Congress
American Satellite Television Alliance
American Sleep Disorders Association
American Society for Psychical Research
American Society of Dowsers
American Spoon Collectors
American Sunbathing Association
American Tolkien Society
American Wooden Money Guild
Americans Combatting Terrorism
Americans for Decency
Americans for Nonsmokers' Rights
America's Society of Separated and
    Divorced Men
AMOA - International Flipper Pinball
    Association
Amputee Shoe and Glove Exchange
Ancient and Honourable Order of Small
    Castle Owners of Great Britain
Ancient Astronaut Society
The Angel Planes
Animal Liberation
Annette Funicello Fan Club

Anonymous Families History Project
Antique and Art Glass Salt Shaker Collectors
  Society
Antique Doorknob Collectors of America
Antique Wireless Association
Aquarian Research Foundation
Archonist Club
Art Dreco Institute
Assassination Archives and Research Center
Association for Astrological Psychology
Association for Gravestone Studies
Association for Research and Enlightenment
Association for the Study of Dada and
  Surrealism
Association for the Study of Food and Society
Association for Transpersonal Psychology
Association of Acrobats
Association of Balloon and Airship
  Constructors
Association of Black Storytellers
Association of Bottled Beer Collectors
Association of Brewers
The Association of Comedy Artists
Association of Concern for Ultimate Reality
  and Meaning
Association of Old Crows
Association of Oldetime Barbell and
  Strongmen
Association of Space Explorers - U.S.A.
Astro-Psychology Institute
Astromusic
Atlantis Research Group
Awareness Research Foundation
Baker Street Irregulars
Bald-Headed Men of America
Balloon Post Collectors Club
Barbara Eden International Fan Club
Barber Coin Collector Society
Baronial Order of Magna Charta
Baseball Hall of SHAME
Bass'n Gal
Bat Conservation International
Beach Boys Stomp Fan Club
BeachFront U.S.A.
Beauty Without Cruelty U.S.A.
Beaver Defenders
Beer Can Collectors of America
Beer Drinkers of America
Benevolent and Loyal Order of Pessimists
Best Candidate Committee
Better World Society
Bicycle Network
Big Deal
Big Thicket Association
Bikers Against Manslaughter
Black Filmmakers Hall of Fame, Inc.
Black Rock Coalition
Bloomsday Club
Blue Blazes Irregulars
Bobs International
Bohemia Ragtime Society
Boise Peace Quilt Project
Bonsai Clubs International

Borderland Sciences Research Foundation
Boring Institute
Boston Star Trek Association
Bowhunters Who Care
Bram Stoker Memorial Association
Bread and Roses
Brewmeisters Anonymous
Brewster Society
Brotherhood of Knights of the Black Pudding
  Tasters
Brotherhood of the Knights of the Vine
Bull Elephants
Bureau of the Budget in Exile Unrequited
  Marching and Chowder Society
Burlesque Historical Society
Burlington Liar's Club
Bus History Association
Business Card Collectors International
Butterfly Lovers International
Buxom Belles, International
Caithness Paperweight Collectors Society
California Wilderness Survival League
Campaign for World Government
Cartoonists Northwest
Cash Free America
Catalyst
Catgut Acoustical Society
Center for Bigfoot Studies
Center for Reflection on the Second Law
Central Intelligence Retirees Association
Cher'd Interest
Cherokee National Historical Society
Children of the Confederacy
Children of the Green Earth
C.H.U.C.K.
Church of Monday Night Football
Cigarette Pack Collectors Association
Circumnavigators Club
Circus Fans Association of America
Circus Historical Society
Circus Model Builders, International
Citizens Against Government Waste
Citizens Against PAC's
Citizens Against UFO Secrecy
Citizens for a Debt Free America
Citizens for a Drug Free America
Citizens for Common Sense
Citrus Label Society
Civil War Token Society
Classic Bicycle and Whizzer Club of America
Clowns of America, International
Club of the Friends of Ancient Smoothing
  Irons
Coalition for Non-Violent Food
Coalition to Abolish the Draize Rabbit
  Blinding Tests
Coalition to Protect Animals in Entertainment
Coalition to Stop Government Waste
Coca-Cola Collectors Club International
The Coin Coalition
Coleopterists' Society
Collectors of Unusual Data - International
Colonial Order of the Acorn

Columbus: Countdown 1992

Combined Organizations of Numismatic Error Collectors of America

Comedy Prescription

Comedy Writers Association

Committee Against Registration and the Draft

Committee for a Voluntary Census

Committee for Immediate Nuclear War

Committee for National Arbor Day

Committee for the Advancement of Role-Playing Games

Committee for the Scientific Investigation of Claims of the Paranormal

Committee on Public Doublespeak

Committee on the Present Danger

Community Dreamsharing Network

Companions of Doctor Who Fan Club

Compassion for Animals Campaign

Concerned American Indian Parents

Concerned Pet Owners' Association

Confederate Stamp Alliance

Consciousness Research and Training Project

Conservative Action Foundation

Constantian Society

Cookie Cutter Collectors Club

Coronary Club

Council for a Livable World

Council for Alternatives to Stereotyping in Entertainment

Count Dracula Fan Club

Count Dracula Society

Countdown 2001

Cowboy Artists of America

Cowboys for Christ

Cowsills Fan Club

Crazy Horse Memorial Foundation

Crossword Club

Crowncap Collectors Society International

Crystal StarGate

Cult Awareness Network

Dairy Shrine

Dean Martin Association

Death Row Support Project

Debtors Anonymous

Dedicated Wooden Money Collectors

DeLorean Motor Club of America

Depression After Delivery

Desert Fishes Council

Dignity After Death

Dinosaur Society

Diving Dentists Society

DOC (Doctors Ought to Care)

Dracula and Company

Dream Factory

Drug Policy Foundation

Dude Ranchers' Association

E. P. Impersonators Association International

Earth Save Earthstewards Network

Earthwatch

Eastern Coast Breweriana Association

Edsel Owner's Club

Elephant Interest Group

Eleventh Commandment Fellowship

Elves', Gnomes', and Little Men's Science Fiction, Chowder and Marching Society

Elvira Fan Club

Elvis Lives on Fan Club

Elvis Our Guardian AngEL, Elvis Presley Fan Club

Elvis Presley Burning Love Fan Club

Elvis Teddy Bears

Elvisly Yours

Emil Verban Society

EMILY's List

Emotions Anonymous

Empire State Tattoo Club of America

Engelbert's Goils

The Engelettes

Engel's Angels in Humperdinck Heaven Fan Club

Enterprise II International

Ephemera Society of America

Eric's Wasted Worldwide Repair Society

Ernest Fan Club

Errors, Freaks and Oddities Collector's Club

Escapees, Inc.

Exotic Dancers League of America

Experimental Aircraft Association

Explorers Club

Extra Miler Club

Fabulous Fifties Ford Club of America

Fair-Witness Project

Fairy Investigation Society

Famous Personalities' Business Card Collectors of America

Fan Association of North America

Fan Tek

Far and Wide Tape Club

Fat Lip Readers Theater

Fathers Day Council

Feathered Pipe Foundation

Federation of Historical Bottle Clubs

Fellowship for Intentional Community

Ferret Fanciers Club

Figural Bottle Openers Collectors Club

Finding Our Own Ways

Fire Collectors Club

Fire Mark Circle

First Fandom

Flat Earth Research Society International

Floating Homes Association

Fly Without Fear

Flying Chiropractors Association

Flying Dentists Association

Flying Eagle and Indian Head Cent Collectors

Flying Funeral Directors of America

Flying Physicians Association

Flying Veterinarians Association

Football Hall of Shame

The FORUM

The Fossils

Foundation for Research on the Nature of Man

Fran Lee Foundation

Franchise of Americans Needing Sports

Free Territory of Ely-Chatelaine

Freedom From Religion Foundation
Friends of Astrology
Friends of Old-Time Radio
Friends of the Tango
Friends of the Trees Society
Frog Pond - Frog Collectors Club
Front Striker Bulletin
Frontlash
Fund for Constitutional Government
Fund for Open Information and
   Accountability
Fund for UFO Research
Fundamentalists Anonymous
Fur Farm Animal Welfare Coalition
Galactic Hitchhiker's Guild
The Galactic Society
Gamblers Anonymous
Gambling Chip Collectors Association
Gay and Lesbian History on Stamps Club
Gaylactic Network
Ghost Research Society
Gilligan's Island Fan Club
The Giraffe Project
Girl Friends
Girth and Mirth
Globetrotters' Club
Gnomes Anonymous
Gold Prospectors Association of America
Golden Companions
Golden Rule Foundation
Golden Rule Society
Goldfish Society of America
Good Bears of the World
Good Samaritan Coalition
Goose and Gander, Society for the
   Preservation of First Wives and First
   Husbands
Government Accountability Project
Graham Brothers Truck and Bus Club
Grandmothers for Peace
Grandparents Anonymous
Gray Panthers
Greater Washington, DC Association of
   Professionals Practicing the Transcendental
   Meditation Program
Ground Saucer Watch
Guardian Angels
Gungywamp Society
GWTW Collectors Club
Gypsy Lore Society
Handwriting Analysts, International
Happy Hours Brotherhood
Harley Hummer Club
Harmony International
Haunt Hunters
Having Fun With Elvis
Hawkwatch International
Highamerica Balloon Club
Hocker International Federation
Holiday Institute of Yonkers
Hollywood Studio Collectors Club
Holyearth Foundation
Horseless Carriage Club of America

Houdini Historical Center
Howdy Doody Memorabilia Collectors Club
Hubcappers
Hug Club
Humans Against Rabbit Exploitation
Humor Association
Humor Correspondence Club
Humor Project
Humor Stamp Club
Humorolics Anonymous
Humper Dears
Ice Screamers
Iceberg Athletic Club
Icelandic Horse Adventure Society
Idealist International, Inc.
Imaginary Basketball Federation
Immortalist Society
Impotents Anonymous
Ingglish Speling 3soesiaesh3n
Inner Peace Movement
Institute for the Development of the
   Harmonious Human Being
Institute for UFO Contactee Studies
Institute of Pyramidology
Institute of Strategic Studies on Terrorism
Institute of Totally Useless Skills
Intercontinental UFO Galactic Spacecraft
   Research and Analytic Network
International Academy of Twirling Teachers
International Arthurian Society, North
   American Branch
International Association for Near-Death
   Studies
International Association for the Fantastic in
   the Arts
International Association of Jim Beam Bottle
   and Specialties Clubs
International Association of Pipe Smokers
   Clubs
International Association of Professional
   Bureaucrats
International Association of Sand Castle
   Builders
International Automotive Hall of Shame
International Balut Federation
International Banana Club
International Barbed Wire Collectors
   Association
International Barbie Doll Collectors Club
International Beer Tasting Society
International Betta Congress
International Brick Collectors' Association
International Brotherhood of Magicians
International Brotherhood of Old Bastards
International Bus Collectors Club
International Catacomb Society
International Chain Saw Wood Sculptors
   Association
International Chili Society
International Chinese Snuff Bottle Society
International Coalition Against Violent
   Entertainment
International Connoisseurs of Green and Red
   Chile

International Correspondence of Corkscrew Addicts
International Diastema Club
International Dull Folks Unlimited
International Dull Men's Club
International Edsel Club
International Errol Flynn Society
International Esperantist League for Go
International Fantasy Gaming Society
International Federation of Magical Societies
International Federation of Pedestrians
International Federation of Sound Hunters
International Federation of Tiddlywinks Associations
International Fire Buff Associates
International Flying Farmers
International Flying Nurses Association
International Fortean Organization
International Foundation for Gender Education
International Frankenstein Society
International Guild of Candle Artisans
International Hug Center
International Imagery Association
International Jugglers Association
International Laughter Society
International Mailbag Club
International Maledicta Society
International Map Collectors' Society
International Mothers' Peace Day Committee
International New Thought Alliance
International Old Lacers, Inc.
International Order of E.A.R.S.
International Order of Hoo-Hoo
International Order of the Armadillo
International Order of the Golden Rule
International Organization of Nerds
International Organization of Wooden Money Collectors
International Paintball Players Association
International Petula Clark Society
International Playing-Card Society
International Polka Association
International Primate Protection League
International Primitive Money Society
International Pumpkin Association
International Rose O'Neill Club
International Sand Collectors Society
International Save the Pun Foundation
International Sled Dog Racing Association
International Society for Astrological Research
International Society for Humor Studies
International Society for Philosophical Enquiry
International Society for the Study of Dendrobatid Frogs
International Society for the Study of Time
International Society of Animal License Collectors
International Society of Copier Artists
International Society of Copoclephologists
International Society of Flying Engineers
International Society of Folk Harpers and Craftsmen
International Society of Psychology of Handwriting
International Sourdough Reunion
International Stiltwalkers Association
International Stop Continental Drift Society
International Twins Association
International Veterinary Acupuncture Society
International Watch Fob Association, Inc.
International Wizard of Oz Club
International Wood Collectors Society
International Zebu Breeders Association
J. Allen Hynek Center for UFO Studies
James Bond 007 Fan Club
James Bond 007 Fan Club
James Buchanan Foundation
James K. Polk Memorial Association
Japanese Animation Network
Jazzmobile
Jews for Jesus
Jim Smith Society
Jim's Neighbors
Johnny Alfalfa Sprout
Johns and Call Girls United Against Repression
Joygerms Unlimited
Judson Welliver Society
Junior International Club
Kangaroo Protection Foundation
Keltic Society and the College of Druidism
Kentucky Callers Association
Knife and Fork Club International
Knifemakers Guild
Knights of the Square Table
Labologists Society
Ladies Against Women
LADIES - Life After Divorce Is Eventually Sane
Ladyslipper
Largesse
Last Chance Forever
Laugh Lovers
Lead Belly Society
Left Green Network
Lefthanders International
Leif Ericson Society International
Leonard Nimoy Fan Club, Spotlight
Liberace Club of Las Vegas
Liberator Atlanta
Liberty Bell Matchcover Club
Liberty Seated Collectors Club Life Understanding Foundation
The Lifestyles Organization
Lilliputian Bottle Club
Little Big Horn Associates
Little People of America
Live-Free International
London Club
Lone Indian Fellowship and Lone Scout Alumni
Loners of America
Loners on Wheels
Lord Ruthven Assembly

Lost in Space Fannish Alliance
Lottery Collectors Society
Love-N-Addiction
Love Notes
Love Token Society
Lovers of the Stinking Rose
Loyal Order of Catfish
Lovers Macro Society
Mad World Campaign
Magic Lantern Society of the United States
  and Canada
Magical Youths International
Make-A-Wish Foundation of America
Male Liberation Foundation
Man Watchers
Man Will Never Fly
Memorial Society Internationale
Marble Collectors Society of America
Marble Collectors Unlimited
Martin Van Buren Fan Club
Marx Brothers Study Unit
Mechanical Bank Collectors of America
Mega Society
Men International
MEND - Mothers Embracing Nuclear
  Disarmament
Mend Our Tongues Society
Men's Rights
Men's Rights Association
Messies Anonymous
MetaScience Foundation
Michigan/Canadian Bigfoot Information
  Center
Midwest Decoy Collectors Association
Mikes of America
Military Vehicle Preservation Association
Millennium Society
Mind Development and Control Association
Mind Science Foundation
Miniature Armoured Fighting Vehicle
  Association
Miniature Book Society
Miniature Donkey Registry of the United
  States
Miniature Golf Association of America
Miniature Piano Enthusiast Club
Mining Club
Miss Mom/Mister Mom
Mister Ed Fan Club
Mistresses Anonymous
Moles
Monarchist Alliance
Monkees Buttonmania Club
Monmouth Antiquarian Society
Monorail Society
Monty Python Special Interest Group
Mother's Day Council
Mothers Without Custody
Motor Bus Society
Motor Maids, Inc.
Motor Voters
Mount Rushmore Memorial Society
Mountain Gorilla Project

The Mouse Club
Munsters and the Addams Family Fan Club
Mushroom Caucus
Mutual UFO Network
Mythopoeic Society
Names Project Foundation
Napoleonic Society of America
National Alliance of Supermarket Shoppers
National Amusement Park Historical
  Association
National Anxiety Center
National Arbor Day Foundation
National Association for Outlaw and
  Lawman History
National Association for the Advancement of
  Perry Mason
National Association for the Advancement of
  Time
National Association for the Preservation and
  Perpetuation of Storytelling
National Association for the Preservation of
  Baseball
National Association of Breweriana
  Advertising
National Association of Full Figured Women
National Association of Milk Bottle Collectors
National Association of Non-Smokers
National Association of Timetable Collectors
National Association of Wheat Weavers
National Association to Advance Fat
  Acceptance
National Black on Black Love Campaign
National Carousel Association
National Chastity Association
National Christmas Tree Association
National Circus Preservation Society
National Clogging and Hoedown Council
National Coalition of IRS Whistleblowers
National Coalition on Television Violence
National Committee for Responsible
  Patriotism
National Committee for Sexual Civil Liberties
National Congress for Men
National Cowboy Hall of Fame and Western
  Heritage Center
National Displaced Homemakers Network
National Elephant Collectors Society
National Fantasy Fan Federation
National Father's Day Committee
National Federation of Grandmother Clubs
  of America
National Fishing Lure Collectors Club
National FRUMPS of America
National Guild of Decoupeurs
National Headache Foundation
National Hemlock Society
National Historical Fire Foundation
National Hobo Association
National Horseshoe Pitchers Association of
  America
National Investigations Committee on
  Unidentified Flying Objects
National Leather Association

National Little Britches Rodeo Association
National Lum and Abner Society
National Mother's Day Committee
National Odd Shoe Exchange
National Old-Time Fiddlers' Association
National Order of Trench Rats
National Organization for Changing Men
National Organization for Men
National Organization for the Reform of
 Marijuana Laws
National Organization of Mall Walkers
National Organization Taunting Safety and
 Fairness Everywhere
National Organization to Insure Survival
 Economics
National Peace Day Celebrations
National Police Bloodhound Association
National Pop Can Collectors
National Privy Diggers Association
National Puzzlers' League
National Pygmy Goat Association
National Reamer Collectors Association
National Scrabble Association
National Seafood Educators
National Society for Prevention of Cruelty to
 Mushrooms
National Society for Shut-Ins
National Space Club
National Space Society
National Square Dance Convention
National Story League
National Task Force on Prostitution
National Tattoo Association
National Thanksgiving Commission
National Toothpick Holder Collector's
 Society
National Tractor Pullers Association
National Velthrow Association
National Write Your Congressman
Native Daughters of the Golden West
Native Sons of the Golden West
The Naturist Society Naturists and Nudists
 Opposing Pornographic Exploitation
Negative Population Growth
New Moon Matchbox and Label Club
New Tribes Mission
9 to 5, National Association of Working
 Women
1904 World's Fair Society
No Business As Usual
No Kidding!
North American Bungee Association
North American Fuzzy Information Processing
 Society
North American Swing Club Association
North American Tiddlywinks Association
North Central Name Society
Northeast Rat and Mouse Club
Northern Cross Society
Notch
Nudist Information Center
Occidental Society of Metempiric Analysis
Occupied Japan Club

Of a Like Mind
Official Betty Boop Fan Club
Official Gumby Fan Club
Official Rocky Horror Fan Club
Old Boys Network Turtle Club
Old Mine Lamp Collectors Society of America
Old Old Timers Club
Old Sleepy Eye Collectors' Club of America
Old Timers' Club
Oldtime Radio-show Collector's Association
OMB Watch
Omega Project
On the Lighter Side, International Lighter
 Collectors
1% for Peace
One Person's Impact
The One Shoe Crew
Open Minded Comics Club
Optimist International
Organ Clearing House
Organization for Collectors of Covered
 Bridge Postcards
Original Gilligan's Island Fan Club
Ornamental Fish International
Our World—Underwater Scholarship Society
Outward Bound
Over the Hill Gang, International
Overachievers Anonymous
Overseas Brats
Paddle Steamer Preservation Society
Pagan/Occult/Witchcraft S IG
Pagans for Peace Network
Pansophic Institute
Parachute Study Group
Parapsychological Association
Parapsychological Services Institute
Parapsychology Foundation
Parapsychology Institute of America
Parents' Music Resource Center
Patrexes of the Panopticon
Peaceful Beginnings
Peanut Pals
Pelican Man's Bird Sanctuary
Penny Resistance
People Against Telephone Terrorism and
 Harassment
People, Food and Land Foundation
People Organized to Stop Rape of
 Imprisoned Persons
People's Music Network for Songs of
 Freedom and Struggle
Phenix Society
Pia Zadora Fan Club
Pilgrim Society
Pilots for Christ International
Pinochle Bugs Social and Civic Club
Pipe Collectors Club of America
Placename Survey of the U.S.
Plain Talk
Planetary Citizens
Planetary Society
Poets for Christ
Polar Bear Club—U.S.A.

Police Insignia Collector's Association
Polka Lovers Klub of America
Popular Culture Association
Porlock Society
Possum Growers and Breeders Association
Potato Eaters
Praed Street Irregulars
Prairie Chicken Foundation
Princess Kitty Fan Club
Private Citizen, Inc.
Procrastinators' Club of America
Professional Comedians' Association
Professional Psychics United
Project Blue Book
Project Starlight International
Project to Research Objects, Theories, Extraterrestrials and Unusual Sightings
Project VISIT—Vehicle Internal Systems Investigative Team
PSI Research Psychic Detective Bureau
Psychic Science International Special Interest Group
Psychical Research Foundation
Psynetics Foundation
Puns Corps
Puppeteers of America
Puzzle Buffs International
Quixote Center
Race Track Chaplaincy of America
Radical Women
Radio Association Defending Airwave Rights
Rat, Mouse and Hamster Fanciers
Rathkamp Matchcover Society
Re-Geniusing Project
Reagan Alumni Association
Redeem Our Country
Redheads International
Remain Intact Organization
Republican Women of Capitol Hill
Retired Greyhounds as Pets
Rhino Rescue U.S.A.
Richard III Society
Riot Relief Fund
Rockette Alumnae Association
Rocky Mountain Llama and Alpaca Association
Rodeo Historical Society
Role Playing Game Association Network
Ronald Reagan Philatelic Society
Roo Rat Society
Route 66 Association
Royal Association for the Longevity and Preservation of the Honeymooners
Sand Collectors International
Sarcastics Anonymous
Sasquatch Investigations of Mid-America
Save America's Forests
Save Life On Earth
Save Our Barns Committee
Science Fiction Poetry Association
Science Fiction Research Association
Science Frontiers
Scientific Instrument Society
Scientific Marriage Foundation
Scripophila Helvetica

SEARCH Foundation
Second Wives Association of North America
Seed Savers Exchange
Senior Masters
Sensitives of America Club
Sex Addicts Anonymous
Sex and Love Addicts Anonymous
Sexaholics Anonymous
Ships-in-Bottles Association of America
Shoplifters Anonymous
Shroud of Turin Research Project
Silent Running Society
Single Gourmet
Single Mothers by Choice
Single Persons for Tax Equality Association
Singles in Agriculture
Sinistral Sig
Sleep Research Society
Slow Food Foundation
Smoker's Rights Alliance
Smurf Collectors
Snow Biz
Society for Creative Anachronism
Society for Musteline Arts and Literature
Society for Scientific Exploration
Society for the Application of Free Energy
Society for the Eradication of Television
Society for the Furtherance and Study of Fantasy and Science Fiction
Society for the Investigation of Recurring Events
Society for the Investigation of the Unexplained
Society for the Philosophy of Sex and Love
Society for the Preservation and Advancement of the Harmonica
Society for the Preservation and Appreciation of Antique Motor Fire Apparatus in America
Society for the Preservation and Encouragement of Barber Shop Quartet Singing in America
Society for the Preservation and Enhancement of the Recognition of Millard Fillmore, Last of the Whigs
Society for the Preservation of Beers from the Wood
Society for the Second Self
Society for the Study of Myth and Tradition
Society for the Systematic Documentation of Paranormal Experiments
Society for Utopian Studies
Society of American Fight Directors
Society of California Pioneers
Society of Earthbound Extraterrestrials
Society of Flavor Chemists
Society of Geniuses of Distinction
Society of Inkwell Collectors
Society of Limerents
Society of Ornamental Turners
Society of Phantom Friends
Society of Political Item Enthusiasts
Society of Saunterers, International
Society of Scribes
Society of the President Street Fellows

Society to Curtail Ridiculous, Outrageous and Ostentatious Gift Exchange
Society to Preserve and Encourage Radio Drama, Variety and Comedy
Sod House Society
Solo War-gamers Association
Somatics Society
Son of a Witch
Sons and Daughters of the Soddies
Sons of Confederate Veterans
Sons of Sherman's March to the Sea
Sons of the Desert
Sons of the Whiskey Rebellion
South African Bird Ringing Unit
Space Settlement Studies Program
Spark Plug Collectors of America
Spiritual Counterfeits Project
Sports Hall of SHAME
Star Trek Welcommittee
Starfleet Command
Starships of the Third Fleet
Starthrowers
Still Bank Collectors Club of America
Still Waters Foundation
Stonehenge Study Group
Stop War Toys Campaign
Stumpwork Society
Sugar Packet Collectors Club
Survival Research Foundation
Tall Clubs International
Tara Collectors Club
Tattoo-a-Pet Tattoo Club of America
Tax Free America
Terrarium Association
Thermometer Collectors Club of America
Thimble Collectors
International Third Generation
1334 North Beechwood Drive Irregulars
Three Stooges Fan Club
Tippers Anonymous
Tippers International
Tonga and Tin Can Mail Study Circle
Treasure Hunter Research and Information Center
Tree-Ring Society
TreePeople
Trekville U.S.A.
Triplet Connection
Triskaidekaphobia Illuminatus Society
True Life Institute
20/20 Vision National Project
Twins Foundation
Twirly Birds
UFO Information Retrieval Center
Uglies Unlimited
U.N.C.L.E. HQ
Uncle Remus Museum
United Flying Octogenarians
United Serpents
United States Amateur Ballroom Dancers Association
United States Amateur Dancers Association
United States Amateur Tug of War Association
U.S. Boomerang Association

U.S. English
United States Korfball Federation
United States Othello Association
U.S. Psychotronics Association
U.S. Trivia Association
The Universal Coterie of Pipe Smokers
V Fan Club
Vacation Exchange Club
Vampire
Vampire Information Exchange
Vampire Pen Pal Network
Vampire Research Center
Vegetarian Resource Group
Vestigia
Viewers for Quality Television
Visual Lunacy Society
Voltaire Society
Voluntary Census Committee
Wabash, Frisco and Pacific Association
Wages and Not Tips
Walden Forever Wild
Walking Association
Walter Koenig International
Watchdogs of the Treasury
We Love Lucy/The International Lucille Ball Fan Club
Welcome to Our Elvis World
Werewolf Research Center
Whimsical Alternative Political Action Committee
Whirly-Girls (International Women Helicopter Pilots)
Whiskey Painters of America
White House Historical Association
Wilderness Leadership International
Wilhelm Furtwangler Society of America
William Shatner Connection
Windmill Study Unit
Wine Appreciation Guild
Witches Anti-Discrimination Lobby
Women in the Wind
Women on Wheels
Wooden Canoe Heritage Association
Workshop Library on World Humour
World ArmWrestling Federation
World Championship Cutter and Chariot Racing Association
World Day for Peace
World Government of the Age of Enlightenment —U.S.
World Organization for Modelship Building and Modelship Sport
World Organization of China Painters
World Pumpkin Confederation
World Science Fiction Society
World Timecapsule Fund
World Watusi Association
Worldloppet
World's Wrist-wrestling Championship
Xerces Society
Yarns of Yesteryear Project
Zane Grey's West Society
Zeppelin Collectors Club
Zimmerman Registry
Zinfandel Club

For Ruth "Gram" Moore, who
started a special club of her own

ORGANIZED OBSESSIONS

A A A A A A A A

Abbott and Costello Fan Club (ACFC)
PO Box 262
Carteret, NJ 07008-0262

Fans and admirers of the comedy team of Bud Abbott (1896-1974) and Lou Costello (1906-59), which attained peak popularity on the stage, the screen, and the airwaves from 1941 to 1951. The club seeks to keep alive the spirit of good-natured buffoonery (*heyyyy* Ab-bott!) and slapstick which characterized A&C's work. Founded in 1968. 15,062 members. Contact Billy Wolfe, Founder & Director.

Absurd Special Interest Group (ASIG)
2419 Greensburg Pike
Pittsburgh, PA 15221

Members are a special interest group of Mensa interested in absurd humor. Group objective is simple "amusement." Has a staff of one and a "minuscule" budget. Members remain amused via the monthly *Atrocity* newsletter (available for $8 per year). Founded in 1979. 222 members. Contact Henry Roll, Executive Officer.

Abundantly Yours (AY)
PO Box 151134
San Diego, CA 92115   (619) 286-4206

An organization for "abundant-size" men and women and their adult loved ones or "treasured skinny people," AY hopes to educate and enlighten fat people about themselves and to promote the motto of "being the best you are regardless of size." The group encourages members to focus on what is right about themselves instead of what is wrong and works to dispel myths about fat people, including the one that portrays them as undisciplined, self-hating, compulsive overeaters.

The group believes that good health and happiness is a function of participation in various activities and overweight people tend to limit themselves in those areas. So it sponsors camping and theater trips and other projects designed to serve lonely, isolated people who are overweight and to motivate them to participate more fully in life. AY organizes *The Lighter Side of Big*, an annual comedy-variety show and raises funds through the Abundantly Yours Too resale shop of previously owned fashions for big people. Founded in 1979. 2100 members. Contact Joyce L. Rue-Potter, Founder & Director.

Academy of Accounting Historians (AAH)
James Madison University
School of Accounting
Harrisonburg, VA 22807   (703) 568-6607

Accounting institutions, accountants, university libraries, and individuals interested in accounting and/or business history (a great moment in accounting history—invention of the ledger). The group encourages research, publication, teaching, and personal exchange in all facets of accounting history and its relationship to business and economic history. AAH maintains the Accounting History Research Center, in conjunction with Georgia State University, to promote research in accounting history as well as the Tax History Center (in conjunction with the University of Mississippi) to promote research in tax history. Semiannually it issues the gripping *Accounting Historians Journal.* Founded in 1973. 850 members. Contact Ashton C. Bishop, Secretary.

Academy of Psychic Arts and Sciences (APAS)
100B Turtle Creek Village, Suite 363
PO Box 191129
Dallas, TX 75219   (214) 788-1833

Open to persons and organizations interested in psychic phenomena, parapsychology, metaphysics, and "new age" spiritual issues of personal growth, self-responsibility, and creative living, APAS promotes a professional approach to the study and practice of parapsychology and metaphysics. Founded in 1970. Contact Timothy Dexter Latus, President.

Academy of Science Fiction, Fantasy, and Horror Films (ASFFHF)
334 W. 54th St.
Los Angeles, CA 90037   (213) 752-5811

Members include actors, writers, producers, directors, special effects people, and other individuals connected with the film industry as well as people in the field of education and fans of the genres. The group bestows the annual *Saturn Awards* to the outstanding science fiction, fantasy, and horror films of the year and also recognizes artists in these genres in the fields of acting, music, direction, writing, cinematography, special effects, makeup, film criticism, set decoration and design, stop motion animation, publicity, and advertising.

The Academy holds special screenings for members, who include directors Wes Craven, Roger Corman, Joe Dante, William Friedkin, and Martin Scorsese, author Ray Bradbury, Mistress of the Dark Elvira, and other, more anonymous folks. Memberships start at $100 per year. Affiliated with The Count Dracula Society, described elsewhere in this book (likely under "C"). Founded in 1972. 3000 members. Contact Dr. Donald A. Reed, President.

Accordion Federation of North America (AFNA)
11438 Elmcrest St.
El Monte, CA 91732   (213) 686-1769

A group dedicated to the advancement of the accordion and acquainting the nonaccordion-loving public with the instrument's myriad possibilities and musical advantages (for instance, it's portability allows the accordionist to play while on roller skates or in the bath). Members include music school operators, teachers, instrument wholesalers, music publishers, and professional accordionists dedicated to the advancement of the accordion in all areas. The Federation seeks to recognize outstanding ability and conspicuous service to the accordion industry. It conducts an annual four-day music festival with competitions for students at all levels of study, which attracts 2500 contestants each year. Founded in 1957. 80 members. Contact Peggy Milne, Executive Secretary.

ACT UP

135 W. 29th St., 10th Floor
New York, NY 10001 (212) 564-2437

Members are "united in anger and committed to direct action to end the AIDS crisis." ACT UP seeks to increase public awareness and government involvement in the fight against AIDS, conducting rallies and demonstrations aimed at public figures or institutions that the group feels should be doing more to combat AIDS. The group lobbies for quicker availability of experimental AIDS drugs. News on the AIDS front is conveyed through the quarterly *ACT UP Reports* newsletter.

Adult Video Association (AVA)

270 N. Canon Dr., Suite 1370
Beverly Hills, CA 90210 (818) 882-6323

Trade organization that believes adults should be able to watch what they want (videos with lots of skin) in the privacy of their own homes. AVA challenges the constitutionality of laws affecting adult videos, typically citing the First Amendment with such expressions as, "The First Amendment was not created to protect only 'mainstream' expression. Rather, the purpose of the first Amendment is to protect those ideas and opinions which are considered less than popular."

AVA calls on members to, "Defend your constitutional right to see, hear, read and learn OR pay the price of losing your fundamental freedoms to the Troops of Tyranny!" And furthermore, "Our voices do represent the majority but our apathy is permitting a well-financed, well-oiled, highly vocal minority to bully the rest of us into silent submission. We must send a message that we will no longer tolerate the reign of tyranny perpetrated by these thugs in three-piece suits."

It may not come as a surprise that members hail from the video industry, including distributors, writers, directors, actors, and retail store owners. Membership fees are based upon occupation (ranging from $25 to $1000 per year). Administrative Director Gloria Leonard is an announced candidate for President of the U.S. Founded in 1987. Contact Ron Sullivan, Chairman.

Agatha Christie Appreciation Society Postern of Murder (ACAS)

61 E. Northampton St., No. 206
Wilkes-Barre, PA 18701 (717) 829-5717

Individuals interested in the works of Agatha Christie (1890-1976) and in mystery fiction. Co-founder Dorothy Carr says the idea came about after she and two friends attended a local Sherlock Holmes Group dinner and decided it was high time that Christie was paid her due with at least a hot meal. The group claims that it is the "first official Agatha" society. It does not charge dues, but members, upon joining, promise to continue "a Christie for Christmas," by giving her books as gifts. Three meetings are held a year, with the meeting theme related to a title from one of Christie's books. Members read the book in advance and are given some type of puzzle to solve about the story. In 1990, several members went to England to purchase Christie Centenary Memorabilia for members. Founded in 1990. 150 members. Contact Dorothy M. Carr, President.

Air Mail Pioneers (AMP)
468-D Calle Cadiz
Laguna Hills, CA 92653   (714) 581-6246

Former employees of the U.S. Post Office Department, Air Mail Service, who served between May 15, 1918 and August 31, 1927 during the inaugural stages of air mail delivery, seeking to record the history of the Air Mail Service and preserve the mementos of that enterprise before Father and Mother Time assign everything to the dead letter office. The Pioneers donate historical material to the Smithsonian Institution in Washington, DC and other museums. Founded in 1943. 150 members. Contact Jerome Lederer, President.

Aladdin Knights of the Mystic Light (AKML)
Route 1
Simpson, IL 62985   (618) 949-3884

Members include collectors, dealers, users, and admirers of Aladdin lamps and memorabilia. The group strives to preserve information on kerosene lighting and electric Aladdin lamps and encourages Aladdin collecting and camaraderie among collectors (hey buddy, nice lamp). Members are enlightened via the *Mystic Light of the Aladdin Knights*, a bimonthly newsletter. Founded in 1973. 1000 members. Contact Dr. J. W. Courter, Bright Knight.

Alan Thicke Fan Club (ATFC)
PO Box 724
Altadena, CA 91003

Fans of Canadian actor Alan Thicke, best known for his role on the television situation comedy *Growing Pains*, and, to a lesser degree, for the 1983 *Thicke of the Night*, a late-night variety show that you may not remember because it didn't last very long. Members are from the U.S., France, Canada, Australia, Italy, Philippines, Japan, and other parts of the world. The group promotes Mr. Thicke's career through distribution of a membership kit and notifies members of public appearances by Mr. Thicke. ATFC holds an annual softball picnic with Mr. Thicke and fans and is an avid supporter of Juvenile Diabetes Association since Thicke's son, Brennan, has diabetes. Publishes *All About Alan*, an annual journal chronicling the ongoing adventures of Mr. Thicke. Founded in 1984. Contact Dawna Kessell, President.

Alferd E. Packer Society (AEPS)
603 3rd St. NE
Washington, DC 20002   (202) 547-4396

Group dedicated to the preservation of the memory of Alferd E. Packer (1842-1907), America's only convicted cannibal (unless you consider Jeffrey Dahmer). Packer was convicted of cannibalism following the mysterious disappearance of his five companion prospectors during a journey to the San Juan Mountains in 1874. Founded in 1979. 20 members. Contact Wesley McCune, Chaplain.

All American Association of Contest Judges (AAACJ)
1627 Lay Blvd.
Kalamazoo, MI 49001   (616) 343-2172

Members are technically trained to adjudicate drum and bugle corps, color guard, drill team, baton corps, and chorus contests and parades. AAACJ seeks to improve the caliber of bands and drum and bugle corps and serve as a vehicle for the instillment of teamwork, cooperation, sportsmanship, and Americanism into the youth of America through competition. It publishes the quarterly *On Parade.* Founded in 1932. 462 members. Contact Granville B. Cutler, Executive Officer.

All Together (AT)
405 N. Wabash Ave., Suite 3612
Chicago, IL 60605   (312) 467-0465

Members are folks with alternative lifestyles ("gays, swingers, cohabitants, bisexuals, singles, divorced people, *new* women"). AT seeks to eliminate economic discrimination against such people, with particular emphasis on insurance, credit, and legal affairs, and to develop a central resource for both those with alternate lifestyles and those "within the establishment." It provides consulting services and compiles clipping file on alternate lifestyles. All Together is conducting research on growth, needs, desires, and future of emerging lifestyles. Founded in 1975. Contact Lloyd M. Levin, President.

Alternative Resource Center (ARC)
PO Box 429
5263 Bouldercrest Road
Ellenwood, GA 30049   (404) 961-0102

ARC provides resources to encourage conscientious holiday observance, especially church-oriented celebrations, and responsible behavior in daily life. In addition to conducting annual campaigns to decommercialize Christmas and Easter, ARC publishes the *Simply Delicious Cookbook, Alternative Celebration Catalogue,* and *Guide to World Hunger Organizations.* Founded in 1973.

Alternative to the New York Times Committee (ANYTC)
3419 Irwin Ave.
Riverdale, NY 10463   (212) 796-6028

ANYTC members are scholars and journalists concerned with the lack of diversity in the major American news media. Working for effective freedom of the press, the group hopes to develop a national, daily newspaper adversarial to and competitive with *The New York Times* and other similar daily news monopolies. ANYTC believes that such an adversarial relationship "is the premise of a free society in all spheres," and that the *New York Times* has a "monopoly influence in the sphere of Western foreign policy, defense and strategy." Founded in 1981. Contact Lev Navrozov, Co-Director.

Always Causing Legal Unrest (ACLU)
PO Box 2085
Rancho Cordova, CA 95741-2085   (408) 427-2858

Rowdy bunch of feminists, anti-pornography activists, and individuals interested in an "alternative to First Amendment fundamentalism." Urges corporations to place public safety and welfare and women's rights over profit and the "fundamentalist" emphasis on trademark laws, private property rights, and individual privacy. Promotes the use of humor in generating public awareness of what the group sees as an overemphasis on conservative values. Above and beyond laughter, encourages women to learn self defense and weaponry. Sponsors Pushing Buttons Campaign, in which buttons bearing slogans against media violence and for women's self-defense are worn in an effort to gain widespread public and legislative awareness and support. Founded in 1990. 200 members. Contact Steven Paskey.

Amalgamated Flying Saucer Clubs of America (AFSCA)
PO Box 39
Yucca Valley, CA 92286   (619) 365-1141

They're out there. Somewhere. Purpose of AFSCA is to inform the public about "the reality of flying saucers (extraterrestrial spacecraft piloted by advanced men and women from other planets and star systems) and of their plan for imparting their advanced knowledge to the people of the Earth in order to resolve present world problems." The group serves as a source of "contactee-oriented" flying saucer information, including books, photographs, "contactee" reports, and space tapes ("tape recorded messages from space people"). Local units hold public meetings to promote knowledge of flying saucers and serve as sources for information and literature in their areas. The quarterly newsletter *Flying Saucers International* provides information on sightings of unidentified flying objects, interplanetary travel, and communications with extraterrestrial beings. Founded in 1959. 5600 members. Contact Gabriel Green, President.

American Accordion Musicological Society (AAMS)
334 S. Broadway
Pitman, NJ 08071   (609) 854-6628

Another group of accordion enthusiasts united for the common causes of accordionistic study, research, and knowledge. AAMS operates a library of 500 volumes on music and its history and maintains a collection of records, tapes, and scores. The group has established a museum of antique accordions and sponsors an annual composition contest. Founded in 1970. 175 members. Contact Stanley Darrow, Secretary.

American Accordionists' Association (AAA)
PO Box 616
Mineola, NY 11501   (516) 746-3101

And yet another accordion group, evidence of a groundswell of accordion interest in the 90s. Members are certified accordion instructors, students, manufacturers and importers of accordions, and publishers and arrangers of accordion music. AAA promotes the accordion through contests, concerts, granting of scholarships, and commissioning of contemporary American composers to write for the accordion. Founded in 1938. 17,000 members. Contact Faithe Deffner, CEO & President.

American Alligator Farmers Association (AAFA)
5145 Harvey Tew Road
Plant City, FL 33566   (813) 752-2836

Yup, got me a farm full of gators. Members include the rare individual holding an alligator farming permit as well as just plain interested individuals and companies. AAFA promotes the alligator farming industry through research, education, and representation. All the news that's fit for farmers is provided in the *Gator Talk* newsletter; members gather for the annual Crocodilian Congress.

Yeeeeehah. Founded in 1986. 42 members. Contact Tracy Howell, President.

American Alpine Club (AAC)
113 E. 90th St.
New York, NY 10128   (212) 722-1628

A group of people who have made mountain ascents, conducted explorations in the Arctic or Antarctic tracts, or contributed to the literature or science of mountaineering, recent glaciology, or alpine art. The Alpine club conducts scientific studies and explorations and encourages mountaineering safety. Annually it publishes *Accidents in North American Mountaineering,* must reading for the Alpine set. Founded in 1902. 1600 members. Contact Patricia A. Fletcher, Librarian.

American Armwrestling Association (AAA)
PO Box 132
Scranton, PA 18504   (717) 342-4984

AAA sponsors local, state, and national seated and standing arm-wrestling competitions, one of the more exciting spectator sports. To keep members up to date on the latest in arm-wrestling lore, it publishes the *Armbender,* a quarterly magazine. Founded in 1971. 5000 members. Contact Bob O'Leary, Founder & Chairman.

American Association - Electronic Voice Phenomena (AA-EVP)
726 Dill Road
Severna Park, MD 21146   (301) 647-8742

Engineers, physicists, and other individuals interested in evidence of postmortem survival, particularly verbal communication from the deceased through tape recorders, televisions, and other electronic equipment. The group investigates evidence that suggests postmortem survival of individual consciousness. It encourages research and development of equipment used in members' work. Focus is on EVP, which members and researchers believe come from other dimensions. These voices are tape-recorded and members claim varied success with soliciting answers to direct questions. Members (still living) are available to speak and give demonstrations to local groups. The group conducts the Taped Survival Project, wherein members submit an audiocassette containing information that they will attempt to communicate after their deaths to other members. No word on success of this venture. Founded in 1982. 200 members. Contact Sarah Estep, Founder & President.

American Association for Parapsychology (AAP)
23101 Sherman Place
PO Box 225
Canoga Park, CA 91305   (818) 883-0840

AAP encourages interest in the expanding field of parapsychology, promoting the exchange of information between the public and those in the field. The group tries to bridge the gap between academic parapsychology and the experimental ESP participation among laymen. It hopes to stimulate interest in scientific research and encourage public involvement in future research. AAP offers a complete course in parapsychology including basic theories, principles, and histories of phenomena involving telepathy, clairvoyance, hypnosis, sensory awareness, psychometry, psychokinesis, and the human aura. Founded in 1971. Contact Ralph Merritt Ph.D., Executive Officer.

American Association of Aardvark Aficionados (AAAA)
PO Box 200
Parsippany, NJ 07054   (201) 729-4176

An association for people with a "bent for the unusual" and/or a "exhibiting a bizarre sense of humor" who profess an affection or enthusiasm for the "noble" aardvark and are interested in promoting and enhancing its image. At first glance, a rare combination of characteristics yet 700 folks belong to this organization. According to the Aardvark Aficionados, the aardvark is a mammal belonging to the order *Tublidentata*, the family *Orycteropodidae*, and the genus *Orydteropus*. The aardvark is the single member of this family of mammals, and is therefore something of a lonely mammal hat on the evolutionary coat tree. Residents of central and southern Africa, mature aardvarks generally are four feet long and armed with a two-foot tail and an 18-inch tongue, which they use to snag termites and ants (the tongue, not the tail). The ears are tubular and 150 to 210 millimeters in length, enabling them to pick up the sound of a violin being plucked with a chicken feather at more than 500 yards. Aardvark president Robert Bogart says that the proper greeting when one sights an aardvark is, "Hark! Vark!" but admits that aardvark sightings are rare in North America.

Nonetheless, AAAA observes National Aardvark Week the first week in March, during which it holds the annual Miss American Aardvark Contest at such select sites as the Philadelphia Zoo. It publishes *Aardvark Tales*, an annual newsletter, as well as an *Annual Press Release*. A4 also issues the *American Aardvark Calendar*, which begins in March with National Aardvark Week and includes often overlooked holidays and events. Founded in 1975. 700 members. Contact Robert L. Bogart, President.

American Association of Handwriting Analysts (AAHA)
820 W. Maple
Hinsdale, IL 60521   (708) 325-2266

The swanky swirl in your "s" and the wildly undulating cross to your "t" indicate a person with a strong passion for doing the unexpected, or perhaps merely showing up unexpectedly. Members include persons who have completed a recognized course in handwriting analysis, passed examinations by a committee of the AAHA, and displayed proficiency in the science of analyzing character from handwriting. The group promotes professionalism in the "science of analyzing character through examination of all forms of writing." Individuals who have passed an exam on the guiding principles of graphology are eligible for associate membership. AAHA seeks public recognition of handwriting analysis as an important aid in the solution of problems involving personality and identification of signatures or writing. Publications include *Handwriting, An Analysis Through Its Symbolism*. Founded in 1962. 400 members. Contact Liz Mills, President.

American Association of Meta-Science (AAMS)

PO Box 1182
Huntsville, AL 35807   (205) 881-7165

AAMS studies, explores, and observes paranormal phenomena, including UFOs. Presently inactive, at least in this dimension, the group assists members and others in developing psychic and spiritual abilities and provides a channel for bringing paranormal discoveries into everyday life. Founded in 1977. 200 members. Contact William F. Sowder, President.

American Atheists

PO Box 140195
Austin, TX 78714   (512) 458-1244

Where have you gone, Madalyn Murray O'Hair? Members of American Atheists include families supporting the aims of the society, which are atheism, separation of state and church, and taxation of the church on real estate, income, business, and other profits. The group presents the American Atheist of the Year Award annually and sponsors the American Atheist Radio series and American Atheist Forum TV series nationwide. AA publishes *American Atheist Magazine*, a journal of atheist news and thought containing articles on current events and controversies. Founded in 1958. 100,000 members. Contact Dr. Madalyn Murray O'Hair, Founder.

American Banjo Fraternity (ABF)

271 McKinley St.
Pittsburgh, PA 15221   (412) 271-2712

People who enjoy pickin', including players, collectors, and historians of the classic standard five-string banjo (no accordions). ABF seeks to perpetuate the instrument's music and performing technique as it was used for entertainment and concert purposes from 1885 to 1915. Banjo news is relayed through the quarterly *Five Stringer* newsletter, which includes banjo music transcriptions. Founded in 1948. 288 members. Contact Norman W. Azinger, Executive Secretary.

American Barefoot Club (ABC)

c/o American Water Ski Association
799 Overlook Dr.
Winter Haven, FL 33884   (813) 324-4341

Enthusiasts of barefoot water skiing dedicated to serving as the sanctioning body for official activities concerning the sport, which requires that members water ski (sans skis) on the bottoms of their feet. The group establishes rules and regulations for tournaments and similar events and bestows the Man of the Year award to individual contributing most to the sport in a nonathletic capacity. This award may go to deserving women as well. The Barefoot National Competition is held in August. Founded in 1977. 2500 members. Contact Don Mixon, President.

American Bladesmith Society (ABS)

PO Box 68
Braddock Heights, MD 21714   (301) 371-7543

Bladesmiths dedicated to the preservation of hand-forged and art blades, united to encourage and promote interest in the traditional blade. ABS educates the public on the forged blade's quality and art value and has established the Bladesmith School in Washington, Arizona to provide instruction in ancient metallurgy and Damascus steel making, handle making, folding-knife making, and engraving. The group holds lectures and demonstrations on forging, blade design, frontier bladesmithing, and blacksmith techniques. It also issues stamps to mark individual blades and certifies bladesmiths as apprentices. Founded in 1976. 168 members. Contact W. F. Moran Jr., Board Chairman.

American Breweriana Association (ABA)
PO Box 11157
Pueblo, CO 81001   (719) 544-9267

Lovers of the golden suds. Members include collectors of brewery advertising and antiques, brewery historians, breweries, beer distributors and retailers, industrial workers, and beer workers. ABA promotes increased public knowledge of brewing techniques and preserves the memories and artifacts of historic breweries in the U.S. The group provides an exchange service allowing collectors of beer labels, coasters, crown caps, openers, and printed material to exchange duplicates with other members. One day, it hopes to establish a museum of brewery history and advertising. The brewmeisters assist members with research regarding brewery history and the industry and publish the bimonthly *American Breweriana Journal*, which contains book reviews, calendar of events, finance report, and a membership directory, as well as the quarterly *Anheuser-Busch and Budweiser Collectors Club Newsletter*. Founded in 1982. 1500 members. Contact Christine Galloway, Executive Director.

American Business Card Club (ABCC)
PO Box 460297
Aurora, CO 80046-0297   (303) 690-6496

A club for business card collectors and enthusiasts, promoting recognition of the business card as both an art form and an advertising and marketing tool. The group encourages the exchange of business cards (of course) among collectors and fosters appreciation of outstanding concepts in business card design and production. It operates the Business Card Hall of Fame, which honors imaginative, creative, and effective business card designs. Founded in 1980. 300 members. Contact Avery N. Pitzak, President.

American Carousel Society (ACS)
470 S. Pleasant Ave.
Ridgewood, NJ 07450

Round and round we go. Members are folks interested in the preservation of the art of the antique wooden carousel. These lovers of wooden ponies promote, especially in hobbyists and collectors, knowledge and appreciation of carousel art. ACS makes available repair techniques to the amateur restorer and issue a census of existing U.S. carousels. Founded in 1978. 900 members. Contact Mary Fritsch, Secretary Treasurer.

American Citizens Committee on Reducing Debt (AC-CORD)

P.O. Box 1962
Midland, MI 48641-1962

ACCORD believes that federal expenditures must not exceed revenues. The nonpartisan group promotes this novel stance, calling for the resolution of the national debt "problem" ($3.25 trillion at last count) and the elimination of annual deficits, although it does not favor any specific budgetary remedy. ACCORD currently figures the national debt places a burden of $37,000 per household. It seeks to create public awareness of Congressional voting records on issues affecting the national debt. ACCORD members are encouraged to withhold votes from federal office seekers who do not act to contain the debt. Memberships are $10 per year and the committee promises at least four newsletters. Founded in 1990. 55 members. Contact B.C. Hurley, President.

American Coaster Enthusiasts (ACE)

PO Box 8226
Chicago, IL 60680

So you think you have your ups and downs? ACE members are roller coaster enthusiasts interested in the history, preservation, and present-day operation of roller coasters. Purposes are to promote, organize, and increase the appreciation of the roller coaster. ACE provides people who need to know with general roller coaster data, including designer information and park updates. It also aids individual park owners and coaster operators with design decisions and seeks to save vintage wood coasters from demolition. The Enthusiasts support the arts of coaster model building and photography and serve as a haven for coaster postcard collectors. The group hopes to establish an amusement park/roller coaster museum which will contain permanent exhibits, photograph galleries, models, coaster cars, and a rehabilitation workshop. Members are updated on gut-wrenching thrills through the quarterly *Rollercoaster!* magazine. Founded in 1978. 3500 members. Contact Ray Ueberroth, President.

American Collectors of Infant Feeders (ACIF)

5161 W. 59th St.
Indianapolis, IN 46254   (317) 291-5850

ACIF members are devoted to the study of infant feeding devices from early pottery feeding vessels through glass nursers of the 1950s to plastic nursers of the 1980s. Included are glass, tin, pewter, porcelain, and silver bottles, pap boats, medicine spoons, and other related feeding items. It publishes *Keeping Abreast*, a quarterly newsletter. Founded in 1973. 135 members. Contact Jo Ann Todd, Secretary Treasurer.

American Council of Spotted Asses (ACSA)

2126 Fairview Place
Billings, MT 59102   (406) 259-4926

Members are owners of spotted asses (donkeys or burros) and interested individuals united to promote the breed. Spotted asses are an endangered species of the donkey and the council believes there are only 450 registered in the world. Founded in 1962. 180 members. Contact John Conter, President.

American Crime Fighters (ACF)
5466 Lake Ave.
Sanford, FL 32773

A group for people interested in learning to protect themselves against crime, but not with guns except in extreme cases. ACF urges direct action against attackers and household intruders, encouraging the use of household objects such as shovel handles and table legs as weapons to be used for self-protection and the protection of young children. Founded in 1983. 100 members. Contact Dr. Merle E. Parker, Chairman.

American Divorce Association of Men (ADAM)
1008 White Oak
Arlington Heights, IL 60005 (708) 870-1040

The ad in the newspaper says: "Now you don't have to lose your money, your home or your kids when you get divorced. ADAM is here to protect your rights. You'll get strong, effective advice and support from ADAM. We're a group of highly qualified divorce lawyers and counselors who will answer by telephone any of your questions on divorce at no charge." Members promote divorce reform and the implementation of new divorce procedures, obviously catering to the male viewpoint. ADAM provides individual divorce counseling and divorce mediation, educational and therapeutic meetings, investigative services, and lawyer referral lists. It also supplies strategic laymen and legal knowledge, educational services, guidance in legal self-representation, and human relations consulting. It maintains a women's council known as *EVE.* Founded in 1970. 12,000 members. Contact Louis J. Filczer, Executive Director.

American Fancy Rat and Mouse Association (AFRMA)
9230 64th St.
Riverside, CA 92509 (714) 685-2350

Enthusiasts and owners of fancy rats and mice (rats and mice putting on airs?). The rat and mouse group promotes and encourages the breeding and exhibition of fancy rats and mice as show animals and pets and tries to foster and maintain excellence in judging and show management. And it of course maintains records of champions for fancy rats and mice. A big occasion for the rat and mousers is the bimonthly fancy rat and mouse show and display at county fairs, parks, and public buildings, where they occasionally come into contact with less fancy cousins. Rodent news is carried in the *American Fancy Rat and Mouse Association-Yearbook* and the *Rat and Mouse Tales,* a bimonthly newsletter. Founded in 1983. 150 members. Contact Karen Hauser, Founder.

American Federation of Astrologers (AFA)
PO Box 22040-2040
Tempe, AZ 85285 (602) 838-1751

When you wish upon a star . . . "The world's largest astrological membership organization" whose members include local associations and individuals in 38 countries interested in the advancement of astrology through research and education. It maintains a special library on astrology and offers a full range of astrology books, videos, audio cassettes, aids, software, and calendars. AFA conducts computer-assisted astrological examinations of persons interested in the field and issues a quarterly newsletter. Every two years (during even-numbered years) AFA holds a five-day convention featuring workshops by world renowned astrologers and exhibits. To be a member, one must have an interest in astrology and agree to conform to the code of ethics, which, among other items, directs that a "precise astrological opinion cannot honestly be rendered with reference to the life of an individual unless it is based upon a horoscope cast for the year, month, day, and time of day plus correct geographical location of the place of birth of the individual..." Founded in 1938. Contact Robert W. Cooper, Executive Secretary.

American Go Association (AGA)
PO Box 397, Old Chelsea Station
New York, NY 10113-0397   (718) 768-5217

One, two, three... Go Association members are united to conduct nationally rated and sanctioned Go tournaments, including the U.S. championship. Invented in China in approximately 2000 B.C., Go has a simple rule structure, great subtlety, and many levels of play. Or at least that's what the Go Association says. It maintains a numerical rating system and publishes the quarterly *American Go Journal.* Founded in 1933. 1400 members. Contact Roy Laird, Editor.

American Gourd Society (AGS)
PO Box 274
Mt. Gilead, OH 43338   (419) 946-3302

Club for people interested in gourds and gourdcraft, which involves making interesting things out of gourds (yes sir, I built this entire home out of gourds...). The gourd people promote the fine art of gourdcraft and the raising and use of gourds for both decorative and practical purposes. AGS disseminates information on culture, harvesting, curing, uses of gourds for gourdcraft, and members' experiences with gourds (how well I remember my first gourd). It issues *The Gourd,* a quarterly newsletter on culture and crafting of gourds and new uses of gourds. AGS meets annually during October in Mt. Gilead (bring your own gourd). Founded in 1970. 2500 members. Contact John Stevens, Secretary.

American Guild of English Handbell Ringers (AGEHR)
1055 E. Centerville Station
Dayton, OH 45459-5503   (513) 438-0085

Members are church and school groups and individual musicians interested in the art of English handbell ringing and dedicated to the exchange of ideas related to techniques of ringing, composing, arranging, and conducting handbell music. The English handbell is a very popular Christmas instrument, and members tend to be extremely busy with their handbell choirs during the holidays. The tuned handbell has its clapper rigidly mounted and hinged so that striking is possible in only two directions. A restraining spring prevents the clapper from lying against the bell when held upright. "Any bell which is suspended and tapped or which can be rung by jiggling with the mouth downward, indicating a clapper mounted to permit it to swivel, is not an English handbell." Don't be misled.

The Guild publishes *Overtones,* a bimonthly magazine listing upcoming events and stories of interest to handbell ringers. The Guild encourages participation in area and national festivals and holds workshops. Founded in 1954. 7800 members. Contact Vic Kostenko, Executive Director.

American Hair Loss Council (AHLC)
100 Independence Place, Suite 207
Tyler, TX 75703 (903) 561-1107

Dermatologists, plastic surgeons, cosmetologists, barbers, and others interested in the phenomenon known as hair loss (hair today, gone tomorrow, ha!). The council reports that it provides nonbiased information regarding treatments for hair loss in both men and women. AHLC facilitates communication and information exchange between professionals in different areas of specialization. The group publishes the quarterly *Hair Loss Journal* reporting on hair loss and treatment and holds an annual conference. Founded in 1985. 320 members. Contact Mike Mahoney, President.

American Handwriting Analysis Foundation (AHAF)
1211 El Solyo Ave.
Campbell, CA 95008 (408) 377-6775

Individuals with an interest in handwriting analysis seeking to advance graphology (the art and science of determining qualities of the personality from the script) as a helping profession. The AHAF provides a certification program for members and has established a code of ethics. It fosters research in handwriting analysis and cooperation among all handwriting analysts and handwriting societies. Founded in 1967. 415 members. Contact Dorothy W. Hodos, Administrative Assistant.

American Hobbit Association (AHA)
Rivendell-EA
730-F Northland Road
Forest Park, OH 45240 (513) 742-4384

Members are fans of British writer J.R.R. Tolkien (1892-1973) and his works, including *The Hobbit* and *The Lord of the Rings* trilogy. AHA seeks to inform and unite Tolkien fans worldwide and encourages members to form local subgroups. The group sponsors trips to local Tolkien events and maintains a library of 300 books and paraphernalia by or about Tolkien. AHA holds a monthly council to discuss Tolkien's works and related topics, play Tolkien games, and have costume parties. Hobbit news is reported six times per year in *The Rivendell Review*, which includes reviews of Tolkien-related merchandise, short stories, artwork, and association news. Members sit down annually to an elegant Hobbit Dinner. Founded in 1977. 175 members. Contact Renee Arwen Alper, Executive Director.

American Humor Studies Association (AHSA)
300 Orange Ave.
University of New Haven
West Haven, CT 06517 (203) 932-7000

Members include academics, general readers, and professional humorists who wish to encourage the study and appreciation of American humor from interdisciplinary perspectives. The group delivers papers at the annual Modern Language Association and the American Literature Association conventions. AHSA insists on taking dangerous ground for an academic group: papers "should not be over-written and boringly stated, but interesting, significant—

even amusing, enjoyable." Examples of recent programs include "Mark Twain's Cultural Environment," "Pure and Driven: The Black Comedy of Virginity in Barthelme's and Sexton's Rewritings of 'Snow White,'" and "The Absurd and Other Forms of the Comic in the Twentieth-Century American Novel."

The AHSA issues the journal *Studies in American Humor* as well as *To Wit*, a newsletter published twice per year with information on research in progress, notices of books and other publications, bibliographical items, information on humor resources other than the traditionally scholarly ones, and "as the auction ads say at the end, 'items too numerous to mention,' according to the whims, more likely the special (even more likely the spatial) needs of the editors." Founded in 1974. 400 members. Contact David E.E. Sloane, Executive Director.

American International Checkers Society (AICS)
11010 Horde St.
Wheaton, MD 20902   (301) 949-5920

A group seeking to advance the proud game of international checkers in the United States of America. International checkers differs from conventional checkers in that 20 "men" are used (rather than 12), the board has 100 squares, and people with funny accents often command the board. AICS conducts state and local tournaments leading to an annual national tournament of international checkers which may well lead to the international tournament of international checkers. Founded in 1967. 128 members. Contact Jack Birnman, Secretary Treasurer.

American Kitefliers Association (AKA)
1559 Rockville Pike
Rockville, MD 20852-1651   (408) 647-8483

Members are "big kids" interested in kite building, kiting events, and the advancement of kites (on the ground and in the air). AKA sponsors an annual four-day convention (usually in October) which features kite competitions, workshops, and The Great Kite Auction. The group publishes *Kiting*, a bimonthly journal filled with club news, competition results, reports on kiting events around the country, announcements of coming events, club profiles, "how to make or fly your kite better" information, and lots of kite store ads.

The AKA advises on kite safety: never fly in wet or stormy weather; never fly near power lines; never use metallic flying line; do not fly near trees, streets, or airports (it is considered bad form to have your kite tangle with a 747); and do not fasten yourself to your line unless you have a quick release mechanism (even worse form is becoming airborne with your kite). An individual membership for a year is about $20. Toll-free 800-AKA2550. Founded in 1964. 4000 members. Contact David Gomberg, President.

American Lock Collectors Association (ALCA)
36076 Grennada
Livonia, MI 40151   (313) 522-0920

Members are collectors of old locks, including heavy-duty factory locks, padlocks, combination locks, handcuffs, shackles, and leg irons. Members also enjoy collecting keys to the locks, as well as big things that use locks, such as safes. Every other month or so, the association issues a newsletter, with information on upcoming events, locks for sale, and recent lock collecting show. Founded in

1970. 250 members. Contact Charles W. Chandler, Executive Officer.

American Mead Association (AMA)
PO Box 206
Ostrander, OH 43061 (614) 666-4253

The diverse membership includes beekeepers, home winemakers, small winery owners, and history enthusiasts. The group promotes the production, consumption, and appreciation of mead, a fermented beverage made of water, honey, and yeast. AMA publishes a semiannual newsletter known as *Mead Letters* and the annual *Meadmaker's Journal.* Founded in 1986. 100 members. Contact Pamela J. Spence, Director.

American Mensa
2626 E. 14th St.
Brooklyn, NY 11235 (718) 934-3700

Members are "persons who have established, by a score on a standard intelligence test, that their intelligence is higher than that of 98 percent of the population." Mensa seeks to identify and foster human intelligence and to provide a stimulating intellectual and social environment for its members, who have an IQ of 132 or above. It maintains the Mensa Education and Research Foundation, which encourages and supports research in the social and psychological sciences, especially projects that concern the intellectually gifted. Two-thirds of Mensas are male, while 52% of all members are single, making Mensa a prime mecca for single semi-geniuses in search of the perfect other. Members are kept updated through the *Interloc* newsletter (10 per year) and the *Mensa Bulletin/International Journal* as well as the quarterly *Mensa Research Journal.* Bunny Warsh of Colton, CA met her husband through a personal ad in the *Mensa Bulletin.* "I joined Mensa when I was 28, and as soon as I stopped wasting my time on men not intelligent enough to talk to, I did just fine," says Warsh. Founded in 1960. 55,000 members. Contact Sheila Skolnik, Executive Director.

American Miniature Horse Association (AMHA)
2908 SE Loop 820
Ft. Worth, TX 76140 (817) 293-0041

Individuals interested in wee horsies, the American miniature horse breed. These folks promote the breed and maintain a permanent registry. AMHA publishes *Miniature Horse World,* a bimonthly magazine providing articles by breeders and experts in the field (also includes show calendar). Founded in 1978. 4400 members. Contact Russell Walker, Executive Secretary.

American Miniature Horse Registry (AMHR)
PO Box 3415
Peoria, IL 61612-3415 (309) 691-9661

More lovers of little horses. Members are breeders and owners of American miniature horses. AMHR informs members of shows and other activities and maintains a breed registry and a (small) hall of fame. It publishes *Pony Journal,* a bimonthly covering Shetland miniature horse breeding, sales, and shows. Founded in 1970. 1300 members. Contact Barbara Stockwell, Secretary Treasurer.

American Name Society (ANS)

Baruch College
Department of Foreign Languages and Comparative Lit.
New York, NY 10010   (212) 505-2177

Name that name. ANS is a professional society of onomatologists, including linguists, geographers, literary historians, and others interested in the study of the etymology, origin, meaning, and application of place names and personal names. Members are also interested in scientific, popular, and commercial nomenclature and the publication of dictionaries, monographs, and pamphlets in the field of onomatology. ANS conducts research on the origin and meaning of names and issues the aptly named *Names,* a quarterly journal containing articles on onomastics. Founded in 1951. 900 members. Contact Prof. Wayne H. Finke, Executive Secretary Treasurer.

American Ostrich Association (AOA)

1227 W. Magnolia, Suite 210
Ft. Worth, TX 76104   (817) 926-1366

Members are people who promote ostrich raising as a potential source for food, leather, and feathers. Provides those who need to know information about raising ostriches. According to the AOA, breeding ostriches is a growing industry, with more than 10,000 ostriches living in the U.S.A., some in high rises. Founded in 1987. 650 members. Contact Susan Cook Adkins, Executive Director.

American Pain Society (APS)

5700 Old Orchard Road, 1st Floor
Skokie, IL 60077-1024   (708) 966-5595

Just tell me where it hurts. Members of the Pain Society include physicians, dentists, psychologists, nurses, and other health professionals interested in the study of pain. Purposes are to promote control, management, and understanding of pain through scientific meetings and research activities and develop standards for training and ethical management of pain patients. Founded in 1977. 1600 members. Contact Jeffrey W. Engle, Executive Director.

American Pencil Collectors Society (APCS)

2222 S. Millwood
Wichita, KS 67213   (316) 263-8419

Time to get the lead out. Members are interested in collecting writing instruments of all kinds. APCS publishes *The Pencil Collector,* a monthly. Founded in 1958. 625 members. Contact R. J. Romey, President.

American Physicians Poetry Association (APPA)

230 Toll Dr.
Southampton, PA 18966   (215) 364-2990

Your stomach I fear is a dreadful mess/ Please pay the receptionist before I take out the rest. Physicians dedicated to the principle that sensitivity in the practice of medicine can be maintained and developed through poetry. APPA provides a forum of communication for doctor-poets and assists members in publishing and reading poetry. The group presents educational programs, holds reading sessions, and publishes the annual *American Physi-*

cians Poetry Association Newsletter. Founded in 1976. 150 members. Contact Richard A. Lippin M.D., Executive Director.

American Poultry Historical Society (APHS)
USDA - Extension Service
South Building, Room 3334
Washington, DC 20250 (202) 447-4087

A place for chicken lovers to dream. The Society locates, collects, and preserves records, pictures, and other materials related to the development of the poultry industry. A committee of 30 individuals selects persons of outstanding achievement for inclusion in the Poultry Industry Hall of Fame, Beltsville, MD. The group publishes the *Poultry Industry Hall of Fame Booklet* and *American Poultry History 1823-1973.* Founded in 1952. 240 members. Contact Richard Reynnells, Secretary.

American Puffer Alliance (APA)
1 Gold St., Suites 22-ABC
Hartford, CT 06103 (203) 547-1281

Smoke 'em if you got 'em. The Puffer Alliance works to end "the current anti-smoking crusade and restore the rights and freedoms of smokers." To this end it conducts research and offers organizing assistance. Founded in 1984. Contact Foster Gunnison Jr., Administrator.

American Roque League (ARL)
PO Box 2304
Richmond, IN 47375 (317) 962-7191

Individuals interested in promoting the game of roque, a game combining elements of croquet and billiards. We do not know if this is played on a lawn or a table or both. The group holds local and state tournaments and distributes *Roque—Official Rules and Regulations.* Founded in 1902. Contact Jack R. Roegner, Treasurer.

American Rubberband Duckpin Bowling Congress (ARDBC)
Hempfield Highlands Mobile Park
4A Cardinal Dr.
Jeannette, PA 15644 (412) 523-8006

ARDBC sanctions rubberband duckpin bowling leagues. Rules of play (which escaped our review), certification of equipment and lanes, and recognition of record scores are carried out in cooperation with the Oldtimers' Rubberband Duckpin Bowling Association, a group of older souls who've been knocking down duckpins longer. ARDBC publishes *The Duckpinner.* Founded in 1945. 2500 members. Contact Wilbur Ammon, Executive Secretary.

American Satellite Television Alliance (ASTA)
16 Broadway, Suite 400
Valhalla, NY 10595 (914) 997-8192

Dish owners (as distinguished from plate collectors), this is your opportunity to fight back! The ASTA works to defend satellite dish owners against discriminatory zoning and covenant restrictions. Its position is that satellite dish installation is a federally protected right. "I have spoken to countless dish owners and dealers who have been forced to devote tremendous time and expense to exercise their rights," says Court Newton, ASTA's executive director. "Many have had to pay legal fees from $1,500 to $15,000 to defend their dishes." ASTA lobbies government for satellite owners' rights and sponsors research and educational programs. The group plans to broaden its scope to include other areas of interest to satellite television owners. Founded in 1991. Contact Courtland G. Newton Jr., Executive Director.

American Sleep Disorders Association (ASDA)
604 2nd St. SW
Rochester, MN 55902   (507) 287-6006

Having trouble catching some zzzzzzs? ASDA members include sleep disorders centers and individuals united to provide full diagnostic and treatment services and to improve the quality of care for patients with all types of sleep disorders. The group trains and evaluates the competence of individuals who care for patients with sleep disorders and conducts research programs, including a cooperative case study series on all patients seen by sleep disorders centers throughout the country. Members are lulled bimonthly by the journal *SLEEP.* Founded in 1975. 1400 members. Contact Carol C. Westbrook, Executive Director.

American Society for Psychical Research (ASPR)
5 W. 73rd St.
New York, NY 10023   (212) 799-5050

The Society investigates and disseminates information about telepathy, visions and apparitions, dowsing, precognition, psychokinesis (mind over matter), automatic writing and other forms of automatism, psychometry, dreams, clairvoyance, clairaudience, predictions, the physical phenomena of mediumship (such as materialization, telekinesis, rapping, and other sounds), and other unclassified parapsychological phenomena. Membership in ASPR does not imply acceptance of any particular phenomenon. The group works to collect, classify, study, and publish firsthand reports of these phenomena and is served by its 9000-volume library on psychical research. The Society publishes the *Journal of the American Society for Psychical Research,* a quarterly research journal on parapsychological or paranormal subjects. Founded in 1885. 2000 members. Contact Donna L. McCormick, Director of Administration.

American Society of Dowsers (ASD)
PO Box 24
Brainerd St.
Danville, VT 05828   (802) 684-3417

Members are amateur and professional dowsers and others interested in locating water, oil, mineral deposits, and various objects and information with or without the use of forked sticks, pendulums, and rods. ASD promotes fellowship and the teaching of dowsing skills, informing the public on the significance and uses of dowsing. The Society holds no corporate views on the nature of dowsing phenomena and has adopted no standard technique, preferring to let members dowse as they go. It maintains a library of books and pamphlets on dowsing and other forms of extrasensory perception. Dowsing news and tips are reported in the quarterly

The American Dowser. Founded in 1961. 3500 members. Contact Donna Robinson, Director.

American Spoon Collectors (ASC)
4922 State Line
Westwood Hills, KS 66205   (913) 831-0912

Collectors of antique and modern souvenir spoons who share their interest through meetings on local, regional, national, and international levels. ASC publishes the monthly *Spooners Forum.* Founded in 1974. 500 members. Contact Bill Boyd, Sponsor.

American Sunbathing Association (ASA)
1703 N. Main St.
Kissimmee, FL 34744   (407) 933-2064

ASA is the largest, oldest, and "most respected nudist organization in North America." The Sunbathers promote "improved health— physically, psychologically, and spiritually—through nudism and the realization that true modesty is not related to the wearing of clothing." Or better, "being nude is being natural," particularly when everyone else is naked. The group stresses that nudists are not opposed to wearing clothes, particularly when participating in hazardous household activities such as "frying bacon." The ASA philosophy is "clothed when practical, unclothed when possible." Members belong to some 200 local clubs.

ASA publishes *The Bulletin* 11 times per year, a newspaper providing information on nudist camps, local nudist organizations, and the nudist movement worldwide. It also issues the *Nudist Park Guide,* a directory of North American nudist parks and clubs and a *North American Guide to Nude Recreation* for the traveling nudist. The association also sells other books, t-shirts, towels, videos, and the prerequisite visors. Founded in 1931. 36,000 members. Contact Arne Eriksen, Executive Director.

American Tolkien Society (ATS)
PO Box 373
Highland, MI 48357-0373   (813) 585-0985

Another group dedicated to the study and appreciation of the works of J.R.R. Tolkien (1892-1973), English author and scholar, ATS facilitates contact between members and conducts seminars and an annual limerick contest. The group sponsors the annual "Hobbit Day" (September 22) and "Tolkien Week" (the week surrounding the 22nd), all the while providing information and speakers for programs relating to the works of Tolkien. It publishes *Minas Tirith Evening Star,* a quarterly journal. Founded in 1975. 475 members. Contact Phil Helms, President.

American Wooden Money Guild (AWMG)
PO Box 30444
Tucson, AZ 85751

Finally, a group willing to take wooden nickels. Members are "lignadenarists," numismatists, and others interested in wooden money either as collectors or dealers. AWMG issues several wooden nickels annually and maintains a collection of wooden money. The Guild's newsletter *Old Woody Views* covers the hobby of collecting wooden money, as does its *Encyclopedia of Wooden Money.* Founded in 1975. 350 members. Contact Matt Welch, Club Administrator.

Americans Combatting Terrorism (ACT)

PO Box 370
Telluride, CO 81435

Members include 250 corporations, 50 individuals, 30 news media affiliates, 20 nonprofit groups, and 15 government representatives seeking to reduce what the organization believes are the primary causes of terrorism (deadly armed people with a grudge). ACT provides corporate and governmental policy statements on censorship, disinformation, justice, and secrecy. The group, which trains and educates members using security penetration and terrorist scenario exercises, maintains a library of 30,000 microfiche documents related to terrorism (for members only). Founded in 1978. 365 members. Contact Thomas P. O'Connor, Executive Director.

Americans for Decency (AFD)

871 Post Ave.
Staten Island, NY 10310   (718) 442-6088

"Decency Belongs Everywhere" is the motto of the AFD, a loosely formed group of individuals and organizations whose goal is to "promote decency in America." AFD describes its goals as conservative and traditional, objecting to "free access to marijuana, pornography, and classroom sex education" and to the "loud and vulgar so-called music with suggestive lyrics that is constantly broadcast."

As opposed to what it opposes, AFD supports respect for life and death; sanctity of marriage; the belief that abortion is murder; nonsanction of vulgarity on television and radio; rejection of the Equal Rights Amendment; eradication of pornography; and rejection of the gay and lesbian way of life. AFD refuses to buy newspapers and magazines featuring stories and photographs that contain pornography or emphasize sex. It encourages letter-writing campaigns to government representatives, television networks, and sponsors, and refuses to buy manufacturers' products if they sponsor telecasts the group considers offensive. AFD does not patronize theaters and other places of amusement that "have no sense of decency in their shows."

AFD holds no meetings, collects no dues. It continues to sponsor the Americans for Decency Postage Stamp Project, which is attempting to convince (so far with no luck) the U.S. Postal Service to issue an Americans for Decency Stamp. Wonder what it thinks of the Elvis stamp? Founded in 1975. Contact Paul J. Gangemi, Founder.

Americans for Nonsmokers' Rights (ANR)

2530 San Pablo Ave., Suite J
Berkeley, CA 94702   (415) 841-3032

ANR seeks to protect the rights of nonsmokers in the workplace and other public settings. It maintains the American Nonsmokers' Rights Foundation, which promotes smoking prevention, nonsmokers' rights, and public education about passive smoking. ANR publishes the *Smokefree Travel Guide, Legislative Approaches to a Smokefree Society,* and *Matrix of Major Local Smoking Ordinances in the U.S.* Founded in 1976. 15,000 members. Contact Mark Pertschuk, Executive Director.

America's Society of Separated and Divorced Men (ASDM)
575 Keep St.
Elgin, IL 60120   (312) 695-2200

Members are separated and divorced men. Goal is to assist men "in fighting the divorce racket." ASDM is dedicated to the elimination of unreasonable alimony, child support, custody, and property settlement awards. The Society reports that it is likewise devoted to establishing respect for marriage in the courts and to upholding the rights of fathers to their children. ASDM supports the development and maintenance of certain experimental federal and Supreme Court suits and works at educating the public about divorce customs and practices. It conducts interviews with divorced and separated men to discuss their situations and offer help if possible. Also provides pro-male attorney referrals. Founded in 1968. Contact Richard Templeton, President.

AMOA - International Flipper Pinball Association
141 W Vine St.
Milwaukee, WI 53212   (414) 263-0233

"Dedicated to worldwide pinball promotion," and particularly, league play, IFPA is funded by the Amusement and Music Operators Association (AMOA) and the world's four leading flipper pinball manufacturers: Data East Pinball, Midway Manufacturing (makers of Bally machines), Premier Technology (manufacturers of Gottlieb machines), and Williams Electronics Games. Members include both "street" and arcade operators, distributors and other manufacturers doing business in the coin-op industry, and adult and youth players.

The International Flippers hold an annual world championship called "Flipper Frenzy," with competitions for open team, women's team, singles (men and women), and youth competition. One highlight of the frenzy is the "Single Flibber Doubles" tournament, in which two people are on the same machine at the same time, each handling a flipper button. At the first Flipper Frenzy in 1991, players converged on Chicago from 20 states as well as from Canada, Scotland, Spain, and England.

IFPA publishes a variety of pamphlets and guides, including a sheet on historic pinball moments (*1930—Little Whirl-Wind, the first upright pin game is invented; 1931—Baffle Ball becomes the first commercially successful pin game; 1991-Checkpoint, the first pinball with player-select music*), and a glossary of pinball terms (*nudging—the most common term used to refer to the body-English players employ when playing a machine*). It also issues the *IFPA Tournament and League Primer.* Founded in 1990. Contact Doug A. Young, Executive Director.

Amputee Shoe and Glove Exchange (ASGE)
PO Box 27067
Houston, TX 77227

A free information exchange which facilitates swaps of unneeded shoes and gloves by amputees. The Shoe and Glove Exchange attempts to match amputees who need the opposite shoe or glove, who are about the same age, and who have reasonably similar tastes. All mailings of shoes or gloves are between the amputees matched. The Exchange serves men, women, and children. Founded in 1959. 175 members. Contact Dr. Richard E. Wainerdi, Director.

Ancient and Honourable Order of Small Castle Owners of Great Britain
900 McKay Tower
Grand Rapids, MI 49503 (616) 458-1464

Members, many of them American, are owners of ancient edifices in Great Britain, The Ancient Order is a tongue-in-cheek organization whose stationery shows a wine bottle, wine glass, and a radiator surrounding a castle. The radiator represents the castle owner's biggest headache, the heating problem. Motto is "Tax Vobiscum" (Tax Be With You). Contact Hollis M. Baker, Secretary.

Ancient Astronaut Society (AAS)
1921 St. Johns Ave.
Highland Park, IL 60035-3105 (708) 295-8899

Motto is, "Come Search With Us!" Members are open-minded individuals united to determine whether earth was visited in prehistoric times by extraterrestrial beings and whether advanced civilizations existed on earth prior to recorded history. They come from all 50 states and 88 other countries (members, not aliens).

Founder Gene Phillips says that the idea for the AAS came to him after viewing a television special based upon Erich von Daniken's book, *Chariots of the Gods.* Daniken is a member, of course. The AAS conducts member field expeditions to remote areas to examine evidence of technologically advanced civilizations and extraterrestrial intervention, as well as more mundane trips to museums and archaeological sites. As Phillips notes: "If human intelligence on Earth *did* occur all of a sudden as we are taught, then surely it did not *evolve*, but was brought here, in one form or another. *Mankind* is, of course, the best evidence of the intervention of intelligent beings from outer space. Either we are their *product*, or we are their *descendants*. (Emphasis is Mr. Phillip's.)

AAS publishes *Ancient Skies* (in English and German), a bimonthly newsletter, and sponsors world conferences, the next of which will be held in Las Vegas in August of 1993. Dues are $12 for one year. Founded in 1973. 6000 members. Contact Gene M. Phillips, Founder.

The Angel Planes (TAP)
2595 Chandler, #12
Las Vegas, NV 89120 (702) 736-1604

Volunteer pilots whose mission is to fly blood to central blood banks before it deteriorates. The Angels are also dedicated to making emergency flights to rural hospitals to deliver special types of blood, picking up blood from mobile blood drives so that the blood can be prepared for transfusion within six hours of its donation, and transporting critical care (but not trauma) patients as well as delivering donated organs. TAP publishes *Plane Talk*, a quarterly newsletter. Founded in 1985. 500 members. Contact Ann Mishoulam, President.

Animal Liberation (AL)
319 W. 74th St.
New York, NY 10023 (212) 874-1792

Vegetarians opposed to all animal experimentation that involves the cutting, maiming, inflicting of pain and stress, or killing of animals. Other members are individuals who are sympathetic to the cause of animal welfare reform. AL seeks to promote animal welfare and educate the public on the benefits of a vegetarian diet (love that broccoli). Founded in 1971. 300 members. Contact Dudley Giehl, President.

Annette Funicello Fan Club (AFFC)
Box 134
Nestleton, ON, Canada L0B 1L0 (416) 986-0196

Fans of Annette Funicello (1942-), the terminally perky movie actress and former Mickey Mouse Club Mouseketeer. Part of American folklore, the Mickey Mouse Club was a popular television series which ran from 1955 through 1959. The young actors that appeared on the show were of course known as Mouseketeers, and Funicello was one of the most popular. The club monitors Funicello's personal and professional activities, including her peanut butter commercials. AFFC publishes the *Annette Fan Club Newsletter* and *Annette Featurette* journal. Founded in 1961. 300 members. Contact Mary Lou Fitton, President.

Anonymous Families History Project (AFHP)
Department of Individual and Family Studies
101 Alison Hall
University of Delaware
Newark, DE 19716 (302) 451-6522

Steering committee of 12 is composed of faculty members at colleges and universities, mostly historians. Participating scholars encourage their students to write the social histories (as distinct from genealogies) of their own families and to deposit them in the Anonymous Family History Archive at the University of Minnesota, a component of the Social Welfare History Archives Center. Founded in 1971. Contact Prof. Tamara K. Hareven, Director.

Antique and Art Glass Salt Shaker Collectors Society (AAGSSCS)
1618 S. Main St.
Clyde, OH 43410 (419) 547-7231

Members are collectors of Victorian and art salt shakers. The Salt Shakers encourage communication among members and provide for the exchange of information. The Society publishes the *The Pioneer*, a quarterly association and industry newsletter. Founded in 1983. 100 members. Contact Dick and Mary Ann Krauss, Co-Presidents.

Antique Doorknob Collectors of America (ADCA)
PO Box 126
Eola, IL 60519 (708) 357-2381

Get a load of those doorknobs. ADCA is a group of collectors and antique dealers interested in antique doorknobs and related hardware. It publishes the *The Doorknob Collector*, a bimonthly newsletter containing historical articles and calendar of events. Founded in 1981. 183 members. Contact Raymond J. Nemec, Secretary Treasurer.

Antique Wireless Association (AWA)
Main St.
Holcomb, NY 14469   (716) 657-7489

Members are radio historians and collectors interested in documenting the history and technology of the wireless, the work of its pioneers and early broadcasting, and all phases of communication. These people are primarily concerned with wireless or radio transmitting or receiving apparatus used in wireless telegraphy and/or telephony during the early years of radio broadcasting. AWA has created a museum of 25,000 historical items and develops and presents historical radio and radio film programs. It annually sponsors several historical radio meets. Founded in 1952. 3600 members. Contact Bruce L. Kelley, Director.

Aquarian Research Foundation (ARF)
5620 Morton St.
Philadelphia, PA 19144   (215) 849-3237

Say, it's the dawning of the age of the Aquarian Research Foundation. ARF conducts research in discovering ways people can help bring a new age of love and peace into the world. To accomplish this goal, it provides printing apprenticeships to peace activists. *Aquarian Alternatives*, a newsletter published six to 10 times per year, provides information on alternative life-styles, new age and birth control information, and related subjects. ARF also publishes *The Natural Birth Control Book* and materials on new developments in the alternative movement. Founded in 1969. Contact Art Rosenblum, Director.

Archonist Club (ARCLUB)
682 Callahan Pl.
Mendota Heights, MN 55118

A civic, quasi-religious association that reports it has Christian orientation and a semi-select membership. Archonism is defined as "a positive interpretation of the Divine Will in relation to civic affairs and to political matters; the essential concept is decision of matters on the basis of merits in logic and in morality." The group opposes public funding for political campaigns, believing that the electoral process is "corrupt and prone to Zionist influence." It advocates a wide-ranging and somewhat discombobulated series of proposals, including disengagement from foreign interests of "questionable merits," renunciation of Zionism and of "criminal Israel," advocacy of an Archonist Constitution for the U.S., de-emphasis of sports in American culture, "rational constraints on irresponsibly behaving carriers of AIDS," equal protection without reverse discrimination, and restoration of voluntary prayer in public schools.

ARCLUB is also involved in such areas as analysis of human issues in Archonist perspective and promotion of human interests defined by Archonist ideology. Additionally, it strives for public enlightenment, selective development of nuclear power and alternative sources of energy, and equitable reforms in taxation.

Last but not least, the Archonist Club has organized the Klinger Plan "for effective coordinated action by conscientious persons who cannot accept military service in a Zionist-related war." Inspired by the character of Klinger of the television show *MASH*, the plan states that "in the event of conscription for a pro-Zionist purpose, our advisees will assume the guise of lesbian-oriented transsexuals, in lesbian hangouts, in the company of pro-Archonist, anti-Zionist lesbians." That should fool them. As a sideline, the group conducts sociological research on transsexualism, perhaps in order to better prepare for possible long-term impersonation. Founded in 1967. Contact William L. Knaus, Regent.

Art Dreco Institute (ADI)
1709 Sanchez
San Francisco, CA 94131   (415) 647-7532

Artists, art dealers, collectors, historians, and other individuals interested in Art Dreco, an art form characterized by a total disregard for public taste and fashion. The Institute recognizes "found" or utilitarian objects and acknowledges such facets as Sports Dreco, Television Dreco, and Architectural Dreco, proving that it is open-minded about trash. ADI maintains that Art Dreco has existed since the beginning of time, although the late 19th century, 1930s, 1940s, and 1950s have produced it most prolifically. Objectives are to make the public more aware of Art Dreco, give "bad taste" a higher aesthetic standing than it currently enjoys, and teach people how to recognize bad art when they see it. The group lectures, sponsors film festivals featuring selections of "loathsome" movies, and authenticates Dreco *objects d'art.* The Institute maintains the Dreco hall of fame, museum, and biographical archives. Publications include the *Art Dreco Catalog.* Founded in 1973. 250 members. Contact Paul Drexler, Director.

Assassination Archives and Research Center (AARC)
918 F St. NW, Suite 510
Washington, DC 20004   (202) 393-1917

If you're looking for conspiracy evidence, perhaps here's a place to start. AARC is an organization of independent researchers, academics, and private citizens with an interest in political assassinations. AARC operates the research center created for the study of political assassinations throughout American and world history, while focusing on the post World War II era with extensive collections on the John F. Kennedy and Martin Luther King, Jr. assassinations. Founded in 1984. 300 members. Contact Bud Fensterwald, President.

Association for Astrological Psychology (AAP)
83 Porteous Way
Fairfax, CA 94930   (415) 453-5857

Members are psychologists, counselors, and astrologers working to enhance the credibility of astrology in the mental health professions. AAP establishes general guidelines for the application of astrology in the fields of counseling and psychotherapy. It issues *The Astrotherapy Newsletter.* Founded in 1967. 300 members. Contact Glenn Perry Ph.D., President.

Association for Gravestone Studies (AGS)
46 Plymouth Road
Needham, MA 02192   (617) 455-8180

A group of historians, archaeologists, anthropologists, genealogists, folklorists, art historians, and other individuals and organizations interested in the study and preservation of old gravestones. AGS seeks to promote public awareness of and education on the preservation of gravestones. It serves as an information clearinghouse for the public and aids community restoration programs by encouraging orderly and systematic recording practices and by conducting restoration workshops. The group publishes the *Association for Gravestone Studies Newsletter,* which presents information about projects, literature, and research concerning gravestones, including folk art carvings, lettering, epitaphs, shapes, materials used, and symbolism. AGS also publishes the book *A Graveyard Preservation Primer,* regional cemetery guides, and material on preservation of gravestones and graveyards. It produces the slide show *Early New England Gravestones and the Stories They Tell.* Founded in 1977. 900 members. Contact Rosalee F. Oakley, Executive Director.

Association for Research and Enlightenment (ARE)
215 67th St.
Virginia Beach, VA 23451   (804) 428-3588

ARE seeks to give physical, mental, and spiritual help through investigation of the 14,250 "readings" left by Edgar Cayce (1877-1945), a clairvoyant diagnostician who is said to have "possessed an utterly amazing ability to describe, in a kind of self-imposed hypnotic sleep, individuals and events which he had never seen." The group coordinates a medical research program with the ARE Clinic in Phoenix, AZ. With regard to medical data from the Cayce readings, ARE recommends that, except for noncritical home remedies, all medical information should be used under supervision of a licensed physician. It has a 50,000-volume library on metaphysics, psychic phenomena, and related subjects. The Edgar Cayce Foundation has custody of the readings and conducts a continuous program of indexing, extracting, microfilming, and otherwise organizing the material in the files; all data files are open to the public. The group issues several publications, including *Venture Inward,* a bimonthly magazine focusing on readings given by Cayce; includes book reviews and general information on metaphysical and paranormal ideas and subjects. Founded in 1931. 90,000 members. Contact Charles Thomas Cayce Ph.D., President.

Association for the Study of Dada and Surrealism (ASDS)
University of Southern California
Department of French and Italian
Taper 126 University Park
Los Angeles, CA 90089   (213) 740-3700

North American branch of the International Association for the Study of Dada and Surrealism (Paris, France). Members include scholars, collectors, teachers, students, and others interested in the Dada and Surrealist movements in literature and the arts. ASDS desires to facilitate studies on the men and women, ideas, and works connected with these movements. The Dada movement in art and literature flourished from 1916 to 1920, declaring a program of protest against civilization and rejecting all previous art by means of violent satire and incongruous humor. Several of its chief exponents were later associated with the surrealist movement in art. ASDS publishes the annual *Dada-Surrealism.* and sponsors an annual conference in conjunction with the Modern Language Association. Founded in 1964. 150 members. Contact Albert Sonnenfeld, President.

Association for the Study of Food and Society (ASFS)

Texas A&M University
Department of Sociology
College Station, TX 77843   (409) 845-4944

Just yesterday I was wondering about the sociocultural aspects of the Big Mac as I waited patiently in line for a chance to drive to the drive-through window and collect my food in recyclable bags from teenagers occupying an economic strata one short step above the minimum wage while suffering from oily glands and hormonal fits. Like me, ASFS members are an interdisciplinarian lot dedicated to the study of how food and society relate, interlock, and feed off one another. A sort of deep structural look at the cultural identity of food, probing the existential conditions of "we eat, therefore we are," and "we are what we eat," which, come to think of it, is probably how Mr. Potato Head came to be.

Members include social scientists, nutritionists, dieticians, and folklorists. ASFS examines issues such as nutrition education, food policy and programs, hunger and food security, malnutrition, eating behaviors, food habits and practices, dietary change, nutritional epidemiology, applied nutrition, agricultural development, foodways, and food production, distribution, and purchasing. The group publishes a newsletter which includes information about resources related to food and society, book reviews, short papers, teaching information, and announcements. It also has published *Teaching Food and Society*, a collection of instructional materials. ASFS holds an annual conference and membership is $40 per year ($10 for students). Founded in 1986. 61 members. Contact William Alex McIntosh, President.

Association for Transpersonal Psychology (ATP)

PO Box 3049
Stanford, CA 94309   (415) 327-2066

A membership branch of the Transpersonal Institute, ATP is a group of professional and nonprofessional individuals interested in the development of the transpersonal orientation, toward the "realization of transpersonal, positive, personal and species-wide human capacities and potentialities." No, we don't know what that means either. ATP encourages theoretical and applied scientific transpersonal research as a "vital part of psychology, education, religion, philosophy and other related fields." The organization is concerned, like so many of us are, with "transpersonal values, unitive consciousness, and transcendence of the self." ATP holds meetings and lectures concerned with transpersonal phenomena and publishes the *Journal of Transpersonal Psychology*, containing information on theory, research application in transpersonal psychology, psychotherapy, spiritual disciplines, consciousness research, and cross-cultural issues. Founded in 1971. 2600 members. Contact Miles A. Vich, Editor.

Association of Acrobats (AA)

6 Walworth Ave.
Newport, NSW 2106, Australia   2 991851

A worldwide association with members (amateur and professional acrobats) from 30 countries. AA works to create a better understanding of the background and techniques of acrobatics and strives to further knowledge of celebrated performers and their work in all branches of acrobatics, including the circus, theater, and cabaret. It offers correspondence courses, which apparently teach acrobatics by mail, and publishes the monthly *World Acrobatics*. Founded in 1954. 1460 members. Contact R. P. H. Samuels, Secretary & Editor.

Association of Balloon and Airship Constructors (ABAC)
PO Box 90864
San Diego, CA 92169   (619) 270-4049

Association of lighter-than-air technologists who just can't seem to keep their feet on the ground. Members believe in the utility of a broad spectrum of lighter-than-air craft for modern applications. Projects range from solo hot air or gas airship and balloon projects to industrial or government-funded major programs. ABAC provides research and referral services to members requesting help with their own projects. It maintains a library of 1500 volumes and archives containing reports, memoranda, notes, proposals, Navy and Air Force manuals, and rare and otherwise unpublished items on rigid airship operations, flight training, and hot air balloon construction. Founded in 1974. 250 members. Contact Donald E. Woodward, Executive Officer.

Association of Black Storytellers (ABS)
PO Box 27456
Philadelphia, PA 19118   (215) 898-5118

Members are black storytellers (yes, really) and enthusiasts seeking to establish a forum to promote the black oral tradition and to attract an audience. ABS works for the reissue of out-of-print story collections, bestows the Zora Neale Hurston Award to pioneers in black storytelling, and holds the annual National Festival of Black Storytelling. Founded in 1984. 175 members. Contact Linda Goss, President.

Association of Bottled Beer Collectors (ABBC)
4 Woodhall Road
Penn
Wolverhampton, W. Midlands WV4 4DJ, England   902 342672

99 bottles of beer on the wall (hey, careful, that's my collection). A club for enthusiasts of bottled beer collecting, ABBC informs members of available bottled beers and communicates with breweries and related organizations. Founded in 1983. 150 members. Contact R. T. Heath, Chairman.

Association of Brewers (AOB)
Box 287
Boulder, CO 80306-0287   (303) 447-0816

Members are interested in the home brewing of beer, including beer retailers, consumers, wholesalers, and manufacturers. AOB disseminates information for home brewers and those interested in the art of home brewing and commercial brewing on a small scale ("microbreweries" and "brewpubs"). It operates the Institute for Brewing Studies and takes the testing very seriously.

AOB publishes *Beer and Brewing: National Conference for Quality Beer and Brewing*. Other publications include *Brewery Operations: Practical Ideas for Microbrewers* and *Microbrewers Resource Handbook and Directory*, which lists brewers, suppliers, manufacturers, and consultants and contains a handbook of guidelines for starting a brewing operation. It also issues *New Brewer,* a bimonthly magazine providing technical, production, and business information to commercial brewers, restaurateurs, and pub owners. Last, but not least, the Association of Brewers publishes the bottom of the alphabet title, *Zymurgy: The Magazine for the Homebrewer and Beer Lover,* a quarterly magazine containing product reviews, a problem-solving column, recommendations for beginning brewers, and news from home brew clubs (batch 144-a came out better than we, hic, expected). It also includes calendar of events, competition news, recipes, brewers portraits, and British and Canadian brewing notes.

AOB gathers the members at the annual National Micro-brewery Conference and sponsors the annual National Homebrewers Conference. Founded in 1978. 9000 members. Contact Charles N. Papazian, President.

The Association of Comedy Artists (TACA)
PO Box 1796
New York, NY 10025   (212) 864-6620

Members are comedians, comedy buffs, comedy club owners, comedy writers, critics, members of the press, talent agents, and other interested individuals dedicated to the advancement of comedy as a serious art form. TACA seeks to gain greater public recognition and status for comedy by promoting the highest professional standards in the field. It conducts professional training courses, lectures, and seminars on comedy as art. The association sponsors the Comedy Arts Institute, which offers classes in comedy writing, improvisation, stand-up comedy, and seminars. And it holds the annual New York Festival of Comedy as well as the occasional Women in Humor Conferences. Founded in 1978. 2000 members. Contact Barbara Contardi, President.

Association of Concern for Ultimate Reality and Meaning (ACURM)
15 St. Mary St.
Toronto, ON, Canada M4Y 2R5   (416) 922-2476

No, not an offshoot of the Woody Allen Fan Club, but a mature group of philosophical educators yearning to study how man in the past answered the question of existence in order to help modern man "understand his own mystery, uniqueness, and originality." We wish them good luck.

Objectives include fostering universal brotherhood and understanding, promoting interdisciplinary scientific research, and "encouraging a universal dialogue about ultimate reality." These and the infinite number of related issues are examined in the quarterly *Ultimate Reality and Meaning.* Founded in 1976. Contact Prof. Tibor Horvath SJ, Director.

Association of Old Crows (AOC)
1000 N. Payne St.
Alexandria, VA 22314   (703) 549-1600

Professional association of scientists, engineers, managers, operators, educators, military personnel, and others engaged in the science of electronic warfare and related areas. The term "Old Crows" emerged during World War II when the U.S. and allied bombing raids were first outfitted with radio and radar receivers and transmitters, code named "Ravens." Operators were known as "Raven Operators" and later as "Old Crows." AOC works for the advancement of electronic warfare in full cooperation with the U.S. Department of Defense and is dedicated to national security and a strong defense posture for the U.S. and its allies. It provides members with information on new developments in electronic warfare technology, training, operations, and doctrines. Founded in 1964. 25,000 members. Contact Gus Slayton, Executive Director.

Association of Oldetime Barbell and Strongmen (AOBS)

611 Banner Ave., Suite 4D
Brooklyn, NY 11235   (718) 648-5254

Hear ye, hear ye, the strongmen are about to lift. Members are strength athletes, weightlifters, and others interested in muscle promotions. The group promotes bodybuilding and contests of strength and works to preserve the history of "physical culture." Former champions flex and preen at an annual reunion banquet. 200 members. Contact Vic Boff, President.

Association of Space Explorers - U.S.A. (ASE-USA)

35 White St.
San Francisco, CA 94109   (415) 931-0585

Rather exclusive club of astronauts, cosmonauts, and other space travelers from 18 countries who have made at least one orbit around the earth, presumedly while in a spacecraft. ASE provides a forum for discussion of global issues, encourages cooperation among nations in the exploration and development of space for the benefit of humanity, and promotes the use of space sciences and technology to improve the social, economic, and cultural conditions of humankind. In particular, ASE looks to space to resolve world problems regarding energy, natural resources, and environmental pollution. The space travelers work to educate young space explorers about the importance of international cooperation and to increase awareness and understanding of the significance and achievements of space exploration. The group holds an annual week-long congress and makes available *The Home Planet*, a composite of photos of Earth taken from space interwoven with quotations by the astronauts and cosmonauts. Founded in 1985. 150 members. Contact John Fabian, President.

Astro-Psychology Institute (API)

2640 Greenwich, Suite 403
San Francisco, CA 94123   (415) 921-1192

For those continually experiencing that Uranus kind of day and looking for a change, API may be the answer. It seeks to educate the public on the effects and influence of planets and celestial bodies on the lives of humans and other forms of life. As part of its quest for planetary truth, API publishes *New Age Astrology*, a yearbook providing information on "the changes in planetary patterns and the way they affect the twelve zodiacal types/signs during the ensuing twelve month period." Other publications include the annual *New Age Astrology Guide*, and *Astro Rhythms, Astrology, The Star Science from A-Z*, and *Five Keys to Inner Wisdom*. Founded in 1979. Contact Milo Kovar, Director.

Astromusic

PO Box 118
New York, NY 10033 (212) 942-0004

Individuals interested in celestial music or "the music of the spheres," which is defined as a person's horoscope or actual birth chart translated into a musical composition. Integrating music and astronomy, the composition is a musical interpretation of planetary positions and angular separations at the time of an individual's birth, intended to enhance meditation, relaxation, and healing. The association provides cassettes of compositions and holds four to six conferences per year as well as an annual Astro World Congress. Founded in 1980. 500 members. Contact Gerald Jay Markoe.

Atlantis Research Group (ARG)

F.G. Lanham Federal Building
819 Taylor St.
Box 17364
Ft. Worth, TX 76102-0364

Way down, in a hole in the ocean, the Atlantis Research Group conducts research and serves as a clearinghouse of information regarding underwater archaeology in the North Atlantic. ARG focuses on efforts to uncover "artifacts and civilizations of man's far-distant past." Founded in 1989. 8 members. Contact Charles William Horton, President.

Awareness Research Foundation (ARF)

DeSoto Square
35 Ritter Road, Apt. 29
Hayesville, NC 28904 (704) 389-8672

Members are interested in metaphysics, space ships, reincarnation, and "cosmic truths." ARF strives to educate individuals in multilevel and multiplane awareness, the first step of which is comprehending the phrase, "multilevel and multiplane awareness." It seeks to "help people accomplish their missions in their present incarnations" even though time may well be on their side. The group contends that there are seven universes, each with a governing lord, and believes that each person experiences stages of evolution before joining the human race (rock, snail, game show host). ARF delivers messages from higher beings (as well as book reviews and health articles) in *Meet the Lords*, a quarterly newsletter. Other publications include *My Visits to Other Planets* and *Technique of Past Lives Recall.* Dues are $15 bucks annually, payable now rather than in the next life. Founded in 1969. Contact Helen I. Hoag, Executive Director.

Baker Street Irregulars (BSI)

34 Pierson Ave.
Norwood, NJ 07648 (201) 768-2241

A group of people interested in the fictional detective Sherlock Holmes, his fictional biographer Dr. Watson, and writings about them, the Irregulars study and explicate on Sherlock Holmes and his world. BSI sponsors the Silver Blaze Handicap (a horse race) and awards Irregular Shillings to members who have shown serious interest over a period of years. It publishes the *Baker Street Journal: An Irregular Quarterly of Sherlockiana*, available for $15 per year. Once a year the Irregulars gather for dinner, toasts, stories, and awards. Founded in 1934. 275 members. Contact Thomas L. Stix Jr., Wiggins.

Bald-Headed Men of America (BHMA)
3819 Bridges St.
Morehead City, NC 28557   (919) 726-1855

Members are some of the many, many bald-headed men who agree with the philosophy "bald is beautiful." Dedicated to the belief that bald-headed men (whether maintaining chrome-dome, balding pate, or simple bald spot) have extra individual character, BHMA strives to cultivate a sense of pride for all bald-headed men and to eliminate the loss of self-esteem associated with the loss of hair (I am bald and I am beautiful). The group promotes National Rub a Bald Head Week. The founder gives speeches and makes television appearances proclaiming "the fun of being bald." The bald-headed ones operate a hall of fame and publish the *Chrome Dome*, a newsletter covering conventions and other activities for bald-headed men. BHMA sponsors an annual conference which is always held on the second Saturday in September at Morehead City, NC. Founded in 1974. 20,000 members. Contact John T. Capps III, Founder.

Balloon Post Collectors Club (BPCC)
PO Box 25
Deerfield, IL 60015   (312) 948-9440

A unified front of collectors of balloon philately and related materials, the Balloon Post Collectors gather and distribute philatelic and other information concerning ballooning. The group is currently researching how the U.S. celebrated the bicentennial of ballooning. The latest hot-air is reported in the quarterly *Balloon Post News* and the periodic *Balloon Stratosphere Flights*. BPCC meets annually on Memorial Day weekend. Founded in 1970. 600 members. Contact Stephen Neulander, President.

Barbara Eden International Fan Club (BEIFC)
1332 N. Ulster St.
Allentown, PA 18103   (215) 434-2977

For individuals dreaming of Genie, BEIFC attracts people interested in the activities of actress Barbara Eden (1934-). The club informs members of upcoming appearances, compiles statistics of Eden's TV and film credits from 1956 to the present, and maintains biographical archives and a hall of fame. Its *Barbara Eden International Fan Club-Newsletter* is a bimonthly containing television and movie credit updates and color photos. Founded in 1977. 300 members. Contact Kenneth A. Bealer, President.

Barber Coin Collector Society (BCCS)
PO Box 382246
Memphis, TN 38183-2246

BCCS promotes the advancement of knowledge regarding barber coinage, a practice many people know nothing about, hence the organization. Barber coinage is covered exclusively in its quarterly *Barber Coin Collectors Journal*. Founded in 1989. 500 members.

Baronial Order of Magna Charta (BOMC)

PO Box 601
Wayne, PA 19087

Foreground: Members of the Order are lineal male descendants of the 25 earls and barons and five nonsurety supporters who forced England's King John to sign the Magna Charta and were elected to be the first official guardians of adherence to the charter by the Magna Charta Earls and Barons in 1215.

Deep background: The original Magna Charta, or Magna Carta, was a definitive statement of feudal law and general charter of liberties. It became a symbol of protection against oppression and now is also defined as any document constituting a fundamental guarantee of rights and privileges. The term Magna Charta, and the style and wording of the original charter have been adopted, in part, into succeeding charters of England and other English colonies; it is an integral part of U.S. constitutional law and legislation.

Back to the Baronial Order: BOMC promotes literary study and social intercourse among members and fosters admiration and respect for related principles of constitutional government (ah yes dear boy, very good statement, that liberty phrase). The Order promotes awareness of the Magna Charta's history and perpetuates the memory of those 20-some earls and barons and five nonsurety supporters of the Magna Charta, observing June 15-19 as the anniversary of the granting of the charter. Annually, BOMC holds a commemorative church service and reception and bestows the Magna Charta Day Award at Arch Street Presbyterian Church, Philadelphia, PA. Founded in 1898. 375 members. Contact Andrew R. Sullivan, Marshall.

Baseball Hall of SHAME (BHS)

PO Box 31867
Palm Beach Gardens, FL 33420

Pete Rose seems a sure bet to be inducted into this hall. Members are fans, players, coaches, managers, owners, umpires, broadcasters, sportswriters, and other individuals associated with baseball. The Hall seeks to recognize and dishonor "hilarious bloopers and wacky blunders" in baseball history, including horrible hitting, pitiful pitching, and foolish pitching, while paying a lighthearted tribute to baseball. The members are solicited for nominations to the Hall and eventually elect the new inductees. The Hall officially recognizes all persons submitting nominations that are accepted. An annual induction ceremony is held (no word on whether inductees attend) and a museum is planned to house memorabilia from shameful moments in baseball history. BHS has published the *The Baseball Hall of Shame.* (volumes 1-4). Founded in 1983. 752 members. Contact Bruce M. Nash, Co-Founder.

Bass'n Gal

PO Box 13925
2007 Roosevelt
Arlington, TX 76013   (817) 265-6214

Members are women interested in the sport of bass fishing and dedicated to bringing together other women anglers and encouraging preservation of natural resources. To help improve members' skills as anglers, the club promotes the exchange of techniques and ideas and holds eight tournaments annually. The group strives to bring an end to discrimination against women in participation of certain outdoor activities, dispelling old beliefs that women do not have the skill or experience to compete with their male counterparts on the same level. It attempts to stimulate the public awareness (what kind of lure?) of bass fishing as a major sport and a relaxing pastime, and works to introduce youth to the pleasures of fishing. It maintains the library of Bass'n Gal Classic Films, bestows scholarship to women seeking to further their education in an outdoor-related field, and publishes *Bass'n Gal Magazine* on a bimonthly basis. Founded in 1976. 26,376 members. Contact Sugar Ferris, President.

Bat Conservation International (BCI)
PO Box 162603
Austin, TX 78716   (512) 327-9721

Somebody has to stick up for these critters. Members are individuals in 50 countries working to document the value and conservation needs of bats. BCI seeks to increase public awareness of the ecological importance of bats and promote bat conservation and management efforts. It publicizes conservation of the flying fox bat, found on Pacific islands. BCI publishes the quarterly and succinctly named *Bats*. It also issues *America's Neighborhood Bats* (the kind that fly in the bathroom), *Why Save Bats, Bats, Pesticides and Politics,* and instructions for building a bat house (the construction of which will surely start the neighbors talking). Founded in 1982. 8500 members. Contact Toni Turner.

Beach Boys Stomp Fan Club (BBSFC)
22 Avondale Road
Wealdstone
London HA3 7RE, England   81 8634031

Wouldn't it be nice if individuals from Australasia, Europe, the Far East, and the United States who are fans of the Beach Boys formed a club? The Stomp disseminates information to members about the group, its activities, and its recordings. It publishes a newsletter on a bimonthly basis and holds an annual conference, which is always in September. For the record, original members of the American rock 'n' roll group included Brian Wilson (1942-), Dennis Wilson (1944-83), Carl Wilson (1946-), Bruce Johnston (1942-), Alan Jardine (1942), and Michael Love (1941-). Founded in 1977. 850 members. Contact Mike Grant, Executive Officer.

BeachFront U.S.A. (BFUSA)
PO Box 328
Moreno Valley, CA 92337   (714) 684-2532

Members advocate the concept of nudism as "wholesomeness of the human body and its natural functions and activities." Representing the nudist and naturist communities, BFUSA promotes the legalization of clothes-optional recreation at designated beaches and other public sites and seeks to educate the public on the nudist/naturist culture. The group sponsors summer expeditions to established nude beaches and maintains the Callen-Davis Memorial Fund to provide funding for legal action to secure nudist rights. BFUSA markets items of interest to supporters and publishes the *Free Beach News,* a monthly newsletter containing association news, updates on California free beaches, and news of the Callen-

David Memorial Fund. The group also issues *No-Wear Land: Selected Spots for Clothing Optional Recreation* and produces map and description/updates of clothing-optional beaches in southern California. Membership fees are $15 per year for single individuals and $20 per year for families. Founded in 1985. 113 members. Contact Bob Campbell, President.

Beauty Without Cruelty U.S.A. (BWC)
175 W. 12th St., No. 16-G
New York, NY 10011   (212) 989-8073

Affiliated with the American Fund for Alternatives to Animal Research, BWC opposes the painful and destructive use of animals in the production of apparel and toiletries. It informs the public of the suffering of both wild and farmed furbearing animals, of trapped wild animals, and of animal products in and laboratory testing of cosmetics. BWC sponsors fashion shows of simulated fur garments and other garments without fur to demonstrate the humane alternatives to real fur.

BWC provides members with a list of cruelty-free products and where to find them and publishes *The Compassionate Shopper*, a quarterly newsletter providing names and addresses of manufacturers that do not test products on animals. The group maintains a celebrity committee and has the support of some 360 celebrities who disapprove of the use of fur in apparel, including Don Henley, Olivia Newton-John, Loretta Swit, Robert Redford, Sting, Dennis Weaver, and River Phoenix. Membership fee for BWC is $15 per year. Founded in 1972. 7000 members. Contact Dr. Ethel Thurston, Chairwoman.

Beaver Defenders (BD)
Unexpected Wildlife Refuge
PO Box 765
Newfield, NJ 08344   (609) 697-3541

An organization for those interested in preserving and protecting wildlife, especially beavers. Purpose of the Beaver Defenders is to educate the public and maintain a 450-acre wildlife refuge. The Defenders conduct research on beavers and publish *The Beaver Defenders*, a quarterly containing editorials, selected articles, essays, and poems (about beavers). Founded in 1970. 200 members. Contact Hope Sawyer Buyukmihci, Secretary.

Beer Can Collectors of America (BCCA)
747 Merus Ct.
Fenton, MO 63026-2092   (314) 343-6486

Individuals of all ages and interests who collect beer cans and related items. BCCA presents the "Can of the Year Award" for the best designed beer can currently on the market and maintains the can hall of fame. President Dan Hicks recalls first being attracted to beer cans because "they kind of look neat."

"You get a feeling for a certain can, and you like it, you desire to have it, you work on acquiring it," says Hicks, describing the can wooing process. "When you do get it, you like to look at it. Me personally, when I go after a can, I have a shelf in my basement that's for the Can of the Month." The group publishes the bimonthly *News Report* with all the hot news on cans as well as *American Beer Cans 1975-1988* and a catalog of all known beer cans (U.S. and foreign). BCCA sponsors the annual CANvention, which is always held in September. Founded in 1970. 4500 members. Contact Dan Hicks, President.

Beer Drinkers of America (BDA)
150 Paularino, Suite 190
Costa Mesa, CA 92626   (714) 557-BEER

For all you do, this group's for you. Individuals over 21 years of age advocating da right of Americans to drink beer responsibly. Also stands with cold one in hand against excessive government regulation and taxation of beer. BDA emphasizes moderation among adults who choose to drink beer, and concern for community health and safety. The group believes beer should not be taxed disproportionately to other consumer products and works to remind government officials that "the majority of beer drinkers are responsible people." BDA sponsors the Beer Drinkers of America's Party Smart Education Project and addresses legislative concerns involving proposed increases of beer excise taxes and advertising bans. Founded in 1987. Contact William Schreiber, Executive Director.

Benevolent and Loyal Order of Pessimists (BLOOP)
PO Box 1945
Iowa City, IA 52244   (319) 351-2973

Group motto is: "In front of every silver lining there's a dark cloud." Alternative motto is "the other line always moves faster." BLOOP is a tongue-in-cheek organization of pessimists, founded to counteract the insidious spread of optimists' clubs. It publishes the semiannual *BLOOP Newsletter* and convenes annually on the Saturday closest to the April 15th IRS tax-filing deadline (and the anniversary of the sinking of the Titanic), an event frequently held in Iowa City, IA. According to the Royal Order, the date is "always tentative to allow for missed plane connections and other expected natural disasters." The "lowlight" of the evening is the awarding of a trophy resembling the shape of a horse's rear end to the Pessimist of the Year.

Jack Duvall, current pessimistic president, is a pseudonym adopted by all BLOOP presidents because the name "seems to embody pessimists everywhere." The current Mr. Duvall was recently contacted by an ad agency representing the Vernor's soft drink about lending his voice to a radio commercial, although Duvall admits that he has not heard from the agency for a while and, true to his pessimistic nature, he's "not waiting by the phone to hear from them." Patron saint of the group is Mark Twain. A certificate "For Meritorious Achievement in Pessimism" is available for $10. But hey, why bother to join? We're all going to die anyway. Founded in 1975. 200 members. Contact Jack Duvall, President.

Best Candidate Committee (BCC)
1400 20th St. NW, Suite 114
Washington, DC 20036   (202) 833-8160

Goal of the group is to dream the impossible dream: to improve the quality of Congress by encouraging the selection of the "best" candidates for election. To this noble end, it conducts research and evaluates the performance and potential of candidates. Founded in 1976. Contact Harry DeWitt, Chairman.

Better World Society (BWS)
1100 17th St. NW, Suite 502
Washington, DC 20036   (202) 331-3770

A consciousness-raising group of people, corporations, founda-
tions, governments, government agencies, and nonprofit organizations that uses television programming to foster international
awareness and concern for issues relating directly to the sustaina-
bility of life on earth. BWS encourages citizens of all nations to
develop a sense of common responsibility for the fate of life on
earth and to undertake constructive action to redirect nations
toward progress and world peace. The group regards the control,
reduction, and elimination of nuclear arms as the most critical
challenge facing humanity and is also concerned with global
environmental problems such as acid rain, deforestation, ocean
pollution, soil erosion, pesticide abuse, and desertification. Founded
in 1985. 7500 members. Contact Victoria G. Markell, Executive
Director.

Bicycle Network (BN)
PO Box 8194
Philadelphia, PA 19101   (215) 222-1253

BN advocates the bicycle as a healthful, low-cost, and energy
efficient means of transportation. Members demonstrate the
practical importance of bicycle transit and pedal technology
worldwide. The Network works for the "velorution" on a global
basis. According to the network, "velorution" is the French-
Canadian word for "bicycle revolution." The group addresses
issues such as safe and practical cycling facilities (parking, commut-
ing, and transport), cyclist education, bicycle integration with public
transportation, and the role of the bicycle in developing countries.
Members receive *Cycle and Recycle* three times per year and meet
annually in Montreal, Quebec. Founded in 1976. 500 members.
Contact John Dowlin, Editor.

Big Deal (BD)
2119 College St.
Cedar Falls, IA 50613   (319) 266-8669

A group for people interested in political satire (so what).
Publishes *Big Deal* magazine. Founded in 1984. 40 members.
Contact Gerald Baker, Executive Director.

Big Thicket Association (BTA)
Box 198 - Highway 770
Saratoga, TX 77585   (409) 274-5000

Conservationists and others interested in preserving the wilderness area of southeast Texas known as the "Big Thicket," a
threemillion acre area containing a wide variety of both tropical and
temperate vegetation. The Big Thicket is one of the major resting
places along the Gulf Coast for migratory birds with at least 300
species, many endangered, having set up permanent residency in
the Big T. An 84,550-acre parcel of the Big Thicket was named a
national preserve on Oct. 11, 1974. The group maintains a museum
in Saratoga, TX, which attempts to interpret the area and serve as
an information center for visitors and researchers. The BTA
sponsors environmental education programs, hiking tours, and
seminars and maintains a nature trail in Lance Rosier Memorial

Park. Every spring the group gathers for the Big Thicket Day Festival in Saratoga. Members receive the bimonthly *Rattler Tattler* newsletter. Founded in 1964. 200 members.

Bikers Against Manslaughter (BAM)

5455 Wilshire Blvd., Room 1600
Los Angeles, CA 90036   (213) 932-1277

Motorcyclists and motorcycling organizations united to reduce the number of motorcycle accidents and fatalities in the United States. Members provide reciprocal assistance in areas such as emergency repairs, housing, and transportation. BAM provides nationwide legal and legislative services and conducts seminars on legal services aiding motorcyclists. Founded in 1982. 100,000 members. Contact Bill Bish, Director.

Black Filmmakers Hall of Fame, Inc. (BFHFI)

405 14th St., Suite 515
Oakland, CA 94612   (415) 465-0804

BFHFI studies and preserves the contributions of black filmmakers to American cinema, while seeking to educate the masses about these movie makers. It fosters cultural awareness through educational, research, and public service programs in the film arts. The Hall sponsors a film-lecture series, the Black Filmworks Festival, and the annual International Film Competition. BFHFI publishes the annual *Black Filmworks* and conducts workshops and classes. Founded in 1973. 500 members. Contact Mary Perry Smith, President.

Black Rock Coalition (BRC)

PO Box 1054, Cooper Station
New York, NY 10276

Artists, musicians, writers, and supporters of alternative/black music, performed by groups such as *Living Colour*. BRC works to foster change in the conventional operation and classification of black music and musicians within the entertainment industry, seeking to counteract competition among musicians through networking programs and the sharing of resources. The Coalition opposes what the group terms the American "apartheid-oriented" rock circuit, which BRC feels perpetuates racism, commercial restrictions, and double standards within the music industry that may deter black artists from receiving the same musical freedom of expression and marketing privileges afforded white artists. BRC promotes, produces, and distributes alternative/black music and provides information, technical expertise, and performance and recording opportunities for "musically and politically progressive musicians." It publishes the *Ravers* newsletter four to six times per year. Founded in 1985. 50 members. Contact Donald C. Eversley, Executive Officer.

Bloomsday Club (BC)

c/o Old York Books
122 French St.
New Brunswick, NJ 08901   (201) 249-0430

Members are dedicated to reading, writing about, researching, and holding social gatherings focusing on the writings of Irish writer James Joyce (1882-1941), who developed a stream of consciousness style that avoided most of the formal rules of grammar, including punctuation. Yes, he wrote, *"And then I asked him with my eyes to ask again yes and then he asked me would I yes to say yes my mountain flower and first I put my arms around him yes and drew him down to me so he could feel my breasts all perfume yes and his heart was going like mad and yes I said yes I said yes I will Yes."*

The organization name is derived from the major character in Joyce's novel *Ulysses*, Leopold Bloom. Members read, write about, research, and hold social gatherings focusing on the writings of Joyce. Currently the group is compiling an annotated edition of Joyce's works. Founded in 1975. 150 members. Contact E. T. Cecile Hopkins.

Blue Blazes Irregulars (BBI)
Team Banzai
PO Box 24590
Denver, CO 80224   (303) 671-TREK

Fans of sci-fi spoofster Buckaroo Banzai, the main character in the book and film *The Adventures of Buckaroo Banzai*. Buckaroo, for those unfamiliar with him, is a neurosurgeon and the leader of a blues band, the Hong Kong Cavaliers, who travels through the eighth dimension to battle aliens, utilizing his vast knowledge of medicine, science, music, racing, and foreign relations. The Irregulars disseminate information about the characters and actors (among them, Jeff Goldblum, Peter Weller, John Lithgow, Ellen Barkin, and Christopher Lloyd) who appeared in the film. The group proudly publishes a newsletter called *World Watch One*. Founded in 1984. 7000 members. Contact Mr. Pecos, Director.

Bobs International (BI)
Route 1, Box 120
St. Peter, MN 56082   (507) 931-6667

Group that answers the question, "what about Bob?" Members are people from countries around the world (seven, really) who are named Bob or would like to be named Bob. BI strives to assure members that Bob is not a boring name. It maintains the Famous Bobs Gallery, featuring items such as BOBsleds and shishkaBOB. Members receive all the news that Bobs need through the newsletter *Yessirree Bob*. Founded in 1986. 500 members. Contact Bob Idso, Big Bob.

Bohemia Ragtime Society (BRS)
5095 Picket Dr.
Colorado Springs, CO 80918   (719) 528-1547

BRS encourages the preservation of classical ragtime music, serving as a forum for the performance and discussion of ragtime. To get the word out, it quarterly publishes *The Top Liner Rag*. Founded in 1990. Contact Nick Taylor, President.

Boise Peace Quilt Project (BPQP)
PO Box 6469
Boise, ID 83707   (208) 378-0293

Individuals working to produce peace quilts as gestures of international goodwill and as awards for peacemakers. Local project has produced two Soviet friendship quilts sent to the national Soviet Women's Committee as a symbol of goodwill, hope, and peace. A joint Soviet-American Peace Quilt was made in cooperation with Soviet women and presented at the bilateral arms talks in Geneva, Switzerland. BPQP sponsors the National Peace Quilt Project, a patchwork quilt made with fifty squares (one representing each state) based on children's drawings. It publishes *Peaceful Pieces*, a semiannual newsletter containing articles on the fiber arts and social activism, as well as *How to Start a Peace Quilt Project in Your Own Community.* The group holds a weekly quilting meeting. Founded in 1981. 50 members. Contact Heidi Read, Manager.

Bonsai Clubs International (BCI)
2636 W. Mission Road, No. 277
Tallahassee, FL 32304

Individuals (3500) and clubs (200) interested in practicing bonsai (the art of growing miniature trees in containers). Purpose is to assist bonsai clubs and educate the public through programs, activities, ideas, and educational exhibitions. Bonsai news is reported in the bimonthly *Bonsai Magazine.* Founded in 1958. 3700 members. Contact Virginia Ellermann, Business Manager.

Borderland Sciences Research Foundation (BSRF)
PO Box 429
Garberville, CA 95440   (707) 986-7211

An organization for individuals who take an active interest in the "borderland between the visible and invisible manifestations of reality," including the fields of parapsychology, the occult, psychic research, hypnosis, dowsing, radiesthesia, radionics, flying saucers, electricity and the evolving soul, hollow earth mysteries, telepathy, commercials on television, and other phenomena. BSRF explores phenomena which orthodox science cannot or will not investigate. It offers recognition, understanding, and encouragement to individuals who are having unusual experiences of the borderland type or are conducting research in the occult. The Foundation publishes the bimonthly *Journal of Borderland Research.* Founded in 1945. 1000 members. Contact Thomas Joseph Brown, Director.

Boring Institute (BI)
PO Box 40
Maplewood, NJ 07040   (201) 763-6392

Humor and health organization whose purpose is to spoof celebrities, sports, films, television, politics, and social events and trends and provide serious commentary on the effect of boredom on individuals and society. The Institute bestows the *Most Boring Films of the Year* awards and issues a list of *Most Boring Celebrities of the Year.* In January it releases the annual Fearless Forecasts of TV's Fall Flops and at some point in the year sponsors National Anti-Boredom Month. During Anti-Boredom Month, the Institute "focuses on the ways boredom affects people, often playing a role in decisions to drop out of school, to abuse alcohol and drugs, and contributing to marital problems as well as worker burn-out."

The Boring Institute publishes *Ten Secrets to Avoid Boredom* and *Boring Stuff: How to Spot It & How To Avoid It.* Membership is $20 per year and includes *Ten Secrets, Boring Stuff,* an "official" boring certificate, and The Boring Party campaign button and membership card. Sister organization is the National Anxiety Center, described elsewhere. Founded in 1984. 1000 members. Contact Alan Caruba, Founder.

Boston Star Trek Association (BSTA)

PO Box 1108
Boston, MA 02103-1108   (617) 894-BSTA

A group going boldly where many groups have since gone, tracking the adventures of the USS Enterprise. BSTA claims to be the "oldest continuous Star Trek Club in the United States." Members are fans of the science fiction television show *Star Trek*, which aired from 1966-69, and the current series *Star Trek: The Next Generation*. Although most activities are centered in New England, members are drawn from across the country and include individuals interested in any aspect of science fiction, fantasy, horror, animation, costuming, other television shows, and gaming.

The trekkies promote the ideals of the Star Trek universe, where men and women lounge casually in form-fitting v-neck shirts and short tight pants. BSTA has built a replica of a full-size starship bridge and calls it the USS Goddard, named after the father of modern rocketry. It uses the Goddard for fundraising and as a video set. At the annual BASH, a Star Trek convention put on by BASH, Conventions, Inc., the group performs a humorous play (usually a *Star Trek* parody), which it says is "serious fun."

BSTA also operates the Media Science Fiction Group for individuals with a special interest in films and television programs and bestows Fantastic Film Awards. It publishes *The Newsletter at the End of the Universe*, a bimonthly with updates on *Star Trek* and related programs, association activities and programs, reviews, and submissions from members. To be a part of this "Infinite Diversity in Infinite Combinations," the fee is $15 per year. Founded in 1973. Contact Maryhelen Shuman-Groh, Coordinator.

Bowhunters Who Care (BWC)

PO Box 269
Columbus, NE 68601   (402) 564-7176

Members are archery clubs and bowhunting enthusiasts as well as manufacturers and retailers of archery equipment working together to promote and enhance the sport of bowhunting. Who Care seeks to increase understanding and appreciation of bowhunting among the nonhunting public and to improve hunter-landowner relations. Founded in 1977. 2000 members. Contact C. A. Saunders, Acting President.

Bram Stoker Memorial Association (BSMA)

29 Washington Square W., Penthouse N
New York, NY 10011   (212) 982-6754

BSMA seeks to preserve the works and memory of Bram Stoker (1847-1912), Irish author noted for his use of Gothic tradition with supernatural themes (as in his book, *Dracula*). It maintains the Bram Stoker Wall of Fame, Bram Stoker Memorial Library, and a nice photograph collection. Founded in 1985. 260 members. Contact Jenny O'Casey, Executive Director.

Bread and Roses (B&R)

78 Throckmorton Ave.
Mill Valley, CA 94941   (415) 381-0320

Volunteer entertainers and others who work together to bring free, live entertainment to people in local institutions such as prisons, convalescent homes, and psychiatric wards. Entertainers donate their time and talents to people who "desperately need and appreciate the pleasure and human contact that live entertainment can bring." The performers benefit from a "sympathetic, noncommercial environment in which to perform." The name Bread and Roses comes from a song written for a textile strike in Massachusetts in 1912: "... hearts starve as well as bodies, give us bread and give us roses." Founded in 1974. Contact Mimi Farina, Executive Director & Founder.

Brewmeisters Anonymous (BA)
6707 S. McKemy, No. 16
Tempe, AZ 85283 (602) 897-1775

Members are united to promote the appreciation of beer and improvement of the quality and methods of home brewing, while remaining anonymous. Founded in 1986. 35 members. Contact Clark Nelson, Contact.

Brewster Society (BS)
100 Severn Ave., Suite 605
Annapolis, MD 21403 (301) 365-1855

A group for those inclined to look at the world with kaleidoscope eyes. Members are designers, collectors, and lovers of kaleidoscopes dedicated to the idea that kaleidoscopes allow one to see the world differently (nicer patterns). The Society bestows the Brewster Award for creative ingenuity and maintains a kaleidoscope museum. It publishes the *News Scope,* a quarterly with a calendar of events, new designs, feature articles, and information on antique kaleidoscopes. The group's annual meeting includes a State-of-the-Scope Expo. Membership is $25 per year. Founded in 1986. 600 members. Contact Cozy Baker, Executive Secretary.

Brotherhood of Knights of the Black Pudding Tasters (BKBPT)
Boite Postale 65
F-61400 Mortagne au Perche, France 37 521762

A group of individuals united to promote black pudding, with the big event being an annual black pudding contest. The Brotherhood documents various types of black pudding, preserves traditional recipes, develops new recipes in collaboration with other culinary societies, and upholds the traditions of French cooking. It promotes appreciation of the province of Perche in France, its countryside, monuments, history, and products. Founded in 1962. 2000 members. Contact Jean Claude Gotteri, Great Master.

Brotherhood of the Knights of the Vine (BKV)
PO Box 13285
Sacramento, CA 95813 (916) 269-1021

Group seeks to promote wine as a healthy, hygienic beverage. Members include vintners, grape growers, wine wholesalers and retailers, professors of enology (the study of wine and wine-making), and wine lovers with an interest in American grapes and wine. The Brotherhood bestows titles of Supreme Knight, Master Knight, and Knight or Gentlelady for services rendered to the cause of vines and wines of America. BKV sponsors Knights of the Vine Scholarship Fund at various universities and maintains a wine museum at Historic Buena Vista Winery in Sonoma, CA. It publishes *The Arbor,* a semiannual magazine containing articles about wine and its history, book reviews, membership directory (geographically arranged), recipes, calendar of events, and obituaries. The Knights sponsor an annual world congress, with the 1992 meeting held in Chateauneuf-du-Pape, France. Founded in 1971. 1500 members. Contact Norman E. Gates, Grand Commander.

Bull Elephants (BE)
House of Representatives
2372 Rayburn Office Building
Washington, DC 20515   (202) 225-5805

A support group for male members of the staffs of Republican Congressmen, congressional committee employees who are Republicans, and Republican leadership employees and appointees. The Bulls meet to exchange ideas and discuss mutual problems and issues and to hear speakers on current problems. Founded in 1951. 200 members. Contact Ron Hardman, Chairman.

Bureau of the Budget in Exile Unrequited Marching and Chowder Society (BOBEUMACS)
PO Box 519
Garrett Park, MD 20896   (301) 942-5031

Possible winner of longest acronym contest. This informal society provides an opportunity for former Budget Bureau employees to gather together and exchange accounting and other ribald financial jests. Members also get together for lunch every six months. Founded in 1972. 330 members. Contact Roy Gootenberg, Executive Director.

Burlesque Historical Society (BHS)
Exotic World
29053 Wild Road
Helendale, CA 92342   (619) 243-5261

Hubba hubba. Society is supported by donations of materials and funds from persons interested in maintaining a museum of burlesque, which includes books, magazines, photographs, newspaper clippings, films, costumes, displays, posters, and other items relating to burlesque shows and dancers. It maintains a small library, videotapes, the Burlesque Hall of Fame, a museum, and a school for strippers. BHS publishes the magazines *Jennie Lee, The Bazoom Girl* and the *Legend of Jennie Lee.* The annual reunion is in May. Founded in 1963. 500 members. Contact Dixie Evans, Executive Officer.

Burlington Liar's Club (BLC)
149 N. Oakland Ave.
Burlington, WI 53105   (414) 763-3341

Me and my wife Morgan Fairchild were thinking of joining, but first we had to meet with President Bush to plan his campaign. Ya, that's the ticket. BLC is out "to foster and perpetuate the American heritage of tall story telling." Originally founded in 1929 as the Liars Club, which disbanded in 1980, the group was reestablished in 1981 under the current name. BLC sponsors the annual "World's Champion Liar" contest, with the winner announced on New Year's Eve. The winner receives a "parchment" certificate proclaiming him or her as the World's Champion Liar. The contest is open to the general public. The club issues *50 Plus Years of Championship Lies,* containing a brief history of the club and a list of "champion lies" since 1929. To become a member, send one dollar and a lie. Founded in 1981. 50,000 members. Contact Dan Reed, Vice President.

Bus History Association (BHA)
965 McEwan
Windsor, ON, Canada N9B 2G1   (519) 977-0664

Welcome to the wacky world of buses. Sure, they're big and lack romance and frequently suffer from exhaust problems, but some people love 'em. Group is composed of historians worldwide interested in motor buses and bus transportation, as well as employees of bus companies, transit and intercity operating bus companies, and motor bus manufacturing firms. BHA collects and preserves historical data, photographs, equipment lists, and manufacturer's specifications. It cooperates with the bus industry in preserving historical archives, including biographies of pioneers in the field. The group keeps members informed through the quarterly *Bus Industry Magazine* and holds an annual tour. Founded in 1963. 600 members. Contact Bernard Drouillard, Secretary Treasurer.

Business Card Collectors International (BCCI)
PO Box 466
Hollywood, FL 33022

BCCI is a group of people interested in promoting and furthering worldwide the novel hobby of collecting business cards. It provides information on new and unusual cards and conducts research on history of business cards. BCCI facilitates card trading among members and the exchange of data and ideas. Founded in 1976. 70 members. Contact Bill Weinstein, President.

Butterfly Lovers International (BLI)
210 Columbus Ave., No. 611
San Francisco, CA 94133   (415) 864-1169

A group of people interested in butterflies, hoping to educate the masses regarding the habits and characteristics of various types of butterflies and the need to protect endangered butterflies. The Butterfly Lovers collect arts and crafts featuring butterflies, including books, photographs and artifacts. Founded in 1975. Contact Dr. Stevanne Auerbach, Director.

Buxom Belles, International (BBI)
27856 Palomino Dr.
Warren, MI 48093   (313) 754-5731

Assists overweight men and women, on a group therapy basis, in their efforts to lose weight. Conducts weight loss contests and holds group discussions on diets and individual problems of reducing. Publishes the monthly *Buxom Belle Courier* and holds an annual convention, usually in May and usually in Detroit, MI. Founded in 1956. 1000 members. Contact Joan Klauka, President.

C C C C C C C C C

Caithness Paperweight Collectors Society (CPCS)
Caithness Glass PLC
Inveralmond
Perth, Tayside PH1 3TZ, Scotland   738 37373

Individuals in seven countries who collect or purchase paperweights made from Caithness glass, a specially developed colored
glass encased in crystal and named for the county in Scotland where
it is produced. The different colors found in the glass—peat,
heather, moss, and twilight blue—were originally inspired by the
surrounding landscape. Founded in 1976. 3000 members. Contact
Mrs. F. Anton, Secretary.

California Wilderness Survival League (CWSL)
PO Box 2220
Central Valley, CA 96019-2220   (916) 275-5825

Trying to survive in the modern world? Ever thought about
foraging in the wilderness? A full-scale retreat from urban calamity?
A chance to erect a new world order with only your heavily armed
friends participating? CWSL is a group of people interested in
enhancing and applying wilderness and modern survival skills as
well as folks interested in safe campsites and retreat facilities.
Membership is open to individuals and families outside of California
but is by invitation only. CWSL seeks to establish recreation,
camping, and retreat grounds and facilities and promote safety and
survival skills.

For members mutual benefit and safety, the Survival League
encourages friendship among members. It publishes the *California
Wilderness Survival League Newsletter,* a quarterly which reviews
current situations in the world and contains a calendar of events. It
holds an annual retreat for members intent on surviving. Founded
in 1984. 937 members. Contact Rudy W. Maich, President.

Campaign for World Government (CWG)
552 Lincoln Ave., No. 202
Winnetka, IL 60093   (708) 446-7177

CWG works for the establishment of a universal world federation, with a democratic structure and civilian law enforcement upon
individual citizens, as in the U.S. system of government. It's open
to all nations who are willing to undertake and abide by an overall
constitution. CWG publishes the *World Federation - Now* newsletter covering issues related to world federation. Founded in 1937.
300 members. Contact Georgia Lloyd, Executive Secretary.

Cartoonists Northwest
PO Box 31122
Seattle, WA 98103   (206) 448-2464

A group of cartoonists, writers, publishers, illustrators, agents,
and others interested in promoting cartooning as an art form.
Although regional by name, members are accepted nationwide. CN
provides information on all aspects of the cartooning profession to
amateur, aspiring, and practicing cartoonists. The group provides
networking opportunities and referral services and publishes
Penstuff, a monthly newsletter containing the president's column,

comic strip reviews, comic book/publishing news, speaker previews and reviews, and trivia. Founded in 1981. 400 members. Contact Elizabeth W. Pankey, President.

Cash Free America (CFA)
PO Box 367
Deer Park, NY 11729   (516) 243-3860

Organization seeking to replace paper money and coins with checks, credit, and debit cards. Believes there is a correlation between the existence of paper money and the prevalence of crime and that its system will allow police to more easily trace criminal "paper" trails. It encourages banks to issue debit cards, consumers to use them, and retail stores to accept them. Founded in 1989. Contact Vito Verga, President.

Catalyst
250 Park Ave., S.
New York, NY 10003   (212) 777-8900

A national research and advisory organization that helps corporations foster career and leadership development of women, Catalyst works to identify and analyze impediments to women's progress in the corporation, balancing work and family, and managing a diverse work force. The group develops cost-effective and transferable models that help employers manage the two-gender work force. It publishes the monthly *Perspective on Current Corporate Issues* as well as research reports, career guidance books and pamphlets, policy planning tools for managing a diverse work force, and other publications on leadership development and career and family issues. The group also holds an annual awards dinner. Founded in 1962. Contact Felice N. Schwartz, President.

Catgut Acoustical Society (CAS)
112 Essex Ave.
Montclair, NJ 07042

Physicists, engineers, instrument makers, musicians, and others interested in violin acoustics. Members congregate for periodic discussions of plate vibrations, varnish, damping factors, tap tones, air resonance, special properties of the slip-stick action of the bowed string, and other aspects of violin construction and sound. CAS studies factors affecting the quality of old Italian violins and modern instruments. The group is responsible for developing and constructing eight new instruments of the violin family. CAS sponsors musical compositions for new instruments and keeps members up on breaking violin news through the semiannual *Journal of the Catgut Acoustical Society* and the *Newsletter of the Catgut Acoustical Society.* It annually holds the International Symposium on Musical Acoustica. Founded in 1963. 800 members. Contact Carleen Maley Hutchins, Secretary.

Center for Bigfoot Studies (CBS)
10926 Milano Ave.
Norwalk, CA 90650-1638   (714) 351-9034

Seeks to establish the physical reality of Bigfoot and solicit the support of scientists and colleagues with more than an armchair interest in the topic. Sometimes called "Sasquatch" or "Uncle Phil," Mr. Bigfoot is a large, man-like critter reputedly inhabiting wilderness regions of North America. According to CBS, the name derives from an anglicized version of the Coast Salish Native American word meaning "Wild Men of the Woods." The Center disseminates news about the international Bigfoot phenomenon (for instance, the Abominable Snowmen of the Himalayas, the Yowie of Australia, Ye Ren of China, and the Almas from the Soviet Union) and frequently conducts field investigations and produces written reports on the outcome of those studies. It maintains extensive files along with a footprint casting collection. CBS speculates that a prime spot of Bigfoot activity is the High Uinta Mountains in Utah (maybe it's those signs along the mountain roads declaring "Caution—Bigfoot Crossing"). Believes, in the words of a Professor Markotic, that "it is not of cardinal importance if such beings exist or not, because even if they do not exist, they are a part of folklore all around the world and, therefore, provide legitimate reason for study and examination."

The Center has published the *Bigfoot Directory* and occasionally, when the mood strikes, issues the newsletter *BigfooTimes*. It also has issued *Big Footnotes*, a comprehensive bibliography covering more than 400 years of literature concerning Bigfoot, the abominable snowmen, and related beings. A work in progress is entitled *A History of the Bigfoot Mystery*. Periodically holds a conference, with the next one slated for Los Angeles in the year 2000. Membership is $30 per year. Founded in 1984. Contact Daniel Edward Perez, Founder.

Center for Reflection on the Second Law (CFRSL)
8420 Camellia Dr.
Raleigh, NC 27613 (919) 847-5819

Works to increase public understanding of the need to "live softly on the earth," which includes recycling, reducing consumption of non-renewable resources, preserving wilderness areas, and encouraging wildlife protection. It testifies at legislative hearings, reviews books, and issues a monthly letter on the relationship between the human and the earth. "Second Law" refers to the second law of thermodynamics, which states that things tend to become disorderly rather than orderly and energy dissipates; once something is used, it is thereafter less useful. One gets older, not younger, according to this law, which explains the mid-life crisis. The group interprets this as a call to use "earthstuff sparingly."

CFRSL holds a three-day conference each year dealing with some aspect of ecology and the human fit in the natural world. The Center has close ties with the Riverdale Center for Religious Research in the Bronx, a theological and philosophical house of study focused on the relationship between the human and creation, and the North American Conference on Christianity and Ecology, a group seeking to sensitize the Christian conscience on the subject of ecology. Founded in 1980.

Central Intelligence Retirees Association (CIRA)
PO Box 1150
Ft. Myer, VA 22211

CIA and government retirees with at least ten years of service with the Central Intelligence Agency. Sponsors various activities, although travel to Beirut is not among them. Founded in 1975. 2400 members.

(CPRI)

Cher'd Interest (CI)
5807 Hornet Dr.
Orlando, FL 32808   (407) 299-6830

Fans of actress and singer Cher (1946-), whose movies include *Moonstruck, Silkwood,* and *Mask,* and recordings such as *If I Could Turn Back Time* and *I Got You Babe* (with ex-hubby Sonny Bono). Group is dedicated to helping promote Cher's career (although she does seem to be doing pretty well on her own). CI facilitates the collection of Cher memorabilia and provides a forum whereby members can communicate their appreciation to Cher. Has published a book, *25 Years with Cher.* Founded in 1987. 350 members. Contact Linda Huston, Director.

Cherokee National Historical Society (CNHS)
PO Box 515
Tahlequah, OK 74465   (918) 456-6007

Persons and organizations interested in preserving the history and tradition of the Cherokee Indian Nation. CNHS plans to mark locations of historic significance to the Cherokees, including graves of officials and other prominent persons of the Nation. In addition to sponsoring educational, charitable, and benevolent activities for Cherokees and their descendants, the group operates Cherokee Heritage Center, which includes the Cherokee National Museum, Cherokee Arboretum and Herb Garden (including trees and plants used traditionally by Cherokees for food, fiber, and medicines), and the Cherokee National Archives of documents, papers, books, and other materials on Cherokee history and development. CNHS maintains a "living" Indian Village, circa 1700-50 and a Rural Cherokee Museum Village, circa 1875-90. It annually presents *The Trail of Tears,* an outdoor epic symphonic drama relating to Cherokee history in the southern highlands and the Southwest. Founded in 1963. 900 members. Contact Marilyn G. Moss, Executive Director.

Children of the Confederacy (CofC)
328 North Blvd.
Richmond, VA 23220   (804) 355-1636

Boys and girls from infancy to age 21 who are lineal or collateral descendants of men and women who served honorably in the Confederate Army, Navy, or civil service as well as children who are lineal or collateral descendants of members of the United Daughters of the Confederacy and the Sons of Confederate Veterans. Group sponsors educational, patriotic, memorial, historical, and benevolent activities and conducts programs on the "true history" of the South, the War Between the States, and the Confederate forces. It observes Confederate memorial days and seeks letters, diaries, scrapbooks, reminiscences, and relics for state archives. Founded in 1954. 3926 members. Contact Marion H. Giannasi, Office Manager.

Children of the Green Earth
PO Box 31550
Seattle, WA 98103   (206) 781-0852

Individuals with an interest in promoting and organizing responsible children's tree planting projects and other educational activities. The Green Earth Kids seek to "regreen the earth through the spiritual and practical act of planting trees" and by helping children on a local, national, and international basis care for trees, seeds, and seedlings in places where planting them will help to renew the land. It focuses on enhancing children's practical work with the earth, and on assisting children of other cultures who are doing similar work. Founded in 1980. 450 members. Contact Michael Soule, Executive Director.

C.H.U.C.K.
PO Box 188
Sayville, NY 11782   (516) 567-1130

CHUCK, or the Committee to Halt Useless College Killings, is a group of national fraternities and sororities, parents, schools, PTAs, and alcohol-related groups. CHUCK aims to alert parents, students, educators, and lawmakers to the dangers of fraternity hazings (initiation activities), lobby for antihazing legislation, and share documentation of incidents and related information through public speaking appearances. Founded in 1978. 100 members. Contact Eileen Stevens, President.

Church of Monday Night Football (CMNFB)
PO Box 2127
Santa Barbara, CA 93102   (805) 687-8420

"Monday night football" fans who consider Monday nights the best time to view professional football and maintain that Sunday is for family, friends, and conventional worship. Main activity of the Church is watching professional football on Monday nights, commencing with a "holy huddle" before each kickoff. The group has petitioned the commissioner of the National Football League to consider scheduling the Super Bowl on a Monday night. CMNFB encourages "pilgrimages" to live Monday night professional football games and holds an annual holy huddle on Super Bowl game day. Founded in 1979. 2500 members. Contact S. Richard "Rev." Slade, President.

Cigarette Pack Collectors Association (CPCA)
61 Searle St.
Georgetown, MA 01833   (508) 352-7377

Collectors of cigarette packs, tins, and advertising materials. Emphasis is on obsolete U.S. brands but international wrappers are also collected. CPCA promotes interest in the preservation of obsolete cigarette packs, encourages active trading among collectors, and acts as a forum for members to exchange information on the history of the cigarette industry. It publishes the *Brandstand,* a bimonthly newsletter. Founded in 1976. 250 members. Contact Richard W. Elliott, President.

Circumnavigators Club (CC)
24 E. 39th St.
New York, NY 10016   (212) 724-4448

Members have crossed all meridians of longitude, thus completing a global circumnavigation, and have more than a superficial interest in other countries. CC strives to extend points of friendly contact among those who go to the ends of the earth in the cause of commerce, research, exploration, big game hunting, military news, maritime or government service, or for the simple pleasure of travel. Founded in 1902. 1000 members. Contact Helen Jost, Executive Secretary.

Circus Fans Association of America (CFA)
PO Box 59710
Potomac, MD 20859-9710   (313) 234-8496

Members share an enthusiasm for the circus as an institution and the desire to preserve the big top for future generations. The group strives to create a true understanding and appreciation of the educational and recreative value of the circus. CFA is organized into statewide (and provincial) units known as "tops" (circus parlance for tent), while local units are known as "tents" (civilian lingo for tents) and bear names of outstanding circus personalities. It publishes *White Tops*, a bimonthly journal containing circus reviews, interviews with performers, and other circus news and views. The group meets annually. Founded in 1926. 2500 members. Contact Irvin C. Mohler, Secretary Treasurer.

Circus Historical Society (CHS)
3477 Vienna Court
Westerville, OH 43081   (219) 926-2020

A group of circus managers, employees, and fans interested in collecting and preserving historical material on circuses throughout the world. Members, who cooperate with other groups to select performers to be honored by the Circus Hall of Fame in Sarasota, Florida, maintain collections of circusiana that they're willing to talk about, write about, and use as an economy of exchange. CHS publishes the bimonthly *Bandwagon Magazine* with some 50 pages of circus nostalgia, and meets annually, often with the accompaniment of circus entertainment. Founded in 1939. 1400 members. Contact Dale C. Haynes, Secretary Treasurer.

Circus Model Builders, International (CMB)
347 Lonsdale Ave.
Dayton, OH 45419   (513) 299-0515

Members are folks 16 years of age or older who own or have built miniature models of circus equipment. Or youths age eight to 15 who show a serious interest in the circus and intend to pursue the hobby of circus model building. CMB works to perpetuate the circus as an amusement by designing and constructing circus models and publicly displaying them as a reminder that the circus is a great institution. It focuses on bringing together circus hobbyists through mutual problem solving and the exchange of ideas, plans, and specifications involving circus model construction. The group publishes the bimonthly magazine, *The Little Circus Wagon*. Founded in 1936. 1900 members. Contact Sally Conover Weitlauf, Secretary Treasurer.

Citizens Against Government Waste (CAGW)
1301 Connecticut Ave. NW, Suite 400
Washington, DC 20036   (202) 467-5300

Wonder if the phrase "tilting at windmills" means anything to members of CAGW? Citizens Against Government Waste is a bipartisan organization that seeks to educate the public, individuals in public administration, and Congress on eliminating waste, mismanagement, and inefficiency in government spending. It promotes the need to reduce the federal deficit and seeks to create public support for programs designed to reduce waste in spending, such as those proposed by the Foundation for the President's Private Sector Survey on Cost Control. Always vigilant, the organization seeks to expose cases of fraud which may occur at any level of the government. It publishes the quarterly newsletter *Government Waste Watch* and the quarterly *War on Waste Digest*. Founded in 1984. 350,000 members. Contact Alan Keyes, President.

Citizens Against PAC's (CAP)
2000 P St., NW, Suite 408
Washington, DC 20036   (202) 463-0465

Bipartisan organization of individuals who believe that political action committees (PACs) undermine the integrity and independence of elected officials and corrode the representative nature of government. Concerned primarily with the result of PACs on congressional elections, CAP compiles statistics on campaign finances. Contact Philip M. Stern, Founder & Co-Chairman.

Citizens Against UFO Secrecy (CAUS)
3518 Martha Custis Dr.
Alexandria, VA 22302   (703) 931-3341

Volunteer researchers specializing in the acquisition and analysis of documentation by local, state, and federal agencies concerning unidentified flying objects. Purpose is to promote greater freedom of official UFO information and to demand full accountability of the government and its agencies for the past, current, and future policies, programs, and projects relating to UFOs and the collection and processing of UFO data. CAUS demands access to official files documenting UFO sightings, intelligence analyses, directives, reports, and other results of the government's UFO research. It lobbies for the right of citizens to become participants of the decision-making process of UFO policymakers in domestic and foreign government agencies. Founded in 1978. 100 members. Contact Larry W. Bryant, Administrator.

Citizens for a Debt Free America (CDFA)
2550 S. Sunny Slope Road
New Berlin, WI 53151   (414) 782-1305

Cooperative network of grassroots groups and interested persons attempting to roll back the national debt with private contributions to the U.S. Department of the Treasury. Their nobel objectives are to honor our predecessors, ensure hope and opportunity in the U.S., and restore a legacy of liberty and initiative for future generations. CDFA seeks to inspire public servants to meet the challenge of working toward a debt-free nation by the year 2000 (time's running out with trillions of dollars yet to go). According to the CDFA, citizen contributions have exceeded $12 million since 1983. CDFA asks interested citizens to send debt reduction donations to the Treasury Department of Public Debt. The network publishes *Silver Linings*, a quarterly newsletter. Founded in 1983. Contact Kay M. Fishburn, Coordinator.

Citizens for a Drug Free America (CDFA)
2230 George C. Marshall Dr., Suite 123
Falls Church, VA 22043   (703) 207-9300

A coalition of individuals seeking to mobilize an effort to "win the war on drugs" and achieve "a drug free America" by the year 2000 (the year 2000 seems to be a very big year for citizen groups, who may soon be scanning the calendar for new dates). CDFA (oh no, acronym deja vu) plans to develop the project *Be Your Best*, which will encourage a positive, healthy lifestyle with emphasis on exercise, diet, and moral and self-worth values for young people. It's also working on Operation Open Door, a program which will keep school doors open until six o'clock in the evening. The group works to gain support for the formation of a specially appointed presidential commission to recommend a long-term game plan to restore "traditional American values and ethics to society." Founded in 1984. Contact Roger Chapin, President.

Citizens for Common Sense (CCS)
1713 J St., No. 211
Sacramento, CA 95814   (916) 448-DUKE

Republican grassroots organization working to heighten public awareness of and mobilize action on proposed local and national legislation that the group feels will endanger "American freedoms." CCS is currently campaigning against proposed legislation that would allow election-day voter registration—current law requires that voters be registered at least 29 days prior to an election and popular theory holds that lastminute registrants are not likely to be Republican. CCS is chaired by former California Governor George Deukmejian, who periodically emits *Dukegrams* to the faithful. Founded in 1987. 50,000 members. Contact Brian F. Lungren, Executive Director.

Citrus Label Society (CLS)

Collectors, historians, dealers, librarians, state historical societies, and others interested in collecting fruit crate labels for historic and artistic value. Yes, fruit crate labels. CLS promotes citrus label collecting, gathers and preserves information about the citrus industry, and assists members in buying, selling, and trading labels. The group conducts research on early lithography houses that printed citrus labels and publishes the quarterly *Citrus Peal*. Founded in 1981. 250 members.

Civil War Token Society (CWTS)
PO Box 330
Garnerville, NY 10923   (914) 362-0934

No, not subway tokens; civil war tokens. Members are collectors of civil war tokens issued by merchants to serve as emergency one-cent coins when federally issued coins vanished from circulation after the government suspended specie payments from 1862-64. Many tokens served as advertisements for merchants and their businesses; others contained patriotic inscriptions and designs. CWTS works to promote the educational, historic, and scientific study of Civil War tokens. Publishes the quarterly *Civil War Token Journal*. Founded in 1966. 850 members. Contact Donna Morgan, Secretary.

Classic Bicycle and Whizzer Club of America (CBWCA)
35769 Simon
Fraser, MI 48026   (313) 791-5594

Bicycle enthusiasts dedicated to the preservation, restoration, and enjoyment of classic balloon tire and other special interest bicycles and whizzers (gee) of the 1930-1960 era. (But what's a whizzer?) Motto is, "Preserving Yesterday for Tomorrow." In addition to balloon tires, "the classic bicycle is usually decked with a horn tank, lights, chain guard, large seats, spring action, and other evidences of luxury." The whizzer is usually a balloon tire bike with a *motor attached*. Activities of the club are "family oriented and include rides, parades, shows, swap meets, picnics, and good old-fashioned get-togethers." The Club publishes the monthly newsletter *Coaster*, featuring listings of swaps, rides, and shows, and parades. CBWCA's Saline-Ann Arbor Swap Meet in Michigan is the largest event of its kind in the country and is held on the last Sunday of April every year. A year's membership is $18. Founded in 1980. 535 members. Contact Ron Klaus, President.

Clowns of America, International (COAI)
PO Box 570
Lake Jackson, TX 77566-0570   (409) 297-6699

A group for the serious-minded "joey." Members are professional and amateur clowns, magicians, puppeteers, jugglers, and others who present a humorous program for the circus, radio, television, stage, and screen. Other members include friends of clowns and persons interested in clowning as a profession or hobby. Activities include training sessions, entertaining in parades, circuses, and shows (as well as charity events involving children, senior citizens, and hospitalized individuals), and sponsorship of the Clown Hall of Fame at Develan, WI. Promotes Aug. 1-7 as International Clown Week. Conducts research programs on clown art and publishes *The New Calliope*, a bimonthly magazine containing information on props, make-up, costuming, and other great stuff on the art of being a clown. Every spring the COAI holds a convention with various competitions, seminars, lectures, and dealer demonstrations. New member fee is $25. Founded in 1968. 5400 members. Contact Don Berkoski, President.

Club of the Friends of Ancient Smoothing Irons (CFASI)
PO Box 215
Carlsbad, CA 92008   (619) 729-1740

Members include collectors of old smoothing irons and people just interested in the irons. The club collects information on smoothing irons and compiles statistics having to do with ancient smoothing irons. Has published *The Evolution of the Sad Iron* and the *Encyclopedia of Smoothing Irons*. Founded in 1972. Contact Edna M. Glissman, U.S. Representative.

Coalition for Non-Violent Food (CNVF)
PO Box 214, Planetarium Station
New York, NY 10024   (212) 873-3674

Organizations and individuals who promote reduction in the pain and suffering of farm animals by advocating eating only nonviolent foods. Nonviolent foods are pacifist by nature and further defined as those not derived from animals killed for their meat. The Non-Violent Foodsters hope to reduce the number of animals used for food and encourage alternatives to animal food products. The Coalition advocates refining current agribusiness methods in order to reduce the pain and distress suffered by factory farm animals. And, of course, it promotes vegetarianism. Founded in 1986. Contact Henry Spira, Coordinator.

Coalition to Abolish the Draize Rabbit Blinding Tests (CADRBT)

PO Box 214, Planetarium Station
New York, NY 10024   (212) 873-3674

Organizations concerned with the "quality of life, focusing on the massive suffering of animals." CADRBT works to continue the campaign against the 40-year-old Draize test which forces chemicals into the eyes of conscious rabbits to observe the subsequent damage. It conducts boycotts and demonstrations and encourages corporate funding to develop innovative, nonanimal testing methods. The Coalition promotes research and procedures that do not involve the use of animals and works to phase out all animal testing methods. Founded in 1979. 400 members. Contact Henry Spira, Coordinator.

Coalition to Protect Animals in Entertainment (CPAE)

PO Box 2448
Riverside, CA 92516   (714) 682-7872

A task force of United Activists for Animal Rights, CPAE is a network of organizations interested in protecting animals in the entertainment industry. The network provides follow-up investigation and action on reported animal abuse cases. It hopes to reduce the profiting aspect of animal cruelty in movies, TV, commercials, circuses, zoos, rodeos, and other areas of entertainment. CPAE was originally formed to investigate alleged abuses uncovered in the 1987 movie *Project X*. The film was used by many animal rights groups as an example of the detrimental effects of animal research; it was later alleged that chimpanzees used in the movie had been abused during pre-production and filming. CPAE works to relieve the American Humane Association of its duties, because the group feels the AHA, which was present on the *Project X* set, is neglecting its responsibilities. Founded in 1987. Contact Nancy Burnet, Executive Director.

Coalition to Stop Government Waste (CSGW)

508 W. 26th St., 10th Floor
New York, NY 10001   (212) 633-6625

Individuals who support legislative measures and programs to curb what the group considers waste and corruption in government, such as military overspending on supplies and the alleged 1988 Pentagon contract kick-backs. Stop Government Waste is currently lobbying for the passage of a bill that would reform procurement procedures. It bestows the Whistleblower Patriot Award to government whistleblowers and Congressional Patriot Award to members of Congress who assist whistleblowers. Founded in 1985. 80,000 members. Contact Loebe Julie, President.

Coca-Cola Collectors Club International (CCCI)

PO Box 49166
Atlanta, GA 30359-1166   (601) 206-0040

A club for people interested in the history and memorabilia of The *Coca-Cola* Company, serving as a market for buying, trading, and selling collectibles related to the soft drink manufacturer. Collectible items which The *Coca-Cola* Company has used for advertising since the soft drink formula was created in 1886 include lithographs, glasses, bottles, mugs, change trays, serving trays, tiffany-style lamps, mirrors, clocks, and calendars. (In fact, *Coca Cola* now operates retail outlets that sell only collectibles and other related knick-knacks, but this group is not connected to company.) CCCI issues a monthly newsletter and holds annual international and regional conventions. Annual dues are $25. Founded in 1975. 6500 members. Contact Joel Burcham, President.

The Coin Coalition (TCC)
1000 Connecticut Ave., Suite 304
Washington, DC 20036   (202) 659-4805

With corporations and trade associations as members, the group lobbies for and promotes the design and use of a one-dollar coin to substitute for the dollar bill, which TCC believes should be phased out of use. Founded in 1986. 23 members. Contact James C. Benfield, Executive Director.

Coleopterists' Society (CS)
Field Museum of Natural History
Division of Insects
Chicago, IL 60605   (312) 922-9410

Professionals and amateurs with an interest in Coleoptera (garden variety beetles). The beetle lovers promote the advancement of the science of coleopterology by conducting seminars, workshops, and field expeditions. It alerts the faithful to news in the field through the quarterly *Coleopterists Bulletin: An International Journal Devoted to the Study of Beetles*. Founded in 1969. 600 members. Contact Margaret K. Thayer, Treasurer.

Collectors of Unusual Data - International (COUD-I)
2312 Shields Ave.
St. Louis, MO 63136   (314) 388-0087

Individuals who collect unusual facts and information for personal enjoyment (just for the sheer wonder of it all). The group's interest focuses on paranormal and occult events and phenomena such as perpetual motion devices, arcane aspects of the Kennedy assassination, and strange meteorological events. It disseminates information gathered from newspapers and other sources dealing with paranormal phenomena, and it answers requests for information on paranormal phenomena. Founded in 1985. 40 members. Contact Raymond Nelke, Founder.

Colonial Order of the Acorn (COA)
200 E. 66th St., Apt. E-507
New York, NY 10021   (212) 838-5632

The Colonial Order is a group of male descendants of residents of the North American colonies which became the 13 original states. Members are primarily from New York, though COA accepts members from other parts of the U.S. *Acorn* signifies the members of the 13 colonies who were the "Acorns from which grew the Tall Oak of the U.S." A better slogan than "The acorns which became the meal of the English squirrel."

Objectives are to cherish and perpetuate American traditions and associations, promote patriotism and loyalty to American national institutions, and encourage social intercourse among the descendants of the nation's founders. It also hopes to stimulate vigilance and united action in the preservation and promotion of political theories and principles of America's forefathers without regard to political party divisions or ecclesiastical denominations. Ancestors need not be connected with the military, and activities are not confined to commemoration of events related to war and government. Acorn collects and preserves records of colonial incidents and encourages preparation and study of historical and patriotic papers. Every 12 to 14 years or so, it publishes the *Yearbook*. Founded in 1894. 135 members. Contact Sidney Hughes, Chancellor.

Columbus: Countdown 1992 (CC 1992)
166-25 Powells Cove Blvd.
Beechhurst, NY 11357 (718) 767-8380

Institutions, organizations, and individuals interested in celebrating the quincentenary of the arrival of Christopher Columbus in the Caribbean in 1492. CC 1992 promotes planning of art exhibits and dramatic readings. Founded in 1984. Contact Dr. Anne Paolucci, President.

Combined Organizations of Numismatic Error Collectors of America (CONECA)
PO Box 932
Savannah, GA 31402 (912) 232-8655

Coin collectors interested in mint errors and varieties on U.S. and foreign coins. CONECA provides authentication, education, research, and evaluation services and sponsors trade-pals programs to acquaint members with others who have similar specialty interests. It publishes the monthly *Errorscope* and holds the annual Errorama coin show and symposium. Founded in 1983. 700 members. Contact J. T. Stanton, President.

Comedy Prescription (CP)
PO Box 61315
Denver, CO 80218 (303) 832-2296

Comedy Prescription uses comedy improvisation as a therapeutic tool to offer physical, mental, and emotional healing, learning, and communication. CP provides a supportive format for people to express the silly, humorous, and creative parts of themselves. The group designs comic presentations for businesses, schools, and hospitals. Founded in 1983. Contact Emily Oldak, Executive Officer.

Comedy Writers Association (CWA)
PO Box 023304
Brooklyn, NY 11202-0066 (718) 855-5057

A chuckle-heavy group whose members write humorous material for performers and periodicals. CWA offers assistance to comedy writers in creating and marketing their work. It issues the annuals *Comedy Buyer's Bulletin, Comedy Writer's Bulletin,* and *How to Sell Comedy Material* as well as the monthly *Latest Jokes.* Members gather annually in New York City. Founded in 1977. 125 members. Contact Robert Makinson, Director.

Committee Against Registration and the Draft (CARD)
731 State St.
Madison, WI 53703 (608) 257-7562

National and local organizations united to oppose reactivation of the Selective Service System and beginning of inductions through either the Military Selective Service Act or a compulsory national service program. With the Armed Forces actually downsizing at the moment, their fears may not be realized. Objectives are to participate in public education and political action; to initiate and maintain contacts with the media to keep the public informed; to secure support and participation from a variety of people and organizations; to assist in the anti-draft work of cooperating organizations. Offers referral to a national network of anti-draft activists and draft counselors. Sponsors the National Un-Registration Campaign, which receives the names of individuals currently registered with the Selective Service who would like to revoke their registrations. Publishes the quarterly *Anti-Draft*, and the bimonthly *CARD News Service*. Founded in 1979. 300 members. Contact Gillam Kerley, Executive Director.

Committee for a Voluntary Census (CVC)

PO Box 338
Warminster, PA 18974   (215) 675-6830

A committee of the Society for Individual Liberty, CVC believes that questions on the U.S. Census which go beyond counting the whole number of persons in each state are unconstitutional and a violation of privacy. The Committee works with supportive legislators to pass laws which make responding to such questions strictly voluntary. To get its point across, the group engages in advertising, publicity programs, and demonstrations to enlist public support. It also conducts seminars in census resistance (don't answer the doorbell, avoid people walking around with clipboards, etc.) CVC, which provides legal defense for persons who refuse to respond to census questions, reports that 300,000 persons resisted the 1970 census and over two million persons resisted the 1980 census. Founded in 1970. Contact Donald Ernsberger, Director.

Committee for Immediate Nuclear War (CINW)

2001 S.W. 98th Terrace
Ft. Lauderdale, FL 33324   (305) 475-9576

A tongue-in-cheek campaign that promotes global nuclear war as a solution to such problems as "boredom, soap operas, and peddlers on 14th Street" in New York City. The Immediate Nuclears seek to draw voter attention to the "silliness" of nuclear war by supporting "political candidates who also promote immediate nuclear war." The Committee studies and conducts seminars on the "beneficial effects of global nuclear war." Founded in 1983. Contact Richard Grayson, President.

Committee for National Arbor Day (CNAD)

PO Box 333
West Orange, NJ 07052   (201) 731-0840

Members are tree experts, horticulturists, and tree lovers united to bring trees into focus as a very necessary part of everyday life-economically, aesthetically, environmentally, and by contributing to the mental and physical well-being of all people. Founded in 1936. 50 members. Contact Harry J. Banker, Chairman.

Committee for the Advancement of Role-Playing Games (CARPG)
8032 Locust Ave.
Miller, IN 46403 (219) 938-3382

Individuals interested in role-playing games. According to the group, role-playing games are improvised, open-ended stories in which the referee or gamemaster sets the scene and players describe the actions of individual characters. Play depends on imagination and group interaction within elaborate rule systems. CARPG promotes the recreational and educational benefits of role-playing games and their use in psychological and sociological Founded in 1988. Contact William A. Flatt, Chair.

Committee for the Scientific Investigation of Claims of the Paranormal (CSICOP)
PO Box 229, Central Park Station
Buffalo, NY 14215 (716) 834-3222

Group of debunkers of paranormal phenonmena (UFOs, astrology, and psychic incidents) which counts among its members psychologists, philosophers, astronomers, science writers and others interested in the field of the paranormal. Independently functioning groups are concerned about biased, pseudoscientific media presentations of claims of paranormal occurrences, fearing that the ready acceptance of such claims erodes the spirit of scientific skepticism and opens the populace to gullibility in other areas. CSICOP encourages evaluative research in the paranormal and provides a "dissenting scientific point of view" through aggressive challenge. It bestows the annual *In Praise of Reason Award* to individuals best applying reason and scientific evidence in solving social problems, and the annual *Responsibility in Journalism Award* for fair reporting of paranormal claims. The group publishes *The Skeptical Inquirer*, a quarterly journal containing reports, articles on paranormal occurrences and trends, news and comments, book reviews, and letters from readers. Founded in 1976. 200 members. Contact Paul Kurtz, Chairman.

Committee on Public Doublespeak (CPD)
National Council of Teachers of English
1111 Kenyon Road
Urbana, IL 61801 (217) 328-3870

A committee of the National Council of Teachers of English comprising some 30 NCTE members who are "charged with identifying deceptive language used by those in government, business, education, and other areas of society." Doublespeak is described as "language used to lie or mislead while pretending to tell the truth." Four kinds are identified: euphemisms, specialized jargon, gobbledygook (or bureaucratese), and plain ol' inflated language. Committee objectives are to study dishonest and inhumane uses of language, especially as transmitted through the mass media; bring these misuses to public attention; and propose classroom techniques for the study of public language.

Current examples of everyday doublespeak overheard by the Committee include "pre-enjoyed car" (used car), "food and beverage consultant" (waiter), "delivery ambassador" (pizza delivery person), and "vocational relocation" (you've been fired). The group presents the annual Doublespeak Award to call attention to the misuse of language (recent winners were the Department of Defense for its use of elaborate euphemisms during the "armed situation" in the Persian Gulf and President Bush for, among other offenses, advocating "no new taxes" while promoting "tax revenue increases") and the annual George Orwell Award to pay tribute to outstanding contributions to the study of public language. The Committee publishes the *Quarterly Review of Doublespeak*, discussing current examples of doublespeak, articles, book reviews, cartoons, and other materials illustrating, criticizing, and analyzing doublespeak. Available for $8 per year. Founded in 1972. 30 members. Contact William Lutz, Chairman.

Committee on the Present Danger (CPD)
905 16th St. NW, Suite 207
Washington, DC 20006   (202) 628-2409

CPD promotes better understanding of foreign and defense policy issues. It believes that the U.S. must strengthen its defense effort and modernize weapons systems to meet growing Soviet military strength. Ah, did you say "present danger?" A group whose time may have passed. Founded in 1976. 178 members. Contact Charles Tyroler II, Director.

Community Dreamsharing Network (CDN)
PO Box 8032
Hicksville, NY 11801   (516) 796-9455

Individuals interested in discussing and analyzing their dreams in a group setting (I had a dream that I was in a group setting talking about my dreams). The group believes that dream analysis and exchange encourages better mental health, imparts an "exciting and entertaining" awareness of another reality, focuses creativity in writing and arts, promotes holistic growth, and leads to a better understanding of people, cultures, and religions. The Dreamsharing Network works to organize local dreamsharing groups and encourages networking between these groups (according to CDN, several hundred cost-free groups of four to 12 members meet regularly to discuss dreams). The Network sponsors training sessions in dream interpretation methods and travels to other metropolitan centers to organize similar community dreamsharing and switchboard activities. It publishes the quarterly newsletter *Dream Switchboard*, a collection of networking ads (four issues for $5). The Network also responds to public inquiries on the meaning of dreams. Founded in 1982. 50 members. Contact Harold Roger Ellis, Ph.D.

Companions of Doctor Who Fan Club (CODW)
2412 Peachwood Circle, NE
Atlanta, GA 30345   (404) 634-7538

Fans of the *Doctor Who* television show, a science fiction/fantasy serial that aired in London on the BBC network in 1963 and has been running for 25 years (the series has also been running in the U.S.). It operates through local chapters known as TARDISes, which are governed by the High Council of Time Lords. These admirers of the good doctor publish *Timelog* once or twice a year, a magazine containing stories, poems, songs, puzzles, and artwork contributed by fans. Nearly every other month (and sometimes more often) it issues the *Unpaid Scientific Advisor*, which contains club and chapter news, interviews, articles on the show's actors and actresses, information on available Doctor Who paraphernalia, convention information, and television show reviews. Founded in 1981. 1000 members. Contact Glyn Davis, President.

Compassion for Animals Campaign
PO Box 52193
Philadelphia, PA 19115   (215) 860-2113

A group promoting public awareness of animal testing performed in the cosmetic and pharmaceutical industries. It encourages support for those companies that do not employ animal testing and provides strategies to encourage companies to abandon animal testing. The Campaign also offers consulting services for manufacturers seeking alternative testing methods. Founded in 1987. 10,000 members. Contact Maria Liberty, Spokesperson.

Concerned American Indian Parents (CAIP)
CUHCC Clinic
2016 16th Ave., S.
Minneapolis, MN 55404   (612) 627-6888

CAIP serves as a network for American Indian parents and others interested in abolishing symbols that are degrading to Native Americans, such as the Redskins and Indians logos adopted by sports teams in the U.S. The group seeks to make the future easier for Native American children by educating the public about the racial messages inherent in such symbols. Founded in 1987. Contact Fred Veilleux.

Concerned Pet Owners' Association (CPOA)
American Philatelic Building
PO Box 8067
State College, PA 16803   (814) 692-8484

Participants include pet owners, manufacturers of pet-related products, consumer groups, veterinarians, and kennel owners. The group exists to champion the rights of pet owners and advocate informed consumer choice in selecting pet-related products and services. It serves as a watchdog organization monitoring pet-related product manufacturers and conflicts of interest in the business practices of veterinarians. Founded in 1989. Contact Jacqueline Marie Dorney, Director.

Confederate Stamp Alliance (CSA)
PO Box 1816
Kernersville, NC 27285

Professional and amateur philatelists and historians interested in the Confederate States of America, especially in its postal history and stamp issues. CSA maintains library and archives at Wineburgh Philatelic Research Library in Dallas, TX. Founded in 1935. 800 members. Contact Brian Green.

Consciousness Research and Training Project (CRTP)
Box 9G
315 E. 68th St.
New York, NY 10021

To teach, sponsor, and conduct research into the nature of human consciousness, parapsychology, and paranormal healing and new dimensions of human potential are the goals of CRTP. The group sponsors introductory level and advanced courses in paranormal healing, training seminars, research group meetings, and workshops on meditation for professionals. It studies and evaluates health regimens and therapies. Founded in 1980. 800 members. Contact Joyce Goodrich Ph.D., President.

Conservative Action Foundation (CAF)
316 Pennsylvania Ave. SE, Suite 401
Washington, DC 20003   (202) 547-0200

Another group in need of a new agenda. CAF seeks to establish a network of intellectuals, activists, and others to promote Americanism, individualism, free enterprise, and military strength. The group has launched a "private initiative war against Moscow" to supplement what the foundation describes as failed attempts by other conservatives to force substantive government action against communist imperialism (so they're the ones who changed the Soviet/CIS/Baltic outlook). It operates the Coalition Against Nuclear Annihilation, which works to promote the Strategic Defense Initiative program. Founded in 1983. Contact R. David Finzer, Chairman.

Constantian Society (CS)
123 Orr Road
Pittsburgh, PA 15241   (412) 831-8750

A group that believes in the King and I. The Constantian Society operates as a network for monarchists, particularly those in the Americas, enabling said monarchists to meet and contact other monarchists. The Society attempts to foster interest in the monarchy system and existing monarchies and royalty, while working for the restorations of deposed monarchs (the current most popular form of monarchy). The Society presents the *Michael Krupensky Award* (named after Michael Krupensky) annually to a nonmember who has made an outstanding contribution to the monarchist cause. CS maintains photo and biographical archives as well as committees on the monarchies and royal families of Spain, Iran, and Hawaii. Founded in 1970. 500 members. Contact Randall J. Dicks, Governor & Editor.

Cookie Cutter Collectors Club (CCCC)
5426 27th St. NW
Washington, DC 20015   (202) 966-0869

Collectors, tinsmiths, and individuals in the antique and flea market business interested in the collection of cookie cutters and other cookie shaping tools, such as molds and rollers. The Cookie Cutters research, record, and share information on cookie-shaping devices and certain workable recipes for special cookie cutters. Members collect cutter-related materials and discuss recipes and other uses of cutters. CCCC keeps abreast of new cutter sources and special offers, keeping members updated through the quarterly newsletter *Cookie Crumbs* and the bimonthly newsletter, *Cookies*. Founded in 1971. 600 members. Contact Phyllis S. Wetherill, Founder.

Coronary Club (CC)
9500 Euclid Ave.
Cleveland, OH 44106   (216) 444-3690

Heart patients, doctors, nurses, therapists, educators, and other health professionals involved in cardiac care. The Club seeks to provide members with information on all facets of heart care and rehabilitation via a bulletin written by cardiologists in lay language. It publishes the monthly *Heartline,* a nontechnical newsletter on heart care and rehabilitation covering surgery, medication, diet, exercise, depression, stress management, and new research developments. Founded in 1969. 9000 members. Contact Kathryn E. Ryan, Administrative Assistant.

Council for a Livable World (CLW)
20 Park Plaza
Boston, MA 02116   (617) 542-2282

With a reported 100,000 supporters, CLW enthusiasts include scientists, academics, professionals, and others who are concerned about the present course of the arms race and are interested in the related issues of foreign and defense policies. A political organization dedicated to working for practical, attainable measures to reduce the risk of war, the Council strives to diminish international tensions, facilitate progress toward general and comprehensive disarmament, and strengthen national security through national arms control. It brings distinguished scholars and scientists to Washington, D.C. for discussions with key members of the Administration and the Congress. The Council endorses and raises funds for Senate and House candidates, concentrating efforts on the U.S. Senate, "which has unique powers in foreign affairs and military spending." It publishes the monthly *Candidate Profiles* and the annual *Nuclear Arms Control Voting Record.* Founded in 1962. Contact Jerome Grossman, President.

Council for Alternatives to Stereotyping in Entertainment (CASE)
139 Corson Ave.
Staten Island, NY 10301   (718) 720-5378

Individuals in the arts and entertainment industry who seek to educate the public on the widespread, undesirable effects inflicted upon the entertainment industry by stereotyping. CASE disseminates information on self-image, reality perception, and receptivity to accurate performance feedback. The organization publishes the quarterly *Case Cares* and holds an annual conference in New York City. Founded in 1982. 25 members. Contact Michael Johnson, Secretary.

Count Dracula Fan Club (CDFC)
29 Washington Square W., Penthouse N
New York, NY 10011   (212) 982-6754

Individuals interested in the literary and historical aspects of Bram Stoker's book *Dracula,* as well as characters and personalities in the horror, magic, and fantasy genres. The Fan Club of the Big Dripper sponsors movie showings and trips (hey, Transylvania next stop) and maintains a big research library of 25,000 books in the horror genre along with the Dracula Museum. The group distributes first-edition books in good condition for collection purposes and offers lonely vampire lovers a pen pal network. Publishes the *Dracula News-Journal,* a bimonthly which includes nonfiction vampire news. Also CDFC publishes *Count Dracula and the Unicorn, Dracula Made Easy, How to Become a Vampire in Six Easy Lessons,* and other limited edition vampire stories.

Founded in 1965. 5090 members. Contact Ann Hart, Executive Secretary.

Count Dracula Society (CDS)
334 W. 54th St.
Los Angeles, CA 90037   (213) 752-5811

Academicians, teachers, writers, librarians, movie producers, and others devoted to the serious study of horror films and Gothic literature. CDS presents Mrs. Ann Radcliffe Awards in literature, movies, and television and the annual International Cinema Achievement Award, Horace Walpole Gold Medal, and Rev. Dr. Montague Summers Memorial Award. It maintains the Horror Hall of Fame and publishes the *The Count Dracula Quarterly*. Membership starts at $20. Founded in 1962. 1000 members. Contact Dr. Donald A. Reed, President.

Countdown 2001
110 N. Payne St.
Alexandria, VA 22314   (703) 684-4735

Individuals and organizations interested in working toward "creating the best possible 21st century." Participants in the countdown recognize that the "launching of a new millennium is the greatest teachable moment of our lifetimes." The group provides organizational support including training seminars and workshops on topics such as strategic planning and visioning, creativity and decision-making, and education for the future. It sponsors the *Agenda for the 21st Century Project*, which provides teachers with multidisciplinary materials to help students develop knowledge, skills, and perceptions necessary to be effective citizens in the world of tomorrow. Founded in 1985. Contact Dr. Sherry L. Schiller, President.

Cowboy Artists of America (CAA)
PO Box 396
Blue Springs, MO 64015   (816) 224-2244

Professional fine artists specializing in Western subject matters and who have a Western background. CAA educates collectors and the public in the authentic reproduction of the American West, as it was and is. Founded in 1965. 27 members. Contact T. M. Watson, Business Manager.

Cowboys for Christ (CFC)
PO Box 7557
Ft. Worth, TX 76111   (817) 834-6841

Interdenominational organization seeking to bring the gospel of Jesus Christ to the livestock industry. Or more precisely, to those who work in the industry, not the livestock themselves, who generally have no use for organized religion. CFC, working in conjunction with local churches to provide evangelistic outreach services, conducts fellowship and worship services at rodeos, livestock shows, and cattle and horse conventions. It publishes the *Christian Ranchman*, a monthly tabloid providing Christian testimonies and news of the ministry. Founded in 1971. 83,000 members. Contact Ted K. Pressley, President.

Cowsills Fan Club (CFC)
PO Box 83
Lexington, MS 39095

The club promotes the career of the family musical group the Cowsills. Formed in the mid-1960s (and currently making a comeback), the Cowsills produced such unforgettable hits as *The Rain, the Park, and Other Things* and the theme from the rock musical *Hair*. The Fan Club publishes the quarterly *Cowsill Connection*, which includes updates of concert dates and reviews. Founded in 1990. 100 members. Contact Marsha E. Jordan, President.

Crazy Horse Memorial Foundation (CHMF)
The Black Hills
Ave. of the Chiefs
Crazy Horse, SD 57730   (605) 673-4681

CHMF seeks completion of the memorial to North American Indians begun by sculptor Korczak Ziolkowski (1908-82). The completed memorial is to be a statue, 563 feet high and 641 feet long, depicting the Sioux leader Crazy Horse astride his pony and pointing to the lands of his people. Ziolkowki's wife and children are continuing work on the statue, which is being carved from Thunderhead Mountain in South Dakota. The Foundation maintains a museum of art and artifacts of Indian tribes from many areas of the United States and a museum-studio of American and European antiques, art objects, marble, bronze, and mahogany sculpture. It operates a library of 15,000 volumes on Indian culture, heritage, arts, crafts, and history. The Foundation offers scholarships and plans to establish a university and medical center for Native Americans. Interested parties are updated through the quarterly *Crazy Horse Progress* newsletter. Other publications include *Korczak: Storyteller in Stone* (biography), *Crazy Horse and Korczak*, and *Korczak, Saga of Sitting Bull's Bones*. Founded in 1948. 23 members. Contact Ruth Ziolkowski, Board Chairman.

Crossword Club (CC)
Hilberry Farm
Awbridge Hill
Romsey, Hants. SO51 0HF, England   794 524346

A group of folks united to promote the art of solving and creating crossword puzzles. CC provides members with high quality crossword puzzles, sponsors competitions, and maintains a 200-volume library of books of and about crosswords, crossword dictionaries, and general dictionaries. Founded in 1978. 650 members. Contact Brian Head, Secretary.

Crowncap Collectors Society International (CCSI)
4300 San Juan
Fairfax, VA 22030

"Our hobby is not just for little kids and eccentrics," proclaims CCSI somewhat defensively. Members are serious collectors of the crown closure bottle caps found on soda and beer bottles. Membership is evenly split between those who collect all crowns and those who specialize in beer, soda, domestic, and other crowns. The crown closure bottle cap was invented by William Painter and usually carries a design representing the soda or beer manufacturer on its feat surface. CCSI publishes the quarterly newsletter, *CrownCappers' Exchange* and holds a "Crownvention." Dues are $10 a year. 85 members. Contact John Vetter, President.

Crystal StarGate (CSG)
PO Box 1761
San Marcos, CA 92069   (619) 741-8148

A group of craft and wiccan practitioners, users of nature magic, and individuals interested in the psychic and supernatural. CSG seeks to "awaken a sense of oneness in ourselves and our world" while enhancing the "joy of being alive" without external substances such as drugs and alcohol. It encourages an exchange of thought and feelings among members as well as an attitude of a love of life and love of learning. CSG offers classes in nature magic and sponsors herbal walks. It publishes *Wanderment*, a bimonthly newsletter and catalog. Founded in 1977. 170 members. Contact Aline Gray, Manager.

Cult Awareness Network (CAN)
2421 W. Pratt Blvd., Suite 1173
Chicago, IL 60645   (312) 267-7777

CAN is an educational organization of volunteers interested in freedom from mind control. The Network offers information and counsel to persons concerned about destructive cults and serves as a national referral network for connecting concerned families with religious, legal, and medical sources. The group seeks to understand tactics of mind control and coercive persuasion in order to provide protection from those persons who take advantage of people through such tactics. CAN opposes deceptive recruitment, fraudulent solicitation of funds, illegal immigration, child abuse and neglect, trafficking in drugs, smuggling, and using unpaid or low-paid labor working long hours to staff lucrative businesses. Founded in 1974. 2000 members. Contact Cynthia S. Kisser, Executive Director.

Dairy Shrine (DS)
c/o American Breeders Service
PO Box 459
DeForest, WI 53532   (608) 846-3721

Persons interested in the dairy industry, including cattle breeders and educators. The gist of the Shrine is a portrait gallery and museum in Ft. Atkinson, WI "to honor great dairymen of the past, recognize great dairymen of the present, and inspire dairy leaders of the future." The Dairy Shrine library includes some 200 volumes and photographic records of cattle selected as breed champions at national shows, plus volumes of collegiate and 4-H dairy judging contest winners. Founded in 1949. 12,900 members. Contact Liz Henry, Secretary.

Dean Martin Association (DMA)

Hamway House
249 London Road
Croydon, Greater London CR0 2RL, England

Everybody loves somebody sometime, and these people are in love with entertainer Dean Martin (1917-), king of the martini, formerly of Martin and Lewis (Jerry), and one of the original Rat Pack (Sinatra). DMA promotes and publicizes Martin's career. Founded in 1960. 3000 members. Contact Bernard H. Thorpe, President.

Death Row Support Project (DRSP)

PO Box 600
Liberty Mills, IN 46946   (219) 982-7480

A project of Church of the Brethren that links 1500 concerned individuals with prisoners who have been sentenced to death. DRSP believes correspondence is a way of serving Jesus and brightening the lives of prison inmates. It works to educate the public about prison life and disseminates information opposing the death penalty. Founded in 1978. Contact Rachel Gross, Coordinator.

Debtors Anonymous (DA)

PO Box 20322
New York, NY 10025-9992   (212) 642-8220

Fellowship of men and women who share their experience, strength, and hope with each other that they may solve their common problem of compulsive debting. DA has adapted the Twelve Steps of Alcoholics Anonymous World Services for compulsive debtors, establishing and coordinating self-help support groups for people seeking to live prosperously without incurring unsecured debt. It helps members develop workable savings plans for long-term goals and become responsible shoppers. DA publishes *Ways and Means*, a bimonthly newsletter. Founded in 1976. Contact Diana D.

Dedicated Wooden Money Collectors (DWMC)

1028 Azalea Ct.
La Marque, TX 77568   (409) 935-2136

Wooden money collectors united to advance the knowledge of official wooden money along educational, historical, and scientific lines and further cooperation among all persons interested in the issue, circulation, classification, collection, exhibition, use, and preservation of all wooden money. Members of the group also exchange ideas and hold discussions on topics related to . . . wooden money and its collection. Publishes *Timber Lines*, a monthly newsletter. Founded in 1976. 350 members. Contact Ruby Threlkeld, Secretary.

DeLorean Motor Club of America (DMCA)

17552 Metzler Lane, Suite A
Huntington Beach, CA 92647   (714) 847-9940

Owners and enthusiasts of the DeLorean automobiles produced by the DeLorean Motor Company from 1981 through January, 1983. DMCA participates in the manufacture of (and search for) parts and in the hunt for adequate service. The group informs members of new ideas, parts availability, and technical data regarding the DeLorean. It serves as liaison among members and companies providing specialized products and services. Members are kept informed through the quarterly *DeGull Wing* newsletter. Founded in 1982. 4000 members. Contact Patti Nolan, President.

Depression After Delivery (DAD)
PO Box 1282
Morrisville, PA 19067   (215) 295-3994

A group for women who have experienced postpartum adjustment problems, depression, or psychosis as well as professionals in the health care industry. The group, with its interesting acronym, provides support to members and their families and acts as a clearinghouse for information on postpartum depression and psychosis. DAD holds the annual Postpartum Support International/Depression After Delivery National Conference. Founded in 1986. 10,000 members. Contact Nancy Berchtold, Executive Director.

Desert Fishes Council (DFC)
PO Box 337
Bishop, CA 93514   (619) 872-8751

Scientists, resource specialists, members of conservation organizations, and individuals concerned with long-term environmental values. Originally concerned with native fish of the Death Valley region, the group's interest has spread to habitat integrity within all deserts of Mexico and the southwestern U.S. The Desert Fishes promote proper management of this resource and encourage research relative to desert ecosystems. Founded in 1970. 500 members. Contact E. P. Pister, Executive Secretary.

Dignity After Death (DAD)
613 Cedar Circle
Spencerport, NY 14559   (716) 352-1105

Seeks "to boycott and protest the commercialization and marketing of John Lennon after his death." DAD traces merchandisers of items using the former Beatle's name, publishes lists of their names, and circulates lists to alternative newspapers around the country. It urges people to register complaints against store owners carrying "tasteless Lennon items" and offers lectures on how an individual can change a pattern in society and on using the media to bring about social change. Founded in 1980. Contact Laura Lyn Senft, Founder.

Dinosaur Society (DS)
PO Box 171
Newton Lower Falls, MA 02162   (617) 527-7796

A group striving to bring about "an end to dinosaur abuse!" The Dinosaur Society is an international organization promoting research and education in the study of dinosaurs in "this pioneering effort to end decades of exploitation of dinosaur science." The board of directors includes author Michael Crichton, director Sir David Attenborough, paleontologist and author Dr. Robert Bakker, and *NOVA* executive producer Paula Aspell.

The Society asserts that dinosaurs are misrepresented by merchandisers and assists in accurately revising products portraying dinosaurs to reflect current scientific knowledge. Cited examples of dinosaur misrepresentation range from "the taildragging Sinclair Dino to the U.S. Post Office stamps wrongly labelled *Brontosaurus.*"

"Dinosaurs make millions of dollars for merchandisers of products from toilet paper to ravioli," reports the Society. "Yet dinosaur science is suffering from a critical financial crisis. There are less than 30 researchers exploring for dinosaur worldwide today, on a total budget of less than $1 million."

The Society publishes *Dinosaur Data,* a quarterly newsletter for members, and it cooperates in the publication of *Dino Times,* a monthly newspaper (slogan: "All the News That's Old") offering children accurate and timely information on new dinosaur discoveries. The newspaper is in response to "dinosaur abuse" in books and films, in which "children are not only misinformed about the evolution of life but turned away, often permanently, from the world of science."

Membership fees for the Society, which largely go to support dinosaur projects, start at $25 and are tax deductible. Founded in 1991. 5000 members. Contact Don Lessen, Founder.

Diving Dentists Society (DDS)
1101 N. Calvert St.
Baltimore, MD 21202 (301) 837-5852

North American dentists interested in scuba and other forms of diving. The Diving Dentists perform root canals and research (though not while underwater) and propose solutions to the dental problems of scuba divers (make sure you brush after each dive). Founded in 1978. 100 members. Contact Leonore Chizever, Executive Director.

DOC (Doctors Ought to Care)
1423 Harper St.
Augusta, GA 30912 (404) 721-2269

A physician-led organization of medical students, teachers, parents, and other concerned individuals working to prove that doctors do care about health issues, even if the evidence suggests otherwise. DOC works through school programs, health professionals' offices, hospitals, media, and Super Health 2000, a health promotion effort which attempts to counter the effects of advertising. It seeks to launch a broad health promotion effort aimed at educating the public, particularly teenagers and children, on the "lethal" lifestyles of cigarette smoking, alcohol dependency, drug abuses, poor nutrition, and teenage pregnancy. The group publishes *DOC News and Views,* a quarterly newsletter fighting advertising and promotion of unhealthy products by the tobacco and alcohol industry. The letter includes information on anti-smoking and anti-drinking campaigns being promoted by DOC. Founded in 1977. 6000 members. Contact Alan Blum M.D., Chairman.

Dracula and Company (DC)
PO Box 994
Metairie, LA 70004-0994 (504) 734-8414

Individuals interested in preserving interest in horror films and literature. It publishes *The Haunted Journal* and *Nocturnal News* as well as *The Vampire Journal.* Founded in 1977. 300 members. Contact Thomas Schellenberger, President.

Dream Factory (DF)
315 Guthrie Green
Louisville, KY 40202   (502) 584-3928

Volunteers devoted to granting the dreams of chronically or critically ill children. DF hopes to bring smiles to the faces of seriously ill children and promote a better family atmosphere during a prolonged illness. The group involves the community in granting wishes to children and raises funds necessary for making dreams come true, including fulfilling requests for photographs of celebrities, arranging trips to Disney World and Buckingham Palace, and building a home. The group sponsors annual summer camps. Founded in 1980. 1000 members. Contact Denis P. Heavrin, Executive Director.

Drug Policy Foundation (DPF)
4801 Massachusetts Ave. NW, Suite 400
Washington, DC 20016   (202) 895-1634

DPF promotes alternative methods (such as legalization, decriminalization, and medicalization of currently illegal substances including marijuana and heroin) to curb drug abuse while protecting the rights of the individual. The group assists in litigation to change federal drug possession laws and maintains the Medical-Legal Advocacy Project to provide legal aid in cases involving medicine and law. The Foundation believes that legal drugs, clean needles, and effective drug treatment would vastly improve the health of addicts, slow the spread of AIDS, and decrease crime. While supporting vigorous police action against drug traffickers, DPF strongly opposes the use of urine tests in employment. Founded in 1987. 1000 members. Contact Arnold S. Trebach, President.

Dude Ranchers' Association (DRA)
Box 471
Laporte, CO 80535   (303) 493-7623

Whoa, boy. Dude ranchers from ten western U.S. states and Canada are members, as are individuals and business firms interested in ranching. DRA seeks to exchange ideas for the betterment of the ranchers and guests, publicize the advantages of a western ranch vacation, cooperate with federal land agencies, and preserve and protect wildlife, parks, and forests. It issues the annual *Dude Ranch Newsletter* and the *Dude Rancher Magazine/Directory*. Founded in 1926. 94 members. Contact Amey Grubbs, Executive Director.

E ᴱ ᴱ ᴱ ᴱ ᴱ ᴱ ᴱ ᴱ

E. P. Impersonators Association International (EPIAI)
c/o Rising Sun Productions
PO Box 1126
Seattle, WA 98111-1126

Wouldn't you like to go to a meeting of this group. EPIAI is a group of Elvis impersonators who obviously admire the music and career of the King of rock 'n' roll enough to become the King. The E.P. Impersonators seek to enhance public awareness of humanitarian gestures made by Presley. When not in full Elvis attire, the pseudo-Elvises conduct letter-writing campaigns, raise funds for charitable causes in Presley's name, and maintain the E.P Impersonators Hall of Fame. Founded in 1977. 200 members. Contact Sandel DeMastus, President.

Earth Save (ES)
706 Frederick St.
Santa Cruz, CA 95060 (408) 423-4069

Individuals interested in the ecological balance of the earth, the twist being that they believe that dietary choices affect the environment as well as the individual's health. Contact Patricia Carney, Executive Director.

Earthstewards Network
Box 10697
Bainbridge Island, WA 98110 (206) 842-7986

A project of the Holyearth Foundation in which individuals interested in taking responsibility for serving and improving their world becoming earthstewards. Earthstewards are defined as individuals "connected by a network of communication and consciousness, who know the power of their thoughts and actions and are directing them in the service of their brothers and sisters and of their planet." The Network encourages members to develop a personal program of commitment toward earth stewardship based on the Seven Fold Path of Peace, a program recognizing the rights of all living things and a "total connectedness between all beings." It organizes the Peacetree and Urban Peacetree programs, bringing together youths from the U.S., the USSR, India, Costa Rica, and Northern Ireland to reforest desert areas, rainforests, and over-paved cities. The group sponsors a U.S./USSR(CIS) children's art and photography exchange and goodwill visits to the former Soviet Union. It also brings together American Vietnam veterans and Soviet Afghanistan veterans to discuss and explore peace. Founded in 1980. 1800 members. Contact Danaan Parry, Director.

Earthwatch
680 Mt. Auburn St.
Box 403
Watertown, MA 02272 (617) 926-8200

Research and educational organization that allows individuals who have an avocational interest in science and the humanities to become working members of research teams led by highly qualified scientists. Team members support, physically and financially, ongoing scientific research projects in exchange for being able to work as research assistants for a two- or three-week period. Teams consist of two to 20 people with projects involving field work in most disciplines of the sciences (archaeology, earth, marine and life sciences, zoology, ornithology, astronomy, ecology, and marine science) and in the humanities (anthropology, folklore, and history). The group currently sponsors 110 research expeditions a year. Two to four times a year it issues the *Earthcorps-Our Daily Planet*, a newsletter containing alumni information, interviews, and list of sponsored projects. Other publications include *Earthwatch*, a bimonthly magazine containing information on current issues and a list of expeditions which members may join. Founded in 1971. 45,000 members. Contact Brian A. Rosborough, President.

Eastern Coast Breweriana Association (ECBA)
2212 Baker Dr.
Allentown, PA 18103   (215) 797-2566

Collectors of beer and brewery advertising items. Purposes are to unite individuals interested in promoting breweriana and to preserve for posterity the history of the brewing industry. Founded in 1970. 500 members. Contact William K. Fatzinger, President.

Edsel Owner's Club (EOC)
West Liberty, IL 62475   (618) 754-3516

Owners and others interested in the preservation and restoration of the Edsel automobile. The Edsel, produced by the Ford Motor Company in the late 1950s, was phased out of production in 1959. Local groups hold individual meets. The national group publishes the quarterly *Big E* and *Greenline*, a monthly newsletter. It also holds an annual car show during the first weekend in August. Founded in 1967. 1800 members. Contact Perry E. Piper, Co-Founder.

Elephant Interest Group (EIG)
106 E. Hickory Grove
Bloomfield Hills, MI 48013   (313) 540-3947

EIG's members are university faculty and students, farmers, zoo keepers, circus animal trainers, and others interested in the study and saving of elephants. The Group promotes interest in and increases public knowledge of elephants and works to protect elephant species. According to EIG, recent estimates of the wild elephant population are about one half of the 1972 estimate (currently 785,000). In North America some 700 captive elephants currently reside. EIG reports that "the major dangers to the elephant population are diminishing habitat, poaching, and natural causes" and that the elephant is critical to the continuation of the ecosystem, since it is an "indicator species."

The EIG is part of a larger conservationist effort trying to prevent the elephant population from reaching critical numbers and becoming an endangered species. To this end, it collects and disseminates information needed for education, research on, and conservation of elephants.

The logo of the EIG is a sketch of Ahmed, "the African elephant that became a walking legend while still alive." According to the Group, hunters were after Ahmed's huge tusks (over nine feet long and about 148 pounds each), a situation that ignited a worldwide protest and a decree by the late president of Kenya, Mzee Jomo Kenyatta, that Ahmed be protected. Lucky Ahmed died a natural death in 1974 at 55 years of age and is now preserved at the National Museum of Nairobi, Kenya, where "he has become a symbol of elephant conservation" (and also extremely leathery).

EIG maintains a small library on elephants and related species and works in cooperation with the American Society of Mammalogists, East African Wildlife Society, International Union for Conservation of Nature and Natural Resources, and World Wildlife Fund. Once a year or so it sends a newsletter updating members on activities and irregularly issues a journal appropriately named *Elephant*, which, when it does come out, includes articles, news items, and correspondence "written for a wide audience ... covering living and extinct elephants, captive and wild populations." Currently, eight back issues are available. Membership in the Group is $20 annually. Founded in 1977. 500 members. Contact Hezy Shoshani.

Eleventh Commandment Fellowship (ECF)
PO Box 14667
San Francisco, CA 94114   (415) 626-6064

Individuals of all faiths who accept and practice the 11th Commandment as an environmental ethic. Articulated by Roderick Nash and later expanded by Vincent Rossi and based on interpretive readings of Holy Scripture, the 11th Commandment states: "The earth is the Lord's and the fullness thereof; thou shall not despoil the earth nor destroy the life thereon." Objectives are to promote and urge the practice of the 11th Commandment as a benevolent and healing ethic of the environment, teach the commandment's implications, and address what the Fellowship feels are the spiritual roots of environmental problems. The group believes that environmental problems of pollution require a change in human attitudes based on a sense of the sacredness of nature and an acknowledgment of an urgent need to reintegrate human society into the earth's environment. Founded in 1979. 3800 members. Contact Frederick W. Krueger, Coordinator.

Elves', Gnomes', and Little Men's Science Fiction, Chowder and Marching Society (EGLMSFCMS)
PO Box 1169
Berkeley, CA 94701   (415) 848-0413

A club for science fiction and fantasy enthusiasts existing to promote the enjoyment of the genres in all their forms. The Chowder and Marching Society bestows the annual Invisible Little Man Award for unsung service to the field of science fiction. It publishes the *The Rhodomagnetic Bulletin*, a monthly newsletter. Founded in 1949. 100 members. Contact Dave Nee, Coordinator.

Elvira Fan Club (EFC)
14755 Ventura Blvd., 1-710
Sherman Oaks, CA 91403

A group for fans of Elvira, Mistress of the Dark, keeper of the cleavage, entertainer and hostess of a horror film television series.

Elvis Lives on Fan Club (ELFC)
10631 N. 190th Ave.
Bennington, NE 68087   (402) 238-2868

Fans of rock 'n' roll singer Elvis Presley desiring to promote a good public image of Presley and his music. ELFC contributes to charitable causes in Presley's name and participates in gatherings of groups with similar interests. It holds an annual meeting during the month of August in Memphis, TN. Founded in 1979. 35 members. Contact Connie Quinn, Executive Officer.

Elvis Our Guardian AngEL, Elvis Presley Fan Club
6061 Glenwood Dr.
Huntington Beach, CA 92647

Long-winded name for a group of Elvis fans united to share experiences and keep alive the memory of Presley. The club disseminates information on conventions relating to Elvis and provides contacts with merchandisers of Presley memorabilia. It publishes the bimonthly *Guardian AngEL News*. Founded in 1965. 100 members. Contact Judy McPhail, President.

Elvis Presley Burning Love Fan Club (EPBLFC)
1904 Williamsburg Dr.
Streamwood, IL 60107 (312) 882-1061

Another hunka hunka fans of Elvis. Supports charities in Presley's memory with funds raised through auctions, raffles, and conventions featuring Presley memorabilia. EPBLFC publishes *Burning Love,* a quarterly newsletter containing news of new record releases, books, videos, commemorative items, and other memorabilia. Founded in 1983. 650 members. Contact Bill De-Night, President.

Elvis Teddy Bears (ETB)
744 Caliente Dr.
Brandon, FL 33511 (813) 684-6522

Yes, the Elvis phenomenon is big. Really big. ETB president Mary Ann Parisi says that in 1975 she decided to start the Elvis Teddy Bears after being "lucky enough" to shake Elvis's hand and receive a scarf from the King (he was still alive then). Parisi recalls seeing Elvis perform six times, with her first sighting occurring in 1950. Her international club publishes *The Proud Mary* quarterly, with news on members, Elvis, and Elvis collectibles. The group commemorates *Elvis Week* during August each year with such activities as a sock hop, notalgia concert, candlelight vigil, video marathon, a karate tournament, and the Elvis Memorial Dinner. The Teddy Bears note that the official word out of Graceland is that Elvis was of Irish descent (O'Presley?). Founded in 1976. 89 members. Contact Mary Ann Parisi, President.

Elvisly Yours (EY)
PO Box 315
London NW10, England 71 7392001

They're everywhere. Fans of Elvis Presley from some 50 countries, with a mailing list of 50,000 Elvis fanatics. EY works to perpetuate the memory of Presley and his music by operating exchange and charitable programs and conducting trips to Presley's home, Graceland, in Memphis, TN. Elvisly supplies Elvis souvenir items wholesale and retail to members and publishes *Elvisly Yours* six times per year (and the *Elvisly Yours Fan Club Newsletter* four times per year). It also publishes an annual full color calendar and the books *Elvis a King Forever, The Best of Elvisly Yours,* and *Elvis in Quotes.* EY holds a twice yearly conference on January 8 and August 16 (dates of Presley's birth and death, respectively) in London, England. Founded in 1978. Contact Sid Shaw, President.

Emil Verban Society (EVS)
Motorola, Inc.
1350 I St. NW
Washington, DC 20005 (202) 371-6900

A club for hard-luck, diehard Chicago Cubs fans (is there any other type?). EVS seeks to honor present and former Cubs' players while deriving its name from Emil Verban, former second baseman for the Chicago Cubs and St. Louis Cardinals. Some 10 times per year it publishes the imaginatively titled *Memo* and biennially gathers to lunch. Founded in 1975. Contact Bruce C. Ladd Jr., Founder.

EMILY's List (EL)
1112 16th St. NW, Suite 750
Washington, DC 20036   (202) 887-1957

Political network for Democratic women that raises "early" money for pro-choice Democratic women running for high office. "Members receive a profile about each candidate that assesses the political situation of the race and gives the candidates positions on a wide range of issues." Members than decide where they want their money to go, writing checks to the candidates of their choice and forwarding them through EMILY's List. Members agree to make a biannual membership contribution of $100 or more, and to make gifts of at least $100 to two recommended candidates.

During the 1990 cycle, members contributed $1.5 million to 14 pro-choice Democratic women candidates, helping to elect seven members of Congress and two Governors, Ann Richards of Texas and Barbara Roberts of Oregon. Members receive the quarterly *Notes from EMILY*. EMILY is an acronym for *Early Money is Like Yeast*—"it makes the dough rise." Founded in 1985. 3400 members. Contact Ellen Malcolm, President.

Emotions Anonymous (EA)
PO Box 4245
St. Paul, MN 55104   (612) 647-9712

"Fellowship of men and women who share their experience, strength and hope with each other, that they may solve their common problem and help others recover from emotional illness." The group uses the Twelve Steps of Alcoholics Anonymous World Services, adapted to help with emotional problems. It disseminates literature and information and provides telephone referrals to local chapters. Founded in 1971. Contact William Roath, Coordinator.

Empire State Tattoo Club of America (ESTCA)
27 Mt. Vernon Ave.
PO Box 1374
Mt. Vernon, NY 10550   (914) 664-9894

International organization of tattoo artists and individuals with tattoos working to increase public awareness of tattoo art. Founded in 1974. 1000 members. Contact Joe Kaplan, President.

Engelbert's "Goils" (EG)
10880 Kader Dr.
Cleveland, OH 44130   (216) 842-3199

A club for admirers of the music and career of singer Engelbert Humperdinck (1936-), the "King of Romance." "Enge" keeps the "Goils" supplied with information on his concert tours, new record releases, and other pertinent information regarding his career. The purpose of the club "is to support Englebert in a dignified and responsible manner and to show respect for his talent, his person, and his right to privacy wherever he appears." Primarily active in the Cleveland, OH, area, although membership is spread across the U.S. and, to a smaller extent, overseas. Publishes *Goil Talk*, a bimonthly newsletter reporting Engelbert news, tour itineraries, record releases, and memorabilia for sale. Club dues are $18 per year. Founded in 1971. 325 members. Contact Jeanne Friedl, Co-Director.

The Engelettes (TE)
59-82 58th Ave.
Maspeth, NY 11378   (718) 326-0860

More fans of singer Engelbert Humperdinck, dedicated to keeping members apprised of Humperdinck's personal and television appearances and record releases. The club also arranges group outings to concerts. Founded in 1971. 200 members. Contact Martha Bologna, President.

Engel's Angels in Humperdinck Heaven Fan Club (EAHHFC)
3024 4th Ave. Carney
Baltimore, MD 21234   (301) 665-0744

Fans of (guess who?) the Engelbert of Humperdinck. The Angels support and promote Humperdinck's career through regular meetings, video viewings, and concert attendance. Founded in 1971. 81 members. Contact Jean Marshalek, President.

Enterprise II International
15527 Scenic Haven
Houston, TX 77083   (713) 530-3218

Fans of the syndicated television series *Star Trek* and the current series *Star Trek: The Next Generation.* Provides information on the stars of both series, *Star Trek* movies, and other related topics. The group holds an annual convention attended by various Star Trek characters and opened an elevator at a shopping center with James Doohan (Scotty). Members have won a variety of prizes for their uniforms. A bimonthly newsletter, *Communicator,* keeps the fleet updated. Membership fee is $20 per year. Founded in 1986. 35 members. Contact Ray Tanyer, Captain.

Ephemera Society of America (EPHSOC)
PO Box 37
Schoharie, NY 12157   (518) 295-7978

Libraries, schools, and individuals interested in, or concerned with, the collection, preservation, study, and educational use of printed and handwritten ephemera, "the window into the center of a culture." Or more casually referred to as "stuff." The society defines ephemera as the minor transient documents of everyday life, printed matter of current and passing interest (previously known as paper collectibles). Collections include such items as tickets, letterheads, posters, labels, timetables, trade cards, valentines, bills of lading, magazines, newspapers, greeting cards, catalogs, maps, rewards of merit, political and campaign material, and menus. The primary mission of the Society is to put members in touch with each other and with sources of information on the collecting and conservation of ephemera. It publishes the *Ephemera Book-Catalog,* the *Ephemera Journal* and the quarterly *Ephemera News.* The Society sponsors an annual conference and ephemera fair. Membership fee is $25 per year. Founded in 1980. 800 members. Contact William Frost Nobley, President.

Eric's Wasted Worldwide Repair Society (EWWRS)
1053 Inkster Blvd.
Winnipeg, MB, Canada R2X 1P1

Great name for whatever it is. Club unites admirers of Eric Hysteric and his music. The group informs members of Hysteric's new releases, concerts, and special appearances. It also maintains biographical archives and a hall of fame dedicated to Eric Hysteric. Founded in 1985. Contact J. C. Mitch Impudent, Wasted Poobah.

Ernest Fan Club (EFC)
1219 McGavock St.
Nashville, TN 37203

Hey Vern, here's some fans of Ernest P. Worrell, a nearly irritating character portrayed in movies and television commercials by actor and comedian Jim Varney (1949-). Ernest's people seek to promote entertainment and humor, using Ernest as an example. EFC makes available posters, shirts, tapes, and other items of interest and publishes *KnoWhutImean? News*, a quarterly newsletter. Founded in 1984. 17,000 members. Contact John Cherry, President.

Errors, Freaks and Oddities Collector's Club (EFOCC)
1903 Village Road W.
Norwood, MA 02062-2524   (617) 769-6531

Philatelists interested in the production of postage stamps and the variations that occur as a result of mistakes in, or testing of, production equipment. And some members are interested in errors in stamp designs and cancellations. Objectives are to learn about the causes of EFO (short for errors, freaks, and oddities) material and to disseminate that information and to be aware of current trends in philately and EFO value determination. Founded in 1978. 350 members. Contact James E. McDevitt, Secretary.

Escapees, Inc. (S-K-Ps)
Route 5, Box 310
Livingston, TX 77351   (409) 327-8873

No, not a prison group but families who live or plan to live in recreational vehicles. The S-K-Ps (clever, no?) promote the concept of the nomadic lifestyle housed in RVs and offer a support network for fellow travelers. The group aims to further the enjoyment of "RVing" through camp-outs and rallies. To this end it maintains a network of 12 nonprofit, co-op campgrounds where club members can stay free of charge or at a low cost. The club publishes *Escapees: Magazine for RV'ers*, a bimonthly. newsletter containing articles on maintenance, book reviews, chapter news, list of employment opportunities, product evaluations, and research reports. It also publishes the books *Survival of the Snowbirds, Encyclopedia for RVers, Home Is Where You Park It*, and *Full-Time RVing: Is It for You?* Reunions are held during a semiannual national rally (with exhibits), the annual Escapade, and various regional rallies. Founded in 1978. 15,000 members. Contact Joe Peterson, Founder & President.

Exotic Dancers League of America (EDLA)
29053 Wild Road
Helendale, CA 92342   (619) 243-5261

"The striptease is an original American Art—as American as baseball and Indians and apple pie." Did you know that football legend Knute Rockney got his idea for the Four Horsemen backfield while watching a chorus line in a burlesque theater? This bit of burlesque trivia was brought to you courtesy of the Exotic Dancers League of America, located just off Route 66 in beautiful Helendale. Members are women who perform in night clubs and theaters as exotic dancers (also known as ecdysiasts, strippers, or burlesque dancers) and others interested in preserving the vanishing art of burlesque.

The League strives to promote and improve the image of "a fine old American tradition" and to fight the trend of pornography. It sponsors an occasional contest to choose *Miss Striptease USA* on the basis of beauty of face and figure, talent, personality, and showmanship. EDLA also holds the annual *Diamonds of Burlesque Reunion* in the spring, featuring the *Miss Exotic World* contest to select "a well-educated and excellent dancer to enhance and uphold the true image of burlesque." The group also attempts to present annual Fanny Awards, recognizing excellence in the art of striptease. The League collects photographs, playbills, books, costumes, and historical material about burlesque and maintains a burlesque hall of fame and museum, with a collection of more than 1000 photos of the all-stars of burlesque from 1920 through 1960. EDLA was founded by the late stripper Jennie Lee. Current leader Dixie Lee was known as "The Marilyn Monroe of Burlesque," and according to the Exotic Dancers League, was the first woman Joe DiMaggio dated after breaking up with Monroe. Founded in 1953. 656 members. Contact Dixie Evans, President.

Experimental Aircraft Association (EAA)
EAA Aviation Center
Oshkosh, WI 54903-3086   (414) 426-4800

But will it fly? Members are individuals interested in sport and recreational flying. EAA promotes building of aircraft in high school industrial arts classes through Project School Flight. It maintains an aviation reference archive and 30,000 volume library and conducts research programs and specialized education courses. EAA operates EAA Kermit Weeks Flight Research Center, in conjunction with the EAA Aviation Foundation. The group publishes the monthly *EAA Experimenter: The "How to" Magazine for the Aircraft Builder*, providing technical and how-to information on building light aircraft from kits or as homebuilts. The fliers hold an annual conference with exhibits in Oshkosh, WI., usually during the first week of August. Founded in 1953. 125,000 members. Contact Paul H. Poberezny, Chairman.

Explorers Club (EC)
46 E. 70th St.
New York, NY 10021   (212) 628-8383

The "World Center for Exploration." EC is an international organization of professional explorers and scientists dedicated to the advancement of field research, scientific exploration, and the ideal that it is vital to preserve the instinct to explore. The Club encourages the exploration of land, sea, the air, and space and hopes to steer young people toward careers in field science and engineering. One of the traditions of the club, the Explorers Club Flag, has flown at both poles, real high mountain peaks, and deep dark jungles and is loaned to individual club members when they venture forth on a noncommercial expedition. "Each flag is numbered and develops a history as it goes out with various members on successive expeditions over the years."

The Club publishes the quarterly *Explorers Journal*, containing articles, editorials, and book reviews on a wide spectrum of expeditionary work and written in a popular vein. It also updates members on club activities via the quarterly *Explorers Newsletter*. The annual Explorers Club dinner is held usually in April and usually at the Waldolf Astoria Hotel in New York City. Club members are selected based on their field experience and exploratory activities; student memberships are also available. Honorary president is Sir Edmund Hillary of mountain climbing fame. Founded in 1904. 3200 members. Contact Eileen Harsch, Manager.

Extra Miler Club (EMC)
PO Box 90101
Henderson, NV 89009   (702) 565-4567

A group for people on the go-go. Members are avid travelers whose goal is to visit every U.S. county and record such visits as well as other travel goals such as visiting points of the highest and lowest elevation in each state. Founded in 1973. 55 members. Contact Roy A. Carson, President.

F F F F F F F F F F

Fabulous Fifties Ford Club of America (FFFCA)
PO Box 286
Riverside, CA 92502   (714) 354-5667

Members are dedicated to the restoration, preservation, and enjoyment of passenger cars and commercial vehicles built by the Ford Motor Company in the years 1949-1960, including Lincolns, Edsels, and Mercuries. Publishes bimonthly *Keystone Times* and holds an annual national meet, with judged competition. Founded in 1973. 700 members. Contact Leonard Raimondo, President.

Fair-Witness Project (FWP)
4219 W. Olive St., Suite 247
Burbank, CA 91505   (213) 463-0542

Individuals with a scientific or journalistic background and others interested in the investigation of paranormal phenomena or events. Purpose of the group is to screen, select, and objectively investigate specific cases of "high-strange singularity" involving the supernatural or the paranormal and disseminate verifiable facts on such cases to the public. The project does not argue for or against specific conclusions in a given case. Founded in 1984. 500 members. Contact William L. Moore, President.

Fairy Investigation Society (FIS)
1 Lakelands Close
Stillorgan
Blackrock, Dublin, Ireland

Ah, the wee little people are making their visits again, you say? Time to contact the FIS. Members are persons who sincerely hold the fairy faith (the Society is appropriately located in Ireland, where those with the faith outnumber without). Reports of fairy sightings are welcomed by the society's Fairy Investigation Bureau (FIB) and for eventual publication. Anonymity of contributors is respected. Founded in 1927. Contact Mr. Leslie Shepard, Executive Officer.

Famous Personalities' Business Card Collectors of America (FPBCCA)
PO Box 8028
Ann Arbor, MI 48107

Objective is to encourage the collecting and trading of business cards of famous people. To aid in the collecting, Fab Card Collectors publishes an annual *Celebrity Directory*. Founded in 1983. 30 members. Contact Terry Robinson, Executive Officer.

Fan Association of North America (FANA)
505 Peach Road
Orlando, FL 32804

Individuals united to promote, collect, and conserve folding fans and rigid handscreens. Encourages people to appreciate fans. Former president Grace Grayson says that the paper fans are romantic. "I'm taken with how beautiful they are, and how fragile, and the lovely aura of femininity behind the fan," says Grayson, who has more the 450. "It's all so very romantic. You can practically smell perfume and see moonlight." Yes, and please pass the wine. The association issues the *FANA Quarterly* and gathers annually. Founded in 1982. 262 members. Contact Wendy Blue, President.

Fan Tek (FT)
1607 Thomas Road
Ft. Washington, MD 20744   (301) 292-5231

Individuals interested in science fiction, fantasy, and gaming. FT seeks to promote creativity and enjoyment in space science, computers, writing and editing, drawing, historical reenactment, costuming, and laser and special effects technology. Members also work "secretly toward the Revival of the Empire and the resurrection of Darth Vader." FT publishes *The Castle*, a quarterly newsletter containing short fiction, science fiction and fantasy art, classified ads, and convention updates. Founded in 1982. 3000 members. Contact Bruce Evry, Executive Officer.

Far and Wide Tape Club (FWTC)
PO Box 51
Lively, ON, Canada P0M 2E0   (705) 692-3374

Not enthusiasts of masking tape but folks seeking to promote friendship through taped correspondence known as *tapespondence*. FWTC provides taped programs for institutes for the blind and for blind individuals. It assists individuals with personal taping. The group maintains a 10,000-tape library of old-time radio programs, documentaries, and old country and western music. Members meet annually at a picnic. Founded in 1967. 300 members. Contact Ross V. Smith, Director.

Fat Lip Readers Theater (FLRT)
PO Box 29963
Oakland, CA 94604   (415) 664-6842

Members are individuals who do not look upon being fat as an illness and are not intent on finding its cure who perform original scripts dramatizing the experience of growing up fat and female in America. FLRT is determined to fight misinformation and stereotypes about being fat within a theatrical and entertaining medium. To educate others it conducts workshops and classes for universities, professional associations, medical and health workers, and the public. FLRT makes available its videotape *Nothing to Lose*. Founded in 1981. 12 members. Contact Laura Bock.

Fathers Day Council (FDC)
47 W. 34th St.
New York, NY 10001   (212) 594-5977

Manufacturers of products for men, as well as newspapers, magazines, radio, and television stations and major retail corporations. FDC encourages participation in the celebration of Fathers' Day by increasing public awareness of "the fundamental values of fatherhood and their effect on American life styles and family integrity." It bestows the annual National Father of the Year and Regional Fathers of the Year awards. Founded in 1934. 2000 members. Contact Theodore M. Kaufman, Executive Director.

Feathered Pipe Foundation (FPF)
PO Box 1682
Helena, MT 59624   (406) 442-8196

FPF provides opportunities for people to become healthier in body, mind, and spirit. The Foundation sponsors retreats and training intensives year-round at Feathered Pipe Ranch near Helena, MT. It conducts educational seminars and sponsors educational tours throughout the world with leaders in the field of conscious evolution. Primary focus of the tours is experiential learning in places of pilgrimage and power centers such as India, Tibet and Nepal, the Great Pyramid in Egypt, and Machu Pichu in Peru. FPF publishes *Circle* three times per year, a newsletter with information on seasonal events in and around Montana related to personal and community awakening and empowerment. Founded in 1975. 300 members. Contact India Supera, Executive Director.

Federation of Historical Bottle Clubs (FOHBC)
14521 Atlantic
Riverdale, IL 60627   (708) 841-4068

Antique bottle collectors clubs (110) and interested individuals (500) seeking to educate and inform the public on antique bottle collecting. FOHBC maintains the National Bottle Museum in Ballston Spa, NY which displays antique bottles of various categories. The group encourages the writing of research and true stories related to bottles. The organization presents awards to individuals and clubs for best educational display of bottles and for other competitions. It also maintains a bottle hall of fame and publishes

The Federation Glassworks. Founded in 1969. 610 members. Contact Barbara Harms, Treasurer.

Fellowship for Intentional Community (FIC)
Center for Communal Studies
8600 University Blvd.
Evansville, IN 47712   (812) 464-1727

Communities (25), organizations (10), and individuals (60) promoting the establishment of communal, cooperative living groups. FIC encourages increased public awareness, understanding, and acceptance of "intentional communities." The Fellowship demonstrates and facilitates application of communal experiences to the larger society, citing intentional communities as models of ecological options, opportunities for personal and community development, and methods for nurturing peaceful social transformation. The group promotes the exchange of information, skills, and economic support among existing and newly formed intentional communities. Founded in 1948. 95 members.

Ferret Fanciers Club (FFC)
711 Chautauqua Ct.
Pittsburgh, PA 15214   (412) 322-1161

Members are veterinarians and ferret owners. Ferrets are domesticated European polecats that are used to hunt rodents. The Ferret Fanciers Club seeks to facilitate ferret health and preservation and foster ferret information exchange among owners, breeders, and fanciers. It works to promote state legalization of ferrets as household pets, encourages high standards in breeding practices, and promotes the registration of ferrets and ferret shows. The group disseminates medical information on ferrets to healthcare professionals, teaching and research institutions, and animal centers. FFC makes available to the public information on ferret care, nutrition, breeding, and medical requirements. The Fanciers sponsor the Ferret Blood Donor Program, a national program to provide ferret blood donors in medical emergencies. The group also maintains Ferret Rabies Vaccine Program to assist in the development of an effective rabies vaccine for ferrets. Members are updated through the monthly *National Ferret Review.* Everyone gathers at the annual ferret show during November in Pittsburgh, PA. Founded in 1983. 2800 members. Contact Mary Field, Executive Director.

Figural Bottle Openers Collectors Club (FBOC)
13018 Clarion Road
Ft. Washington, MD 20744   (301) 292-2328

Figural, figural, figural. FBOC is a group of collectors of three-dimensional, free-standing figural bottle openers. It conducts research into the origin and manufacture of figural bottle openers and identifies and codes openers. The Club publishes the quarterly *The Opener* and holds an annual conference in May or June. Founded in 1978. 125 members. Contact Phyllis Eisenach, Secretary.

Finding Our Own Ways (FOOW)
PO Box 1545
Lawrence, KS 66044

Members are individuals who are asexual, whose gender is other than male or female and others supporting the group's goals. It seeks to provide members with an opportunity to interact without feeling pressure to define themselves as male or female or to define relationships in terms of one's sexuality. It publishes *Finding Our Own Ways*, a bimonthly newsletter on gender identification, sex roles, asexuality, celibacy, and relationships which includes reviews, essays, poetry, and fiction. Founded in 1987. 40 members.

Fire Collectors Club (FCC)
PO Box 992
Milwaukee, WI 53201

Individuals interested in collecting fire service and insurance related memorabilia including badges, toys, stamps, medals, patches, engines, trucks and equipment, fire marks, and helmets. Founded in 1987. 119 members. Contact David Cerull, President.

Fire Mark Circle (FMC)
c/o Royal Insurance (UK) Ltd.
New Hall Place
Liverpool, Merseyside L69 3EN, England   51 2274422

Collectors of fire marks and similar memorabilia. Fire marks are brass, copper, or lead plates once used by insurance companies to identify the properties they insured from loss or damage by fire. Purpose is to encourage interest in fire marks and other relics of early fire insurance. Founded in 1933. 200 members. Contact R. J. Prideaux, Secretary.

First Fandom (FF)
2209 S Webster St.
Kokomo, IN 46901   (317) 455-1958

Readers, writers, and collectors of science fiction/fantasy publications. Members must prove they read and were interested in science fiction prior to 1938, which essentially eliminates baby boomers. FF seeks to promote and pay homage to the early writers of science fiction and to stimulate and revive interest among older fans. It maintains a hall of fame and holds the annual World Science Fiction Convention. Founded in 1958. 300 members. Contact Ray E. Beam, Executive Officer.

Flat Earth Research Society International (FERSI)
Box 2533
Lancaster, CA 93539   (805) 727-1635

Self-described iconoclastic society whose philosophy is "God exists, right and wrong exist, up and down exist, earth is flat." And, "earth is not a globe." Members are individuals whose outlook is "Zetetic," or characterized by a seeking for truth and the denial of "imaginary" theories. Affiliated with the Covenant Peoples Church. ("God has made an everlasting covenant with every living creature of all flesh and blood on this flat earth.")

The Flat Earthers believe that "science is a religious cult, fanatic in the extreme. We maintain that what is called 'Science' today and 'scientists' consist of the same old gang of witch doctors, sorcerers, tellers of tales, the 'PriestsEntertainers' for the common people. 'Science' consists of a weird, way-out occult concoction of jibberish theory-theology . . . unrelated to the real world of acts, technology and inventions, tall buildings and fast cars, airplanes and other Real and Good things in life . . ."

Having rejected science, members rely only on "provable" knowledge and consequently believe that the "spinning ball" theory regarding the earth is absurd—that, in reality, the earth is flat and infinite in size. "How do we know earth is flat? HOW ELSE? We went out and checked it," reports a jubilant president Charles Johnson.

Members maintain that Australia is not under the world, Australians do not hang by their feet head down, nor do ships sail over the edge of the world to get there; they also assert that continental drift is really the result of the earth and water being "shaken asunder by God." Furthermore, the Society asserts that it can prove that the sun and moon are some 3,000 miles away and both are 32 miles across. FERSI gathers this type of information, disseminates results of its research, and generally seeks to "push forth the frontiers of knowledge in geophysical matters."

The Society publishes the *Flat Earth News*, a quarterly tabloid containing articles decrying modern science for providing a false view of the world. The paper's slogans are "Restoring the World to Sanity" and "Representing the Tiny Few Who Are Reasonable, Logical, and Sane." Also issues *Plane Truth*, a quarterly tabloid concerned with showing the Ten Commandments as a "logical and reasonable means to a better life." Membership includes the *News* and costs $10 per year ($20 for the flat earth map—no globes). Founded in 1800. 2800 members. Contact Charles K. Johnson, President.

Floating Homes Association (FHA)
Box 710, Waldo Point Harbor
Sausalito, CA 94965   (415) 332-1916

Owners and residents of floating homes on San Francisco Bay, CA. FHA attempts to address and solve problems common to the floating home community, for instance, leaks and fish in the bedroom. The group takes political and legal action to protect homeowners' rights and works to improve the image of the floating home community. It publishes *The Floating Times*. Founded in 1985. 300 members. Contact Douglas A. Lawrence, President.

Fly Without Fear (FWF)
310 Madison Ave.
New York, NY 10017   (212) 697-7666

Members are people who are "terrified of airplane travel." Members meet weekly to discuss their fears and to act out reactions to contemplated flight. FWF sponsors talks with ground controllers and safety experts and visits to airports in an effort to help members overcome their phobia. The group conducts "Seminar in the Sky" conditioning flights and lectures on fear of flying to clubs and organizations and has graduated thousands of members who now accept commercial jetliners as a standard mode of transportation, for better or worse. Founded in 1969. 40 members. Contact Carol Gross, Director.

Flying Chiropractors Association (FCA)
7301 Hasbrook Ave.
Philadelphia, PA 19111   (215) 722-7200

Not only do they straighten backs, but they fly. Members are occasionally airborne chiropractic physicians dedicated to promoting fellowship, seeking designation as aviation medical examiners (doctors who examine pilots for their licensure), and encouraging aviation safety. The flying physicians publish the quarterly *D.C. Flyer*. Founded in 1968. 300 members. Contact Dr. W. J. Quinlan, Executive Director.

Flying Dentists Association (FDA)
4700 Chamblee-Dunwoody Road
Dunwoody, GA 30338　　　　　　　　　　　(404) 457-1351

Members of the American Dental Association who have an active aircraft pilot's license. Many members make use of private air travel in conducting their dental practice, yanking a molar here and a canine there while flying through space. FDA publishes the monthly *Flight Watch* and meets annually during June or July. Founded in 1960. 500 members. Contact Dr. Max J. Cohen, Executive Secretary.

Flying Eagle and Indian Head Cent Collectors Society (FEIHCCS)
Allstate Coin Co.
3848 E. 5th St.
Tucson, AZ 85716　　　　　　　　　　　(800) 346-4809

Members are coin collectors of coins minted from 1856 to 1909. The Society publishes *Longacre Ledger*, a quarterly journal containing collector information. Founded in 1990. 300 members. Contact Rich Snow.

Flying Funeral Directors of America (FFDA)
256 Spring Cove Dr.
Elgin, IL 60123　　　　　　　　　　　(708) 931-4232

Lot of people up in the air these days. Members are funeral directors who own planes, have a pilot's license, or are interested in flying, as well as persons associated with allied funeral industries who are licensed pilots. Purposes are to create and further a common interest in flying and funeral service, to join together in case of mass disaster, and to improve flying safety. It publishes the quarterly *Crosswinds*. Founded in 1960. 130 members. Contact William J. Bergan, Secretary Treasurer.

Flying Physicians Association (FPA)
PO Box 17841
Kansas City, MO 64134　　　　　　　　　　　(816) 763-9336

Members are doctors of medicine who have a current pilot certificate and are members of an ethical medical organization. FPA promotes the interests of medicine in aviation, safety, and education. The Flying Physicians publish the *Flying Physician* three times per year, a newsletter for physicians with pilot's certificates which covers medical and aviation topics. Founded in 1954. 1200 members. Contact Don Drake, Vice President.

Flying Veterinarians Association (FVA)
PO Box 1081
Columbia, MO 65205　　　　　　　　　　　(314) 882-7228

Members are veterinarians holding valid private pilot certificates, individuals in the field who have an interest in flying, and nonveterinarians who either teach in veterinary schools or who represent companies serving the veterinary industry. FVA promotes aviation safety through example and education and seeks to increase knowledge and proficiency in the operation of aircraft. It hopes to heighten awareness of and interest in aviation among young people. The group emphasizes utilization of aircraft in veterinary practice. Founded in 1966. 328 members. Contact Robert C. McClure D.V.M., Secretary Treasurer.

Football Hall of Shame (FHS)
PO Box 31867
Palm Beach Gardens, FL 33420

Members are players, coaches, officials, broadcasters, owners, fans, cheerleaders, bands, mascots, and others. FHS seeks to recognize and dishonor "hilarious bloopers and wacky blunders" in both professional and college football history. The Hall solicits nominations for induction and elects new inductees, collects memorabilia from shameful moments in football history, and pays a lighthearted tribute to the sport of football. The Hall officially recognizes persons submitting nominations that are accepted by the hall. FHS has issued two books: *The Football Hall of Shame* and its sequel, *The Football Hall of Shame 2*. Founded in 1985. 382 members. Contact Bruce M. Nash, Co-Founder.

The FORUM (TF)
PO Box 5915
Santa Fe, NM 87502   (505) 983-3962

A research, religious, and educational foundation engaged in the study and exploration of futuristic concepts for the upliftment and understanding of humanity. TF investigates phenomena related to the physical, emotional, mental, and spiritual aspects of the individual. Areas of study, education, and research include parapsychology, psychology, brain radiation, and the dormant powers within man which can be activated through attentive focus. The foundation holds classes, seminars, worship service, and retreats and offers counseling services and directions for participating in a new culture based upon caring and creativity. Founded in 1970. 70 members. Contact Carol Bell Knight, Director.

The Fossils
4245 Garden Lane
Rockford, IL 61111   (815) 282-3421

Fraternal association of individuals who have published, edited, or written for a nonprofessional publication for three or more years. The Fossils work to preserve the history of amateur journalism and provide fellowship for amateur writers. Founded in 1904. 125 members. Contact Keith M. Gray, Secretary Treasurer.

Foundation for Research on the Nature of Man (FRNM)
Box 6847, College Station
Durham, NC 27708   (919) 688-8241

An institution "devoted to advancing the understanding of the human individual, particularly to the scientific discovery of what it is that distinguishes him as a person." FRNM sponsors the Institute for Para-psychology and the Parapsychology Press and conducts research programs. It also offers a summer study program which includes lectures, discussions, and participation in research meetings and projects, and an advanced program giving students intensive training in experimental methods. The group reports on research and theory in the quarterly *Journal of Parapsychology*. Founded in 1962. Contact Dr. K. Ramakrishna Rao, Director.

Fran Lee Foundation (FLF)
565 West End Ave.
New York, NY 10024   (212) 873-5507

Appearing as a spokesperson on radio and television broadcasts, Fran Lee disseminates consumer-related information to the public on such matters as diseases transmitted by pets to humans and the dangers of microwave ovens, cyclamates, swine flu and measles vaccinations, and humidifiers. No relation to Sara. Founded in 1970. Contact Fran Lee, Director.

Franchise of Americans Needing Sports (FANS)
1808 Sherwood
Sacramento, CA 95822   (916) 456-7311

FANS represents the interests of sports fans and consumers, having formulated a "Sports Fans Bill of Rights" which calls for more involvement of sports customers in decisions affecting them, such as sports contract negotiations and stadium relocation. The group had 1984 dedicated in California as the "year of the fan" and represented baseball fans in the 1985 baseball strike negotiations. Goals include developing a system to halt sports franchise relocation and a free agent rating system for sports fans. It also wants consumer input in ticket pricing, stadium construction and design, television programming, All-Star procedures, hall of fame selections, and recommendations for fines or suspensions in cases of player-fan conflicts. The group maintains the FANS Consumer Complaint Board and publishes the quarterly *FANS Sports Page*. Founded in 1981. 2500 members. Contact Michael Ross, Executive Director.

Free Territory of Ely-Chatelaine (FTEC)
Royal Post 100-1000
PO Box 7075
Laguna Niguel, CA 92607   (714) 240-8472

A tongue-in-cheek alliance of households that have declared themselves to be free and autonomous states. FTEC aims to revitalize and restore royalism as a viable socioeconomic and political force. It seeks to educate the public in the art and science of self-government, believing that the present system of nation states is obsolete and that the world is entering an era in which the laws of nature will predominate. FTEC promotes decentralized, monarchical government in which monarchs are selected by democratic vote. Members of the Free State stress nonviolence in all human interactions, maintaining that nations have no right to raise armies or to fight wars. The alliance issues the annual *Royal Post Directory* and the quarterly *Territorial Herald*. It has also published *The Royalist Tradition* and holds an annual banquet. Founded in 1975. 120 members. Contact Marc Eric Augustus Rex, King.

Freedom From Religion Foundation (FFRF)
PO Box 750
Madison, WI 53701   (608) 256-8900

Members are "freethinkers" (including atheists, agnostics,

rationalists, secularists, and humanists) promoting the constitutional principle of separation of state and church. FFRF educates the public on matters relating to nontheistic beliefs and combats fundamentalist thought. It opposes payment of public funds for religious purposes, government favoritism toward religious institutions, illegal activities conducted in the name of religious charities, and the religious campaign against women's rights and civil rights for homosexuals. The freethinkers have helped end prayers in public programs and schools and have stopped the practice by the U.S. Postal Service of giving cancellations to a Catholic group in violation of the Postal Service's own regulations. FFRF reports on legal cases, freethinkers, clergy abuse, and foundation activities in the newspaper *Freethought Today* (10 per year) and has published *The Born Again Skeptic's Guide to the Bible, The Book of Ruth, Woe to the Women - The Bible Tells Me So, Rejecting Religion, Lead Us Not into Penn Station,* and *Just Pretend: A Freethought Book for Children.* Founded in 1978. 3400 members. Contact Anne Nicol Gaylor, President.

Friends of Astrology (FA)
535 Woodside Ave.
Hinsdale, IL 60521   (708) 654-4737

FA seeks to raise the standards of astrology through scientific research and educational programs. Their monthly magazine *Friends of Astrology Bulletin* contains astrological lessons, book reviews, and zodiac sign and monthly lunar forecasts (and includes personality analyses of newsworthy figures). Founded in 1938. 500 members. Contact Gladys Hall, President.

Friends of Old-Time Radio (FOTR)
PO Box 4321
Hamden, CT 06514   (203) 248-2887

A loosely formed organization of individuals who trade and collect recordings of radio shows of the past. Members are updated through the bimonthly *Hello Again* and at the annual convention during October in Newark, NJ. Founded in 1976. 500 members. Contact Jay Hickerson, President.

Friends of the Tango (FT)
99-40 64th Road
Rego Park, NY 11374   (718) 275-9560

Also known as *Agrupacion Amigos del Tango,* FT is a group of individuals interested in tango dancing and music, and in the life and career of Argentinean tango singer Carlos Gardel (1890-1935). Besides promoting Gardel's posthumous career and tango music and dancing, FT conducts two to three dance classes a year, holds monthly dance and tango shows in New York City, and sponsors the Friend's Quartet, which conducts charitable performances at universities and public libraries. Members receive the bimonthly *Agrupacion Amigos del Tango* (in English and Spanish) and the monthly *Tango!,* with a calendar of hot tango events. Founded in 1977. 480 members. Contact Abel Malvestiti, President.

Friends of the Trees Society
PO Box 1064
Tonasket, WA 98855   (509) 486-4726

Friends of the Trees promotes reforestation and sustainable

agriculture, conducting workshops on reforestation, permaculture, and related topics. The Friends relate news on projects and events in the *International Green Front Report*. Founded in 1978. Contact Michael Pilarski, Executive Officer.

Frog Pond - Frog Collectors Club (FP)
PO Box 193
Beech Grove, IN 46107

A group uniting collectors of objects depicting frogs, such as figurines, toys, and jewelry. Serving as a forum for contact among collectors worldwide, FP bestows the monthly *Froggie Person Award* and publishes the *Frog Collectors Club Members' Directory*, (with photos of new members!). Member activities are reported in the bimonthly *Ribbit, Ribbit* ($2.50 for a sample issue). Founded in 1985. 400 members. Contact Merelaine Haskett, Director.

Front Striker Bulletin (FSB)
3417 Clayborne Ave.
Alexandria, VA 22306   (703) 768-3932

FSB is a group for collectors of matchcovers, matchboxes, ephemera, specialty items, and labels. The club promotes matchcover collecting to preserve the history of the hobby and the match industry. FSB issues the *Front Striker Bulletin* and meets annually. Founded in 1986. 700 members. Contact Bill Retskin, Editor & Publisher.

Frontlash
815 16th St., NW
Washington, DC 20006   (202) 783-3993

A group of high school and college students, young workers, youth and student organizations, and individuals involved in civil rights and labor movements. Purpose is to increase the political and labor participation of young people, minorities, senior citizens, and workers through voter registration and turn-out campaigns. Frontlash operates on the principle of coalition politics, believing that meaningful social progress in America may only be made possible through cooperative efforts of groups having a stake in long-range political and economic reform. Quarterly it updates members through the newsletter, *Making Democracy Work*. Founded in 1968. Contact Joel Klaverkamp, Executive Director.

Fund for Constitutional Government (FCG)
122 Maryland Ave. NE, Suite 300
Washington, DC 20002   (202) 546-3732

A publicly supported foundation that seeks to expose and correct corruption, illegal activities, or lack of accountability in the federal government. FCG conducts research, public education, and litigation in cases with a large public impact, of precedent-setting value, and which, if rectified, will help preserve an open and accountable government.

FCG sponsors a number of activities, including the Project on Military Procurement, which exposes fraudulent and wasteful weapons systems of the Department of Defense; the Investigative Journalism Project, which provides financial support for investigative projects; the Government Accountability Project, which supports "whistleblowers" by furnishing legal counsel and referral services and by exposing harassment and retaliation; and the KAL

Project, which supports the investigation of the 1983 incident in which a Korean airliner was shot down over the Soviet Union. The group has published the book, *More Bucks, Less Bang.* Founded in 1974. 14 members. Contact Anne B. Zill, President.

Fund for Open Information and Accountability (FOIA)
PO Box 022397
Brooklyn, NY 11202

FOIA works to help enforce the constitutional guarantee, under the Freedom of Information Act, of the people's right to know. It organizes around issues of government secrecy in conjunction with a network of national and grassroots organizations and provides support for lawsuits to expose government misconduct, such as the cases of atomic veterans and sanctuary congregations. FOIA operates Files Clinic to assist individuals in obtaining and interpreting released documents. The group publishes *Our Right to Know,* a quarterly journal. Founded in 1977. Contact Adele Oltman, Acting Director.

Fund for UFO Research (FUFOR)
PO Box 277
Mt. Rainier, MD 20712   (703) 684-6032

FUFOR conducts research on the U.S. government's involvement with UFOs, the abduction phenomenon, and case investigations. It reviews research proposals and approves those that promise to advance scientific knowledge and public understanding of UFO phenomena, such as explaining what Grays, or people from outer space, look like: bald, egg-shaped head, ear holes but not ears, huge black eyes that look like wraparound sunglasses, skinny limbs, four fingers with some webbing, and gray skin. "The generally accepted description of a Gray has only been around for about 10 years," notes FUFOR chairman Bruce Maccabee. "One doesn't know if these things are seen naked or in a suit" (when they come to the office they're always in suits).

"They do not have the proportions of human beings," continues Maccabee. "The feature that's most universally reported around the world by abductees is large black eyes." So if you spot a blue-eyed alien, you've got a rare one. To get the word out on alien characteristics and fashion and other UFO-related matters, FUFOR issues the *Fund for UFO Research-Quarterly Report,* a newsletter covering the activities of the association and major UFO events. Founded in 1979. Contact Bruce S. Maccabee Ph.D., Chairman.

Fundamentalists Anonymous (FA)
PO Box 20324, Greeley Square Station
New York, NY 10001   (212) 696-0420

FA is an organization of former members of fundamentalist religious organizations, including pentecostal or charismatic as well as family and friends of fundamentalists. Fundamentalism, according to FA, tends to foster authoritarian leaders and strict regimentation of members' personal lives, therefore posing a mental health hazard to its adherents. FA describes the fundamentalist mindset as authoritarian (believing it has a monopoly on truth), intolerant, compulsive about control, unable to tolerate ambiguity and uncertainty in life, and inclined to view all matters as black and white, right and wrong, and good and evil, FA offers support to those who feel harmed by the fundamentalist experience and provides guidance to individuals suffering psychological and social difficulties as a result of their experiences with fundamentalism. FA is not considered to be a religious group or anti-Christian. It updates members through the quarterly *FA Networker* and *Speak Out America*. Founded in 1985. 60,000 members. Contact James Luce, Assistant Executive Director.

Fur Farm Animal Welfare Coalition (FFAWC)
405 Sibley St., Suite 120
St. Paul, MN 55101   (612) 293-0349

Veterinarians, farmers, and others interested in animal welfare belong to FFAWC, which promotes humane care practices for farm animals and establishes care guidelines and conducts veterinarian inspections. It publishes *American Fur*, a quarterly magazine. Founded in 1985. 2000 members. Contact Robert Buckler, Executive Director.

Galactic Hitchhiker's Guild (GHG)
PO Box 4229
Bremerton, WA 98312

Members are interested in science fiction, humor, and satire and are dedicated to supporting and promoting British science fiction and satire, particularly Douglas Adams' *The Hitchhiker's Guide to the Galaxy* series. The group also provides a forum for the discussion of related topics. Journeys through the galaxy are charted through the quarterly *Hitchhiker's Guide Supplemental* and a newsletter, *Sub-Etha*. Founded in 1983. 50 members. Contact Brian NcNett, President.

The Galactic Society (TGS)
1078 Ogden Road
Rock Hill, SC 29730   (803) 328-0705

Members are physicists, engineers, economists, and executives as well as institutions seeking to intensify human development by accelerating exploration into space. If your interests include human potentials psychology, alternative technology, economic astronomy, psychological astronomy, interspecies communication, extragalactic astronomy, and tachyon physics, this group may be for you. TGS bestows the *Robert Page Burruss Award* for outstanding effort toward making deep-space, manned missions a reality. It holds an annual conference in August with the 1992 meeting taking place in Japan and the 1993 in Moscow. Founded in 1989. Contact J. G. Bowman III, Founder.

Gamblers Anonymous (GA)
3255 Wilshire Blvd., No. 610
Los Angeles, CA 90010   (213) 386-8789

C'mon, lucky seven. GA is a group of men and women who have joined together in order to stop gambling and to help other compulsive gamblers do the same. GA is self-supporting, declines outside contributions, and neither opposes nor endorses outside causes. Founded in 1957. Contact Karen H., Executive Secretary.

Gambling Chip Collectors Association (GCCA)
500 Yosemite Dr.
Milpitas, CA 95035   (415) 941-5000

Individuals interested in collecting, trading, buying, and selling gambling chips (everyone needs a hobby). GCCA facilitates interaction among members (hey, those are very nice chips—thank you very much) and provides poker chip classifications and chip codes. On the subject of antique and new chips, it has published *Antique Gambling Chips, Ivory Poker Chips,* and other books and supplements. Founded in 1987. 35 members. Contact Steve Bowling, Executive Officer.

Gay and Lesbian History on Stamps Club (GLHSC)
PO Box 3940
Hartford, CT 06103   (203) 653-3791

A study unit of the American Topical Association, GLHSC is a group of individuals interested in learning about and promoting stamp collecting and its connection to gay and bisexual history. The G&L History on Stamps Club works to bring together persons with an interest in gay and bisexual heritage as it pertains to philatelic literature and stamp collecting and exhibiting. The Club disseminates information related to gay and bisexual philately, including aspects of mythology, flora, and fauna and profiles historical persons reputed to be actively or platonically gay or bisexual who have been honored on postage stamps. GLHS points out that although some of the figures under the unit's purview of study are popularly believed to be gay or bisexual, the sexual preference of these persons cannot be decisively determined by a group of stamp collectors. Members are updated through the quarterly *Lambda Philatelic Journal.* Founded in 1982. 248 members. Contact Ed S. Centeno, President.

Gaylactic Network (GN)
PO Box 1051, Back Bay Annex
Boston, MA 02117-1051

Members are gay men, lesbians, and others interested in science fiction and fantasy. The group promotes the genres of science fiction and fantasy in all media, dealing specifically with material related to homosexuality. It provides members with a network for shared information and interests. Quarterly the group publishes short stories, book reviews, and artwork in the *Gaylactic Gayzette.* Founded in 1987. 115 members. Contact Franklin Hummel, Director.

Ghost Research Society (GRS)
PO Box 205
Oaklawn, IL 60454   (708) 425-5163

Who you gonna call? The Ghost Research Society is interested in supernatural or preternatural phenomena, seeking to substantiate claims that man exists after death and that ghosts inhabit the earth. GRS investigates ghosts, hauntings, and poltergeists and conducts expeditions to "haunted" sites. To spread the word on ghosts, the group sponsors lectures, speaking engagements, psychic discussions, and "ghost tours" and reports on the paranormal in the *Ghost Trackers Newsletter* (three per year). GRS also publishes the annual *Astrology Directory* and the annual *International Directory of Psychic Sciences,* a directory of over 240 groups, organizations, and individuals involved in parapsychology and the occult. Founded in 1981. 160 members. Contact Dale Kaczmarek, President.

Gilligan's Island Fan Club (GIFC)
1993 Indian Trails Ct.
Lakeland, FL 33813   (813) 644-8472

Fans of the television situation comedy *Gilligan's Island,* which aired on the CBS television network from 1964 to 1967 and detailed the adventures of Gilligan, the Skipper too, the Millionaire (Thurston Howe III) and his wife (Lovey), the Movie Star (Ginger Grant), and the Professor (Roy Hinkley) and Mary Ann (Summers), all on Gilligan's Island. As the story goes, they were on a three-hour tour when the weather starting getting rough and their tiny ship (the Minnow) was tossed. If not for the courage of the fearless crew, the Minnow would have been lost. Gilligan and crew beached on an uncharted desert island inhabited only by television comedy writers.

Goals of the Fan Club are to study the origination and production of the series. It recognizes individuals involved directly and indirectly in the production of the show and has presented plaques to honor cast members and the creator of the series. Founded in 1987. 180 members. Contact Ronald A. Turner, Founder & President.

The Giraffe Project (TGP)
PO Box 759
Langley, WA 98260   (206) 221-7989

Honors and publicizes the acts of individuals who "stick their necks out" for the common good in a manner that involves physical, financial, or social risk. Develops educational programs for schools and universities. Inspirational stories are reported on in the quarterly *Giraffe Gazette.* Founded in 1983. 2500 members. Contact John Graham, Executive Director.

Girl Friends (GF)
2228 Lansing Ave.
Portsmouth, VA 23704   (804) 397-1339

A group for black women "who have been friends over the years" Primary aim is to "keep the fires of friendship burning." Girl Friends conducts charitable projects and contributes annually to a selected charity. Members continue the chatter through the annual *The Chatterbox* and the biennial *Chatterletter.* The Girl Friends gather annually (usually in May), with the 1992 gathering set for Pittsburgh, PA, the 1993 in Dallas, TX, and the 1994 in Columbia, SC. Founded in 1927. 1200 members. Contact Rachel Norcom Smith, Executive Officer.

Girth and Mirth (G&M)
PO Box 14384
Chicago, IL 60614   (312) 776-9223

A social club for gay men over age 21 who are overweight or sympathetic to overweight men. G&M provides heavyset gay men the opportunity for group and personal interaction through social gatherings including luncheons, picnics, banquets, and trips. It publishes the monthly *Girth Shaking News/Midwest* and *Midwest*

Malegram (for members only). Founded in 1980. 200 members. Contact Lee Gardener, Founder.

Globetrotters' Club (GT'S)
BCM/Roving
London WC1N 3XX, England

Individuals in 37 countries interested in economical international travel and opportunities to meet people of other countries. The Club offers information on most inexpensive and practical methods of traveling. It also provides a mutual aid column for members looking for traveling companions or advice about a specific area to visit. Members are updated through the bimonthly newsletter *Globe*. Founded in 1947. 1500 members. Contact Joanna Amos, Secretary.

Gnomes Anonymous (GA)
The Church House
Church St.
Bicknoller, Somerset TH4 4EL, England

A club for people of all ages interested in gnomes but who prefer to remain anonymous. Purpose of GA is to "unite gnomes and their human keepers." The group offers children's services and conducts research on gnome behavior and locations. Members are kept informed of gnome happenings through the *Gnome News* (three per year). Founded in 1978. 1000 members. Contact Alex Adams, Executive Officer.

Gold Prospectors Association of America (GPAA)
PO Box 507
Bonsall, CA 92003   (619) 728-6620

A group of recreational gold prospectors and miners seeking gold in them thar hills. GPAA seeks to promote prospecting as an environmentally compatible operation, further knowledge of gold mining, and help small miners attain big prospecting success. GPAA has established the Institute for Legislative Action to preserve the Mining Law of 1872, which upholds Americans' rights to utilize public lands for prospecting. The group offers educational classes and seminars on geology, assaying and refining, gold metallurgy, and dowsing. It also sponsors shows featuring equipment demonstrations, lectures, gold panning, contests, and displays and presents awards for prospecting, panning, dredging, and mucking. GPAA publishes the bimonthly *Gold Prospector* magazine providing reports, new product information, and lists of dealers and new members, as well as the periodic *Pick and Shovel Gazette*, the *U.S. Mining Laws Handbook*, and the *GPAA Mining Claims Guide*. Founded in 1965. 84,000 members. Contact George Massie, President.

Golden Companions (GC)
PO Box 754
Pullman, WA 99163   (509) 334-9351

A group of avid travelers over the age of 49 (hey, that's not so golden!) seeking to assist members in finding travel companions. The Golden Companions offer travel information and tour discounts. As an aid to its member travelers, it provides a mail exchange service and organizes local social activities including tours and cruises. Bimonthly the group reports on travel destinations, types of travel, and members' personal travel accounts in the *The Golden Traveler*. The newsletter includes a networking column that lists members interested in vacation-home exchanges. Founded in 1987. 1000 members. Contact Joanne R. Buteau, President.

Golden Rule Foundation (GRF)

RR 4, Box 284
Mifflintown, PA 17059-4284   (717) 436-6940

Motto is, "It is better to kick-off than receive." No, that can't be it. How about "do onto to others as they would approve for someone to do onto you, particularly if there's no way to trace back the weapon." That's far too cynical a statement for the members of the Golden Rule Foundation, composed of benevolent souls dedicated to securing liberty, freedom, and justice for all people by respecting individual rights (what a neat idea). Objectives are to open the minds, hearts, and doors of people around the world (after of course, knocking) and foster dialogue among the world's people in order to solve mankind's problems through responsible negotiation. The Golden Rulers report on progress in the periodic *Towards a More Perfect World*. Founded in 1937. Contact Stan C. Barner II, President.

Golden Rule Society (GRS)

PO Box 809
Boynton Beach, FL 33425   (407) 732-7354

Christian and Jewish people organized to combat prejudice, poverty, crime, and injustices in the U.S. GRS believes that non-Jews must support Jews in their fight against anti-Semitism and that Arabs are fighting and winning a propaganda war financed by money from oil. GRS works to end anti-Semitism within the church and support the separation of church and state. Founded in 1988. 76 members. Contact Melvin Cohen, President.

Goldfish Society of America (GFSA)

PO Box 1367
South Gate, CA 90280   (213) 633-6016

A club for the universal first pet, the one that dies after eating itself to death because too much food was dumped in the bowl in the mistaken belief that a fat goldfish is a happy goldfish. Belly up, it's less a pet and more a conversation piece. No matter, they're cheap and tiny and easily replaced. To belong to GFSA, it helps if you have an interest in goldfish. If you belong, you get information on breeding, feeding, and care of goldfish. To keep members up to date on breaking goldfish news, the group issues the monthly *Goldfish Report* and various beginners' guides, most of which begin: "For optimum pet survival rates (and months of exciting fish watching), do not overfeed the goldfish." Founded in 1972. 1500 members. Contact W.J. Parsonson, Treasurer.

Good Bears of the World (GBW)

Box 8236
Honolulu, HI 96815   (808) 942-0200

Hailing from ten countries, GBW members are promoters and collectors of teddy bears who gather annually for a teddy bear jubilee, where the teddy bears and their owners are known for kicking up their paws and heels. The group upholds the teddy bear as a symbol of love and affection and believes teddy bears spread comfort to old and young people. So it distributes teddy bears to children in hospitals, battered and abused children, AIDS patients, Alzheimer's patients, victims of violent crimes, and senior citizens in institutions. The good news bears sponsor Good Bear Day on October 27, the birthday of Theodore Roosevelt, who inspired a toymaker to create the "teddy" bear when he refused to shoot a bear on a hunting trip in Mississippi in 1902. GBW provides information of interest to teddy bear collectors and aficionados in the quarterly *Bear Tracks.* The journal contains updates on den activities, articles on teddy bears and bearmobilia, book reviews, calendar of events, chapter news, member profiles, and an annual list of life members and dens. Founded in 1969. 10,000 members. Contact Peggy K. Maxwell, Chairman.

Good Samaritan Coalition (GSC)
Hazardous Materials Advisory Council
1110 Vermont Ave. NW, Suite 250
Washington, DC 20005   (202) 728-1460

A group of organizations supporting passage of "Good Samaritan" legislation which would protect from liability volunteer third parties who render assistance at the scene of an emergency involving hazardous material. Entities such as chemical firms, petroleum companies, and liquid propane gas dealers are often called upon to assist police and fire departments in hazardous material emergencies such as train derailments and overturned trucks. Good Samaritan legislation would protect from lawsuit those providing assistance in the event that their actions aggravate rather than alleviate the hazardous condition, provided that assistance is not rendered in a grossly negligent manner. Founded in 1983. 9 members. Contact Paul Rankin, President.

Goose and Gander, Society for the Preservation of First Wives and First Husbands (GGSPFWFH)
155 Mildred Circle
Concord, MA 01742   (508) 369-1878

Couples who have been married at least 25 years to the same spouse, each having no preceding spouse. Further membership requirements are a lifetime of mutual support; common pursuit of excellence; loyalty to friends; devotion to each other; and dedication to public service. The group celebrates longevity in marriage as an important social goal, encourages couples to mate for life, and demonstrates by example the benefits derived from life-long commitment to mutual support and cooperation. The group reports that the symbol of the goose is used because geese mate for life (honk if you love your wife). Founded in 1982. 480 members. Contact Anne Branscomb.

Government Accountability Project (GAP)
25 E St. NW, Suite 700
Washington, DC 20001   (202) 347-0460

Members are federal and corporate employees, union members, professionals, and interested citizens. GAP, a great place to shop for casual wear, provides legal and strategic counsel for corporate and public employees who seek to expose and combat government actions that are repressive, wasteful, illegal, or which present a threat to public health and safety. It seeks to broaden understanding of how the individual can make a difference in preventing and halting government waste. The group offers graduate credit and formal training to lawyers who will assist environmental or nuclear whistle-blowers who can show they were terminated in response to pointing out safety or environmental concerns. GAP holds training seminars for lawyers representing environmental whistle-blowers and citizen activists dealing with environmental concerns. Whistle-blowing is reported on in the quarterly *Bridging the Gap.* Founded in 1977. 6000 members. Contact Louis Clark, Executive Director.

Graham Brothers Truck and Bus Club (GBTBC)
9894 Fairtree Dr.
Strongsville, OH 44136   (216) 238-4956

Members are owners of Graham Brothers trucks and buses which were manufactured from 1923 to 1929 by the Graham Bros. Co. in Detroit, MI and Evansville, IN. The vehicles were sold through Dodge dealers; the buses were used as school buses and parlor coaches. The Club maintains an owners roster and shares information concerning these models. Founded in 1967. 150 members. Contact Edwin L. Brinkman, Founder.

Grandmothers for Peace (GP)
909 12th St., Suite 118
Sacramento, CA 95814   (916) 444-5080

A group of grandmothers and other individuals worldwide who seek an end to the nuclear arms race. GP supports "peace-loving groups in communities across the nation and around the world." Grannies for Peace encourages public involvement in campaigns against nuclear weapons, including vigils at military installations, armaments factories, and the Nevada nuclear weapons test site. It supports nonviolent resistance and efforts toward peaceful coexistence with Russia and the other newly independent Soviet republics. The group facilitates correspondence with women sharing similar beliefs worldwide and publishes the quarterly *Grandmothers for Peace Newsletter.* It also makes available buttons and T-shirts. Founded in 1982. 500 members. Contact Barbara Wiedner, Founder & Executive Director.

Grandparents Anonymous (GPA)
1924 Beverly
Sylvan Lake, MI 48053   (313) 682-8384

Members are grandparents who are denied legal visitation of grandchildren as a result of divorce or a breakdown in family communications. GPA promotes the well-being of grandchildren regardless of race, color, or creed. It is seeking to have March 18 observed in all schools in the United States as Grandparents and Grandchildren Day (presently observed in Michigan). The group disseminates information for establishing observance in other states. Founded in 1976. Contact Luella M. Davison, Founder.

Gray Panthers (GP)
1424 16th St. NW, Suite 602
Washington, DC 20036   (202) 387-3111

Consciousness-raising activist group of older adults and young people united to fight ageism—the discrimination against persons on the basis of chronological age. The Panthers believe that both the old and the young have much to contribute to make our society more just and humane. The group advises, acts as a catalyst for, and organizes local groups of young, middle-aged, and older persons to work on issues of their choosing. GP conducts seminars and research on age-related issues and publishes the *Gray Panther Network*, a quarterly newspaper containing articles on ageism, health care, housing, disarmament, and other intergenerational issues. Progress is also reported on in the bimonthly *Gray Panther Washington Report* and the bimonthly *Health Watch*. Founded in 1970. 6000 members. Contact Frances J. Humphreys, Director.

Greater Washington, DC Association of Professionals Practicing the Transcendental Meditation Program
8701 Georgia Ave., Suite 607
Silver Spring, MD 20910   (301) 495-3111

Ommmmmm. A group of professionals who practice transcendental meditation (TM). Purpose of the group is to introduce non-meditating business leaders and professionals to the benefits of the TM program. It acts as an information clearinghouse and organizational resource for other TM groups. Although activities are concentrated in the Washington, DC area, membership is national. Founded in 1985. 500 members. Contact A. J. Rachele, PR Director.

Ground Saucer Watch (GSW)
13238 N. 7th Dr.
Phoenix, AZ 85029   (602) 942-7216

Members are scientists, engineers, professionals, and educated laymen interested in taking scientific action to resolve the controversial elements in UFO reports. It seeks to bring forth the workable hypotheses and theories of UFO origin and the reasons for their continuing surveillance. Other objectives are to provide an accessible outlet for all interested persons who wish to report any aerial phenomena experiences without fear of ridicule or undue publicity and to "edify a confused media" with factual press releases, lectures, conferences, and interviews. The Watch researches and evaluates all UFO cases to which scientific criteria can be applied and analyzed with the use of specialized talents and instrumentation. It continues to pursue legal action against the federal government with lawsuits and Freedom of Information Act requests for release of UFO materials. Founded in 1957. 500 members. Contact William H. Spaulding, Director.

Guardian Angels (GA)
982 E. 89th St.
Brooklyn, NY 11236   (212) 420-1324

A highly publicized group of unarmed volunteers organized to combat crime in New York City, Philadelphia, PA, Detroit, MI, and other major U.S. and Canadian cities with various degrees of community acceptance. The GA seeks to "provide positive role models for young people" while patrolling subways, buses, streets, ferries, and multiple dwellings. Members wear distinctive red berets and are selected only upon recommendation of other Angels. They must act in a calm manner and be capable of self-defense if attacked by one or more persons. But before being attacked, Angels must undergo three months of physical and legal training. Members make citizens' arrests but their primary impact is one of deterrence; the group reports that often their presence prevents crimes. To help others survive the urban war zone, GA has published the book, *Streetsmarts: The Guardian Angels Guide to Safe Living*. The Angels meet annually. Founded in 1979. 5000 members. Contact Curtis Sliwa, Founder.

Gungywamp Society (GS)
334 Brook St.
Noank, CT 06340   (203) 536-2887

Avocational archaeologists, anthropologists, historians, geologists, astronomers, and interested individuals seeking to protect and preserve sites throughout the northeastern United States that show evidence of ancient and pre-Columbian cultures. GS investigates and studies lithic features, architecture, artifacts, ancient inscriptions, and historic records. It has discovered an archaeological site in Connecticut that shows evidence of serial occupancy since 3000 B.C. The group conducts tours through the Gungywamp Complex, an archaeological area preserved by the group. The Society provides information on archaeological discoveries, ancient inscriptions, translations, and membership updates in the quarterly *Stonewatch*. Founded in 1979. 500 members. Contact David P. Barron, President.

GWTW Collectors Club
8105 Woodview Road
Ellicott City, MD 21043   (301) 465-4632

A group seeking to assist persons who collect or have an interest in memorabilia associated with the 1939 movie *Gone With the Wind*, and the book of the same name by Margaret Mitchell. Purpose is to inform and entertain collectors concerning the movie, book, and actors in the movie. It facilitates correspondence among members and aids members in acquiring items through the club's newsletter. The group maintains historical data, including details of production and costumes. Members are kept updated through the quarterly *GWTW Collectors Club Newsletter*. Founded in 1979. 1000 members. Contact M. Marlene Ridenour.

Gypsy Lore Society (GLS)
5607 Greenleaf Road
Cheverly, MD 20785   (301) 341-1261

Anthropologists, linguists, sociologists, folklorists, educators, and others interested in the study of the Gypsy peoples and analogous itinerant or nomadic groups. GLS works to disseminate information aimed at increasing understanding of Gypsy culture in its diverse forms. The group also seeks to establish closer contacts among scholars in the U.S. and Canada and maintains the Victor Weybright Archives of Gypsy Studies. GLS issues the *Gypsy Lore Society-Newsletter*, a quarterly containing calls for papers, research and conference news, and a bibliography. Various aspects of Gypsy studies are reported on in the semiannual *Journal of the Gypsy Lore Society*. Founded in 1977. 250 members. Contact Sheila Salo, Treasurer.

H H H H H H H H

Handwriting Analysts, International (HAI)
1504 W. 29th St.
Davenport, IA 52804 (319) 391-7350

A group of handwriting analysts striving to elevate handwriting analysis to a professional status, maintain a high standard within the field, and interest educational institutions and the public in the potential of this science. HAI provides educational and research opportunities for handwriting analysts and encourages the exchange of ideas between analysts. It publishes the *Graphological Forum* three times per year. Founded in 1964. 80 members. Contact Robert B. Martin, President.

Happy Hours Brotherhood (HHB)
87 School St.
Fall River, MA 02720 (508) 672-2082

Collectors and readers of dime novels, story papers, and popular literature for the young published during the 19th and early 20th centuries. It seeks to preserve and promote collection of these novels and related material. The group maintains a collection of bibliographic materials on dime novels and more than 50,000 dime novels and story papers. HHB provides members with the *Dime Novel Round-Up*, a periodic magazine devoted to the collecting, preservation, and literature of the old-time dime and nickel novels. Founded in 1925. 400 members. Contact Edward T. LeBlanc, President.

Harley Hummer Club (HHC)
PO Box 7294
Gaithersburg, MD 20898

A club for people who own or are interested in the restoration of American-made two-stroke Harley-Davidson motorcycles produced from 1948 to 1966. Objective is to aid in the preservation and restoration of these motorcycles. Fast-breaking Harley news and views are communicated through the quarterly *HummerNews*. Founded in 1980. 200 members. Contact David M. Hennessey, President.

Harmony International (HI)
PO Box 470168
Tulsa, OK 74147 (918) 622-1444

Women interested in barbershop harmony singing in quartets and choruses belong to HI, which teaches and trains members in singing four-part harmony, barbershop style, without instrumental accompaniment, the parts being tenor, lead, baritone, and bass. HI operates chapters in the U.S., Australia, Canada, Germany, Japan, the Netherlands, New Zealand, Panama, Sweden, and the United Kingdom. The group publishes the quarterly *Pitch Pipe*, which includes articles on choral singing, competition and judging, and leadership skills including management and administration of choral groups. Members meet annually. Founded in 1945. 30,000 members. Contact Sharon Green, Executive Director.

Haunt Hunters (HH)
Goodwilling
2188 Sycamore Hill Ct.
Chesterfield, MO 63017   (314) 831-1379

HH is a division of the Psychic Science Institute serving as a clearinghouse for experiences and information on ghosts, hauntings, extrasensory perception, and other psychic phenomena. The Hunters seek to improve the image of psychic research by creating more positive public relations and by bringing together the qualified psychic researcher and the person having the psychic experience. HH maintains a file of over 300 case histories of psychic phenomena and has published the *Haunt Hunters Handbook for the Psychic Investigator*. Founded in 1965. 300 members. Contact Gordon J. Hoener, Director.

Having Fun With Elvis (HFWE)
5206 Tom Stafford
San Antonio, TX 78219   (512) 661-8955

More fans of Elvis. HFWE publishes the bimonthly *Elvis Footnotes*. Founded in 1980. 125 members. Contact Judy Dial, Coordinator.

Hawkwatch International (HWI)
1420 Carlisle NE, No. 202
PO Box 35706
Albuquerque, NY 87176   (505) 255-7622

Research scientists, raptor biologists, field biologists, and other individuals interested in the conservation of raptor (hawk) populations and their ecosystems. Hawkwatch conducts long-term raptor population monitoring and migration research at sites in western North America and large-scale raptor banding studies for determination of origins and destinations of birds. It sponsors the Adopt-A-Hawk Program to provide funding for raptor banding projects and three to four times a year publishes the *Raptor Watch*, a newsletter with a description of activities, a calendar of events, research findings, conservation news, and activities for children. Founded in 1986. 2000 members. Contact Stephen W. Hoffman.

Highamerica Balloon Club (HBC)
PO Box 99362
Troy, MI 48099   (313) 435-4160

A club for high-flying folks interested in the sport of ballooning, which involves levitating in a large balloon filled with hot air while seated in a gondola or similar carrier. The group holds a weekly balloon launch. Founded in 1968. 300 members. Contact Linden F. Harding, Director.

Hocker International Federation (HIF)
78 Unquowa Place
Fairfield, CT 06430   (203) 255-5907

HIF promotes the playing of hocker, a hybrid sport incorporating aspects of soccer, basketball, volleyball, hockey, and football (but no baseball). The object of the game is to get a 16-inch playground ball down the field and through a set of goalposts. In doing so, the ball may be dribbled, passed, or kicked as long as the player does not long hold onto it. The federation dreams of spreading hocker's popularity to playgrounds and college intramural fields and eventually to have it become a major league sport and possibly an Olympic event. Founded in 1976. Contact Sheila Dearie, Executive Officer.

Holiday Institute of Yonkers (HIY)
Box 266
Hillside, NJ 07205

HIY seeks to research, study, celebrate, and promote interest in holidays in general. It worked to persuade New York Governor Rockefeller to proclaim July 20 as Moon Landing Day. A current endeavor is to encourage celebration of Humanities Day, a proposed international holiday which would fall on December 10. The art of holiday seeking is detailed in the monthly *Holidagology Today.* Founded in 1969. Contact William Bickel, President.

Hollywood Studio Collectors Club (HSCC)
3960 Laurel Canyon Blvd., Suite 450
Studio City, CA 91614   (818) 990-5450

No, they're not collecting entire studios. Just parts of them. Members are movie memorabilia collectors and film buffs as well as interested individuals, clubs, and organizations. The Club promotes interest in collecting movie memorabilia and related items. It also conducts research on motion picture history. And, yes, HSCC encourages trading, buying, and selling among members. What's more, the group encourages the exchange of information and ideas on movies and memorabilia. What a club! It cooperates, yes, cooperates, through publications, with movie museums and halls of fame. Members are kept updated through the *Hollywood Studio Magazine* (15 per year). Founded in 1957. 9000 members. Contact Ralph E. Benner, Executive Officer.

Holyearth Foundation (HF)
Box 10697
Bainbridge Island, WA 98110   (206) 842-7986

The Foundation is an educational organization seeking to facilitate evolution of human consciousness. The group promotes spiritual development that focuses on "collective consciousness" and a "connectedness with all beings" as a means to deal with planetary issues such as peace and ecology. HF maintains the Earthstewards Network (see listing elsewhere) and conducts consulting services and sponsors workshops on conflict resolution, planetary consciousness, and right livelihood.

Areas of interest include principles of aikido as a positive response to conflict, self-healing, examining new models of personal power and group leadership, and discovering and developing personal commitments to the planet and the human family for both adults and children. HF publishes the *Earthsteward Handbook* and gathers annually to elevate the collective consciousness. Founded in 1981. 1800 members. Contact Danaan Parry, Director.

Horseless Carriage Club of America (HCCA)
128 S. Cypress St.
Orange, CA 92666-1314   (714) 538-HCCA

Hobbyists who are interested in the preservation, accessories, archives, and romantic lore of old cars. HCCA annually awards trophies for best regional group publications and for car restorations. It sponsors two tours annually, for larger cars and for one-

and two-cylinder cars. In addition to maintaining a museum and biographical archives, HCCA keeps members up on hot old car news through the bimonthly *Horseless Carriage Gazette*. Founded in 1937. 4700 members.

Houdini Historical Center (HHC)
330 E. College Ave.
Appleton, WI 54911   (414) 733-8445

Individuals interested in preserving the history of magician Harry Houdini (born Ehrich Weiss, 1874-1926). Part of the Outagamie County Historical Society, the group gathers, interprets, and disseminates information and artifacts on the life and times of Houdini. It acts as the caretaker of the Sidney H. Radner Collection of Houdini Memorabilia, "the world's finest collection of artifacts once owned and used by Houdini." The collection includes personal photographs and documents, posters and handbills, as well as handcuffs, leg irons, and lock picks.

HHC sponsors permanent and touring exhibitions, a tour of downtown Appleton (Houdini's home town, located at the top of beautiful Lake Winnebago), and related special events. The group makes available Houdini collectibles (get them fast before they disappear) and publications (a catalog is available). Members receive the Center publication, invitations to center events, and discounts on collectibles and reproductions. All that for $20 per year. Founded in 1990. 30 members. Contact Moira Thomas, Curator.

Howdy Doody Memorabilia Collectors Club (HDMCC)
12 Everitts Hill Road
Flemington, NJ 08822   (201) 782-1159

Fans of *The Howdy Doody Show*, the popular kids' television show which ran from 1947 to 1960 and deeply etched the phrase, "It's Howdy Doody time!" in the minds of bent baby boomers everywhere. The club is also known as the Doodyville Historical Society and as such, it perpetuates the spirit and the history of Doodyville and helps collectors stay in touch with one another. HDMCC campaigns to "Bring back Howdy to TV" and publishes the monthly newsletter, *Howdy Doody Times*. The Doody enthusiasts gather at an annual convention, which in 1991 featured performances by members Buffalo Bob and Clarabell and others connected with the show. Founder Jeff Judson describes himself as "America's Foremost Howdy Doody Collector." Annual dues are $16. Founded in 1978. 225 members. Contact Jeff Judson, Founder & Editor.

Hubcappers
Box 54
Buckley, MI 49620   (616) 269-3555

Persons interested in preserving a piece of automotive history through the collecting of threaded hubcaps manufactured prior to 1930. Objective is to try to locate as many of these hubcaps as possible. The group, also known as the Hubcap Collector's Society, publishes the quarterly *The Hubcapper* and holds an annual swap meet in Hershey, PA. Founded in 1970. 63 members. Contact Dennis H. Kuhn, President.

Hug Club (HC)

PO Box 325
Fishkill, NY 12524

An organization that believes in reaching out and sharing warmth and energy with others through the physical action of hugging. It promotes the therapeutic benefits of hugging which, according to the club, include stress reduction, diminished anger, and strengthened relationships. The Hug Club has established categories of hugging and a formula for hugging frequency (E=MC2=pick up dry cleaning=distance from the sun to the moon=three hugs per hour). It sponsors workshops and lectures on hugging, produces a complete line of Hug Club paraphernalia, and annually issues the *Hug Club Clarion.* Founded in 1980. 6500 members. Contact Ron Monbell, Director.

Humans Against Rabbit Exploitation (HARE)

PO Box 1553
Williamsport, PA 17703   (717) 322-3252

An international coalition of animal protection groups opposing all forms of the exploitation of rabbits. HARE opposes promotion of rabbit as a meat source and encourages avoidance of all products of the rabbit industry and of products that have been tested on rabbits. Particularly focusing on the "factory farming" of rabbits by the rabbit breeding industry, HARE counters these practices through education, legislation, economic boycott, and protest. It stages protests at conferences on rabbit breeding and usage and organizes demonstrations and boycotts against stores and restaurants that sell rabbit meat and against universities offering rabbit breeding courses. Activities and plans are detailed in the quarterly *HARE Lines.* Founded in 1982. 100 members. Contact Dana Stuchell, General Coordinator.

Humor Association (HA)

Box 221
Sharon, MA 02067   (617) 784-2657

Members are interested in introducing humor into the home and workplace on a regular basis. Ha. Founded in 1987. Contact Bernie Delman, President.

Humor Correspondence Club (HCC)

PO Box 023304
Brooklyn, NY 11202-0066   (718) 855-5057

Comedy writers and performers and humor enthusiasts who encourage the initiation of friendship and personal growth through correspondence and exchange of ideas among members. HCC publishes a monthly newsletter called *Latest Jokes* and meets annually in New York City. Founded in 1978. 85 members. Contact Robert Makinson, Director.

Humor Project

110 Spring St.
Saratoga Springs, NY 12866   (518) 587-8770

Health care professionals, educators, counselors, therapists, business executives, and others interested in developing their sense of humor. Members believe humor can be used as a constructive and therapeutic tool, personally and professionally. The group offers public speaking, training, and programs on how to improve and apply one's sense of humor. The Humor Currently developing projects that focus on the medical applications of humor and on the role of humor in parenting and families, Project Humor provides grants to hospitals and organizations for projects and services promoting the positive power of humor. The group issues the no-frills *Directory of People Doing Research on Humor* and the quarterly *Laughing Matters*, a journal that examines the serious implications and applications of humor (and includes interviews with famous humorists and comedians). Founded in 1977. 90,000 members. Contact Dr. Joel Goodman, Director.

Humor Stamp Club (HSC)
PO Box 023304
Brooklyn, NY 11202-0066   (718) 855-5057

Members have a particular interest in stamps that depict humorous themes, comedians, or famous people with wide grins. HSC depicts the humorous state of the stamp world in the annual *Humor Stamp Directory*, listing humorous stamps worldwide. Out to prove that stamps are a laughing matter, the club holds an annual conference in New York City. Founded in 1985. 45 members. Contact Robert Makinson, Editor.

Humorolics Anonymous (HA)
235 Stanyon lane
Bloomingdale, IL 60108   (708) 924-5511

A group of underachievers with low self-esteem, HA is a tongue-in-cheek organization supporting recovering "humorolics, who, having given up humor, find it difficult to maintain the serious, negative outlook on life to which they are committed." The group sponsors workshops to assist people in maintaining a high level of stress in life so "they will die early and be done with it." To help members achieve a deeper, more desirable dour and depressed disposition, HA distributes the Humorolics Anonymous 12-step program and issues *Laugh or Die*, a "silly" newsletter published "twice a year or when I'm inspired, whichever comes first," reports President Bezman. Founded in 1990. Contact Bob Bezman, President.

Humper Dears (HD)
1939 S. Roanoke Ave.
Springfield, MO 65807   (417) 881-5444

A sociological phenomena: another gathering of Engelbert Humperdinck fans, dedicated to supporting and promoting Humper-dinck. It makes available concert itineraries and monitors and reports on appearances of Humperdinck. HD publishes the *The Humper Dears Happening* monthly newsletter. Founded in 1971. 100 members. Contact Velma Miles, President.

Ice Screamers (IS)
Box 538/
2733 Lititz Pike
Lancaster, PA 17601   (717) 569-8284

You scream: members are ice cream and soda fountain enthusiasts. I scream: Or individuals interested in the history of the industry. We all scream: Or collectors of ice cream and soda fountain memorabilia. The Ice Screamers plan to establish an ice cream museum (please turn your attention to the display on the left, where we have a carton of antique chocolate) and cover the state of ice cream art in the quarterly *Ice Screamer*. IS holds an annual conference (with exhibits) during June in Lancaster, PA. Bring your own spoon. Founded in 1981. 500 members. Contact Ed Marks, President.

Iceberg Athletic Club (IAC)
3046 W. 22nd St.
Brooklyn, NY 11224   (718) 648-5254

Membership is limited to men who are devotees of cold water swimming, a condition which so far has severely limited the number of members. IAC has held outdoor winter swims in salt water as cold as 26 or 27 degrees Fahrenheit. The prime cold-weather swimming season begins November 1 and ends on April 1. On the positive side, there's always plenty of room on the beach to spread your blanket. Founded in 1918. 25 members. Contact Vic Boff, President.

Icelandic Horse Adventure Society (IHAS)
Viking Saga Ranch
795 Entrance Road
Solvang, CA 93463   (805) 688-7472

A group of owners and admirers of Icelandic horses who are devoted to promoting public awareness of the Icelandic horse as well as Icelandic history and culture. IHAS sponsors competitions and shows and plans to develop youth, family, senior citizen, and therapeutic programs. The Adventure Society also conducts seminars on breeding, training, and horse care and publishes *Keilir*, a monthly newsletter covering Iceland, Icelandic horses, and association activities. It plans to issue a stud book. 40 members. Contact Elisabeth Haug, Supreme Chieftain.

Idealist International, Inc. (III)
2758 Keller Springs Place
Carrollton, TX 75006   (214) 855-7684

A group of optimistic individuals who "believe in God, the Golden Rule, and that a positive mental attitude is essential to the development and well-being of the individual and the community." III seeks to create an "international community of positive-thinking people with integrity" and works to connect positive people with similar interests and talents. III publishes the semiannual newsletter, *The Idealist Forum* and hosts an annual open house. Founded in 1979. 1200 members. Contact Nancy Greenfield, Executive Director.

Imaginary Basketball Federation (IBF)
Box 5275
Willowick, OH 44095   (216) 946-8278

Individuals who compete in imaginary basketball leagues. Members gather for play-off and all-star tournaments, which are nothing more than figments of their imagination. Founded in 1985. Contact John Bruening.

Immortalist Society (IS)

24443 Roanoke
Oak Park, MI 48237 (313) 548-9549

Scientists, researchers, and interested individuals involved in the study of human life extension. IS promotes research and education in cryobiology, cryogenics, and cryonics. Cryobiology is the study of the effects of extremely low temperatures on biological systems; cryogenics is a branch of physics dealing with the production and effects of very low temperatures; cryonics is the practice of freezing dead human beings in the hope of bringing them back to life at some date in the future when being dead will not necessarily be the end of life, but merely another stage, like middle age, engendering its own after-life crisis.

A related organization, the Cryonics Institute, practices cryonics on members following their deaths, believing that practice makes perfect. IS provides financial support to research projects in life extension science. In conjunction with the American Cryonics Society, it publishes *The Immortalist* monthly newsletter. Founded in 1967. 160 members. Contact Mae Junod, Treasurer.

Impotents Anonymous (IA)

PO Box 5299
Maryville, TN 37802-5299 (615) 983-6064

IA serves as an educational organization providing concerned individuals with information regarding impotency, including medical and psychiatric counseling resources available to impotent males. It also offers group support during pre- and post-treatment. Founded in 1983. Contact Eileen V. MacKenzie, Executive Director.

Ingglish Speling 3soesiaesh3n (IS3)

11 1st St.
London SW3, England 71 5841848

Also known as the English Spelling Association, IS3 works to "propagate better spellings of English for any appropriate purpose" and generally wants to reform and make more understandable the rules of the English language. The group conducts research on historic pronunciation of the English language. The "3" appearing in the association name is being used as the "yert," the 31st letter of the Cyrillic alphabet, about which many people clam to know absolutely nothing. IS3 maintains a library of pronunciation dictionaries and offers typographical advice. Founded in 1974. 90 members. Contact S. S. Eustace, Secretary.

Inner Peace Movement (IPM)

PO Box 4900
Washington, DC 20008 (515) 342-4576

A leadership training program designed "to help man identify and balance the physical, mental and spiritual forces in life so he can mold his own destiny and become the architect of his own success." We assume that women belong as well. IPM believes that meditation and inner guidance will help individuals make mature decisions. The group sponsors local and national workshops for advanced training. The nature of the program evolves with the changing needs of the members. Founded in 1964. 1500 members. Contact Francisco Coll, Founder.

Institute for the Development of the Harmonious Human Being (IDHHB)
PO Box 370
Nevada City, CA 95959 (916) 477-1116

Not a group of barbershop quartets, but individuals and groups studying the ancient teachings of spiritual awakening and personal transformation. Ahh, grasshopper. The Harmonious Human Beings seek to provide public access to information about Voluntary Evolution, an approach to spiritual work on the self. The group promotes the Fourth Way and Sufi teachings, spiritual disciplines dating back to ancient Arab and Greek cultures. The Labyrinth Readers Course fosters new attitudes toward death and dying.

Other educational programs include Gateways books and tapes, sacred theater and dance training, mask initiation workshops, and professional evolutionary marketing seminars. The group offers Zen Basics, an audiocassette training course on essence attention, and publishes *Inner Journeys,* a quarterly newsletter. It also keeps members updated through the monthly *Talk of the Month* and the periodic newsletter *Zen Bo,* which includes information for students of the Zen Basics training course. Founded in 1971. 350 members. Contact Lee Perry, President.

Institute for UFO Contactee Studies
1151 Hidalgo Dr.
Laramie, WY 82070 (307) 742-3399

Supporters are persons interested in the UFO phenomena, that sensation of seeing a spaceship overhead when you least expect it. The Institute sponsors an annual conference for researchers and others who have experienced or are interested in UFOs. It holds the annual Rocky Mountain Conference on UFO Investigation. Contact June O. Parnell Ph.D., President.

Institute of Pyramidology (IOP)
108 Broad St.
Chesham, Bucks. HP5 3ED, England 494 771774

People interested in pyramidology seeking to advance knowledge and research in pyramidology in all its aspects: scientific, prophetic, and religious. The institute's special interest is to make more widely known the "great Divine Revelation enshrined in the Great Pyramid." Each year in March, IOP conducts an annual tour to the Great Pyramid in Egypt and visits the Divine Revelation, or D.R. for short. The group publishes the quarterly *Pyramidology Magazine* instructing members on various methods of using pyramids in their daily lives and has compiled the five-volume *Pyramidology Book,* the perfect gift for those with time on their hands. Founded in 1940. Contact F. Binns, Trustee.

Institute of Strategic Studies on Terrorism
PO Box 3372
Early, TX 76803 (915) 646-8674

Members of the law enforcement and corporate security community who collect, analyze, and study all aspects of terrorism. The Institute provides the most current information and expert training to members regarding counter-terrorism and executive protection tactics. It conducts three-day seminars on threat analysis and risk assessments. Founded in 1984. Contact Arthur E. Gerringer, Director.

Institute of Totally Useless Skills (ITUS)

20 Richmond St.
Dover, NH 03820   (603) 742-6096

ITUS asks that we remember the words of author Tom Robbins: "Life is too serious to be taken seriously." The Institute is a tongue-in-cheek organization for high-minded and refined individuals devoted to acquiring and teaching skills "that add absolutely nothing to society." These include juggling, yodeling, gurning, bandanna stunts, disappearing body parts, crafting the best paper airplane, advanced eye-crossing, apple bouncing, spoon playing, mouth sounds, yo-yo skills, feather balancing, putting a head through a business card (don't try this at home), creative beer can crushing, match tricks, finger stretching, balloon sculpturing, napkin stunts, palm reading, spoon hanging, romantic fortune telling, body tricks, anagrams, hambones, creating symptoms of false physical self-abuse, pen bouncing, mime, learning to make the sound of one hand clapping, plate balancing, pencil tricks, hanging a spoon from the nose, coin tricks, building the longest word (and then pronouncing it), odd finger snapping, brain removal, and developing weird feelings. Members are invited to send in information on their own useless skills and receive a complimentary button for their efforts. The Institute encourages members to "learn everything you'll never need to know" and seeks "to bring instant talent to the untalented, teach members everything they should have learned in sixth grade but didn't, and to boldly go where no curriculum has gone before." The entire course is offered to members on a two-hour videotape.

The Institute sponsors workshops on nonaccomplishment and bestows Practitioner of Uselessness Degree on deserving underachievers. Maintains useless library with very few books. Sometimes publishes a newsletter known as *A Piece of Paper*. The Institute reluctantly admits that while its skills are directly useless, they may not be totally worthless, but may "enhance self-esteem, coordination, concentration, and social interaction. So they're great for parents, recreation leaders, and teachers." Founded in 1987. 250 members. Contact Rick Davis, Master of Uselessness.

Intercontinental UFO Galactic Spacecraft Research and Analytic Network (ICUFON)

35-40 75th St., Suite 4G
Jackson Heights, NY 11372   (718) 672-7948

Participants include organizations, military research scientists, and UFO analytic researchers. ICUFON was established to preserve universal peace and prevent a "space war." It maintains the World Authority for Spatial Affairs (WASA Project), created to encourage the United Nations and national governments to establish official contact and communication with the UFO forces for the "benefit and progress of humanity." It maintains a library of declassified military documents on UFOs. Founded in 1966. Contact Maj. Colman VonKeviczky, Director.

International Academy of Twirling Teachers (IATT)
300 S. Wright Road
Janesville, WI 53545   (608) 754-2239

Just how to you twirl a teacher? Members are people who teach baton twirling, a half-time treat for some and a reason to hit the concession stand for many. Objectives are to raise twirling standards and carry the benefits of twirling to young people worldwide (very good for the wrists and may be used as a protective device). IATT conducts clinics and contests and holds periodic national and international conferences and workshops. Founded in 1971. 9000 members. Contact Don Sartell, Executive Secretary.

International Arthurian Society, North American Branch (IAS/NAB)
Department of French
Dalhousie University
Halifax, NS, Canada B3H 3J5   (902) 494-2430

Members are university professors and other individuals interested in Arthurian literature as well as 150 libraries of universities, seminars, and research institutes. Seeks to further Arthurian studies and encourage exchange of information among members. The group meets annually during May in Kalamazoo, MI. Founded in 1948. 550 members. Contact Hans R. Runte, Secretary Treasurer.

International Association for Near-Death Studies (IANDS)
PO Box 7767
Philadelphia, PA 19101

Members are medical, academic, and health care professionals, laypersons, and individuals who have undergone near-death experiences (NDE), phenomena which occur to people who are very close to physical death or who pass into a temporary state of clinical death. The group relates information emerging from research to appropriate settings, including hospitals and nursing homes, and serves as a fraternal organization for those who have experienced such phenomena. IANDS maintains archives of written and taped accounts of NDE and publishes the *Journal of Near-Death Studies*, a quarterly providing original articles on NDE, out-of-body experiences, death bed visions, comparable experiences occurring under other circumstances, and the implications of such phenomena for the understanding of human consciousness and its relationship to the life and death process. Founded in 1981. 1000 members. Contact Elizabeth W. Fenske Ph.D., President.

International Association for the Fantastic in the Arts (IAFA)
Shippensburg University
Shippensburg, PA 17257   (717) 532-1495

Scholars, educators, writers, critics, and artists sharing an interest in the fantastic, science fiction, horror, and fantasy and their impact on literature, the visual and performing arts, cinema, and other art forms. IAFA serves as a forum for the dissemination of scholarship and the exchange of ideas among members. It encourages work in the field through publications, financial awards, professional support service, and graduate student scholarships. Members are kept informed through various newsletters and the quarterly *Journal of the Fantastic in the Arts,* containing critical commentaries and reviews. During March or April each year, the group conducts the International Conference on the Fantastic in the Arts in Dania, FL. Founded in 1979. 324 members. Contact Donald Palumbo Ph.D., President.

International Association of Jim Beam Bottle and Specialties Clubs (IAJBBSC)
5013 Chase Ave.
Downers Grove, IL 60515   (708) 963-8980

A band of hearty individuals interested in studying, stimulating, and encouraging interest in Jim Beam bottle collecting, presumedly after they're empty. A bit of background: Beam china bottles are manufactured by the Regal China Co. in Antioch, IL. Bottles are most valuable when labels, tax stamps, chains, and other accessories as well as the original boxes are intact. The club publishes the monthly *Beam Around the World.* Founded in 1966. 10,000 members. Contact Shirley Sumbles, Executive Secretary.

International Association of Pipe Smokers Clubs (IAPSC)
647 S. Saginaw
Flint, MI 48502   (313) 235-0581

Members are pipe smokers clubs in Brazil, Canada, England, Germany, Israel, Japan, Netherlands, New Zealand, and the United States as well as pipe and tobacco shops and manufacturers. IAPSC promotes friendship and fellowship among members. It establishes rules for competitive pipe smoking (penalties for illegal puffing, etc.) and holds an annual conference with a pipe smoking contest. Founded in 1949. Contact Paul T. Spaniola, President.

International Association of Professional Bureaucrats (INATAPROBU)
926 National Press Building
Washington, DC 20045   (202) 347-2490

Individuals employed by governments, universities, and industry united to spoof bureaucracy in the hope that looking at it with good-natured humor may bring improvement (not). Motto of the association is "When in doubt, mumble." INATAPROBU seeks to "give recognition to the articulate finger-tappers of the world who, by their steadfast dedication to the principles of dynamic inactivism, have kept things from happening and thereby prevented mistakes from being made." It hopes to encourage "bureaucratic creativity and stimulate innovative approaches to problems . . . within established guidelines." Objectives are to foster professional interdigitation and to give recognition to practitioners of the bureaucratic arts. INATAPROBU suggests that "any good bureaucrat should have a really diversified set of rubber stamps to use on papers that come across his or her desk." In 1972, INATAPROBU challenged the U.S. Postal Service by staging pony express ride from Philadelphia, PA to Washington, DC and won, in some cases, by as much as eight days.

INATAPROBU collaborates in organizing and articulating plans, feasibility studies, reviews, surveys of plans, surveys of feasibility studies, and surveys of reviews. It conducts an examination for Certified Professional Bureaucrats (CPB), conducts seminars, and maintains 29 coordinating committees. The group sponsors international awards banquets (among the awards is the Order of the Bird), an annual taxpayer's dinner, and other activities to enhance the bureaucratic way of life. INATAPROBU has published a variety of books, including *When in Doubt, Mumble, Have Your Way With Bureaucrats, Fuzzify!, Twiggle,* and *The Bureaucratic Zoo.* Founded in 1968. 1800 members. Contact Dr. James H. Boren, President & Chairman of the Board.

International Association of Sand Castle Builders (IASCB)
172 N. Pershing Ave.
Akron, OH 44313   (216) 864-6353

Also known as the International Brotherhood of Silica Structure Engineers, IASCB is a group of beach enthusiasts and seashore environment advocates promoting interest in the art of sand castle building worldwide. It also studies the impact humans have on beaches. IASCB provides support and assistance to people engaged in or seeking to become engaged in sand castle building, helping the builder gain the necessary permits. The group publishes the *Newsletter,* a periodic newsletter and gathers in a frenzy of castle building each year in the spring and during the first week of October at Ocean-Isle Beach, NC. Founded in 1988. Contact Thomas A. Morrison, President.

International Automotive Hall of Shame (IAHS)
515 Alpine Road, Box 324
Fitchburg, MA 01420   (508) 342-0731

Members are automobile manufacturers and dealerships as well as journalists who cover the automobile industry. The Hall seeks to discomfort persons who intentionally or unintentionally discredit or dishonor the American institution of the automobile which the group considers "a genus of technology that is of critical importance to the physical and psychological well-being of our civilization." Wonder where the Japanese stand with this group.

The Hall of Shame bestows the IGGIE Award (Infamous, Grotesque, and Gratuitous Injury to Excellence) annually to the person or organization that commits the "most heinous act of desecration to our beloved automobile." The group annually gathers and discredits. Founded in 1986. 18 members. Contact Bernard A. Fossa, Founder & Chairman.

International Balut Federation (IBF)
PO Box 12-1075
Bangkok 10121, Thailand   2 2713829

Individuals in the Far East and United States united to promote the game of balut, a Filipino dice game with a complicated point system. The Federation participates in tournaments and international championships. Founded in 1972. 400 members. Contact Niels Lumholdt, President.

International Banana Club (IBC)
2524 N. El Molino Ave.
Altadena, CA 91001   (818) 798-2272

Banana enthusiasts from 15 countries with an appreciation of the banana and humor. Purpose is to influence people to smile more often in a world that is "going bananas." IBC promotes a sense of humor, positive outlook, and good health. it organizes parties, picnics, games, photographic outings, seminars, and educational programs on bananas. The group has a banana museum holding more than 12,000 banana artifacts sent by members. Annually the Banana Club awards deserving individuals with a Masters or Doctorate of Bananistry. Members read all about worldwide banana doings in the quarterly *Woddis Newsletter* and glean favorite recipes in the *Banana Club Cookbook*. The lovers of the yellow fruit convene annually. Founded in 1974. 7000 members. Contact L. Ken Bannister, President & Top Banana.

International Barbed Wire Collectors Association (IBWCA)
Sunset Trading Post
Sunset, TX 76270

Not a group whose collection promotes tactile delight. IBWCA members collect antique fencing wire and related collectibles. The group hosts the World Champion Greased Armadillo Races, the Post Hole Digging Contest, and the World's Largest Barbed Wire Collection Contest. It maintains the Barbed Wire Hall of Fame in Wichita, KS and a museum in LaCrosse, KS. IBWCA has published the *Bobbed Wire Bible* and keeps members current on barbed wire news in the monthly *International Barbed Wire Gazette*. The group has also published *Fencin' Tool Bible, Vol. 1*. Founded in 1967. 11,000 members. Contact Jack Glover.

International Barbie Doll Collectors Club (IBDCC)
PO Box 79
Bronx, NY 10464   (212) 885-2439

IBDCC gathers information for Barbie doll collectors and provides them with a forum for communication. The club has donated souvenir books from recent IBDCC conventions to the Smithsonian Institute, the Brooklyn Museum, and the Museum of the City of New York. To keep members abreast of the activities of Barbie, Ken, and all their pals, it issues the bimonthly *Gazette* newsletter. A gathering of the worldwide Barbie clan is planned for 1994. Founded in 1977. 1000 members. Contact Ruth Cronk, President.

International Beer Tasting Society (IBTS)
1800 E. 1st St.
Santa Ana, CA 92705   (714) 973-1345

Beer lovers who want to enjoy beer in the company of other beer lovers. IBTS seeks to grade and savor as many of the world's beers as possible, both as traveling individuals and as a formal beer-tasting organization. A dirty job but someone has to do it. Other group activities include fostering appreciation of the brewer's art and awarding letters of commendation to breweries. Founded in 1954. Contact Martin J. Lockney, Director.

International Betta Congress (IBC)
923 Wadsworth St.
Syracuse, NY 13208   (315) 454-4792

Fanciers of the Betta Splendens and other members of the Betta genus belong to IBC. Bettas are small, brilliantly colored long-finned freshwater fish of southeastern Asia. The club strives to organize Betta fanciers throughout the world, establish and conduct training courses for the certification of judges, and define and establish standards for judging Bettas. It sponsors research and investigation of the betta genus and offers technical assistance in the breeding and raising of Bettas. The group publishes *FLARE*, a bimonthly magazine covering research in breeding and showing of Bettas at IBC-sanctioned Betta shows. Founded in 1965. 600 members. Contact Sally Van Camp, Executive Officer.

International Brick Collectors' Association (IBCA)
8357 Somerset Dr.
Shawnee Mission, KS 66207-1843

A club for people interested in the collection, history, manufacture, and technological aspects of bricks. Yes, bricks. Member Raymond Chase asks, "Why not? I like bricks and I find bricks fascinating. So I joined a group of other people who like bricks and find bricks fascinating." Chase (who has a collection of 1,370 bricks at last count) and the other IBCA brick lovers gather together semiannually to trade bricks. The group publishes the quarterly *Journal of the International Brick Collectors' Association*, a newsletter with fascinating brick tales such as "Bricking in New Zealand" and "Making Brick in Iowa." Founded in 1983. 420 members. Contact Bill Brownlee, Secretary.

International Brotherhood of Magicians (IBM)
103 N. Main St.
PO Box 89
Bluffton, OH 45817   (419) 358-8555

Members are professional and semiprofessional magicians, suppliers, assistants, agents, and others interested in magic. The Brotherhood seeks to advance the art of magic in the field of amusement, entertainment, and culture. It devotes itself to discouraging false or misleading advertising of effects, tricks, literature, merchandise, or actions related to the magical arts and discouraging exposure of the principles of the art of magic (except in books on magic and magazines devoted to such art for the exclusive use of magicians and devotees of the art). The group encourages humane treatment and care of live animals whenever employed in magical performances, including of course the rabbits living in the hat. The members of the Brotherhood receive the monthly *The Linking Ring* and gather annually during July. Founded in 1920. 13,000 members. Contact Marilyn S. Edwards, Executive Secretary.

International Brotherhood of Old Bastards (IBOB)
2330 S. Brentwood Blvd., Suite 666
St. Louis, MO 63144-2096   (314) 544-3311

Fraternal organization that offers members "no committees, no assessments, no responsibilities, no annual dues—just a lifetime membership card and the opportunity to prove you're a real bastard." To help convert the masses to the art and philosophy of old bastardom, IBOB conducts 10 symposia per year. It publishes the *Annual Directory of Bastards Begotten of Royalty and Politicians* and *Ye Olde Bastards Bulletin*, a quarterly newsletter containing jokes, anecdotes, member news, and other amusements. All of the bastards gather annually, with the 1992 meeting set for Brazil in the spring, the 1993 conclave in Belfast, Northern Ireland, and the 1994 session planned for Moscow or Berlin, depending upon how the mood of the head bastards at the time. Founded in

1813. 523,900 members. Contact Brother Cozen P. Bantling, Supreme Archbastard.

International Bus Collectors Club (IBC)
18 Lambert Ave.
Lynn, MA 01902   (617) 592-3390

Another group devoted to collecting items much too large to display on a shelf. Members are bus owners and operators and individuals interested in the motor bus industry who, together as a group, seek to preserve the history of the North American motor bus industry. Members do fun things like construct models (of buses). IBC sponsors events, such as the Bus Bash for which the club organizes a bus gathering to show the public the benefits of buses (one, you can put a lot of people in them and still have room for the groceries). The group provides a listing of historic coaches to be used in movies and films and publishes the *International Bus Collector Journal* three times per year. The bus lovers meet every year on Memorial and Labor Day weekend. Founded in 1976. 979 members. Contact Robert B. Redden, President.

International Catacomb Society (ICS)
61 Beacon St.
Boston, MA 02108   (617) 742-1285

Individuals in eight countries united to preserve and document historical articles, often found in catacombs, related to both the Jewish and early Christian religions at the time of the Roman Empire. ICS encourages study of the period as it relates to both faiths and to pagan beliefs and promotes awareness of the shared Jewish and Christian background as a basis for present understanding between the faiths. The group sponsors exhibits, including a touring exhibit of historical items, maps, photographs, and reproductions. It issues the periodic *ICS Newsletter,* covering the ICS-sponsored exhibits and activities, which involve the preservation of catacombs illustrating the common influences on Jewish, Christian, and pagan funerary practices at the time of the Roman Empire. Founded in 1980. 200 members. Contact Estelle S. Brettman, Executive Director.

International Chain Saw Wood Sculptors Association (ICSWSA)
14041 Carmody Dr.
Eden Prairie, MN 55347   (612) 934-8400

The perfect meeting of large, loud power tools and art. ICSWSA is an international group of chain saw wood sculptors, artists, and interested others working to introduce and promote the art of chain saw sculpting to the public, which so far has managed to pretty much ignore them. The group encourages recycling of tree stumps into works of art and establishes rules and guidelines for chain saw sculpting. As part of its ongoing reasons for being, the saw and sculpt club organizes periodic exhibitions with chain-saw demonstrations and conducts fund-raising events and competitions. Founded in 1985. 30 members. Contact Tom Rine.

International Chili Society (ICS)
PO Box 2966
Newport Beach, CA 92663   (714) 631-1780

Chili enthusiasts who believe that chili cooking is "as American as apple pie." And as similes go, that's as fresh as an armpit after an all-day workout. The group sponsors chili cook-offs in search of the best chili, holding 350 competitions with the winners proceeding to one of 85 regional or state competitions. Contestants who survive the chili wars at this level proceed to the annual World's Championship Chili Cook-Off, where the winner receives a $25,000 prize. The big cook-off is held during October in Rosamond, CA., with all proceeds going to charity. For those desiring to practice the fine art at home, the Chili Society has published the *Official Chili Cookbook.* Founded in 1970. 10,000 members. Contact Jim West, Executive Director.

International Chinese Snuff Bottle Society (ICSBS)
2601 N. Charles St.
Baltimore, MD 21218   (301) 467-9400

Members are collectors, dealers, and museums in 29 countries interested in snuff bottles. The bottles, which were made only in China toward the beginning of the Ch'ing Dynasty (middle 17th century), are generally two to four inches in height and have been rendered in many kinds of materials. They may be inlaid, enameled, carved, painted, or otherwise finished. The Snuff Bottle Society promotes scholarship regarding the nature and sources of snuff bottles and organizes seminars, exhibitions, and museum visits. To keep members up on the latest little bottle news, the group publishes the quarterly *Chinese Snuff Bottle Journal.* ICSBS meets annually during October. Founded in 1968. 600 members. Contact John G. Ford, President.

International Coalition Against Violent Entertainment (I-CAVE)
PO Box 2157
Champaign, IL 61825   (217) 384-1920

ICAVE attempts to keep the public informed about violence in the entertainment media, particularly depictions of physical violence in movies, television shows, toys, sports, music videos, and cartoons. It also provides information regarding war toys. Founded in 1979. Contact Thomas Radecki M.D., Chairman & Research Director.

International Connoisseurs of Green and Red Chile (ICGRC)
311 N. Downtown Mall
Las Cruces, NM 88001   (505) 524-8521

Enthusiasts of green and red chilies. The group conducts research programs on the hot stuff and sponsors competitions. ICGRC, administrated by the Las Cruces Convention and Visitors Bureau, has published the cookbook, *Viva Chile* and sponsors the annual Fiesta de la Salsa. Founded in 1973. 250 members. Contact Helen Revels, Executive Director.

International Correspondence of Corkscrew Addicts (ICCA)
Ambrose House
29 Old Church Green
Kirk Hammerton
York, N. Yorkshire Y05 8DL, England   423 330745

Members are collectors of corkscrews. Once every year they are filled with the need to meet and discuss at length the topic of corkscrews. Founded in 1974. 50 members. Contact J. David Bradshaw, Executive Officer.

International Diastema Club (IDC)
10525 College Circle
Spokane, WA 99218   (509) 468-2306

Members are people with a diastema (a gap between the two front teeth) of at least two millimeters, caused by excess tissue under the upper lip that grows downward, separating the teeth. IDC promotes a humorous approach to the condition, encouraging people with a diastema to make light of the matter and overcome those feelings of nagging self-consciousness. It sponsors contests for spitting seeds the farthest, leaving a corn cob the cleanest, and fitting the greatest number of toothpicks in the gap. "Members vow never to clean off an ear of corn and to enter all spitting contests," says club founder Dale Hempel. Hempel estimates one-quarter of the population has diastema, including Madonna, Michael Keaton, Ernest Borgnine, Sophia Loren, Willie Nelson, Charlie Pride, Willard Scott, Lauren Hutton, and David Letterman. And some say that a gap between the front teeth will be the hottest body trend in the 90s, a situation that obviously pleases Hempel and the IDC. By the way, the club's logo is a bar-circle "no" sign over a perfect set of teeth and its mascot is a beaver. Plans call for a convention in Union Gap, WA. Founded in 1982. 1000 members. Contact Morva Hempel, Secretary.

International Dull Folks Unlimited (IDFUN)
PO Box 23584
Rochester, NY 14692   (716) 253-5794

A club of dull men and women from 12 countries, which "provides an organization of dull pride for all the good and dull people of the earth, regardless of race, creed, religion, nationality, color, sex, or blood type." Motto is, "We're out of it but proud of it." IDFUN advances the controversial belief that even celebrities and influential people can be uninteresting, operating on the premise that "dullness is a balance point between total trendiness and utter boredom." The club was formed by former members of the International Dull Men's Club (see next listing), who charged that the Dull Men were only pseudo-dull and sexist. As originally constituted, the Dull Men barred women on the theory that nothing could be duller than a men's club. "Contrary to myth, there are dull women," reports IDFUN.

In addition to a Dull Hall of Fame, IDFUN maintains a library containing a Roget's Thesaurus, a dictionary, and a *Time* magazine. Annually the group selects the Ten Dullest Americans, a list with no shortage of contenders and which has included former President Gerald Ford, comedian Don Rickles, musician Lawrence Welk, and cartoon character Garfield the Cat. The dull people also bestow bimonthly Dull Lifestyle and Dull Brain awards to prominent individuals who deserve them. The group once held a dull people's parade, with one pickup truck carrying two men drinking generic beer (it was a great success—nobody showed up).

In addition to all the exciting stuff noted above, IDFUN issues the *Dull Membership Booklet*, press releases, "Brown" papers on matters of economic and social importance to dull people, and *The Nobody Register: Who's Nobody, Who Cares?* and plans to publish

Dress to Avoid Bankruptcy, The Browning of America, Dull Men Eat Anything, and *Dullest Rated Almanac* (ratings book of dullest cities in the U.S.). Instead of a conference, the club promotes "periodic relaxing." Founded in 1983. 1000 members. Contact J. D. "Dull" Stewart, Chairman of the Bored.

International Dull Men's Club (IDMC)
300 Napa St, No. 10
Sausalito, CA 94965   (415) 332-8190

Men (and yes, women) united in celebration of dullness. Motto is, "It's the dull that get the job done." Or, "We're out of it and proud of it" (thought that was the other dull group—maybe these groups are so boring they have the same motto). It affirms that "dullness is a quiet state, an unleashed potential—a natural condition, unaffected by foolish fad and fashion." IDMC opposes trendiness such as beansprouts rather than hamburgers, honey rather than sugar, or relationships rather than marriages. "A dull man, like a poised cat, is always ready to do as little as possible to impress others." The women's auxiliary is known as the Plain Janes.

IDMC offers "recognition for the unrecognized, refuge and support in spirit for those who are not born charismatic and respect for the wise and humble among us who have led lives of accomplishment without arrogance." The group sponsors no research or educational programs as "that would be too interesting." Instead, it proudly maintains a 200volume library of *Reader's Digests* and a Museum of the Ordinary, which displays commemorative ashtrays from each of the 50 states, a collection of hubcaps, an outdoor grill, and an exhibit of bowling balls and trophies (sound's interesting . . .). IDMC sponsors the "Club Dead" dating service for dull swingers, featuring trips to the golf courses of New Jersey and the "Motel 6 Extravaganza."

The Dull Men bestow the Ten Dullest People of the Year Award and organized the Committee to Bring Back Calvin Coolidge. In addition to publishing the newsletter *Life in the Slow Lane,* founder Joe Troise has authored the book, *Dare to Be Dull,* which, among other items of discussion, lists suitable hobbies and pastimes for a dull man (lawn care, golf, browsing at Sears, waxing a car, testing the garage door opener, and alphabetizing record albums). Founded in 1980. 650 members. Contact Joe Troise, President.

International Edsel Club (IEC)
PO Box 371
Sully, IA 50251   (515) 594-4284

Individuals in 11 countries interested in the preservation, restoration, and collection of Edsels, the king of cars. IEC publishes *Edseletter,* a monthly newsletter containing association news, statistics, calendar of events, and listings of award recipients, parts wanted, and cars for sale. The group holds an annual rally in August. Founded in 1969. 940 members. Contact Murray and Judy Zegers, Secretaries.

International Errol Flynn Society
327 The Meadway
Tilehurst
Reading, Berks. RG3 4NT, England   734 427588

Individuals in 23 countries interested in the life and career of Errol Flynn (1909-1959), the Australian-born actor specializing in swashbuckling roles who appeared in a number of American films, including the *Charge of the Light Brigade*, the *Adventures of Robin Hood*, and *Gentleman Jim*. The fan club strives to foster international friendship and understanding through appreciation of films featuring Flynn. It also seeks higher standards for film and television presentations and works to combat what the group considers antisocial forms of entertainment such as excessive bad language, violence, and sex as portrayed in cinematic and television productions. The Society celebrates Errol Flynn Day annually on June 20. Founded in 1977. 6000 members. Contact Eric G. Lilley, President.

International Esperantist League for Go (EGLI)
2-26-2, Kojima
Tyohu
Tokyo 182, Japan   3 3823776

Individuals from 29 countries wishing to promote the Esperanto language through the game of *Go* and to popularize *Go* through Esperanto. *Go* is an Oriental game played on a board with black and white stones; the object is to occupy a larger part of the board, sometimes by capturing the opponent's stones. The group translates *Go* terminology into Esperanto. Founded in 1979. 152 members. Contact Minosuke Emori, General Secretary.

International Fantasy Gaming Society (IFGS)
PO Box 3577
Boulder, CO 80307-3577   (303) 441-7727

A group for people interested in fantasy gaming whose purpose is to organize role-playing games using fantasy and espionage scenarios. It publishes the monthly newsletter *The Chaimail* as well as rulebooks on espionage and fantasy gaming and game design handbook. Founded in 1981. 400 members. Contact Paul Hayes.

International Federation of Magical Societies (FISM)
35, rue Vineuse
F-75116 Paris, France   1 47271768

Societies of magicians dedicated to promoting the art of magic. Next conference is in 1994. Founded in 1948. 58 members. Contact Maurice Pierre, General Secretary.

International Federation of Pedestrians (IFP)
3500 Race St.
Philadelphia, PA 19104-2440   (215) 386-1270

National associations, scientific institutes, and individuals in 35 countries working for the protection of the rights of pedestrians, or people who like to walk. IFP coordinates efforts of member associations in such areas as joint research on education, defense, and protection of pedestrians and promotes participation in activities concerned with the environment. The group encourages an international exchange of ideas and publications and represents the interests of pedestrians before the United Nations and other appropriate international institutions. It publishes quarterly *Voice of the Pedestrian*. Founded in 1963. Contact Ralph B. Hirsch, Secretary General.

International Federation of Sound Hunters (IFSH)

Weteringlaan 7
Wassenaar, Netherlands   1751 79438

A coalition of national associations in 10 countries united to encourage the development of audio and video recording for cultural purposes. Founded in 1956. 12 members. Contact Dr. J. J. L. Mees, Vice President & General Secretary.

International Federation of Tiddlywinks Associations (IFTwA)

2 Janmead
Witham, Essex CM8 2EN, England   376 516872

Combined membership of North American Tiddlywinks Association and English Tiddlywinks Association. The primary function of the group is to act as the governing body for international competitions. It also sponsors all-star tours and periodic world matches. Founded in 1972. 250 members. Contact Jon Mapley, Secretary General.

International Fire Buff Associates (IFBA)

7509 Chesapeake Ave.
Baltimore, MD 21219   (301) 477-1544

Persons interested in fires and promoting the welfare of firemen and allied emergency services. IFBA acts as a citizens' public relations group for fire departments. Local groups aid firemen at the scene of fires by serving coffee or food and operating ambulances. The group presents the annual Fireman of the Year and Fire Buff of the Year awards. Founded in 1953. 5000 members. Contact Roman A. Kaminski, Executive Vice President.

International Flying Farmers (IFF)

Mid Continent Airport
PO Box 9124
Wichita, KS 67277   (316) 943-4234

Farm families in the U.S. and Canada in which at least one member holds a pilot's license. IFF promotes the practical use of the airplane in agriculture, encourages soil and water conservation through education derived from aerial conservation flights, and promotes safe flying through continued education and upgrading. Members collectively own 2000 planes, most of which are flown from their privately owned landing strips. Members are kept updated through the *International Flying Farmer* (nine per year). Founded in 1944. 5500 members. Contact T. W. Anderson, Executive Director.

International Flying Nurses Association (IFNA)

PO Box 561218
Harwood Heights, IL 60656

Members are professional nurses or practical/vocational nurses who are also licensed pilots or who hold a student pilot certificate, as well as nursing students and individuals supporting nursing and aviation. Purpose is to exchange ideas and experiences related to aviation and nursing activities. The group publishes *Aero-Nursing News* three times every year. Founded in 1975. 180 members. Contact Terri A. Sinkowski R.N., President.

International Fortean Organization (INFO)
PO Box 367
Arlington, VA 22210-0367   (703) 522-9232

Scientists, scholars, and laypeople from 20 countries concerned with new and unusual scientific discoveries and philosophic problems pertaining to the criteria of scientific theories and validity. Named after Charles Hoy Fort (1874-1932), an American author who researched and documented unusual and unexplained natural phenomena, INFO sponsors investigative teams and issues the quarterly *INFO Journal* containing information on new members, publication reviews, and original research papers. The group meets annually in Washington, DC. Founded in 1965. 1500 members. Contact Raymond D. Manners, President.

International Foundation for Gender Education (IFGE)
PO Box 367
Wayland, MA 01778   (617) 894-8340

IFGE serves as an educational resource for the cross-dressing and transsexual community and those persons affected by or serving that community. It offers walk-in peer counseling and a research library. The Foundation supports a communications network and mutual support system for cross-dressing and transsexual organizations and services worldwide. The group administers the Foundation Trust Fund and Christine Jorgensen Fund. IFGE publishes the *TV/TS Tapestry Journal* three times per year, which includes editorials, entertainment news, personal listing directory, and an updated organizations and services directory. The Institute holds an annual conference, with the 1993 meeting scheduled for Philadelphia, PA. Founded in 1978. Contact Merissa Sherill Lynn, Director.

International Frankenstein Society (IFS)
29 Washington Square, W., Penthouse N
New York, NY 10011   (212) 982-6754

A division of the Count Dracula Fan Club (see separate listing), The International Frankenstein Society has members from seven countries working together to increase enthusiasm for Frankenstein, the main character and title of the novel by Mary Shelley. Frankie, you'll recall, was built out of cadavers, wore big shoes, and had a problem with fire. IFS promotes the exchange of Frankensteinian information and sponsors "ethical, social, moral, and educational activities mixed with good fun." Founded in 1980. 1960 members. Contact Dr. Jeanne Keyes Youngson, President & Founder.

International Guild of Candle Artisans (IGCA)
867 Browning Ave. S.
Salem, OR 97302   (503) 364-5475

A group of people and companies that encourages the study of candlemaking and candle design. IGCA fosters fellowship and seeks to raise and maintain standards of craftsmanship and design. It cooperates with agencies and individuals to increase participation in and appreciation of the art. Monthly, members receive *The Candlelighter*. Founded in 1961. 300 members. Contact Eleanor Wulff, Editor.

International Hug Center (IHC)

115 Glenfield Dr.
Pittsburgh, PA 15235   (415) 682-5053

Individuals in four countries united to promote hugging. IHC attempts to build a network of people who express the interdependence of the human race through the physical act of hugging. Principal program is the observance of International Hug Day on June 15. Annually the group nominates the "10 most huggable people in the world" and plans to publish the *International Hugs Directory*. Founded in 1982. Contact John McKenzie.

International Imagery Association (IIA)

PO Box 1046
Bronx, NY 10471

A group of folks interested in the phenomenon of mental imagery, seeking to integrate a multi-discipline focus into the field. IIA fosters communication and discussion on how imagery can aid in fulfilling human potential and encourages mental imagery research. It publishes *Imagery Today*, a semiannual newsletter, as well as the quarterly *Journal of Mental Imagery*, concerned with the exploration and study of mental imagery phenomena. Founded in 1979. Contact Akhter Ahsen, Chairman.

International Jugglers Association (IJA)

PO Box 3707
Akron, OH 44314-3707   (216) 745-3552

Members are professional and amateur jugglers seeking to preserve and further the art of juggling and promote fellowship among those associated with the art. The world of juggling is vividly portrayed in *Jugglers World*, a quarterly magazine with book reviews, a calendar of events, club and festival listings, and product reviews. Annually during the third week in July the air is afly with objects tossed as the jugglers meet and examine the newest in juggling wares and discuss the business at hand. Founded in 1947. 3000 members. Contact Tom Bennett, Secretary.

International Laughter Society (ILS)

16000 Glen Una Dr.
Los Gatos, CA 95030   (408) 354-3456

Individuals of all ages and professions from 15 countries dedicated to expanding their use of humor and putting more laughter into the world. Promotes laughter (ha!) as a means of improving the quality of life by increasing productivity, creativity, and energy while "immunizing" people against job burn-out, stress-related illness, and depression. ILS promotes a broadened sense of humor as a way to turn negative experiences into positive ones and a means of coping with difficult situations. The group researches and develops humor-related products and services and distributes the *Humor First Aid Kit*, a set of workbook and tapes. Founded in 1981. 2200 members. Contact L. Katherine Ferrari, President.

International Mailbag Club (IMC)

130 Center St.
Findlay, OH 45840   (419) 422-2362

Purpose of the group is "To bring cheer and sunshine into lives of shut-in and handicapped persons through cards and letters." It meets in April annually for an awards presentation. Founded in 1928. Contact Mrs. James T. Shepard, Executive Secretary.

International Maledicta Society (IMS)
PO Box 14123
Santa Rosa, CA 95402-6123   (414) 542-5853

A group of mostly professors of linguistics, English, folklore, sociology, philology, anthropology, psychology, and foreign languages. Well, what do they do? The group promotes, conducts, and supports interdisciplinary research on verbal aggression, pejoration, value judgments, and related subjects in all languages, dialects, cultures, religions, and ethnic groups. In other words, the language of taunting, fighting, cussing, and so on, much of it usually unprintable in family publications. The group maintains a large private library of books and articles on maledicta, including items from 200 cultures and ranging from about 3000 B.C. to the present. It also operates the International Research Center for Verbal Aggression. IMS annually issues *Maledicta: The International Journal of Verbal Aggression,* specializing in uncensored studies and glossaries of offensive and negatively valued words and expressions from all languages and cultures, past and present. The mag covers the origin, etymology, meaning, use, and influence of verbal aggression and verbal abuse of any kind, as well as language usually considered vulgar, obscene, or blasphemous. Founded in 1975. 3000 members. Contact Reinhold A. Aman Ph.D., President.

International Map Collectors' Society (IMCoS)
29 Mount Ephraim Road
Streatham
London SW16 1NQ, England   81 7695041

Members are map collectors, specialist dealers, librarians, and persons working in the field of education in 32 countries. IMCoS promotes map collecting and the study of cartography and its history and encourages map preservation. It publishes the quarterly *IMCoS Journal* and conducts three symposia a year. Founded in 1980. 550 members. Contact Mrs. S. Gole, Executive Chairman.

International Mothers' Peace Day Committee
PO Box 102
West Liberty, WV 26074   (304) 336-7159

The Committee seeks to unite mothers and others worldwide to promote the establishment of the first Sunday in June as International Mothers' Peace Day. The idea originated as Mothers' Peace Day, a day of observance established in 1872 by Julia Ward Howe (1819-1910), peace advocate and composer of The Battle Hymn of the Republic. The modern day group stages letter-writing campaigns and peace demonstrations. Observance of the day is based upon the motto, "Those who nurture life on earth are of one mind in their opposition to those who would destroy it." Founded in 1982. Contact Jeanne V. Schramm, Chairwoman.

International New Thought Alliance (INTA)
5003 E. Broadway Road
Mesa, AZ 85206   (602) 830-2461

A federation of individuals and groups interested in religious-educational philosophy and metaphysics. The group publishes the quarterly *New Thought,* a journal containing articles on enlarging and enriching one's way of life, universalizing vision and consciousness, and developing transcendental faculties. INTA sponsors an annual conference in July. Founded in 1914. Contact Mimi Ronnie, Executive Director.

International Old Lacers, Inc. (IOLI)
218 Via Del Cerrijo
Olivenhain, CA 92024

A group of lace collectors and makers from 17 countries charged with promoting interest in fine old laces and their preservation. Members study the history and learn the names of laces, make lace, and hold lace exhibits. Often their conversation will be laced with references to lace. A large part of their world is in fact laces. The group issues *The International Old Lacers Bulletin*, a quarterly journal with information on local lace workshops and lace days, book reviews, and work advice. Annually members put on their traveling lace and gather during August or September. Founded in 1953. 2155 members. Contact Marji Suhm, Executive Officer.

International Order of E.A.R.S.
12019 Donohue Ave.
Louisville, KY 40243   (502) 245-0643

Members are storytellers and listeners who promote interest in storytelling and conduct storytelling workshops and performances. E.A.R.S. operates the Storytelling Resource Center of books and 2000 cataloged stories on videoand audiotape. The group sponsors storytelling weekends and radio and television programs. It plans to build the Storytelling Theatre and create a Storyteller Wall of Fame. Members tell stories to each other in the quarterly newsletter *Tale Trader*. E.A.R.S. holds the annual Corn Island Storytelling Festival during September in Louisville, KY. Founded in 1983. 600 members. Contact Lee Pennington, Board Chairman.

International Order of Hoo-Hoo (IOHH)
PO Box 118
207 Main St.
Gurdon, AR 71743   (501) 353-4997

Fraternal society of men involved in forest products and the lumber industry, including lumbermen, foresters, officers of lumber associations, and the lumber trade press. Hoo-Hoo sponsors competitions and issues the quarterly *Hoo-Hoo Log and Tally Magazine.* Hoo-Hoo holds an annual conference during September. Founded in 1892. 7300 members. Contact Beth Thomas, Manager.

International Order of the Armadillo (IOA)
PO Box 60305
Jacksonville, FL 32236   (904) 384-8594

Individuals from all walks of life interested in the history and habits of the armadillo, a small, burrowing, armor-plated mammal indigenous to the semitropical regions of the Americas and described, because of their affinity for getting under wheel, as "the Rodney Dangerfields of the highway" or "roadside reminders of mortality." IOA seeks to inform the public of the cultural and ecological value of these creatures, and imparts "armadillo truth, myth, and legend."

The Order offers a variety of "Dillowear" clothing and paraphernalia, including shirts, long johns, belt buckles, and desktop conversation items (such as a hand-painted, cold-cast bronze miniature of the little fellow exiting his tree stump). Founder Robert Graessle says that Dillowear is the "antithesis of Izod. Dillowear is for all of us who aren't comfortable in designer shirts. Some people want to run over armadillos, but a lot of people like them because they are the underdogs." Or under the car. Founded in 1982. 1145 members. Contact Robert L. Graessle, Coordinator.

International Order of the Golden Rule (IOGR)
1000 Churchill Road
Springfield, IL 62702   (217) 793-3322

Service organization of the Order of the Golden Rule comprising funeral directors united for public relations, advertising, and educational purposes. Motto is "service measured not by gold but by the Golden Rule." Contact Karen Wojcicki, President.

International Organization of Nerds (ION)
PO Box 118555
Cincinnati, OH 45211   (513) 941-2624

Although the heyday of the nerd has passed, the peak of nerdity now just a fuzzy, ill-dressed memory, an organization still exists for nerds from all walks of life. Members are individuals who have volunteered or been nominated for membership as nerds. ION considers "nerds" to be people who do weird things, dress funny, or have an unusual attitude. The term "nerd" as used by ION is not meant in a derogatory way; the group considers nerdity a mark of distinction, and seeks to officially recognize nerds everywhere. Most of the members are nominated by friends, although anyone with the right qualifications, which are never specified, can join. The membership kit includes the official nerd record with "You Big Nerd" and "The Nerdy Boogie." ION donates part of the inexpensive, one-time lifetime membership fee to the Muscular Dystrophy Association. The club offers such paraphernalia as *YOU BIG NERD* rubber stamps, *IF U R A "NERD" HONK* bumper stickers, and official NERD clocks (so that nerds can tell time correctly).

According to ION, it was Jerry Lewis, entertainer, and national chairman of MDA, and "one of the biggest nerds" of them all, who inspired the formation of ION. The group keeps all member nerds informed through the annual *Big Nerds News*. Founded in 1984. 11,240 members. Contact Bruce L. Chapman, Supreme Archnerd.

International Organization of Wooden Money Collectors (IOWMC)
PO Box 395
Goose Creek, SC 29445   (803) 797-1260

Hobbyists who collect wooden nickels (hey, you're not supposed to take those!) and other forms of wooden money, as well as coin dealers. Organized as a specialized collectors' group at the 1964 convention of the American Numismatic Association (what a convention that was), the group plans to conduct research on wooden money and to establish a library. It awards prizes to members for the best story about wooden money and keeps members apprised through the monthly *Bunyan's Chips*. Annually in August members gather with pockets full of wooden change. Founded in 1964. 570 members. Contact N. Mack, Treasurer.

International Paintball Players Association (IPPA)
PO Box 90051
Los Angeles, CA 90009   (213) 322-3107

Paintball players, retail stores, manufacturers, distributors, field operators, and others who support the sport of paintball. A variation of the games tag and hide-and-seek, paintball has as its object the capture of the opposing team's flag. Players "tag" with a paintball, a thin-skinned gelatinous capsule that marks the tagged player with a brightly-colored, nontoxic, water-soluble paint, expelled by a carbon dioxide airgun. Players wear protective goggles, and the IPPA claims that the game is safer than many other conventional sports.

The organization seeks to educate the public about the game of paintball and promote a more positive image of the sport. It encourages the international growth of paintball and establishes international standards of safety and competition. It issues the annual *Directory of North American Paintball Fields and Stones* and the bimonthly *Paintball News.* Founded in 1988. 2000 members. Contact Jessica J. Sparks, Executive Officer.

International Petula Clark Society (IPCS)
38 Elmley Way
Margate, Kent CT9 4ES, England   843 291911

Fans of actress and pop singer Petula Clark (1932-), whose hit songs include *Downtown* and *I Know a Place.* Of course, that was in the sixties. The club provides information on Clark's activities and seeks to create friendships between members. In addition to maintaining an archives of photographs, movie stills, press clippings, song sheets, and recordings, IPCS issues the quarterly *Petula & Company.* Founded in 1964. 500 members. Contact Mr. Terry N. Young, Executive Officer.

International Playing-Card Society (IPCS)
188 Sheen Lane
East Sheen
London SW14 8LF, England

Members include collectors, researchers, librarians, museum curators, playing card manufacturers, artists, designers, and game players from 26 countries. The group is all about encouraging the study of the history of playing cards and card playing. Quarterly it sends members copies of the *The Playing-Card* and *Playing-Card World.* Founded in 1971. 375 members. Contact Christopher Rayner, Secretary.

International Polka Association (IPA)
4145 S. Kedzie Ave.
Chicago, IL 60632   (312) 254-7771

IPA is an educational organization concerned with the preservation and advancement of polka music (ah one and ah two). The group pursues the study of polka music, dancing, and traditional folklore. The big event is the annual polka festival in Rosemont, IL., which is usually held during August. The polka enthusiasts also maintain the Polka Music Hall of Fame and museum and present awards to personalities who have made outstanding contributions to the advancement and promotion of polka music. Members are advised of activities monthly through the *IPA News*. Founded in 1968. 1300 members. Contact Fred Hudy, President.

International Primate Protection League (IPPL)

PO Box 766
Summerville, SC 29484   (803) 871-2280

A group of zoologists, primate field workers, anthropologists, other interested individuals, humane societies, and animal welfare organizations united to encourage the conservation and protection of nonhuman primates. IPPL works to protect the native habitat of primates, monitor and reduce international trade and smuggling, and improve conditions of zoo and laboratory primates in nonhabitat countries. It bestows grants for field projects and placement of homeless primates. Primate news is reported in the quarterly *International Primate Protection League-Newsletter,* covering developments in the field of primate protection and conservation. Founded in 1974. 10,000 members. Contact Dr. Shirley McGreal, Chairwoman.

International Primitive Money Society (IPMS)

PO Box 1510
Redlands, CA 92373

Numismatists and enthusiasts of anthropology and archeology dedicated to the study, collection, and trading of stones, metal rings, animal pelts, and other objects used as money in primitive societies. IPMS researches the attributes of primitive money (such as value associations) and related topics (type of wallet or purse necessary to carry large stones or livestock, etc.). Founded in 1974. 90 members. Contact John E. Lenker, Executive Officer.

International Pumpkin Association (IPA)

2155 Union St.
San Francisco, CA 94123   (415) 346-4446

Dedicated folks from four countries united to foster interest in growing giant pumpkins and squash. IPA sponsors the annual World Pumpkin Weigh-Off, a competition designed to locate the largest pumpkin and squash in the world. It disseminates information on pumpkins, which are indigenous to the United States, and studies their role in America's history (for instance, the march of the pumpkins on the British during the Revolutionary War). Founded in 1982. Contact Terry Pimsleur.

International Rose O'Neill Club (IROC)

Box E
Nixa, MO 65714   (417) 725-3291

No, not the television cop. Individuals interested in preserving the works and memory of Rose O'Neill, an artist, writer, and illustrator who created the Kewpie doll in 1909. Kewpie dolls, of course, are plump, cupid-like baby dolls that were first popular prior to World War I. The club issues the quarterly newsletter *Kewpiesta Kourier* and sponsors the annual Kewpiesta conference during April in Branson, MO. Founded in 1967. 1000 members. Contact Jack Crotser.

International Sand Collectors Society (ISCS)
43 Highview Ave.
Old Greenwich, CT 06870   (203) 637-2801

Individuals who collect sand, soil, ore, or minerals. Purpose, other than displaying the stuff as a conversation piece (hey, that's some nice sand you have in that bottle), is to promote the collection, classification, and retention of sand and mineral samples from commercial, historic, recreational, and notable geographic sites. ISCS maintains a museum which contains a collection of 400 specimens. Divisions of the group include Golf Trap, Historic Locations, Mountain Crests, and Ocean Beach. Members receive the quarterly *The Sand Paper* newsletter, which includes information on storage and classification systems. Founded in 1969. 300 members. Contact William S. Diefenbach, President.

International Save the Pun Foundation (ISPF)
PO Box 5040, Station A
Toronto, ON, Canada M5W 1N4   (416) 922-1100

People (writers, performers, public speakers, students, teachers, and other word lovers) out to save an endangered word type known as the pun. In addition to being lovers of word play (in which foreplay is considered use of prepositions and articles in a teasing manner), members are committed to awakening an interest in reading by having fun with words. Full members ("those who have eaten recently") receive the foundation's newsletter which contains a collection of selected puns. The Foundation sponsors competitions and presents prizes for best puns submitted by members. It issues the *Annual Report: The 10 Best-Stressed Puns of the Year* and the monthly newsletter *The Pundit*, containing the best plays on words that the editors can find. The group holds an annual dinner (where? above their heads) on April 1st, where the Punster of the Year is honored and then permitted to eat. A one-year membership is $20. Founded in 1978. Contact John S. Crosbie, Chairman of the Bored.

International Sled Dog Racing Association (ISDRA)
PO Box 446
Nordman, ID 83848   (208) 443-3153

Members are people from nine countries interested in sled dogs and sled dog racing. Obviously, this sport has limited appeal in tropical areas. ISDRA promotes the sport of sled dog racing by stimulating public interest, encouraging cooperation between clubs, and assisting in the standardization of rules and procedures for race management. It sanctions major races and weight pulls and awards Point Championship medals annually. Founded in 1966. 1500 members. Contact Donna Hawley, Executive Director.

International Society for Astrological Research (ISAR)
PO Box 38613
Los Angeles, CA 90038   (818) 333-8702

Members are professional and nonprofessional astrologers working together to provide research data and education for astrologers and interested individuals within the astrological profession. It sponsors workshops, conferences, and a monthly seminar and awards research grants. ISAR issues the quarterly *Kosmos* journal for advanced astrologers. Founded in 1968. 480 members. Contact Carol Tebbs, Secretary.

International Society for Humor Studies (ISHS)
English Department
Arizona State University
Tempe, AZ 85287-0302   (602) 965-7952

He ain't funny, he's my professor. University professors and other individuals interested in linguistic humor belong to this group, which publishes the quarterly *Humor: International Journal of Humor Research*. The journal covers interdisciplinary humor research, including studies in humor theory, research methodologies, and applications of humor studies. ISHS sponsors an annual international conference with exhibits, with the 1992 show set for Paris, France. Presentations include "'Now You See It, Now You Don't': The Myth of Female Humorlessness and Its Eighteenth-Century Origins," "French Jokes About Foreigners," "Humor as Discourse Strategy in Egyptian Arabic Interactions," and, on the lighter side, "What's So Funny About Don Quixote?" The 1993 meeting is planned for Luxembourg and the 1994 show is tentatively set for Ithaca, NY. Memberships start at $35. Founded in 1980. 1000 members. Contact Don L. F. Nilsen, Executive Secretary.

International Society for Philosophical Enquiry (ISPE)
277 Washington Blvd. U.S.
Hudson, NY 12534   (518) 828-1996

Individuals in 21 countries ranked in the top one tenth of one percentile of intellect, as determined by standardized adult intelligence and linguistic ability tests. ISPE helps members enrich their education and experience in an environment of intellectual research, accomplishment, and high achievement. Members progress through various levels within the organization according to their achievements and are encouraged to make original contributions to society. Ten times per year it issues *Telicom*, a journal containing articles, poems, biographies of members, and society news. The group meets monthly in Annandale, VA. Founded in 1974. 450 members. Contact Betty Hansen, President.

International Society for the Study of Dendrobatid Frogs (ISSDF)
495 Ave. F SE
Winter Haven, FL 33880   (813) 293-8424

Individuals interested in the study, promotion, and conservation of the 117 species of Dendrobatid frogs. Dendrobatid frogs are commonly called Poison Arrow frogs and are usually found in Central and South America, meaning you have to travel to visit them. ISSDF assists individuals in communication with foreign governments concerning issues related to the frogs. 150 members. Contact Chance Guyette.

International Society for the Study of Time (ISST)
PO Box 815
Westport, CT 06881

Tick, tick, tick . . . Members are people who have been invited to or have delivered papers to the society at one of its conferences as well as the miscellaneous interested individual approved by the society. ISST encourages the interdisciplinary study of time in all its aspects (backward, forward, standing still). It publishes *Time's News: An Aperiodic Newsletter* once or twice a year, whenever a moment can be spared. The group holds a triennial conference, with the next one scheduled for Cerisy-la-Salle, France in July, 1992 (mark your calendars and set your wrist watches). Founded in 1966. 230 members. Contact Dr. J. T. Fraser, Founder.

International Society of Animal License Collectors (ISALC)
322 2nd St. SW
Cedar Rapids, IA 52404 (319) 366-2427

A group of people interested in collecting animal license tags and certificates and related materials. ISALC compiles statistics and disseminates information about dog licensing laws, license issuances by jurisdiction, and systems of registration. It actually holds competitions to find the oldest dog tag from each state or country. After that fun dies down, it compiles statistics of the oldest-known dog tags issued by each town, city, country, or state agency. The research program has been recently broadened to include a special survey of all known dog tags issued prior to 1900 and all dog tags issued on military installations. Members are kept up to date on licensing news via the quarterly *Paw Prints* newsletter. Founded in 1976. 187 members. Contact Henry M. Keyes, Secretary Treasurer.

International Society of Copier Artists (ISCA)
800 West End Ave., Suite 13B
New York, NY 10025 (212) 662-5533

Artists in Australia, England, Germany, Finland, Italy, Netherlands, and Switzerland who use the photocopier as a creative tool. Other members include libraries, museums, corporations, and collectors. Purpose is to establish electrostatic prints, bookwork multiples, and other unique pieces as legitimate and collectible works of art. ISCA arranges an international traveling exhibition of xerographic prints and book works and seeks to introduce the copier as an art tool to elementary and secondary classrooms. It maintains file of international photocopied art slides and biographical archives. It publishes the *International Society of Copier Artists-Membership List* listing nearly 500 xerographic artists and bookmakers, as well as the *ISCA Quarterly* containing original xerographic prints, postcards, posters, and bookworks created and printed by member artists. Founded in 1981. 160 members. Contact Louise Neaderland, Director.

International Society of Copoclephologists (ISC)
Department 3
Kingfisher Ct.
East Molesey, Surrey KT8 9HL, England 81 9410604

Copoclephologists are not internists but collectors of keys, key rings, and related items. ISC seeks to promote and stimulate interest in copoclephology, an ambitious agenda. It publishes *The Key Ring* magazine. Founded in 1945. Contact Arthur Freakes, Founder & President.

International Society of Flying Engineers (ISFE)
8506 Louis Dr. SE
Huntsville, AL 35802   (205) 881-5653

Yet another group of flying professionals (the skies are littered with doctors, dentists, nurses, farmers, and others winging it to work or play). This one is for engineers who fly as student, private, or commercial pilots. ISFE promotes business flying for engineers, a greater application of engineering to aviation safety and piloting techniques, and engineering registration for flying engineers. It encourages greater acceptance of personal private flying on company business. The group annually publishes *Hangar Flying.* Founded in 1966. 600 members. Contact George Doane, Secretary Treasurer.

International Society of Folk Harpers and Craftsmen (ISFHC)
4718 Maychelle Dr.
Anaheim, CA 92807-3040   (714) 998-5717

ISFHC is a group of folk harpers, folk harp makers, concert artists, and craftsmen in 16 countries. The group collects and distributes historical and current information regarding folk harps and harpers. It also organizes concerts and promotes craft exchange. ISFHC publishes the quarterly *Folk Harp Journal,* which includes book and record reviews, chapter news, and a calendar of events. Founded in 1980. 1300 members. Contact Sylvia Fellows, Secretary.

International Society of Psychology of Handwriting (ISPH)
Istituto di Indagini Psicologiche
Corso XXII Marzo 57
I-20129 Milan, Italy   2 7426489

Physicians, psychologists, psychiatrists, teachers, and others interested in the study in and research of the psychology of handwriting. The group has prepared documentaries on the subject for classroom and public instruction and issues the quarterly *Rivista Internazionale di Psicologia e Ipnosi.* Founded in 1961. 198 members. Contact Prof. Rolando Marchesan, Secretary.

International Sourdough Reunion (ISR)
375 Dell Road
Kelowna, BC, Canada V1X 3P7   (604) 860-9817

Originally pioneers of the Gold Rush days (1897-98) of the Yukon Territory in Alaska and Canada, membership now includes new pioneers of the State of Alaska and the Yukon Territory. A wise move, considering the mortality rate of those born mid-last century. ISR offers a scholarship to a student in the Yukon Territory and Alaska and maintains historical records and information on the Gold Rush. Members gather annually. Founded in 1931. 1500 members. Contact Nora Sinclair, Secretary Treasurer.

International Stiltwalkers Association (ISA)
10810 Cherrygrove Ct.
Louisville, KY 40299   (502) 267-4220

World's worst stiltwalking remark: "Hey, who is that up there?" Never use with NBA centers either. ISA is a group of people interested in walking on stilts. Usually in their spare time, since most employers discourage stiltwalking on the job. The group, which meets annually, develops international unity through the promotion of stiltwalking as a competitive (jostling and racing) and recreational activity, although it's hard to picture looking forward to that weekend jaunt on stilts (and people will stare). In spite of it all, ISA maintains a library of newspapers and magazines dating back to the 1600s and having something to do with stiltwalking (we presume) and keeps the membership somewhat informed through the annual *Stiltwalkers*. Founded in 1981. 500 members. Contact Joe Bowen, President.

International Stop Continental Drift Society (ISCDS)
Star Rte., Box 38
Winthrop, WA 98862   (509) 996-2576

Here's a movement we can all get behind. Or on top of. Members include geologists, geophysicists, geographers, and other technical persons as well as amateur earth scientists and laymen. The group seeks to generate scientific and humorous discussion by challenging the plate tectonics/continental drift theory, which ISCDS believes has become the "established dogma of modern geophysics." Plate tectonics holds that the earth's crust constantly changes and shifts and does not have fixed ocean basins or continents.

Secondary "demands" of the group include cessation of sea-floor spreading; inactivity of large volcanoes; damping of seisms greater than 4.0 on the Richter scale; and the end of "subduction and other crustal discriminations" (remember, this is high humor for geologists).

ISCDS reportedly assigns directors to the earth's crustal plates and supervisors to its tectonic trouble spots. It also conducts ad hoc seminars aimed at individuals who disagree with the society's objectives. The Society, which is pleased to maintain many ad hoc committees to consider tectonic and tectonosociological and tectonocultural and tectononintendo problems, keeps members up to date on drift and other rumors through the quarterly *ISCDS Newsletter*. The newsletter includes a Continental Drift Hit List, a compilation of arguments against the plate tectonics theory. Founded in 1976. 850 members. Contact John C. Holden, President.

International Twins Association (ITA)
511 S. Gilpin St.
Denver, CO 80209

Members are individuals of who came to be during a multiple birth, including both identical and fraternal twins. ITA promotes the spiritual, intellectual, and social welfare of twins throughout the world. Twin spotting reaches its zenith during the annual reunion during Labor Day weekend. Founded in 1932. 800 members. Contact Marilyn Holmes, Secretary Treasurer.

International Veterinary Acupuncture Society (IVAS)
2140 Conestoga Road
Chester Springs, PA 19425   (215) 827-7245

Picture your dog or cat being treated with acupuncture needles. Okay? IVAS members are veterinarians and veterinary students who encourage knowledge and research of the philosophy, technique, and practice of veterinary acupuncture. The group works to maintain high standards in the field and promotes scientific investigation. The Society collects data concerning clinical and research cases where animals have been treated with acupuncture and disseminates the information to veterinary students, practitioners, other scientific groups, and the public. IVAS offers a 120 contact-hour basic veterinary acupuncture course and administers an accreditation examination. Founded in 1974. 400 members. Contact Dr. Meredith L. Snader, Executive Director.

International Watch Fob Association, Inc. (IWFAI)
Route 5, Box 210
Burlington, IA 52601 (319) 752-6749

Collectors of strap-type watch fobs who encourage and promote the study of fobs. IWFAI hopes to interest America's youth in fobs and generally acquires and distributes watch fob information. It demonstrates the educational and recreational aspects of fob collecting. Activities and programs include the annual spring show for collectors to display, trade, buy, and sell fobs. Founded in 1965. 1000 members. Contact R. J. Rothlisberger, Executive Officer.

International Wizard of Oz Club (IWOC)
Box 95
Kinderhook, IL 62345

Persons interested in the wonderful world of Oz and in L. Frank Baum (1856-1919), who created the mythic land in *The Wonderful Wizard of Oz* (published in 1900). IWOC promotes the preservation and study of books, plays, motion pictures, songs, and other by-products of Oz and conducts research on persons other than Baum who contributed to Oz, including Ruth Plumly Thompson, W. W. Denslow, and John R. Neill. The group offers members the opportunity to exchange or auction books and other items. It bestows the annual L. Frank Baum Memorial Award.

Members receive the *The Baum Bugle* three times per year, a journal containing articles and reports on the utopian land of Oz. The mag includes book reviews, a bibliography, the MGM scrapbook, and "Oz in the News" (Tin Man Freezes Up Again!). It also publishes the *Oz Trading Post*, a quarterly list of Oz-related items wanted, for sale, and for trade. And it issues the annual *Oziana* magazine containing stories, games, and puzzles. IWOC makes available maps of Oz, a gazetteer of Oz, a booklet of essays about Oz, and four books (about Oz). On the third weekend in June the merry Ozians gather and make merry, all the while remarking, "Funny, this doesn't look like Kansas." Founded in 1957. 2500 members. Contact Fred M. Meyer, Secretary.

International Wood Collectors Society (IWCS)
13429 Highway 84 N.
Cordova, IL 61242-9708 (309) 765-2312

Scientists, botanists, dendrologists, foresters, wood collectors, hobbyists, and craftsmen who help each other find exotic and colorful wood from historic trees and buildings and from different species of trees worldwide. They share information on books, tools, and methods of turning and finishing. The Wood Collectors encourage the exchange of wood specimens and the adoption of standard methods of sample collecting and standard specimen size. The Society assists in accurate naming and classification of specimens and cooperates with institutions, universities, and schools in augmenting their specimen collections. It issues the monthly *World of Wood,* featuring wood of the month and craft articles. New members are advised by the *Guide for Developing a Wood Collection.* Founded in 1947. 1200 members. Contact A. Dennis Wilson, Executive Officer.

International Zebu Breeders Association (IZBA)
4334 Centergate
San Antonio, TX 78217 (512) 599-1909

A group of Zebu cattle breeders, which are descended from the Asian Zebu oxen (the cattle, not the breeders). IZBA registers and promotes Zebu cattle and holds field days and seminars. It issues the monthly *Zebu Review* newsletter. Founded in 1946. 581 members. Contact Janie Smith, Consultant.

J J J J J J J J J

J. Allen Hynek Center for UFO Studies (CUFOS)
2457 W. Peterson Ave.
Chicago, IL 60659 (312) 271-3611

Individuals throughout the U.S. and abroad who are involved in personal research on UFO subjects and others who wish to be kept informed of the latest research. CUFOS collects and studies UFO sighting reports and promotes public distribution of UFO publications by researchers and other writers throughout the world. It publishes the *International UFO Reporter,* a bimonthly magazine providing news and commentary on all aspects of UFO phenomena. Founded in 1973. 1000 members. Contact Mark Rodeghier, Scientific Director.

James Bond 007 Fan Club (JBFC)
PO Box 007
Addlestone
Weybridge, Surrey KT15 1DY, England 483 756007

Individuals in 40 countries interested in the fiction and motion picture character James Bond, first featured in the novels written by British author Ian Fleming (1908-64) and later portrayed in motion pictures by actors Sean Connery, Roger Moore, George Lazenby, and Timothy Dalton. The group issues *007,* a quarterly magazine, and *007 Extra,* a newsletter published three times per year. Founded in 1979. 2000 members. Contact Graham Rye, President & Editor.

James Bond 007 Fan Club (JBDFC)
Box 414
Bronxville, NY 10708

More fans and enthusiasts of James Bond. Purpose is to unite Bond fans throughout the world. The Club offers members pen pal correspondence, photographs, and free or discount prices on Bond-related merchandise and memorabilia. It keeps members informed of super secret agent news through the semiannual magazine *Bondage* and the newsletter *Bondage Quarterly.* Founded in 1974. 2500 members. Contact Richard Schenkman, President.

James Buchanan Foundation (JBF)
1120 Marietta Ave.
Lancaster, PA 17603   (717) 392-8721

People bonded in the hope of perpetuating the memory of James Buchanan (1791-1868), 15th President of the United States. A primary goal of the group is the maintenance of the Wheatland mansion in Lancaster, PA, former home of Buchanan. Founded in 1936. Contact Sally Cahalan, Director.

James K. Polk Memorial Association (JKPMA)
c/o Polk Home
PO Box 741
Columbia, TN 38402   (615) 388-2354

JKPMA is dedicated to the preservation of the memory of James K. Polk (1795-1849), 11th president of the United States. It conducts educational programs about Polk and his contributions to the U.S., and works to maintain the historic Polk Home in Columbia, TN. Members receive the semiannual *Polk Newsletter* and sit down together for an annual luncheon. Contact James Holtzapple, Director.

Japanese Animation Network (JAN)
9056 W. Broad St., Suite 308
Richmond, VA 23229

Individuals interested in Japanese animation and culture united to promote Japanese animation and the animated works of all nations as a visual and literary art form, an educational tool, and an entertainment form. JAN offers children's services and forums for writers and artists, presents annual awards to members who have contributed significantly to the growth of the organization and to professionals in the animation and comic book industry, and offers a consultation program for Japanese individuals or companies relocating to America or Americans relocating to Japan. It also operates the Animators Hall of Fame. Four to six times per year the group issues *Anime No Shimbun, the Newspaper of Animation,* featuring member-produced artwork. Founded in 1988. 100 members. Contact Roy C. Bruce, Director.

Jazzmobile
154 W. 127th St.
New York, NY 10027   (212) 866-4900

Formed by persons involved in the musical, dramatic, and graphic arts fields who are interested in bringing jazz music to neighborhoods by means of mobile units, the Jazzmobile gives free jazz concerts in the summer throughout the District of Columbia, Maryland, New Jersey, New York, and Pennsylvania. The group is currently studying expansion of the program on a national level. Founded in 1964. Contact S. David Bailey, Executive Director.

Jews for Jesus (JFJ)
60 Haight St.
San Francisco, CA 94102   (415) 864-2600

A group of Jewish people who believe that Y'shua (Jesus) is the Messiah and claim their lives have been changed as a result of that belief. JFJ promotes understanding and reconciliation and helps Christians appreciate the Jewish heritage of the church, partly by conducting research in Jewish-Christian relations and creative communication. The organization provides Jewish evangelism seminars and Messianic music and drama workshops. Divisions include the Liberated Wailing Wall. Members receive the bimonthly *Issues: A Messianic Jewish Perspective,* a journal covering articles, art, poetry, and book reviews relating to contemporary Messianic Jewish alternatives. Founded in 1973. 300,000 members. Contact Moishe Rosen, Chairman.

Jim Smith Society (JSS)
2016 Milltown Road
Camp Hill, PA 17011 (717) 737-7406

A social organization for individuals named Jim Smith, including females, with members in U.S., Canada, Australia, New Zealand, Scotland, and England. Activities include a golf tournament, softball games between teams of Jim Smiths and a research program to draw up a composite Jim Smith. The group is currently researching a book about Jim Smiths throughout history. It publishes the quarterly *Jim Smith Society Newsletter* and holds an annual Fun Festival in the summer. Founded in 1969. 1538 members. Contact James H. Smith Jr., President.

Jim's Neighbors (JN)
3119 Brookview Blvd.
Cleveland, OH 44134-1394

Surprise, surprise, surprise. JN is a group of folks who appreciate the talents and support the career of actor/singer Jim Nabors (1932-), who is best known for his role as Private Pyle in the 1960s television series *Gomer Pyle U.S.M.C.* The Neighbors issue the quarterly newsletter *Nabor's News.* Founded in 1985. Contact Cheryl Yurcak, President.

Johnny Alfalfa Sprout (JAS)
524 Rural Ave.
Williamsport, PA 17701 (717) 322-7370

Johnny A. promotes and provides technical assistance to individuals and organizations interested in raising sprouts, including alfalfa, mung, soy, clover, navy, lentil, pea, oat, and wheat. JAS makes available free seeds and publicizes the attributes of the plants, including their ability to be grown indoors, their high nutritional content, and the fact that they often do not need to be cooked, an advantage in areas where fuel is scarce. The group has published the *Johnny Alfalfa Sprout Handbook* and reprints of sprout literature. Founded in 1984. Contact Ellen Sue Spivack, Executive Officer.

Johns and Call Girls United Against Repression (JACG-UAR)
PO Box 021011
Brooklyn, NY 11202-0022

JACGUAR works to dispel "the notion that there is anything reprehensible or immoral in being a prostitute whose customers are adults, or in being the customer of an adult prostitute." The group hopes to instill in adult prostitutes and their adult customers a sense of self-respect. It works to legally safeguard civil rights and liberties of prostitutes and their customers, and to repeal laws criminalizing prostitution. Members speak out on public issues affecting prostitutes and their customers and testify at legislative hearings. Activities are described in the monthly *Oldest Profession Times.* The group meets annually on the second Tuesday in August. Founded in 1978. 11 members. Contact Hugh Montgomery, President.

Joygerms Unlimited (JU)
PO Box 219, Eastwood Station
Syracuse, NY 13206   (315) 472-2779

A happy coalition of churches, schools, organizations, health and wholeness centers, and interested individuals dedicated to "spreading joy and cheer" throughout the world. JU seeks to "eliminate doom and gloom" and "rid the world of gruff and grumpy grouches" by promoting goodwill and humor (have a nice day!). It conducts Smile Check Up Clinics in hospitals, nursing homes, schools, and fraternal organizations and sponsors the annual Joygerm Parade in Syracuse, NY on the third Saturday of July. It also hosts the annual National Joygerm Day on January 8. Joygerms issues the quarterly newsletter *Infectionately Yours,* which includes updates on local and national activities, member feedback, and poetry. Founded in 1981. 85,000 members. Contact Joan E. White, Founder.

Judson Welliver Society (JWS)
Insurance Information Institute
110 William St.
New York, NY 10038   (212) 669-9201

An exclusive group of former chief presidential speechwriters deriving its name from Judson Welliver, who became the first full-time presidential speechwriter in 1921 during the administration of Warren Harding. The Society recognizes speechwriters as an integral but invisible part of U.S. presidential administrations who often pen classic lines like "Read my lips—no new taxes." The Judson Wellivers facilitate discussion among members and plan to publish a book tracing the writing of famous presidential speeches. The group meets annually over dinner. Founded in 1984. 30 members. Contact Gordon Stewart, Secretary Treasurer.

Junior International Club (JIC)
575 Madison Ave., Suite 1006
New York, NY 10022   (212) 734-3459

A social organization that "mixes young and generally wealthy Europeans who live in New York with their American counterparts." Certainly it is gratifying to know that the young, rich, and restless are not staying home every night, waiting for the phone to ring. JIC sponsors cultural events to benefit charities and organizes a biweekly dinner and dance at nightclubs in New York City. The group has established clubs in Europe and plans to establish similar clubs in other cities. Founded in 1982. 1000 members. Contact Ludovic J. Autet, Founder.

Kangaroo Protection Foundation (KPF)
1900 L St. NW, Suite 500
Washington, DC 20036   (202) 872-8840

Individuals interested in protecting Australia's kangaroos from becoming victims of cruelty and an endangered species. Objectives are to promote the conservation and humane treatment of kangaroos, wallabies, and other land mammals. KPF also works to educate the public about the slaughter of kangaroos in Australia to satisfy the import demands of other nations and to further scientific studies regarding habitat and behavior of wildlife and domestic animals. The group disseminates materials regarding threats to endangered species and urges the reinstatement of a governmental ban on imports of kangaroo hides and products. Founded in 1982. Contact Marian Newman, Program Director.

Keltic Society and the College of Druidism (KS)
Kaer Eidyn
4 A Minto St.
Edinburgh EH9 1RG, Scotland   31 6675788

Persons in 10 countries interested in reviving and maintaining Celtic culture. KS promotes interest in all branches of Celtic culture and shows its relevance in modern society. Areas of concentration include Druidical religion, mythology, paganism, and folklore; poetry and literature; the Celtic languages; music; art, symbolism, and crafts; ancient sites and monuments; and Celtic Christianity. KS encourages the modern expression of Celtic creativity and provides assistance to countries, organizations, and individuals wishing to learn about Celtic culture. The group assists in the training of psychically and spiritually enlightened individuals to act as leaders in the Celtic culture revival. The Keltic Society publishes the annual compilation of poetry, *Awen,* the biennial journal *Inner Keltia,* and the semiannual *Pictish Shaman.* Everyone gathers annually on June 22. Founded in 1980. Contact Kaledon Naddair, Organizer.

Kentucky Callers Association (KCA)
9804 Mary Dell Lane
Vern Creek, KY 40291   (502) 239-1162

Swing that partner off the wall. KCA is a group of square dance callers and their spouses. Purpose is to swing your partner round and round and promote the growth and development of Western-style square dancing. KCA also encourages the development of improved calling and teaching techniques. The group provides callers for square dance groups and conducts periodic seminars for new and experienced callers and provides training for new dancers. KCA meets five times a year on the third Sunday of January, March, May, September, and November in Louisville, KY. Founded in 1957. 53 members. Contact Bill Wise, President.

Knife and Fork Club International (KFCI)
1 Townsite Plaza, Suite 315
Topeka, KS 66603   (913) 232-0892

Motto is "Good food, good company, good minds." KFCI is a

collection of social dinner clubs of business and professional men and women which meet in the evening for the purpose of being entertained by distinguished guest speakers. The club claims that dinner clubs began back in 1898, when a group of men in Kansas City, MO met informally at a dinner with the president of an eastern university who was stopping off on his way west. They had such a good time that the guys decided to meet again, and eventually formed the Knife and Fork Club of Kansas City, the modern counterpart of "The Order of the Good Time" founded in Nova Scotia by Samuel de Champlain and some of his merchant adventurer buddies in 1606. But that's another story. Eventually, the Kansas City club and others like it folded, since good speakers were apparently hard to find.

In 1936, the Knives and Forks were revived by a Mr. Benjamin Franklin, he not of kite flying fame (but the father of the current president). The International group now serves as clearinghouse and coordinator for the local clubs. "Most clubs have five or six programs each year, covering anything of interest to club members—world affairs, adventure, humor, entertainment, and science, to name but a few." The group has "no axe to grind, no political formula to promote, no religious or social prejudice to espouse," but is "a group of compatible families who like to get together for a social and pleasurable evening around a banquet table to listen to a variety of speakers with whom we may agree or disagree. But we are challenged to think, or inspired to be better, or to laugh with the prospect of a better day tomorrow." Founded in 1936. 27,000 members. Contact Ben B. Franklin, President.

Knifemakers Guild (KG)
PO Box 17587
Tampa, FL 33682 (813) 961-0637

Knifemakers and interested others who promote knives and knifemakers. The group also provides technical assistance to knifemakers and encourages ethical and professional business conduct. It holds an annual conference, with a knife show, usually in Orlando, FL. Founded in 1971. 1500 members. Contact Frank Centofante, President.

Knights of the Square Table (NOST)
111 Amber St.
Buffalo, NY 14220 (716) 825-8281

The Knights are people who love to play games, especially chess, through postal correspondence. The club sponsors competitions and publishes the bimonthly *NOST-ALGIA*, which includes games and chess results. During the fall it conducts an annual chess tournament in which participants actually shows up at a single site, although all carry stamps and postcards in their knightly pockets. Founded in 1960. 300 members. Contact Leslie Roselle, Nostmaster.

L L L L L L L L L

Labologists Society (LS)
66 High St.
Puckeridge
Ware, Herts. SG11 1RX, England 920 822405

Also known as the International Society of Label Collectors, LS promotes the hobby of collecting labels and advertising relating to beer and breweries as well as wines and spirits, mineral water, and soft drinks. Members include regular people, brewery officials, and label printing companies in 12 countries. LS makes labels available to members through exchange or sale at reasonable prices and bestows the Label of the Year Award. Founded in 1958. 300 members. Contact G. A. Tubb, Hon. Secretary.

Ladies Against Women (LAW)
48 Shattuck Square, Suite 70
Berkeley, CA 94704 (415) 841-6500

A group of "decent ladies with a moral imperative to return to the Good Old Days" and their male authority figures. Supporting groups include Moral Sorority and Another Mother for World Domination. Motto is "We Have a Monopoly on Morality. God, Inc. Is on Our Side."

LAW conducts seminars for "uppity women," designed to promote stress reduction through apathy. It sponsors consciousness-lowering sessions and supports right-thinking with fundraisers such as the endangered accessories fashion show (Save the Stoles), bake sales for the Pentagon, guest disruptions of women's events, and picket-reception-lines for "real ladies" like Nancy Reagan. Ladies Against Women advocates banning books, not bombs and desires to abolish the environment, since "indoo-routdoor carpeting would be much easier to clean."

Among the more controversial goals of the group is citizenship for sperm and the elimination of masturbation and menstruation. LAW believes it is unladylike to accept money for work and operates a speakers' bureau devoted to issues such as "repealing the women's vote, and the need for a national dress code."

LAW has a men's auxiliary known as For Ladies Against Women (FLAW) and divisions such as Millionaire Mommies With Nannies Against Free Childcare and Younger Ladies Against Younger Women. Members are kept informed of the latest lady news in the *National Embroiderer* newsletter. The group also has published the *LAW Consciousness Lowering Kit* and *Ladyfesto*. Founded in 1980. 12,000 members. Contact Mrs. T. "Bill" Banks, Lady Chair-Man.

LADIES - Life After Divorce Is Eventually Sane
PO Box 2974
Beverly Hills, CA 90213

A support group of ex-wives of famous men that originated during a USA cable show. LADIES seeks to form a network of support among other ex-wives in similar situations, and to assist in creating informal groups called LADIES Too whose members are ex-wives of non-famous men. The group plans to offer discussion panels for other women's groups. Founded in 1983. 15 members.

Ladyslipper
PO Box 3124
Durham, NC 27715 (919) 683-1570

An organization seeking to increase public awareness of the achievements of women artists and musicians and expand the scope and availability of musical and literary recordings by women. Ladyslipper makes available information on recordings by female musicians, writers, and composers and publishes the annual

Ladyslipper Catalog: Resource Guide to Records, Tapes, Compact Discs, and Videos by Women. Founded in 1976. Contact Laurie Fuchs, Director.

Largesse
PO Box 306, Fairhaven Station
New Haven, CT 06513   (203) 787-1624

A network of organizations and overweight individuals concerned about what the group views as "fat oppression" in the U.S. Largesse acts as a support and information resource for people who promote "size acceptance" and oppose bias against those who are overweight. The group believes that "no woman in our society is too thin to feel fat," and that this preoccupation with body shape is an important facet of society's oppression of women. It seeks "the empowerment of all women, regardless of size or shape" and works to educate the women's movement and the public about fat women's issues. Largesse sponsors the Big Sisters Network, a support system for isolated fat women. Founded in 1983. Contact Karen Stimson, Director.

Last Chance Forever (LCF)
506 Ave. A
San Antonio, TX 78218   (512) 655-6049

A group of individuals banded together to shelter and rehabilitate birds of prey. LCF educates the public concerning birds of prey and their relation to the environment. To spread the word on the birds, the group sponsors speaker and slide show exhibitions for civic organizations and schools. LCF also offers tours at summer festivals and environmental exhibits. It issues *Feather in the Wind*, a semiannual newsletter. Founded in 1979. Contact John Karger, Executive Director.

Laugh Lovers (LL)
PO Box 1495
Pleasanton, CA 94566   (415) 462-3470

Individuals devoted to the positive application of humor and laughter in everyday life. LL provides resources and information on research and activities in several fields of humor, conducts workshops and classes at colleges and universities, and is currently developing programs of humor-related activities for children and senior citizens. The club of ha-ha believers publishes the bimonthly *Laugh Lovers News*. Founded in 1980. 307 members. Contact Dr. Virginia O. Tooper Ed.D., Director.

Lead Belly Society (LBS)
PO Box 6679
Ithaca, NY 14851   (607) 273-6615

Fans of blues and folk musician Huddie Ledbetter (1889-1949), better known as Lead Belly, whose best-known songs include *The Midnight Special* and *Goodnight Irene*. LBS promotes an appreciation for Lead Belly's music and seeks to increase awareness of his contributions to blues and folk music. Members receive the quarterly *Lead Belly Letter*, which includes historical articles and facts on Lead Belly. Founded in 1990. 200 members. Contact Sean Killeen, Executive Director.

Left Green Network (LGN)
PO Box 372
West Lebanon, NH 03784   (802) 295-1544

Activists working to "radicalize the Greens and ecologize the Left." LGN promotes independent politics, social ecology, cooperative commonwealth, grassroots democracy, and international solidarity. Its bimonthly magazine *Left Green Notes* includes political news and analysis. Founded in 1988. 400 members. Contact Howard Hawkins, Field Organizer.

Lefthanders International (LHI)
PO Box 8249
Topeka, KS 66608   (913) 234-2177

A group for lefties, dedicated to recognizing lefthanders' accomplishments in areas of sports, entertainment, the arts, and the work world. With 25,000 subscribers, LHI's bimonthly *LEFTHANDER Magazine.* serves the needs and interests of lefthanders worldwide, addressing issues of discrimination and scarcity of products. Each issue provides "how-to" tips on sports and crafts and includes a product catalog of mail order products designed specifically for lefthanders. Subscribers participate in the annual Lefthanders of the Year election. LHI promotes International Lefthanders Day and notes that George Bush is a lefty. Sample copy is of the mag is $2. Founded in 1975. Contact Dean R. Campbell, Publisher & President.

Leif Ericson Society International (LESI)
11 S. Olive St.
Media, PA 19063   (215) 565-3165

Almost one thousand people united to educate the American public on Leif Ericson's discovery of North America in the year 1003. They desire to give Leif Ericson "as much credit for showing the way as others have received for following it." Each year the group celebrates on Leif Ericson Day (October 9) in Philadelphia, PA. Right now, it's busy preparing for the millennium celebration in 2003. LESI maintains a small library and archives which contain substantial research material, data, and opinions regarding the discovery of North America and early North American settlements. It bestows the Viking of the Year Award and sponsors competitions involving the group Viking ship, *Ravnen.* Founded in 1926. 999 members. Contact Ivar Christensen, President.

Leonard Nimoy Fan Club, Spotlight (LNFCS)
77 The Ridings
Ealing
London W53 DP, England   71 9977755

Anglo fans of television and film actor and director Leonard Nimoy (1931-), best known for his role as Dr. Spock in the television and film series *Star Trek.* LNFCS disseminates information on Nimoy's work and activities, offers photographs and a photographic service, and maintains archives of stories, poems, art work, and reviews. It sponsors the annual Leonard Nimoy Conference. Founded in 1982. 400 members. Contact Carol Davies.

Liberace Club of Las Vegas (LCLV)
2994 Talbot St.
Las Vegas, NV 89109   (702) 732-9351

National organization of fans of pianist and flamboyant entertainer Wladziu Valentino Liberace (1919-87). LCLV seeks to perpetuate the memory of Liberace, his music, and sense of fashion. It operates the Liberace Museum, which grants annual scholarships to colleges and universities throughout the U.S. The group issues the semiannual newsletter *Keyboard Magic* and plans to hold an annual birthday celebration in honor of the star spangled pianist. Founded in 1974. 125 members. Contact Pauline Lachance, President.

Liberator Atlanta (LA)
PO Box 694
Norcross, GA 30091

Fans of British science fiction, especially the television show *Blake's 7*. The group puts together a monthly newsletter known as *Xenon Signals* which includes poems, book and movie reviews, and letters from members. LA gathers on the third Sunday of each month in the Norcross, GA area. Founded in 1984. 100 members. Contact Renee L. Groce, President.

Liberty Bell Matchcover Club (LBMC)
6048 N. Water St.
Philadelphia, PA 19120   (215) 424-5218

A group that may strike your fancy. LBMC is a club for matchbox and matchcover collectors. The goal is to inspire and maintain an active interest in the collecting of matchcovers and matchboxes, and to promote good fellowship and fairness. Five times every year the group issues the *Liberty Bell Crier* newsletter. Five times every year the club meets, usually on the fourth Saturday in February, April, June, September, and November. It also holds an annual banquet in September and an annual Christmas/Chanukah party. Founded in 1982. 180 members. Contact Marie E. Harbison, Treasurer.

Liberty Seated Collectors Club (LSCC)
5718 King Arthur Dr.
Kettering, OH 45429   (513) 434-4035

Collectors of 19th century U.S. silver coins who promote study of liberty seated 19th century U.S. silver coins. LSCC determines the rarity and authenticity of these coins and provides identification and descriptions. It publishes the *Gobrecht Journal* three times annually and holds a every year during August. Founded in 1973. 610 members. Contact John W. McCloskey, President.

Life Understanding Foundation
PO Box 729
Stanwood, WA 98292   (206) 387 5133

A religious organization based on pyramidology, the study of pyramids, the pyramid form, and its mathematics and energy. The Foundation believes that the pyramid and its properties can "provide a link to rediscover the ancient sacred sciences." It conducts expeditions to Egypt, South America, and other locations affording the opportunity to study pyramidal structures. The group believes that man did not evolve from the ape, but that his forefathers were "highly evolved initiates." The Foundation conducts correspondence course on pyramids and functions as a pyramid research information clearinghouse. The latest in pyramid news is covered in the bimonthly *Pyramid Guide*. Founded in 1968. 8700 members. Contact William T. Cox, President.

The Lifestyles Organization (TLO)
2641 W. La Palma, Suite A
Anaheim, CA 92801   (714) 821-9953

Participants are persons living an alternative lifestyle. TLO holds seminars, workshops, and panel presentations on topics including ways of living, social recreation, marriage and other interpersonal relationships, swinging, communes, legal and medical aspects of human behavior, and human sexuality. It also offers periodic tours and special events and bestows annual Lifestyles Awards of Recognition. TLO issues the bimonthly *Emerge Playcouple,* sponsors an annual convention with exhibits, and holds an annual couples convention. Founded in 1973. Contact Robert L. McGinley Ph.D., President.

Lilliputian Bottle Club (LBC)
5626 Corning Ave.
Los Angeles, CA 90056

Connoisseurs of those wee vials of spirits. Members are collectors of miniature liquor, wine, beer, and other spirit bottles. LBC exchanges information and bottles with other clubs and collectors. The Lilliputians publish the bimonthly *Gulliver's Gazette* and hold an annual bottle show and sale. Founded in 1971. 450 members. Contact David Spaid, President.

Little Big Horn Associates (LBHA)
PO Box 14708
Ft. Worth, TX 76117-0708   (817) 232-5088

Students, historians, collectors, writers, and others committed to the study of the life of George Armstrong Custer. A U.S. Army officer who served during the Civil War, Custer (1839-76) of course was killed, along with his troops, during the battle of Little Big Horn. The pro-Custer organization seeks to learn and preserve "the truth on the battle of the Little Big Horn," and details of Custer's life. One of its duties is to replace grave markers at the Little Big Horn field in Montana. Almost monthly it issues the *Little Big Horn Associates-Newsletter,* which includes book reviews, a literary section, news of members, and items wanted and for sale. Its annual conference is held during even-numbered years east of the Mississippi River and during odd-numbered years meetings west of the river. Founded in 1966. 1,000 members. Contact Leslie J. Pyatt, Secretary.

Little People of America (LPA)
7238 Piedmont Dr.
Dallas, TX 75227-9324   (214) 388-9576

Adults of the proportionate or disproportionate dwarf types and others 58 inches or under, including teens, young adults, and children. LPA, whose motto is "Think Big," provides fellowship, interchange of ideas, moral support, and solutions to the unique problems of little people. The group promotes good faith, fair dealings, better relations, and understanding of their small size by other members and average-size people. It aids in exchange of information on housing, jobs, clothes, shoes, and education. The group also counsels parents of dwarf children and brings together little couples interested in adoption and adoption agencies that have children of this type available. Members are kept updated through the quarterly newsletter, *LPA Today*. Other publications of the group include *My Child is a Dwarf, Living With Difference*, and *Think Big*. Members meet annually. Founded in 1957. 4500 members. Contact Mary Carten, President.

Live-Free International (L-FI)
PO Box 1743
Harvey, IL 60426   (312) 928-5830

Individuals concerned with long-range survival preparation and self-sufficiency, believing that preparedness and self-sufficiency result in freedom. L-FI strives to develop and promote the philosophy and technology of survival, sponsoring seminars on survival methods and field training events. In addition to helping organize network support systems for individuals and groups seeking freedom through emergency preparedness and self-sufficiency, the group provides contacts and sources for survival writers, organizers, inventors, and instructors. L-FI issues the monthly newsletter *Directions* and the *Survivalist Papers*. Founded in 1974. 1006 members. Contact James C. Jones, President.

London Club (LC)
Route One
Lecompton, KS 66050   (913) 887-6010

Criminologists, members of the press, investigative freelancers, psychics, physicians, educators, and interested individuals dedicated to criminal research specializing in unsolved crimes of the past and present. Goals are to accumulate data; to apply theories and draw conclusions concerning unsolved crimes (such as the Jack the Ripper Whitechapel murders), controversial trial verdicts (such as the Lizzie Borden murder and the Lindbergh kidnapping cases) and theories involving alleged criminal conspiracies both past and present (such as the Lincoln and Kennedy assassinations). The group serves as a clearinghouse and forum for research into unsolved crime by bringing together experts on many levels of criminal investigation. Other case files under current investigation include the Hindenburg disaster in 1937, the Amelia Earhart disappearance in 1937, the Jimmy Hoffa disappearance in 1975, and the Zodiac Killer, who ran amuck in the San Francisco area from 1966 to 1974. The club issues the *London Club Working Papers* and the London Club register, a who's who of membership. To become a member crimebuster, annual dues are $20. Founded in 1975. 100 members. Contact Dennis A. Baranski, Chairman.

Lone Indian Fellowship and Lone Scout Alumni (LIFLSA)
1104 St. Clair Ave.
Sheboygan, WI 53081

LIFLSA creates friendships and promotes intellectual advancement and fellowship, all the while preserving the ideals of the Lone Scouts of America founded in 1915 by W. D. Boyce (who also founded the Boy Scouts of America). The group presents Eagle Feather awards annually for the best poems, articles, stories, and other material printed in the fellowship's magazine and honors the best member worker with the annual Totem Award. It also sponsors a fund to provide seeing eye dogs to the blind. Members receive *Lone Indian Magazine* (10 per year) and attend an annual powwow. Founded in 1926. Contact Ernst T. Grube, Founder.

Loners of America (LOA)
Route 2, Box 85E
Ellsinore, MO 63937   (314) 322-5548

"A club that respects your privacy . . . yet offers many friends and group activities." Members are legally single individuals and mostly retirees who enjoy camping and traveling in RVs, including "people from all walks of life, all forms of careers, all economic levels and ranging in age from the 40s to the 90s." The club promotes fellowship for singles pursuing RV lifestyles (driving the rig, parking the rig, camping out in the rig). The association says that "it is not uncommon for some members to band together to form a caravan (highway travel) throughout an area, state, or crosscountry." Local chapters organize meetings, campouts, and rallies, "to give persons who have no mate an opportunity to enjoy the pleasures of camping with other persons in like circumstances." Friendship and companionship are encouraged, but LOA cautions that it is not a matchmaking club and that it "not only frowns on 'hanky-panky' behavior, but will suspend an offender's membership." Those who marry or pursue the "married lifestyle" have their memberships terminated. The club publishes a monthly newsletter called the *Loners of America News* containing information on campouts and rallies, clubs news, and membership activities. Annual dues are $23. Founded in 1987. 1450 members. Contact Enola Echols, President.

Loners on Wheels (LoW)
PO Box 1355
Poplar Bluff, MO 63901-1355   (314) 785-2420

Another club for legally single people, particularly retirees in the U.S. and Canada, who have a bit of the gypsy in them and who like to dance. Members own and travel in recreational vehicles, such as trailers, campers, and motorhomes. LoW supplies support and companionship for members while respecting their desire to be left alone, sponsoring local and national camp-outs and rallies (most of which offer either line or round dancing, or both, and usually with some instruction). The camping locations are typically on the primitive side and therefore less expensive. Two winter-long rallies take place in the southwest U.S. desert. But take note, "if a man and a woman appear at LoW gatherings traveling in the same rig, their membership is immediately terminated." So come in separate vehicles or risk abandonment by the group. Members who marry or "assume the married lifestyle" can become members of Friendly Roamers, which is open to all (not just ex-members-contact c/o Forrest Forbes, P.O. Box 1716, Lancaster, CA 935391716).

To keep members up to date on activities, RV maintenance tips, and other issues of importance, LoW issues the *Loners on Wheels* monthly newsletter. Noted are those who have "committed matrimony," as well as those who have visited their "last campout." The annual directory includes "an extensive list of members who offer an invitation to visit and come park overnight."

Membership is $26 per year. Founded in 1969. 3000 members. Contact Dick March, President.

Lord Ruthven Assembly (LRA)
University of Northern Colorado
Department of English
Greeley, CO 80639   (303) 351-2971

College and university scholars who research and publish information about the revenant archetype in the disciplines of literature, history, sociology, folklore, psychology, cinema, and the arts. The term *revenant*, which means "one who returns after death or long absence," is used by the assembly primarily to refer to vampires, but can also refer to ghosts and zombies. The assembly's title is derived from the vampire Lord Ruthven, the major character in John Polidori's novel *The Vampyr*. The group bestows the Lord Ruthven Award for the best article or book on revenant research. It publishes the quarterly *The Ruthven Literary Bulletin* and holds the annual International Conference on the Fantastic in mid-March. Founded in 1988. 60 members. Contact Lloyd Worley Ph.D., President.

Lost in Space Fannish Alliance (LISFAN)
7331 Terri Robyn
St. Louis, MO 63129   (314) 846-2846

Individuals interested in the television show *Lost In Space*, which ran from 1965 to 1968 and starred Jonathan Harris (1914-), June Lockhart (1925-), and Guy Williams (1925-89). LISFAN offers LIS information and memorabilia and publishes the semiannual magazine, *LISFAN* and the semiannual *Lost In Space Letterzine*, as well as the *Lost In Space Calendar* and the quarterly *Lost In Space Times/Catalog*. Founded in 1981. 1000 members. Contact Flint Mitchell, President.

Lottery Collectors Society (LCS)
4420 Wisconsin Ave.
Tampa, FL 33616-1031   (813) 839-6245

Individuals interested in collecting items related to lotteries. Members exchange information and hobby materials. LCS publishes the monthly *Lottery Collectors News*, with information on new ticket issues and lottery practices. Founded in 1987. 200 members. Contact Daryl Orr, President.

Love-N-Addiction (LNA)
PO Box 759
Willimantic, CT 06226   (203) 423-2344

Members are self-help support groups as well as individual women who exhibit emotionally addictive and self-destructive behavior in relationships. LNA focuses on relationships that jeopardize the women's emotional and physical well-being. Members seek recovery through the sharing of knowledge and personal experiences. Love-N-Addiction offers consultations and publishes the *Self-Help Group Starter Packet*. Founded in 1986. Contact Carolyn C. Meister, Founder.

Love Notes (LN)
Box 54321
Albuquerque, NM 87153   (505) 293-8540

Promotes love, friendship, and positive relationships among all people as life's highest priority. LN sponsors weekly radio broadcasts and educational programs. Founded in 1986. Contact Ed Ryan, President.

Love Token Society (LTS)
PO Box 1049
Huntingdon Valley, PA 19006   (215) 947-4856

Individuals interested in the collecting and study of love tokens, a coin smoothed and hand-engraved on one side while retaining its original image on the other. The tokens, usually designed on dime-sized silver coins, became popular during the Civil War and were presented to sweethearts as tokens of love. LTS cultivates friendliness among collectors and dealers of such pieces, gathers and disperses information on love tokens, and plans to construct a permanent collection for exhibition and to assemble colored slides of rare or multiple pieces. Token collectors are kept informed of collectibles through the bimonthly *Love Letter*. The group holds an annual conference with exhibits in conjunction with the American Numismatic Association. Founded in 1972. 275 members. Contact Charles H. Godfrey, Secretary.

Lovers of the Stinking Rose (LSR)
1621 Fifth St.
Berkeley, CA 94710   (415) 527-5175

Individual garlic lovers, professional herbalists, gourmet cooks, students of alternative medicine, folklorists, farmers, and organic home gardeners. The Lovers seek to protect garlic in all its varied functions around the world, lobbying against mouthwash companies and others who disparage garlic and its rich odor. LSR cosponsors garlic festivals, maintains the garlic hall of fame, and bestows awards to distinguished garlic lovers, farmers, and cooks. It also sponsors garlic recipe and garlic humor contests and compiles statistics on garlic consumption. The latest on garlic is detailed in the *Garlic Times* (free samples available). Other publications include *The Book of Garlic* and *The Official Garlic Lovers Handbook*. LSR holds the annual Garlic Festival on July 14 in Berkeley, CA. Founded in 1974. 3100 members. Contact L. John Harris, Executive Officer.

Loyal Order of Catfish Lovers (LOCL)
PO Box 3376, Grand Central Station
New York, NY 10163-3376   (212) 697-9191

A group for catfish lovers, particularly people who enjoy eating farm-raised catfish as well as newspaper food editors who enjoy writing about farm-raised catfish (more formally, ictalurus puncta-tus). Motto is "Sic Semper Whiskers!" (Thus Always, Whiskers). The group reports that the six to eight whiskers framing the mouth of the catfish are called "barbels" and function as sensory organs for locating food. They are also important during courtship, when the male catfish sweeps his barbels along the body of the coveted female before mating.

LOCL celebrates National Catfish Month in August, inviting

restaurants to showcase catfish dishes. It sponsors the Catfish Limerick Contest, bestows the Celebrity Catfish Lover of the Month Award, and conducts surveys of catfish enthusiasts. Catfish recipes, celebrity catfish lover profiles (such as NBC *Today Show's* Willard Scott), and other items are covered in the quarterly *Mississippi Prime Times.* The group, which holds the annual World Catfish Festival in Belzoni, MS, notes that the catfish industry contributes more than $300 million to the Mississippi economy each year. Membership fee is $5 and includes bumper sticker ("Honk if you love catfish") and button. Founded in 1989. 3000 members. Contact Diane D'Ambrosio, Membership Chair.

M M M M M M M M

Macro Society (MS)
PO Box 26582
Tempe, AZ 85285   (602) 991-7077

People interested in self-determination through the development of a positive mental attitude. Members strive to provide "happy and healthy alternatives for daily living" through positive thinking, believing one's thoughts determine one's realities. MS sponsors study groups, seminars, classes, and correspondence courses on developing a positive mental attitude and organizes social activities to reinforce these values. Founded in 1975. 8000 members. Contact Thea Alexander, Director.

Mad World Campaign (MWC)
John Francis Plaza
2630 Adams Mill Road NW, Suite 202
Washington, DC 20009-2153   (202) 265-5746

Motion picture aficionados, archivists, preservationists, and others dedicated to the restoration and rerelease of the 1963 motion picture comedy *It's a Mad, Mad, Mad, Mad World,* directed by Stanley Kramer and featuring a cast that included Spencer Tracy, Milton Berle, and Sid Caesar. The original roadshow 70 millimeter Cinerama edition ran 210 minutes and was edited to 162 minutes and later to 154 minutes; the edited scenes were said to have been destroyed. The original version was nominated for six Academy Awards and subsequently won for best sound effects. According to the Mad World Campaign, the cuts were made to increase audience turnover. The group works to locate clippings, stills, and film footage and seeks to convince MGM-United Artists (the owners of the film) to endorse the restoration and permit a search for the missing footage. In 1988, the campaign discovered 21 minutes of 70 millimeter footage cut by the studio from the 210 minute edition and subsequently reedited the film for informational purposes only. Mad World also hopes to inspire the creation of similar campaigns devoted to the restoration of other films produced (and motion picture theaters built) during the 1920s and 1930s, Hollywood's "Golden Age." Mad World issues *Mad World Update* and meets annually, a session which includes a film screening. Founded in 1982. 400 members. Contact Eric K. Federing, Founder.

Magic Lantern Society of the United States and Canada (ML SOCIETY)
897 Belmont St.
Watertown, MA 02172   (617) 484-8077

Magic lantern (lantern slide projectors dating back to the 17th century) collectors and enthusiasts. ML promotes the exchange of information among persons interested in magic lanterns and other kinetic "vintage" type optical toys and collects and tabulates information on magic lantern manufacturers, slide makers, and lantern slide artists. Founded in 1977. 102 members. Contact Richard Balzer.

Magical Youths International (MYI)
61551 Bremen Highway
Mishawaka, IN 46544   (219) 255-4747

Fraternal organization designed to bring together young magicians from around the world. "Although operated by young people for young people, any magician young at heart is welcome to join." Eight times annually it publishes *Top Hat*. Founded in 1955. 250 members. Contact Steve Kelley, Publisher.

Make-A-Wish Foundation of America (MAWFA)
2600 N. Central Ave., Suite 936
Phoenix, AZ 85004   (602) 240-6600

The Foundation grants the wishes of children with life-threatening illnesses, thereby providing these children and their families with special memories and a welcome respite from the daily stress of their situation. MAWFA considers the wish of any child with a life-threatening illness up to the age of 18. Many of the wishes are for trips to Disney World or Disneyland; however, the foundation has also made one child a fireman and another a lawyer with a degree; provided an AirEvac plane for a boy who wanted to die at home; sent a teenager to the Super Bowl; brought a girl from the Midwest to Phoenix, AZ in the winter because she missed the sunshine; and sent birthday greetings to a boy who wanted nothing more. All expenses are covered by the Foundation, which meets annually. Founded in 1980. Contact Janet Hayes, Executive Director.

Male Liberation Foundation (MLF)
701 NE 67th St.
Miami, FL 33138   (305) 756-6249

Individuals who seek to publicize the "new discrimination" against men, including discrimination which caused men "to become the coffee boys, floor sweepers, and delivery boys of the 1980s." MLF believes that men and women have real biological and psychological differences and that public awareness, education, and acceptance of these differences will reduce the divorce rate. The group asserts that men are discriminated against because, according to MLF, women between the ages of 15 and 25 are financially better off than men, yet men pick up the dating tab. Hmmm. The group seeks to educate men about their economic and political potential, supports joint custody and paternal leave for fathers of newborn children, and seeks to defend homemakers from "screaming radical feminists." It also conducts lobbying for changes in Affirmative Action policies, abortion laws, divorce inequities, and sexual harassment rulings. The current MLF position on issues is asserted in the monthly newsletter, *Male Liberation Foundation.* Founded in 1981. 17,000 members. Contact Frank Bertels, Founder & Director.

Man Watchers (MW)
12308 Darlington Ave.
Los Angeles, CA 90049　　　　　　　　　　　　(213) 826-9101

Women aged 18 and older who present "Well Worth Watching" cards to men and select the "ten top men in the world" annually. The group also sponsors the *Man of the 90s* competitions and is currently launching a search for "the type of men women really like" through Man Watcher's Choice (nonbeauty) Pageants. It also produces televised America's Most Watchable Man competitions and publishes the quarterly *Men Watchers Newsletter.* Founded in 1974. 15,000 members. Contact Suzy Mallery, President & Founder.

Man Will Never Fly Memorial Society Internationale
PO Box 1903
Kill Devil Hills, NC 27948　　　　　　　　　　(919) 441-7482

Persons in the news media or aviation and "assorted believers." The society reportedly was founded as a spoof on the First Flight Society, which sponsors the Wright brothers observance. Man Will Never Fly characterizes itself as a tongue-in-cheek, bottle-in-hand group dedicated to proving that birds fly—men drink. Never Fly sponsors an annual social event in Kill Devil Hills on the eve of the celebration of the anniversary of the alleged first airplane flight by the Wright brothers (Dec. 17, 1903). At the Man Will Never Fly gathering, an "unknown international celebrity" discourses on the "unlikely notion that the Wright brothers ever got off the ground." The group gives an annual citation to one or more persons who did the most during the previous year to discourage the idea that flight is a logical thing. In 1967 it established a Hall of Aviation Infamy which gives an award to "some aviation goof-off." Founded in 1959. 5000 members. Contact E. H. North Jr., Thinker.

Marble Collectors Society of America (MCSA)
PO Box 222
Trumbull, CT 06611　　　　　　　　　　　　(203) 261-3223

Marble collectors, dealers, museums, and historical societies united for charitable, scientific, literary, and educational purposes. Objective is to further the hobby of marble collecting. MCSA offers a marble appraisal service and is currently organizing a travelling display for loan to museums. The latest in rollers is covered in the quarterly *Marble Mania,* which in a recent issue said a fond farewell to the late Dumas Walker, a fan (and champion) of outdoor rolley hole marbles who was buried with his favorite marble in his hand. It seems that in the 1960s, Dumas awoke one morning with a vision—if you build it, they will come. Thus inspired, he constructed a marble yard which included bleachers for spectators and lights for night playing. Traffic on the road to the marble yard was so heavy "you'd think there was a roadblock," recalled Walker's nephew. In addition to the newsletter, MCSA issues a price guide and the booklet, *Marbles as Historical Artifacts.* The Society is also preparing a video tape on making marbles. To join, the group requests that wannabe members donate $12 or so (tax deductible, of course). Founded in 1975. 1400 members. Contact Stanley A. Block, Chairman.

Marble Collectors Unlimited (MCU)
Box 206
Northboro, MA 01532 (508) 393-2923

More marble collectors and enthusiasts. The group collects and disseminates historical and bibliographic information on marbles and issues the quarterly *Marble Mart/Newsletter*, which covers meets, auctions, and other events of interest to marble collectors. The newsletter includes listings of items available to buy, sell, or trade. MCU sponsors an annual meet/show with exhibits. Founded in 1978. 600 members. Contact Beverly Brule, Editor.

Martin Van Buren Fan Club (MVBFC)
778 14th St.
San Francisco, CA 94114 (415) 626-9373

Every dead President should have his fan club. MVBFC unites individuals in the U.S. and around the world who are interested in preserving the history and promoting the highlights of the life of Martin Van Buren (1782-1863), eighth President of the U.S. It seeks to bring attention to "the many outstanding and positive things which he did during his lifetime" and actively supports all Van Buren festivities in Kinderhook and Columbia County, New York, where Van Buren apparently was born or lived or jogged through one day.

The MVB admirers publish the annual *OK News*, which features items of interest about the life of Van Buren, member news, trivia, Van Bureniana, and so on. MVBFC holds an annual dinner and seance on the Saturday closest to Martin Van Buren's birthday (Dec. 5). Lifetime dues are in the vicinity of $10, with special rates for seniors and juniors. Members receive a distinctive card, a synopsis of MVB's life, and an official Martin Van Buren Presidential medal issued by the United States Mint. Founded in 1975. 1000 members. Contact Gary L. Holloway, President.

Marx Brothers Study Unit
Darien 28
New Hope, PA 18938 (215) 862-9734

True to the spirit of Groucho, this is a group for those who refuse to join any club that would have them as a member. The Study Unit (and its Marx Brotherhood) unites (loosely) Marxists interested in the lives and careers of Groucho (1890-1977), Chico (1887-1961), and Harpo (1888-1964) Marx, who comprised the classic anarchistic comedy team featured in Hollywood films of the 1930s and 1940s. And it includes folks interested in the short-lived and less zany careers of brothers Gummo (1892-1977) and Zeppo (1901-79).

Originally created as an organization within the National Film Society (which is no longer in business), the Unit acts as an information clearinghouse assisting authors, actors, producers, and other artists interested in accurately depicting the Marx Brothers. A primary activity is the publication of *The Freedonia Gazette*, a semiannual 20-page journal devoted to the lives and careers of the Marx brothers and their effect on popular culture. The Study Unit cautions that semiannual publication is only a theory, since "deadlines are nonexistent and issues are predictably late." In addition to photographs and drawings, the *Gazette* includes "well researched" biographical pieces about particular aspects of the Marxes lives and careers, a two-page column of current news about the influence of the Marxes on the world today, interviews with people associated with the Brothers, book reviews, reviews of stage shows which feature Marx impersonations (remember Gabe Kaplan?), corrections of misleading information on the Marx Brothers from other publications, and questions from readers (usually with answers). "We try to balance the pedantic with the light-hearted to keep the magazine fun, and there's usually a grain of subtle wit throughout each issue," claims the group, but warns, "We don't publish lame attempts at humor just for the sake of including 'humor.'"

Members have access to *Gazette* publisher Paul G. Wesolowski's archive of 100 volumes, 40,000 magazine and newspaper articles dating to 1905, 2000 photographs, and 200 posters. Every year the Study Unit hosts an open house in New Hope, PA, (usually on a day during Memorial Weekend) with 1992's on May 24, the 1993 event on May 30, and 1994 open house on May 29. Members can meet each other, watch rare videotapes, trade memorabilia, and view the archive. For $10, you can either subscribe to the *Gazette* or join the Brotherhood, in which case you can "experience the thrill of belonging to a do-nothing club" while receiving a free subscription to the *Gazette*. "Either way, members receive the same tangible benefits." Founded in 1978. 300 members. Contact Paul G. Wesolowski, Director.

Mechanical Bank Collectors of America (MBCA)
PO Box 128
Allegan, MI 49010   (616) 673-4509

Antique enthusiasts interested in furthering knowledge about antique mechanical banks. MBCA issues the *House Organ* and *Mechanical Banker* three times per year. It also sponsors an annual meeting during the last week in September. Founded in 1955. 290 members. Contact H. E. Mihlheim, Secretary.

Mega Society (MS)
13155 Wimberly Square, No. 284
San Diego, CA 92128   (619) 679-0273

A small group of people who have proven by test to have an intelligence quotient higher than that of 99.9999% of the general population. MS works to provide a forum for individuals of extremely high intellectual ability and seeks to increase knowledge about these intelligence levels. The group derives its name from the prefix mega-, meaning million; theoretically, on any given test or combination of tests accepted for admission purposes by the society, only one person in a million can qualify for membership, which so far limited enrollment. MS publishes the quarterly *Megarian*, which includes a membership directory. Founded in 1982. 20 members. Contact Jeff Ward, Executive Officer.

Men International
1816 Florida Ave.
Palm Harbor, FL 34682   (813) 787-3875

Coalition of men's rights and divorce reform organizations seeking a better male self-image, especially in the role of father. Objectives include obtaining equal rights for men in all areas of law and just and competent administration of domestic relations. MI fights against anti-male discrimination and works to strengthen the family. It also assists men who have been falsely accused of child abuse. The group publishes *The Liberator,* a monthly newsletter and sponsors an annual conference. Founded in 1977. Contact Kenneth R. Pangborn, Executive Director.

MEND - Mothers Embracing Nuclear Disarmament
PO Box 2309
La Jolla, CA 92038   (619) 454-3343

MEND works to achieve global peace and understanding by teaching women and children to become peace educators and citizen diplomats. The group utilizes the universal appeal of parenthood to inspire a mutual commitment among nations toward the reduction and eventual elimination of nuclear weapons. It acknowledges the need for a strong national defense, but believes that without a new approach toward national security, the human race is in danger. MEND conducts the Peace Educators Program, which provides international exchange opportunities and leadership skills training for women and children, and Kids Talk to Kids, a pen pal program between children of the United States and those in India and what used to be called the Soviet Union. Publications include *A Concerned Citizens Introduction to National Security* and *Reflections on War and Peace—Children Speak Out.* Founded in 1985. 2300 members. Contact Maureen King, Executive Director.

Mend Our Tongues Society (MOTS)
2119 College St.
Cedar Falls, IA 50613   (319) 266-8669

A special interest group of Mensa seeking to invent new words for the English language. MOTS conducts linguistic research and publishes *Ferment,* a bimonthly newsletter. Founded in 1982. 64 members. Contact Gerald Baker, Executive Officer.

Men's Rights
PO Box 163180
Sacramento, CA 95816   (916) 484-7333

Another group of men seeking to end sexism in a way that recognizes the social, psychological, physical, legal, and economic problems of men. The club works to correct low standards of male self-image and male health and encourages women to share the burdens of taking the romantic initiative. Men's Rights hopes to eliminate "the dictum that the worst failure a male can commit is the failure to live up to the male role." The group, which seeks to achieve equal opportunity for male parents, believes that "the provider and protector roles have dehumanized, damaged, and limited men." Founded in 1977. Contact Fredric Hayward, Executive Director.

Men's Rights Association (MRA)
17854 Lyons
Forest Lake, MN 55025   (612) 464-7887

Is this a trend or what? MRA is a group of male victims of sex discrimination, actual or potential. The group, interested in obtaining equal rights under the law for all male persons, promotes and fosters the just and competent administration of government, especially of the judicial branch. MRA studies, promotes, and engages in activities that will strengthen the marriage relationship and family life. It supports activities that will restore and maintain the dignity of male persons and offers an attorney referral service to members. Publications include the monthly *The Liberator, Divorce: What Everyone Should Know to Beat the Racket, A Manifesto of Men's Liberation,* and *Rape of the Male.* Founded in 1971. 6500 members. Contact Richard F. Doyle, President.

Messies Anonymous (MA)
5025 SW 114th Ave.
Miami, FL 33165   (305) 271-8404

MA conducts workshops and seminars on housekeeping techniques, hoping to teach chronically disorganized people, known as Messies, to become more organized. MA endorses the Mt. Vernon Method of Cleaning: cleaners begin working in one corner of the house and continue through the house until they have reached the corner in which they began. Sort of a Zen exercise. The group also encourages use of the Flipper System: a series of flip cards containing chores, schedules, menus, and shopping needs. What an idea! MA helps individuals form self-help groups at the local level and publishes the quarterly *Messies Anonymous Newsletter.* Founded in 1980. 3000 members. Contact Sandra Felton, Founder.

MetaScience Foundation (MSF)
c/o MetaScience Annual
Box 32
Kingston, RI 02881

Public and university libraries, parapsychologists, doctors, physicists, and New Age laypersons who enjoy exploring and developing, by use of scientific methods, areas usually neglected by mainstream science. These include futurology, telepathy, precognition, psychokinesis, synchronicity, UFOs, holistic medicine, astrology, graphology, tarot, the multidimensionality of time, and the quantum physics of consciousness. Issues are explored in the *Journal of Occult Studies* and the *MetaScience Annual.* The group meets annually during January in Narragansett, RI. Founded in 1976. 1600 members. Contact Marc Seifer, Director.

Michigan/Canadian Bigfoot Information Center (MCBIC)
152 W. Sherman
Caro, MI 48723   (517) 673-2715

Dedicated to assisting people with a sincere desire for information about the "sasquatch," or "bigfoot," a large, hairy, man-like creature reputedly inhabiting various regions of North America, MCBIC covers northern and midwestern U.S. and eastern Canada. The group seeks to capture sasquatch specimens and conducts overnight vigils in classified areas. MCBIC receives cooperative assistance from anthropologists, wildlife pathologists, and Department of Natural Resources affiliates. Founded in 1970. 4 members. Contact Wayne W. King, Director.

Midwest Decoy Collectors Association (MWDCA)
1100 Bayview Road
Fox River Grove, IL 60021   (708) 639-9392

Decoy collectors who find and preserve old decoys and identify decoy carvers. Provides forum for buying and selling decoys among members. Sponsors annual National Antique Decoy Show during April in St. Charles, IL. Founded in 1966. 610 members. Contact Gene Konopasck, President.

Mikes of America (MA)
PO Box 676
Minneapolis, MN 55440   (612) 827-4868

Hey Mikey! Mikes of America is a nationwide promotional campaign to unite all of the "Mikes" in America to solidify the nominative bond and promote the heritage of the name that has existed "since the time of the Archangels." Mikes of America reports that "Michael" remains the most popular name for boys in America. MA proudly publishes *Mike's World*, a semiannual newsletter. It awards Mike of the Year annually to the Mike judged best at maintaining the visibility of the name. Past winners including Mikhail "Mike" Gorbachev and Chicago Bull Michael Jordan. Founded in 1979. 15,000 members. Contact Michael D. Nelson, President.

Military Vehicle Preservation Association (MVPA)
PO Box 260607
Lakewood, CO 80226   (303) 989-3218

Individuals and groups interested in the preservation, restoration, maintenance, and enjoyment of historic military vehicles. MVPA informs the public of the historical value of collectible military vehicles and serves as a clearinghouse for technical and historical information. It publishes the quarterly *Army Motors* and the bimonthly *Supply Line*. Founded in 1976. 4900 members. Contact Sondra McCoy, Business Manager.

Millennium Society (MS)
6000 Ranleigh Manor
McLean, VA 22101   (703) 522-4482

A group of people representing all six continents who are committed to promoting peace. Objectives are to establish a worldwide scholarship program for young people committed to peace and bring young leaders together for discussions on international peace. MS intends to celebrate the millennium in the year 2000, which seems appropriate. For the World Millennium Charity Ball, the society has chartered the Queen Elizabeth II ocean liner to take 3500 people to Egypt's Great Pyramid of Cheops, a trip which will be somewhat difficult since the pyramid is in the midst of a desert. The group publishes the quarterly *Millennium* magazine and holds an annual charity ball and symposium. Founded in 1979. 1100 members. Contact Cathleen Magennis, President.

Mind Development and Control Association (MDCA)
PO Box 29396
Sappington, MO 63126   (314) 849-3722

Purpose of MDCA is to develop and promote interest in various facets of paranormal and psychic research and to foster awareness and understanding of the forces that influence and shape human existence. The group sponsors research in the field of healing and bio-energy and provides monthly correspondence lessons in psychic arts and sciences as well as classes in psychic development and ESP skills. MDCA maintains a haunted house investigation group and sponsors the Psychic Detective Bureau. Psychic and paranormal news is covered in the quarterly *The Ultimate Energies: Making Your Mind Work for You*, which reports on new age developments, including mind control, psi research, dowsing, and psychoenergies. Founded in 1972. Contact Raymond G. Jaegers, Vice President.

Mind Science Foundation (MSF)
8301 Broadway, Suite 100
San Antonio, TX 78209   (512) 821-6094

MSF conducts research on the human mind, with emphasis on psychoneuroimmunology, creativity, human potential, parapsychology, and memory. It sponsors the annual Imagineer Awards and publishes the quarterly newsletter *Mind Science Foundation-News*, which discusses specific topics such as mind-made health and left and right brain functions. Other publications include *Advancing Frontiers in Alzheimer's Disease Research*. Founded in 1958. Contact Catherine Nixon Cooke, Executive Director.

Miniature Armoured Fighting Vehicle Association (MAFVA)
15 Berwick Ave.
Heaton Mersey
Stockport, Cheshire SK4 3AA, England   61 4327574

Individuals in 50 countries who own, make, and/or collect armoured fighting vehicle (AFV) models as well as those content to merely collect information on AFVs. MAFVA promotes interest in AFVs, other military vehicles, and their associated equipment. It provides a central organization for the collection and dissemination of information and encourages correspondence between those with similar interests. The group publishes the bimonthly *Tankette* and sponsors an annual competition. Founded in 1965. 6700 members. Contact G. E. Gary Williams, President.

Miniature Book Society (MBS)
PO Box 127
Sudbury, MA 01776   (508) 443-2647

Individuals, libraries, book collectors, miniaturists, antiquarian book dealers, and others with an interest in real small books. Recognized as one of the highest expressions of the printer's and binder's arts, miniature books are less than three inches in height, often produced with hand-set type, and released in very limited editions. MBS holds an annual miniature book competition and publishes the annual *Catalog of the Miniature Book Competition* and the quarterly *Miniature Book Society Newsletter*. The group holds an annual conclave with exhibits, usually on Labor Day weekend. Founded in 1983. 475 members. Contact Rev. Joseph L. Curran, Treasurer.

Miniature Donkey Registry of the United States (MDR)
2901 N. Elm St.
Denton, TX 76201   (817) 382-6845

Git along little donkey, git along. A part of the American Donkey and Mule Society, MDR is a group of owners of registered miniature donkeys. Miniature donkeys measure no more than 36 inches high at the withers (whatever donkey withers are), range in color from mouse gray to reddish brown to black, and have a dark stripe that runs down the back and across the shoulders to form a cross. So if you see one wandering in your neighborhood, call the

Registry. MDR assists purchasers in locating breeders in their vicinity and, of course, maintains the miniature donkey registry (a stud book). Founded in 1958. Contact Betsy Hutchins, Secretary.

Miniature Golf Association of America (MGAA)
PO Box 10287
State College, PA 16805 (814) 238-4653

A group dedicated to hitting the golf ball through the windmill. Members are a hearty band of miniature golf course owners, operators, builders, designers, manufacturers, insurers, and purely interested individuals seeking to increase public acceptance of miniature golf as a *serious* sport. The group sponsors competitions and publishes the bimonthly newsletter *Putting Around,* which includes feature articles, promotional ideas, industry updates, and course development and operational tips. It also sponsors an annual conference with exhibits. Founded in 1989. 125 members. Contact Kevin M. Ream, Chairman.

Miniature Piano Enthusiast Club (MPEC)
5815 N. Sheridan Road, No. 202
Chicago, IL 60660 (312) 271-2970

Manufacturers and collectors of miniature pianos (pianos that are very small). MPEC conducts research on the history of miniature pianos and encourages continuing miniature piano education (teach a piano to read). The group maintains a collection of greeting cards and postcards depicting miniature pianos and publishes the quarterly newsletter *Musically Yours!* containing information on new and antique pianos and facts about composers. Members attend an annual miniature piano conference. Founded in 1990. 23 members. Contact Janice E. Kelsh, Executive Director.

Mining Club (MC)
295 Madison Ave.
New York, NY 10017 (212) 532-7649

Social club of persons connected with the mineral industry familiar with the life and language (##!&%*!!) of the mining camps and plants. Members exchange information, often during conversations, about mining camps and plants. Founded in 1930. 641 members. Contact L. John Polite Jr., Executive Officer.

Miss Mom/Mister Mom
PO Box 547
Moab, UT 84532 (801) 259-5090

Self-help support group for single parents (mothers and fathers) offering emotional and moral support. The group provides information and counseling on parenting, substance abuse prevention, building self-esteem, and other issues. "Single parents find comfort in knowing that they are not alone in their struggles, and gain courage from the success of others who were once in their shoes," reports a group official. Miss Mom etc. provides parenting advise, recipes, stories, poems, and insights in the bimonthly newsletter *Miss Mom/Mister Mom.* It holds the annual *National Single Family Convention* during September in Moab. Low income memberships are free, while a donation of $15 is requested from others. Founded in 1986. 5000 members. Contact Tina L. Lopez, Executive Director.

Mister Ed Fan Club (MEFC)
PO Box 1009
Cedar Hill, TX 75104

Haaaaaay Wilber! Fans of the *Mister Ed* television show, which aired from 1961 to 1966 and was about a talking horse (of course) named Ed (Mr.). Group's objective is "betterment of the world" through humor, art, and music, centered around Mister Ed. MEFC bestows the Annual EdWards and operates the Museum of Ed. Members are updated on Ed's activities through the bimonthly newsletter *Ed Magazine.* Founded in 1974. 1000 members. Contact James Burnett, President & Founder.

Mistresses Anonymous (MA)
1320 Spur Dr. S.
Islip, NY 11751

MA is a self-help organization for women involved with married men. The group maintains the Foundation of Mistress Research and issues *Triangle Tabloid,* a newsletter. Other publications include *The Mistress' Survival Manual, The Making of the American Mistress, The Second Wife's Survival Manual, The Passion Factor, How to be a Winner at Love,* and *Look Before You Love.* Contact Melissa Sands, President.

Moles
PO Box 1389
Southampton, NY 11968   (516) 283-6322

A social club of individuals presently or formerly engaged in tunnel, subway, sewer, foundation, marine, subaqueous, or other heavy construction work. The group bestows the annual Moles Award. Three times every year it publishes *Holing Through.* Founded in 1937. 500 members. Contact Arline F. Gallagher, Executive Secretary.

Monarchist Alliance (MA)
PO Box 1973
Lawrence, KS 66044-8973   (913) 842-7160

Members and former members of the Augustan Society, British Commonwealth Alliance, Caroline Society, and Catholic People's Party. MA fosters and maintains an interest in Catholic-Christian monarchy as both a historic divine institution and a present reality preferable to other forms of government. According to the alliance, its political theory and Christian humanistic outlook is based on biblical principles (the Ten Commandments, for instance) and the encyclicals, especially of Pope Leo XIII, Pope Pius X, Pope Pius XI, and Pope Pius XII. The group works to "reestablish a constitutional monarchy in the U.S.," returning to "the strict constructionist aspect of a corrected Constitution," with changes in channels of power and the exercise of religion and the franchise. Founded in 1953. Contact Jovan T. Weismiller.

Monkees Buttonmania Club (MBC)
Liverpool Productions
397 Edgewood Ave.
New Haven, CT 06511   (203) 865-8131

Hey hey we've got buttons. MBC members are collectors of buttons that feature members of the Monkees, the madcap mid-

1960s vocal and acting group that produced several best-selling albums and starred in a successful television series (1966-69) that predated MTV by a couple of decades in its use of video to sell music to unsuspecting teens. The club holds the annual Monkees Convention during August in New York City. Contact Charles F. Rosenay, Executive Officer.

Monmouth Antiquarian Society (MAS)
13998 McCaleb Road
Monmouth, OR 97361

Membership is limited to 600 heads of households and their immediate families who are dedicated to discovering, developing, and perpetuating the pastimes of antiquity. The group conducts festivals, excursions, charitable activities, and research and educational programs. Current projects include the growing of "the world's largest" hedge labyrinth, featuring caverns of the minotaur, a secret garden, oubliettes, hidden slides and trap doors, underground swimming lagoons and caverns, and a catacombs (yes, but where's the television room?). One of the few groups that sponsors competitions in labyrinth running, Renaissance contests of skill, gladiator events, disc golf, and archery. Members receive the quarterly newsletter *Oubliette*, which reports on antiquarian matters of consequence and current research in the field. The group meets during a quarterly festival and conference on the Ides of March, June, September, and December in Monmouth, OR. Founded in 1989. 600 members. Contact Thomas Rocha, President.

Monorail Society (MS)
36450 Diego Dr.
Fremont, CA 94536   (415) 745-7887

Engineers, monorail operators, mechanics, manufacturers, and individuals interested in the history, present day operation, and future of the monorail. MS promotes the single rail transport system as a low cost, safe, efficient transportation alternative. The group encourages study and exchange of information and provides a clearinghouse for dissemination of statistics and data. Members collect monorail postcards and souvenirs and are kept informed of group activities through the quarterly *Monorail* newsletter. Founded in 1989. 46 members. Contact Kim Pedersen, President.

Monty Python Special Interest Group (MPSIG)
2419 Greensburg Pike
Pittsburgh, PA 15221

Members of Mensa International interested in Monty Python, a British satirical comedy group whose members included actors John Cleese, Terry Gilliam, Eric Idle, Terry Jones, Michael Palin, and the late Graham Chapman. The group is also interested in other absurdist humor. MPSIG periodically gathers and publishes the quarterly *Proceedings of the Spanish Inquisition*. Founded in 1982. 106 members. Contact Henry Roll, Coordinator.

Mother's Day Council (MDC)
1328 Broadway
New York, NY 10001   (212) 594-6421

Manufacturers of women's gift products dedicated to the task of increasing the observance of Mother's Day. MDC advances public awareness through newspaper, magazine, television, and radio advertising and bestows the annual Outstanding Mother Awards to mothers who have made an impact on today's perception of American motherhood. The group conducts attitude and market studies on the changing perceptions of Mother's Day. Founded in 1941. 125 members. Contact Theodore M. Kaufman, Executive Director.

Mothers Without Custody (MWOC)
PO Box 27418
Houston, TX 77256 (713) 840-1622

Women living apart from one or more of their minor children for any reason, including court decisions, exchange of custody with an ex-spouse, intervention by a state agency, or childnapping by an ex-spouse. MWOC estimates that 1.5 million mothers live apart from minor children. It provides support to women currently exploring their child custody options during and after divorce. The group helps establish local self-help groups that meet monthly and organizes social events for mothers alone and mothers visiting their children. Members receive *Mother-to-Mother*, a bimonthly newsletter. Founded in 1981. 500 members. Contact Jennifer Isham, President.

Motor Bus Society (MBS)
PO Box 7058
West Trenton, NJ 08628

Hobbyists and others interested in the history of bus lines, terminals, and equipment. The Society sponsors motor coach tours of bus properties and is particularly proud of its 90,000 photographs of buses dating from 1900 to the present. Members receive the monthly *Motor Coach Age*. Founded in 1948. 1200 members. Contact Charles Sullivan, President.

Motor Maids, Inc.
PO Box 1664
Englewood, FL 34295 (813) 474-3970

A club for women motorcyclists. The Maids meet every year. Vrrroom. The group issues an *Advisory Newsletter* quarterly. Founded in 1941. 500 members. Contact Jan S. Barrett, Secretary.

Motor Voters
1350 Beverly Road, Suite 115-240
McLean, VA 22101 (703) 448-0002

Consumers and automotive safety experts united to promote auto safety and consumers' rights. Motor Voters represents the public interest before federal regulatory agencies and Congress and conducts lobbying activities, petition drives, and public awareness campaigns. The group cooperates with other consumer, safety, and public health organizations in advocating improved auto safety. Current activities are reported in the semiannual newsletter *Motor Voter Press*. Founded in 1979. 300 members. Contact Rosemary Dunlap, President.

Mount Rushmore Memorial Society (MRMS)
PO Box 1524
Rapid City, SD 57709   (605) 574-2523

Individuals dedicated to preserving the Mount Rushmore national monument. MRMS conducts fundraising activities and collects information on the Mount, which it then dispenses upon request. Operating in cooperation with the National Park Service, it conducts research activities and collects artifacts related to the Mount. Members receive the quarterly newsletter *Mount Rushmore National Memorial Society.* Contact Carolyn S. Mollers, President.

Mountain Gorilla Project (MGP)
1717 Massachusetts Ave. NW, Suite 602
Washington, DC 20036   (202) 265-8394

A project of the African Wildlife Foundation whose objectives are to work with Rwandan authorities to establish a management plan for the Volcanoes National Park in Rwanda. MGP trains, equips, and funds effective antipoaching forces. It also establishes and supports conservation education programs for Rwandans. The group reports that from 1960 to 1982 the number of gorillas in the area fell from 450 to 245. The project works to safeguard the remaining gorillas and their habitat by addressing economic pressures facing Rwandans which have resulted in agricultural encroachment into the National Park. MGP also encourages controlled tourist development which provides revenue to fund the park and create local employment. Founded in 1978. 4 members. Contact Diana McMeekin, Vice President.

The Mouse Club (TMC)
2056 Cirone Way
San Jose, CA 95124   (408) 377-2590

Collectors of Disney memorabilia including toys, games, and books. TMC provides a network for members to buy, sell, trade, and exchange information on Walt Disney collectibles. It also provides advice on what items may be purchased by mail order through Disneyland. TMC answers questions about old and new merchandise and informs members of the background of collecting interesting Disney artifacts and memorabilia. Bimonthly the group publishes *The Mouse Club Newsletter* and on something of a regular basis holds the Disneyland Collectors Convention. Founded in 1979. 2000 members. Contact Kim McEuen, Executive Officer.

Munsters and the Addams Family Fan Club (MAFFC)
PO Box 69A04
West Hollywood, CA 90069   (213) 650-5112

Fan club for individuals interested in the Addams Family (of television and movie fame) and the Munsters (limited to television). MAFFC facilitates information exchange and offers episode guides, photos, records, t-shirts, videotapes, and other items. The group has a collection of videotapes, records, and memorabilia. The club publishes the quarterly *The Munsters and the Addams Family Reunion* and gathers annually. Founded in 1988. Contact Louis Wendruck, President.

Mushroom Caucus (MC)

2369 Rayburn House Building
Washington, DC 20515   (202) 225-5761

Members are members of Congress from mushroom-producing states united to promote the interests of the U.S. mushroom industry. It coordinates efforts to assist growers and canners in their fight against imported mushrooms that are priced much lower than U.S. mushrooms. Founded in 1978. 60 members. Contact Rep. Richard Schulze, Chairman.

Mutual UFO Network (MUFON)

103 Oldtowne Road
Seguin, TX 78155-4099   (512) 379-9216

Scientists, engineers, doctors, psychologists, technicians, military personnel, computer programmers, pilots, and others seeking to resolve the enigma of unidentified flying objects and investigate UFO sighting reports worldwide. MUFON compiles information on UFO sightings internationally and operates four amateur radio networks which receive and disseminate UFO sighting reports and current UFO information. The group maintains a 350-volume library on UFOs, astronomy, and Bigfoot as well as a file on UFO sighting reports, arranged chronologically by state, province, and country. Committees include Abduction, Animal Mutilations, Astronomy, Humanoid Study Group, Landing Traces and the UFO Telephone Hot Line.

Bob Bletchman, a spokesperson for the group, reports that aliens from outer space are not the products of a few overactive imaginations. "It is not the collective meanderings of a population gone bonkers. (Alien sightings are) based on empirical stuff. This is what very sober persons have witnessed." To get the word out on UFOs, MUFON publishes a monthly magazine called *MUFON UFO Journal*, containing statistics, research reports, book reviews, and information on UFO sightings. It has also published a monograph series covering the reported recovery by the U.S. government of UFOs and alien bodies. The Network holds an annual UFO symposium. Founded in 1969. 2600 members. Contact Walter H. Andrus Jr., International Director.

Mythopoeic Society (MS)

PO Box 6707
Altadena, CA 91003   (818) 571-7727

MS is an educational and literary organization devoted to the study, discussion, and enjoyment of myth, fantasy, and imaginative literature, especially the works of J.R.R. Tolkien, C.S. Lewis, and Charles Williams. The group bestows the Mythopoeic Fantasy Award for fantasy literature and the Mythopoeic Scholarship Award for scholarly work relating to Tolkien, Lewis, or Williams. The Tolkien Society of America is a division. Threes times a year MS publishes *The Mythic Circle,* a magazine of fiction, fantasy, and science fiction. Other publications include an annual membership directory, *Mything Persons,* and the quarterly *Mythlore: A Journal of J.R.R. Tolkien, C.S. Lewis, Charles Williams, General Fantasy and Mythic Studies,* a literary journal interested in the genres of myth and fantasy. And last but not least, issues *Mythprint,* a monthly newsletter covering conferences and other society activities in the genres of myth, fantasy, and imaginative literature.

Founded in 1967. 900 members. Contact Glen H. GoodKnight, Founder.

N N N N N N N

Names Project Foundation (NPF)
2362 Market St.
San Francisco, CA 94114 (415) 863-5511

Ongoing purpose of the foundation is to create a memorial patchwork quilt as an "appropriate, compassionate response" to the AIDS epidemic. Goals of the project are to provide a positive, creative means of expression for persons whose lives have been touched by AIDS, and illustrate the impact of AIDS by emphasizing the "humanity behind the statistics." The close to 400,000 square-foot quilt currently contains more than 13,000 panels from each of the 50 states and 22 foreign countries bearing the names of persons who have died as a result of AIDS. Among materials sewn into the panels are stuffed animals, merit badges, records, feather boas, and a baseball jersey. The foundation encourages support for people with AIDS and their loved ones and raises funds for direct care services for persons with AIDS. Founded in 1987. Contact David Lemos, Executive Director.

Napoleonic Society of America (NSA)
1115 Ponce de Leon Blvd.
Clearwater, FL 34616 (813) 586-1779

Individuals interested in the life and times of Napoleon Bona-parte (1769-1821), the little guy who was Emperor of France from 1804 to 1814. NSA facilitates exchange among individuals interested in Napoleon, offers reprints and synopses of works on Napoleon, and reports on auctions and private sales of Napoleonic memorabilia. It also announces museum shows, movies, and television documentaries dealing with Napoleon, like *Bill and Ted's Excellent Adventure*. The Society, which provides travel notes on Malmaison, Versaille, Fontainebleau, Corsica, Elba, St. Helena, Waterloo, Austerlitz, and other battlefields, conducts an annual Napoleonic tour to France and plans to establish the National Napoleonic Museum and Library. Founded in 1983. 1000 members. Contact Robert M. Snibbe, President & Executive Director.

National Alliance of Supermarket Shoppers (NASS)
2 Broadlawn Ave.
Great Neck, NY 11024 (516) 466-5142

Supermarket shoppers and consumers belong to NASS, which monitors activities of government protection agencies, such as the Federal Trade Commission. NASS takes part in legislative activities concerning consumer issues and conducts negotiations with retailers and manufacturers on consumer complaints. Shoppers are provided with guidance in resolving individual problems. The group operates Project CAPP, a low-income training project that promotes shopper training for welfare recipients. It bestows the Golden Shopping Cart Awards annually to legislators, supermarkets, refunders, manufacturers, managers, and customer relations personnel. The group also sponsors Paperbag Art competitions.

Founded in 1980. 50,000 members. Contact Martin Sloane, Executive Officer.

National Amusement Park Historical Association (NA-PHA)
PO Box 83
Mt. Prospect, IL 60056

Persons interested in the preservation and history of past and present amusement parks. NAPHA promotes the concept of amusement parks as a highly enjoyable recreation. Members preserve and display memorabilia from amusement parks (nice roller coaster you have in basement). The group publishes the bimonthly newsletter, *National Amusement Park Historical News* and holds the annual Amusement Park Nostalgia Show. Founded in 1978. 425 members. Contact James E. Abbate, President.

National Anxiety Center (NAC)
PO Box 40
Maplewood, NJ 07040

A clearinghouse of commentary and information on media-driven "scare campaigns" of every description, including those dealing with food, health, the environment, sex, and the economy. NAC gives advice on how to deal with anxiety effectively. The Center sponsors National Anxiety Month in April and awards the Chicken Little Awards each April 1st to organizations which "have managed to scare the daylights out of countless Americans." The group issues *The National Anxiety Report* and a guide, *Worry Your Way To Success: Ten Secrets of Successful Problem Solving.* Founded in 1990. Contact Alan Caruba, Founder.

National Arbor Day Foundation (NADF)
100 Arbor Ave.
Nebraska City, NE 68410   (402) 474-5655

National associations, corporations, communities, state government agencies, and individuals dedicated to tree planting and conservation. NADF officially promotes the observance of Arbor Day each year and works to create an awareness and appreciation of the fundamental role that trees play in day-to-day existence. The group encourages the young folk to appreciate the joy of trees and initiates programs that encourage the planting of trees. Members receive the bimonthly newsletter *Arbor Day,* which profiles specific trees and reports on the educational efforts of the Foundation. Founded in 1972. Contact John Rosenow, Executive Director.

National Association for Outlaw and Lawman History (NOLA)
615-C N. 8th St.
Killeen, TX 76541   (817) 634-8300

Writers, researchers, memorabilia collectors, photographers, gun collectors, genealogists, historians, and history buffs dedicated to collecting, preserving, and sharing materials on outlaw and lawman history. NOLA also works to preserve historic sites and trails and conducts historical and genealogical research. The group issues the *National Association for Outlaw and Lawman History-Newsletter* six times per year, as well as the *National Association for Outlaw and Lawman History-Quarterly,* a journal featuring articles on outlaws and lawmen of the American old west. During the last week of July it holds an annual conference with exhibits. Founded in 1974. 365 members. Contact Richard J. Miller, Secretary.

National Association for the Advancement of Perry Mason (NAAPM)
2735 Benvenue, #3
Berkeley, CA 94705 (415) 548-4237

Individuals interested in Perry Mason books and the *Perry Mason* television series, which aired on the CBS network from 1957-66 and still pops up on the tube as a movie of the week. Perry Mason, a fictional defense attorney, was the creation of author Erle Stanley Gardner (1889-1970); in the TV series Mason was (and is) played by Raymond Burr. The group provides members with information regarding Perry Mason as he has appeared in books, comics, and radio and the television series. A special treat is the weekly screening of the television series. Founded in 1985. 175 members. Contact Jim Davidson, President.

National Association for the Advancement of Time (NAFTAT)
6201 Sunset Blvd., Suite 114
Hollywood, CA 90028 (213) 936-9876

Anti-nostalgia, pro-future, pro-contemporary culture organization comprised primarily of persons born after 1965 who have an attitude. The group provides a forum for those who feel that interest in the near future is being undermined by a nationwide nostalgia trend. NAFTAT seeks to "reestablish interest in the near future" while promoting an understanding of the past in what NAFTAT feels is its proper perspective. The group believes that "the 80s pop culture is so firmly entrenched in the 60s that kids who would otherwise be discovering the world around them are wishing they had gone to Woodstock." It also believes that marketing aimed at the baby boom generation has created "classic rock" radio and nostalgic television shows that are "crushing creativity or driving it underground." Not one to mince words, the group conducts studies on trends in time perception. It has sponsored Boycott the Past Week and publishes *Clockwise,* a quarterly newsletter. Founded in 1989. 400 members. Contact Bruce Elliot, President.

National Association for the Preservation and Perpetuation of Storytelling (NAPPS)
PO Box 309
Jonesborough, TN 37659 (615) 753-2171

Individuals and organizations interested in the art of storytelling, as both an entertainment and educational tool. Each year the group sponsors the National Storytelling Festival, a weekend event in the fall which draws more than 7000 people. Other activities include workshops, classes, and concerts that provide opportunities to learn about the art and the role it has played in American cultural history. NAPPS sponsors educational programs for teachers, librarians, and others interested in applying storytelling in their work. It maintains a collection of more than 200 hours of audio and video recordings of storytelling material and is currently conducting a search to locate all storytelling organizations, centers, and events in the U.S. The group publishes the annual *National Catalog of*

Storytelling and the quarterly *Storytelling Magazine,* as well as the monthly *The Yarnspinner.* Founded in 1975. 4,500 members. Contact Jimmy Neil Smith, Executive Director.

National Association for the Preservation of Baseball (NAPB)

200 Mimosa Circle
Mandeville, LA 70448   (504) 845-4492

Batter up! Individuals dedicated to the preservation and enjoyment of baseball "in all its glory." NAPB works to pass legislation for the designation of national historic baseball sites, including the birthplace of Babe Ruth, Yankee Stadium, and Wrigley Field. The group promotes the establishment of college-level baseball curricula, studying baseball from a historical, statistical, and sociological perspective. It opposes the use of aluminum bats in major league play and favors natural grass fields over "insulting turf" fields. Founded in 1991. 100 members. Contact Todd J. Rossnagel, Founder & President.

National Association of Breweriana Advertising (NABA)

2343 Met-To-Wee Lane
Wauwatosa, WI 53226   (414) 257-0158

Collectors of brewery advertising such as signs, trays, labels, coasters, mirrors, and tap knobs as well as show promoters, dealers, and individuals involved in the brewery industry. NABA encourages the collection, preservation, and study of American breweriana. It also conducts research on brewery histories and issues the quarterly *Breweriana Collector,* a journal on the history of brewing and beer advertising. Founded in 1972. 1100 members. Contact Robert E. Jaeger, Executive Secretary.

National Association of Full Figured Women (NAFFW)

PO Box 27231
El Paso, TX 79926

NAFFW works to increase public awareness of the contributions of full-figured women to society and to prevent size discrimination. It issues the quarterly *NAFFW News* and the annual *NAFFW Register* and periodically sponsors the Full Figured Fashion Expo and Beauty of a Full Figured Woman seminar. Founded in 1990. 445 members. Contact C. B. Hart, Executive Director.

National Association of Milk Bottle Collectors (NAMBC)

4 Ox Bow Road
Westport, CT 06880

A group dedicated to collecting glass milk bottles and their sealing devices. NAMBC acts as a forum for information exchange, buying, and selling. The milk bottle was patented in 1889 by Dr. Henry Thatcher, whose Common Sense Milk Jar became the model for all bottles that followed. The bottles were machine-made in automatic blowers. Some collectors focus on age and historical position, reflected in bottle shape, size, type of stopper, and type of glass, while others acquire bottles for their company messages and graphics. Some of the most sought-after bottles display wartime exhortations, including early 1940's bottles from Emmet's Diary in New Mexico picturing a man milking a cow, with the slogan, "We're All Pulling for Uncle Sam." NAMBC keeps members

abreast of milk bottle news through the monthly *Milk Route.*
Membership in the group is $15 per year.

National Association of Non-Smokers (NANS)
8701 Georgia Ave., Suite 200
Silver Spring, MD 20910 (202) 667-6653

Nonsmokers and interested individuals united to promote legislation concerning nonsmoking and the rights of nonsmokers. NANS educates youth on the relationship between smoking and health and maintains a toll-free hotline to answer questions about specific nonsmokers' rights. It also offers health, life, automobile, and homeowners insurance, a travel program, and credit cards to members. Founded in 1990. Contact Norman Understein, Executive Director.

National Association of Timetable Collectors (NAOTC)
315 W. Charles St.
Champaign, IL 61820

Collectors of timetables and related artifacts from railroads, airlines, steamships, and bus lines. NAOTC is presently working on a project to compile a catalog of North American timetable issues from 1829 to the present. The group publishes the monthly *The First Edition* and the quarterly *Timetable Collector.* Founded in 1964. 500 members. Contact Richard P. Stair, President.

National Association of Wheat Weavers (NAWW)
Route 1, Box 344
Buhler, KS 67522 (316) 543-2687

Wheat weavers, straw artists, patrons, and others interested in preserving and promoting wheat weaving (also known as corn doll making) and other forms of straw art. The group issues a newsletter known as *Gleanings* and meets annually in August. Founded in 1987. 254 members. Contact Linda Pauls, Executive Officer.

National Association to Advance Fat Acceptance (NAAFA)
PO Box 188620
Sacramento, CA 95818 (916) 443-0303

A self-help organization dedicated to improving the quality of life for fat people. NAAFA encourages the average fat person to improve his/her low self-esteem. Members are both fat and thin; the latter group is composed mostly of husbands, wives, or supporters of fat people. The group opposes discrimination against fat people, including bias in advertising, employment, fashion, medicine, insurance, social acceptance, the media, schooling, and public accommodations. NAAFA monitors legislative activity affecting fat people and has a collection of 60,000 clippings on all phases of obesity. It supports national and local special interest groups, including Couples, Diabetics, Fat Admirers, Fat Men, Feminists, Leadership, Midsize Women, Singles, Teenage, and Women Size 48 and Larger. Founded in 1969. 3000 members. Contact Sally E. Smith, Executive Director.

National Black on Black Love Campaign (BOBL)

111 E. Wacker Dr., Suite 600
Chicago, IL 60601 (312) 644-6610

Individuals and businesses united to promote the motto, "Replace Black on Black crime with Black on Black love" and foster love and respect in all communities where people are inordinately affected by crime. BOBL organizes *No Crime Day* in various communities and *Adopt A Building Program* for businesses. It sponsors youth organizations and seminars in schools and communities to educate the public in ways of dealing with crime. Founded in 1983. Contact Geri Duncan Jones, Executive Director.

National Carousel Association (NCA)

PO Box 8115
Zanesville, OH 43702-8115 (614) 454-0048

NCA promotes the preservation of the American carousel as ride well worth saving. It coordinates seminars on wood carving, restoration, and painting. The group bestows awards to carousel owners who have preserved their carousels, and to members for outstanding preservation efforts. These lovers of wooden horses that go round and round receive the quarterly *Merry-Go-Roundup* and meet annually to discuss the state of carousels. Founded in 1973. 1600 members. Contact William F. Mangels Jr., Executive Secretary.

National Chastity Association (NCA)

PO Box 402
Oak Forest, IL 60452 (708) 687-1767

A group for the sex-confused 90s. NCA members believe in abstaining from premarital sex. They also agree with most of the group's "nineteen desires," which include the desire to marry someone who is one's best friend, the desire to marry someone who will be totally faithful and honest, and the desire to be in love with one's spouse throughout life. The group presents this value system as "a model of logic which will help many people clarify their own goals and methods, whatever they are, regarding relationships." The NCA is not affiliated with any religious organization. Founded in 1988. 600 members. Contact Mary Meyer, President & Founder.

National Christmas Tree Association (NCTA)

611 E. Wells St.
Milwaukee, WI 53202 (414) 276-6410

NCTA represents the Christmas tree industry, seeking to further its national interests and promote Christmas trees in general with promotions such as the National Christmas Tree Contest. The group maintains an information and referral service and provides liability insurance for retailers. Members are updated through the quarterly *American Christmas Tree Journal*, which features state news and annual report on market conditions. NCTA holds a biennial conference and sponsors an annual marketing conference with exhibits. Founded in 1955. 2670 members. Contact Donald L. McNeil, Executive Director.

National Circus Preservation Society (NCPS)
PO Box 3187
Flint, MI 48502 (313) 234-8496

Circus fans whose objectives are to develop and advance information for a better understanding of American circuses, concentrating on the state of the animal participants. NCPS encourages the captive propagation of endangered species and other performing and exhibition animals and encourages humane handling of all circus animals. The group is also active in promoting reasonable and practical legislation, rules, and regulations that affect the health and well-being of circus animals. Its annual conference is held in conjunction with the Circus Fans Association of America. 1000 members. Contact Dale A. Riker, Executive Officer.

National Clogging and Hoedown Council (NCHC)
600 Parkview Dr.
Durham, NC 27712 (919) 477-2417

Dancers, instructors, and parents of dancers desiring to preserve the many regional forms of mountain dancing and promote communication among the rapidly growing number of clogging groups. NCHC works to establish a written clogging nomenclature and compile information and a history of various styles of clogging. The group helps establish judging standards, sponsors festivals, and compiles listing of teams and judges. Members get the latest on clogging steps in *Toe Tapping Talk*, a quarterly newsletter containing information on clogging and supplies (and including a calendar of events). The group holds a semiannual conference and dance. Founded in 1970. 846 members. Contact Betsey Farlow, President.

National Coalition of IRS Whistleblowers
PO Box 4283
Pocatello, ID 83201 (202) 546-5345

A group for people who want to stand up and be counted before they are audited. Members are current and former employees of the U.S. Internal Revenue Service and other concerned Americans united to investigate and identify policies and operations which the coalition feels intrude unreasonably into the lives of private citizens. The group monitors and reports on IRS violations of citizens' constitutional and legal rights. The Coalition works to reduce these intrusions and increase IRS accountability so that the IRS might "more capably perform the basic function originally contemplated in the Constitution and laws of the U.S." Members receive the monthly *National Coalition of IRS Whistleblowers Newsletter*. Other publications include *IRS: An Agency Out of Control, Self-Employed: Target of the IRS,* and *From Saints to Senators: The IRS Hit List.* The group holds an annual conference, with a congress. Founded in 1984. 8000 members. Contact Paul J. DesFosses, President.

National Coalition on Television Violence (NCTV)
PO Box 2157
Champaign, IL 61825 (217) 384-1920

BAM! SLAM! NCTV is an educational and research organization committed to decreasing the amount of violence shown on television and in film. WHACK! The group rates music videos, television shows, and movies and conducts toy reviews and research on sports violence. BONK! NCTV sponsors seminars on organizing school programs on nonviolence and on violent entertainment and public action. WHAMMO! Members keep up on violence in the media and elsewhere in the *NCTV News* (eight per year) and the weekly *TV Monitoring Reports.* CRASH! Founded in 1980. 3500 members. Contact Thomas Radecki M.D., Chairman.

National Committee for Responsible Patriotism (NCRP)
PO Box 665, Grand Central Station
New York, NY 10163 (201) 727-1776

NCRP works with well-established organizations on specific projects that show support for men and women of the U.S. armed forces, respect for law, pride in the national heritage, and love of country. The Committee reports that it was the first organization to coordinate activities on behalf of U.S. POWs in Vietnam in 1969, and in 1970 organized Appreciation Day for law enforcement officers and fire fighters. In 1979, the group conceived Respect America Week and organized 200 national groups (labor, veterans, and fraternal) to support U.S. hostages in Iran. The patriots gather annually during the fall in New York City. Founded in 1967. 160 members. Contact Charles W. Wiley, Executive Director.

National Committee for Sexual Civil Liberties (NCSCL)
98 Olden Lane
Princeton, NJ 08540 (609) 924-1950

Lawyers and scholars in government, sociology, religion, anthropology, and history (with experience in civil liberties) who work toward "dismantling the entire structure of criminality and discrimination surrounding private sexual conduct between consenting adults." This includes repeal of all adultery, fornication, and sodomy laws to the extent that they punish such conduct (very few laws encourage this sort of behavior) and for the removal of all discriminatory practices based on sexual orientation. NCSCL seeks to repeal laws punishing the distribution, importation, or sale of pornographic material to adults. Members are kept up to date on the relationship between law and sex in the quarterly *Sexual Law Reporter.* Founded in 1970. Contact Dr. Arthur C. Warner, Chairman.

National Congress for Men (NCM)
2020 Pennsylvania Ave. NW, Suite 277
Washington, DC 20006 (202) FATHERS

A coalition of organizations and individuals promoting fathers' rights, men's rights, and divorce reform. NCM provides members with a single, national voice advocating respect for the role of fathers in the healthy growth and development of their children and equality in child custody litigation. The group encourages joint custody and enforcement of parental rights and schedules as well as equitable child support guidelines, orders, and enforcement. It works toward the recognition of the validity of traditional male roles in the family and society and equality of the sexes without the denial of the differences between men and women. NCM monitors the news and entertainment media and the advertising industry to identify sexist portrayals of men and women alike, and makes recommendations to Congress. Legislative reports, litigation updates, and research results are part of the monthly *Fathers for Equal Rights Newsletter.* The group also makes available the *National Congress for Men Directory,* which lists organizations active in divorce reform. Founded in 1981. 800 members. Contact Dick Woods, President.

National Cowboy Hall of Fame and Western Heritage Center

1700 NE 63rd St.
Oklahoma City, OK 73111   (405) 478-2250

Interested in preserving the heritage of the American West and in honoring the pioneers who developed the West? Well pilgrim, here's a group for you. The National Cowboy etc. operates the Hall of Fame of Great Westerners, Rodeo Hall of Fame, Gallery of Western Art, the John Wayne Collection, The West of Yesterday, and a museum of Western artifacts. It sponsors the annual Western Heritage Awards for best books, articles, poetry, television productions and motion pictures based on Western history. The group maintains biographical archives and a library of 9000 volumes on the American West. Its quarterly *Persimmon Hill* magazine contains historical and contemporary articles on the American West. The cowboy enthusiasts meet annually during March in Oklahoma City, OK. Founded in 1965. 3000 members. Contact Byron Price, Director.

National Displaced Homemakers Network (NDHN)

1625 K St. NW
Washington, DC 20006   (202) 628-6767

Members are displaced homemakers, displaced homemaker services, persons from related organizations, and supporters. Displaced homemakers are apparently women (mostly) whose chief occupation was maintaining their homes until something displaced them, preventing them from continuing with this work. The Network fosters development of programs and services for the homemakers without a home to make, acting as a clearinghouse to provide communications, technical assistance, public information, data collection, legislative monitoring, funding information, and other services. The group publishes the annual *Displaced Homemaker Program Directory,* as well as the quarterly newsletter *Network News* and the semiannual newsletter *Transition Times.* Founded in 1978. 4000 members. Contact Jill Miller, Executive Director.

National Elephant Collectors Society (NECS)

380 Medford St.
Somerville, MA 02145-3810   (617) 625-4067

Think big. NECS is a group for collectors of elephant memorabilia (the elephants themselves are too bulky to display properly) interested in contributing to and promoting the preservation of the elephant. NECS provides information on the origin, habitat, care, and folklore of the elephant. The group aids members in expanding collections through correspondence with other collectors and works with organizations to prevent the extinction of the elephant. It offers classes to school children in elephant collecting and maintains a small museum. Every so often the group publishes the *Jumbo Jargon* newsletter, with information on collectibles and upcoming elephant events. President Richard Massiglia says that

NECS is "in hiatus at the moment, due to my retirement and putting my new lifestyle in order. I intend to continue with the NECS in the near future." Founded in 1981. 700 members. Contact Richard W. Massiglia, President & Founder.

National Fantasy Fan Federation (N3F)
1920 Division St.
Murphysboro, IL 62966   (608) 684-6090

A correspondence club of persons interested in reading, writing, and collecting science fiction and fantasy books, magazines, articles, and other materials. Activities include an annual story contest. The club issues the bimonthly *The National Fantasy Fan*, covering federation activities, as well as the bimonthly *Tightbeam*. Founded in 1941. 300 members. Contact Lola Ann Center, Secretary.

National Father's Day Committee (NFDC)
47 W. 34th St.
New York, NY 10001   (212) 594-5977

Individuals and organizations "dedicated to building a permanently free democracy through wise parental influence of the young." A main activity of the group is encouraging others to properly observe Father's Day, a national holiday during which fathers are celebrated with ties and tools, created by a congressional act of April, 1972, to be observed on the third Sunday of June. The U.S. president, state governors, and former governors cooperate in observances of the committee, which sponsors an annual award banquet in New York City to honor Father of the Year and fathers in special categories, such as literature, philanthropy, stage, screen, sports, television, and radio. The group also sponsors Regional Father of the Year Award presentations throughout the country. Founded in 1937. Contact Theodore M. Kaufman, Executive Director.

National Federation of Grandmother Clubs of America (NFGCA)
203 N. Wabash Ave., Suite 702
Chicago, IL 60601   (312) 372-5437

Members are women who have grandchildren or have acquired them through marriage or adoption. The group sponsors National Grandmother's Day on the second Sunday in October and raises funds to support research on children's diseases, especially leukemia. NFGCA publishes quarterly *Autumn Leaves*, which includes a memorial list and club highlights. It holds an annual social. Founded in 1938. 8000 members. Contact Margaret Day, Office Manager.

National Fishing Lure Collectors Club (NFLCC)
PO Box 1791
Dearborn, MI 48121   (313) 842-2589

A club of lure, rod, reel, fish decoy, and tackle collectors. Honorary members are individuals who made significant contributions to fishing tackles prior to 1960. The group promotes tackle collecting and classifying and assists members with their appraisal and identification efforts. Members hold trading meetings and give talks at sport shows and for service organizations. Its quarterly magazine *NFLCC Gazette* includes information on tackle companies, tips and ideas, special feature stories, photographs, classified advertisements and drawings. The group meets annually, usually on the first weekend after July 4. Founded in 1976. 3000 members. Contact Rich Treml, Secretary Treasurer.

National FRUMPS of America (NFA)
PO Box 1047
Winter Park, FL 32790   (407) 644-3431

"Ordinary, average, grassroots" folks across the U.S. and in Canada, Mexico, England, New Zealand, and Australia (as well as one women in Moscow) organized to celebrate the joys of things mundane. The group believes that "ordinary" people can be extraordinary, and recognizes them by awarding Frump of the Year to the most deserving. Furthermore, the group has designated October 14th as National FRUMP Day. FRUMP is actually an acronym for frugal, responsible, unpretentious, mature persons. Right.

In addition to such passions as jello molds, lawn work, clipping coupons, and fuzzy slippers, the group believes in recycling discarded trash by making it into useful and/or decorative household items (the milk carton as art). Potential members take a quiz, which includes such questions as "Do you own any Elvis memorabilia?" and "Is your idea of an 'after hours' nightclub a 24-hour supermarket?" Among the many BIG dates on the FRUMPY social calendar are Andy Rooney's birthday on January 14 and July 20th's Ugly Truck Contest in Pelican Rapids, MN.

FRUMP Issues a monthly newsletter, of which it says, "Extremely good looking, intelligent, wealthy, outgoing, friendly, generous people need not write. Everyone else needs the *National Frumps of America Newsletter.*" Also known as the *FRUMP Update*, it includes profiles of the Celebrity Frump of the Month, money saving ideas (recycling out-of-date calendars), polyester fashion tips, the FRUMPY social calendar, unusual recipes (many involving hot dogs and unique treatment of leftovers), novelties, travel tips (traveling to garage sales, how to reach tourist traps by car), and an advice column. Celebrities who have been honored include Barbara Bush, Roseanne Arnold (Barr) and Phyllis Diller, Motel Six spokesperson Tom Bodett, Willard Scott, Erma Bombeck, Mister Rodgers, Peter "Columbo" Falk, Garrison Keilor, and Garfield the Cat. President "Auntie Barbara" has also authored *Auntie Barbara's Tips for an Ordinary Life* (Avon Books). Founded in 1965. 11,000 members. Contact "Auntie Barbara" Hovanetz, President & Founding Mother.

National Guild of Decoupeurs (NGD)
807 Rivard Blvd.
Grosse Pointe, MI 48230   (313) 882-0682

Seeks to distinguish decoupage as an art in itself and one that would be recognized for what it is by an average adult group. NGD identifies authentic decoupage and offers generalized and specialized educational programs, including a correspondence course (learn decoupage at home). The Guild publishes the bimonthly *Decoupage Dialogue* and meets annually, usually in April. Founded in 1971. 430 members. Contact Ann Standish, Executive Director.

National Headache Foundation (NHF)
5252 N. Western Ave.
Chicago, IL 60625   (312) 878-7715

The NHF was established to disseminate information on headache causes and treatment, fund scientific studies, and promote better public understanding of headache problems. It sponsors public education awareness seminars and issues the quarterly *National Headache Foundation-Newsletter.* Founded in 1970. 17,000 members. Contact Seymour Diamond M.D., Executive Director.

National Hemlock Society (HS)
PO Box 11830
Eugene, OR 97440-4030   (503) 342-5748

Individuals supporting the option of active voluntary euthanasia for the advanced terminally ill and the seriously incurably ill. Motto is, "Good Life, Good Death." HS promotes a climate of public opinion tolerant of the terminally ill individual's right to end his or her own life in a planned manner, and, as the Society puts it, "with dignity." The Society believes that the final decision to terminate one's life should be one's own. The group works to improve existing laws on assisted suicide, supporting the right of dying people to lawfully request that physicians help them die. It does not encourage suicide for any primary reason other than terminal illness (such as emotional, traumatic, or financial reasons) and approves of suicide prevention work.

While the group believes that the act of suicide is essentially private and familial, HS does publish informational material "to help members decide the manner of their death." Its *Hemlock Quarterly* is a newsletter focusing on right-to-die issues. Other publications include Derek Humphry's best-selling (and controversial) *Final Exit*, a guide to "selfdeliverance for the dying in the U.S." Humphry started the Society five years after assisting his first wife, who was suffering from cancer, to commit suicide. He later published a book on the incident, *Jean's Way.* The Society derives its name from the root plant *hemlock*, used in ancient Greece and Rome "for rational suicide, which under certain conditions, was acceptable to those societies. The death of Socrates is the most famous example." Founded in 1980. 46,000 members. Contact Derek Humphry, Founder & Executive Director.

National Historical Fire Foundation (NHFF)
6101 E. Van Buren
Phoenix, AZ 85008   (602) 275-3473

You won't want to miss NHFF's Hall of Flame Museum of antique fire fighting vehicles, equipment, documents, and publications. For those who just like reading about fire fighting, the group maintains an 8,000 item library of books, newspaper clippings, manuscripts, and statistics. Founded in 1961. Contact P. M. Molloy, Executive Director.

National Hobo Association (NHA)
World Way Center
Box 90430
Los Angeles, CA 90009   (213) 645-1500

Motto might be: "On the road again." A club for people interested in preserving and maintaining the vagabond lifestyle and historical and contemporary hobo literature. NHA seeks to dispel negative myths about hobos, operating the hobo hall of fame and maintaining biographical archives and a 3000-volume library which includes hobo newspapers and personal history letters. Fellow hobos read all the news they need in the bimonthly *Hobo Times.* Vacationing hobos can pick up the *Hobo Travel Guidebook,* while mere hobo enthusiasts may want to view the videotape, *The Great American Hobo.* The hobos annually gather. Founded in 1979. 2500 members. Contact Garth W. Bishop, Executive Director.

National Horseshoe Pitchers Association of America (NHPA)
Box 278
Munroe Falls, OH 44262   (216) 923-9949

A group solidly supporting the sport of horseshoe pitching on all levels, both as a recreational pastime and competitive sport. NHPA, which has established a unified code of rules, equipment, and playing procedures, sponsors an annual world tournament and other competitive events. The group makes available game-related items including official shoes, trophies, scoresheets, and ringer charts. Founded in 1909. 15,000 members. Contact Donnie Roberts, Secretary Treasurer.

National Investigations Committee on Unidentified Flying Objects (NICUFO)
14617 Victory Blvd., Suite 4
Van Nuys, CA 91411   (818) 989-5942

NICUFO members are interested in investigating "the truth concerning UFOs and associated phenomena." The group probes UFO reports and relates findings to governmental agencies and the public via the press, radio, television, and newsletters. Members are confidentially apprised of UFO activities in the monthly *Confidential Space-Link Letter* and the quarterly *UFO Journal,* which provides accounts of sightings of UFOs worldwide. The group annually meets and also holds monthly UFO, space, and science meeting. Founded in 1967. 1000 members. Contact Dr. Frank E. Stranges, President.

National Leather Association (NLA)
PO Box 17463
Seattle, WA 98107   (206) 789-8990

Individuals and organizations promoting the right of consenting adults to engage in nontraditional sexual practices, particularly those involving sadomasochism, leather, and fetishism (S&M, L&F). NLA seeks to establish and maintain a communication, education, and support network for members of the "leather/SM/fetish community" worldwide. The group conducts political activism and public education to remove misconceptions about and protect the constitutional rights of members.

The Leather Association supports and raises funds on behalf of individuals, corporations, and institutions that work for the decriminalization of all sexual acts between consenting adults. It also conducts outreach programs for women, minorities, the physically challenged, and other groups that have traditionally been excluded from the Leather/SM/fetish community. Additionally, NLA works to preserve records of the history, traditions, and culture of individuals whose sexual practices involve leather, sadomasochism, and fetishism. To get the word out on leather and its properties, the group bestows the annual Man and Woman of the Year awards, publishes the monthly *First Link,* and sponsors the annual Living in

Leather Conference (with exhibits). Founded in 1986. Contact George Nelson, Secretary.

National Little Britches Rodeo Association (NLBRA)
1045 W. Rio Grande
Colorado Springs, CO 80906   (303) 389-0333

NLBRA is a nationwide outdoor sports activity organization for youths featuring all the rugged events of professional rodeo for contestants ages eight through 18. The group aims to perfect standards of competition, rules, and controls for the benefit of youths, safeguard their interests, and promote within them the qualities of good character, sportsmanship, and citizenship. It sponsors the annual National Finals rodeo for competitors who have qualified in local rodeos. Founded in 1952. 5000 members. Contact Jim Chamley, General Manager.

National Lum and Abner Society (NLAS)
Route 3, Box 110
Dora, AL 35062   (205) 648-6110

Individuals interested in the *Lum and Abner* radio series and its creators, Chester Lauck and Norris Goff. The Society operates a tape library of original broadcasts. Members get the latest on Lum and Abner in the bimonthly *Jot 'Em Down Journal* and gather annually during June in Mena, AR. Founded in 1984. 350 members. Contact Tim Hollis, Executive Secretary.

National Mother's Day Committee
1328 Broadway
New York, NY 10001   (212) 594-6421

Affiliated with the aforementioned National Father's Day Committee, the Mom's Day Committee is a group of individuals and organizations "dedicated to building a permanently free democracy through wise parental influence of the young." The group sponsors an annual banquet in New York City to honor Mother of the Year and mothers in special categories. Mother's Day is a national holiday by congressional act in 1914, observed on the second Sunday of May. Founded in 1941. Contact Theodore M. Kaufman, Executive Director.

National Odd Shoe Exchange (NOSE)
PO Box 56845
Phoenix, AZ 85079   (602) 246-8725

NOSE is a service organization which brings together persons with mutual shoe problems (foot amputees and persons having feet which differ physically due to disease, injury, or accident). Some 70% of the population has one foot that's slightly larger than the other. Among roughly one quarter of these people, the difference is as much as one full shoe size or more. Members are matched with others around the country who have the same shoe sizes (but on opposite feet), have similar ages and tastes in shoe styles, and have extra shoes or are seeking someone with whom to exchange mismated footwear. Members then buy two pairs of shoes and send the unused ones to their "sole mates." The group also operates an odd glove exchange program, maintains the National Odd Shoe Foundation, and plans to operate National Odd Shoe Store. It awards certificates of appreciation to people who donate shoes, money, or time. The latest in odd shoe news is covered in the semiannual *Exchange News*. Founded in 1944. 15,000 members. Contact Jeanne L. Sallman, Director.

National Old-Time Fiddlers' Association (NO-TFA)
PO Box 1427
Truth Or Consequences, NM 87901   (505) 894-3503

The Old-Time Fiddlers' are dedicated to the coordination of the revival and preservation of old-time fiddle music within the United States. It sponsors contests and meets annually, fiddles at the ready. Founded in 1967. 2000 members. Contact Wes Nivens, President.

National Order of Trench Rats (NOTR)
PO Box 20538
Veradeton, FL 34203   (813) 751-5997

Fraternal organization of male members of the Disabled American Veterans whose membership is by election. NOTR promotes the fellowship of ex-servicemen "for the further benefit of the disabled man and to provide a fun and philanthropic order for the Disabled American Veterans." It contributes funds to assist in DAV legislative program and hospital work. Officers are given such titles as Golden Rodent, Silver Rodent, Blue Rodent, Bubonic Plague, Black Plague, Hole-y Rat, and Iron Claw. Founded in 1924. 7500 members. Contact Lee A. Henderson, Executive Secretary Treasurer.

National Organization for Changing Men (NOCM)
794 Pennsylvania Ave.
Pittsburgh, PA 15221   (412) 371-8007

NOCM has sponsored the National Conference on Men and Masculinity, participants of which were men "dedicated to the notion of male liberation" who believe that, in order to be emotionally healthy, men must reject "the enslaving macho code of honor" and develop the "feminine" sides of their personalities. NOCM promotes communication between members and other gay-affirmative, pro-feminist, and male supportive groups. It publishes the quarterly *Brother* newsletter, which includes task force updates, interviews and articles concerning men's issues, a calendar of events, and research updates. Contact Geof Morgan, Co-Chairman.

National Organization for Men (NOM)
381 Park Ave. S.
New York, NY 10016   (212) 686-MALE

Men and women united in efforts to promote and advance the equal rights of men in matters such as affirmative action programs, alimony, child custody, men's health, child abuse, battered husbands, divorce, educational benefits, military conscription, and veterans' benefits. NOM maintains the Institute for the Study of Matrimonial Laws, established as a research and education foundation for the study of the nation's divorce, alimony, and custody and visitation laws. The group maintains a 30,000-volume library of newspaper clippings on "the continuing universal battle of the sexes," divorce, and custody cases. It plans to establish the Men's Library and Research Center and Men's Legal Defense Fund. NOM bestows the Wimp Award to any public figure who denigrates the male gender and keeps members informed of the men's rights battlefront bimonthly through *The Quest* newsletter. Founded in 1983. 10,000 members. Contact Sidney Siller, Founder & President.

National Organization for the Reform of Marijuana Laws (NORML)
1636 R St. NW, No. 3
Washington, DC 20009   (202) 483-5500

NORML is a public education organization working to change U.S. policy regarding marijuana. The group seeks an end to all criminal penalties for personal possession, use, and cultivation of marijuana. In support of this goal, NORML provides speakers for interested groups and provides testimony for legislative committees. It also disseminates information on urinalysis testing. Members get the latest news on bogus herb laws through the *National Organization for the Reform of Marijuana Laws-The Leaflet*, a quarterly newsletter reporting on the legal, health, and social aspects of marijuana use. The newsletter updates legislative and NORML activities and contains analyses of government studies and reports on the use and production of marijuana. Other publications include the monthly *Pot-porri* and *Common Sense for America,* a semiannual magazine. Founded in 1970. 80,000 members. Contact Donald B. Fiedler, Director.

National Organization of Mall Walkers (NOMW)
PO Box 191
Hermann, MO 65041   (314) 486-3945

Members walk through shopping malls as a sort of physical fitness program. NOMW supports their desire to hike through shopping paradises by sponsoring walking events and sports and fitness promotional programs and by bestowing awards for distance milestones. The mall walkers receive the quarterly *Heart and Sole Newsletter,* covering health and nutrition issues. Founded in 1988. 5000 members. Contact Thomas Cabot, President.

National Organization Taunting Safety and Fairness Everywhere (NOT SAFE)
PO Box 5743EA
Montecito, CA 93150   (805) 969-6217

Motto is "If it's worth doing right . . . it's worth over-doing." Members of Congress, corporate executives, journalists, scientists, and professionals who advocate free-market and libertarian principles belong to NOT SAFE. The group gleefully provides a platform from which problems of government "stupidity" can be attacked with wit, satire, and overkill. Describing itself as "the world's most sarcastic organization," NOT SAFE uses wooden nickels with slogans such as "Help Abolish Everything" to humorously lampoon bureaucrats. It maintains a file of government-gone-berserk cases and bestows the annual Stir-the-Pot Award to an individual demonstrating "undaunted courage in the face of bureaucratic intimidation." Committees include the Coalition to Ban Cruellers and the Committee to Rename Obscene American Cities. Members are kept somewhat current on stupid government tricks through the annual *Quagmire* newsletter. The group sponsors an annual think-in on February 30 in Montecito, CA.

Items from the NOT SAFE manifesto: the group believes 99% of all aircraft accidents could be eliminated if aircraft were required to taxi to their destinations. It calls for warning labels to be placed on "dangerous" banana peels, supports insect rights, and fights for mandatory motorcycle seatbelts. The group advocates a speed limit of 15 m.p.h. and encourages people to "stay in bed . . . but get plenty of exercise." Other areas of concern include bathtub safety (72,000 accidents per year), satanic rock music, video games, suggestive t-shirts, and the "jinx of junk food." NOT SAFE also cautions against stopping to smell the roses. "Do you realize," says founder Dale Lowdermilk, "that when you smell a flower you are putting your nose near the sexual organ of another species?" Let's be careful out there. Founded in 1980. 1400 members. Contact Dale Lowdermilk, Executive Director & Founder.

National Organization to Insure Survival Economics (NOISE)
12 W. 72nd St.
New York, NY 10023 (212) 787-1070

NOISE is a "one woman crusade to help the victims of divorce." The group(?) promotes programs to find new ways and means to cope with support problems for a family after a divorce (the mailing list for NOISE and the institute contains over 10,000 names). NOISE supports the idea of divorce insurance, to be given as a wedding gift by parents and grandparents or to be taken out at the time of marriage and to insure child support if the marriage should end in divorce. According to director Diana DuBroff, no enforcement laws would be necessary if support were insured and property settled before spouses file for divorce. DuBroff also advocates homemakers' services insurance and seeks to persuade insurance companies to provide Single Parent Living in Poverty (SLIP) coverage by circulating a petition. NOISE sponsors the Institute for Practical Justice, a nationwide educational service which helps people resolve disputes and avoid litigation. Founded in 1972. Contact Diana D. DuBroff, Director.

National Peace Day Celebrations (NPDC)
93 Pilgrim Road
Concord, MA 01742 (508) 369-3751

A volunteer group of interfaith professionals and other interested individuals working to establish the first Sunday in August as the National Day of Peace. NPDC sponsors Celebrations of Peace Day to bring people of all opinions together in unity to reflect on peace and justice and to celebrate life. The group provides information and advice to churches, schools, other peace organizations, and individuals about organizing and conducting Peace Day celebrations. Founded in 1980. Contact Marie M. Strain, President.

National Police Bloodhound Association (NPBA)
RD 1, Box 345
Allenwood, PA 17810 (717) 538-9001

Law enforcement officers at all levels and search and rescue personnel with law enforcement affiliations dedicated to the advancement and training of the man-trailing abilities of the purebred bloodhound in law enforcement and search and rescue. NPBA conducts lectures on topics concerning working bloodhounds. It offers assistance from experts in mountain, desert, swamp, snow, city, and urban trailing. NPBA also makes available technical information on scent, the preservation of scent, and methods of developing cooperation from the departments. The group bestows the annual Sgt. Joe B. Marcum Award, named after Sgt. Marcum, and publishes all the news that a nose needs in the quarterly *Nose News*. Founded in 1962. 300 members. Contact Rebecca J. Shaffer, Secretary.

National Pop Can Collectors (NPCC)
1124 Tyler St.
Fairfield, CA 94533   (707) 426-5553

Collectors of soda cans and other interested individuals working to promote the collection of soda cans and associated items, including advertisements, bottles, openers, trays, and caps. NPCC publishes the monthly *Can-O-Gram* newsletter and holds an annual swap meet during June in Rockford, IL. Founded in 1976. 200 members. Contact Dave Brackett, Director.

National Privy Diggers Association (NPDA)
614 Park Dr.
Mechanicsville, VA 23111   (804) 746-9851

The Diggers are collectors of antique bottles dug from 19th century privies. NPDA promotes the collection and appreciation of antique bottles, provides advice on privy digging methods, and encourages members to locate privy sites and dig for bottles and other artifacts. and provides advice on methods of privy digging. Its monthly newsletter *The Privy* includes information on recent finds, possible locations of privies, and bottle exchange. Members meet annually and also gather for a quadrennial bottle show. Founded in 1985. 85 members. Contact Richard L. Wilcox, President.

National Puzzlers' League (NPL)
Box 9747
North Hollywood, CA 91609   (818) 982-0467

Hobbyists interested in word puzzles. NPL monthly issues *The Enigma*, containing verse puzzles, cryptograms, forms (word squares), and cryptic crossword puzzles. The group meets annually. Founded in 1883. 300 members. Contact Judith Bagai, Editor.

National Pygmy Goat Association (NPGA)
10000 Greenacres Dr.
Bakersfield, CA 93312   (805) 589-8081

Members are pygmy goat breeders, veterinarians, hobbyists, small livestock farmers, and medical research groups. The group encourages breeding and registration of pygmy goats and promotes the breed. The pygmy goat is noted for its hardiness and good nature, its ability to provide milk, its adaptability to climates, and its suitability as a research subject. NPGA sanctions shows and conducts judges' training school and workshops. It issues the quarterly *Pygmy Goat Memo* and meets annually. Founded in 1975. 1600 members. Contact Pam Ames, Business Manager.

National Reamer Collectors Association (NRCA)
Route 3, Box 67
Frederic, WI 54837   (715) 327-4365

Collectors and dealers interested in reamers (orange juicers and lemon squeezers). NRCA promotes reamer collecting and disseminates information about reamers. The group meets annually on the topic of reamers. Founded in 1980. 185 members. Contact Larry Branstad, Board Member.

National Scrabble Association (NSA)
PO Box 700
Greenport, NY 11944   (516) 477-0033

A club for Scrabble players. NSA sanctions, organizes, and publicizes Scrabble crossword game tournaments in the U.S. and Canada, including the biennial National Scrabble Championship. During tournament play, the group awards one Expert Point to each game winner; after a player accumulates 50 points, the NSA awards certification. NSA licenses Scrabble players clubs throughout the U.S. and Canada. The latest on block letters is reported in the bimonthly *Scrabble News.* The group also oversees compilation of the *Official Scrabble Players Dictionary,* which is the word authority of the NSA. Founded in 1972. 9000 members. Contact John D. Williams.

National Seafood Educators (NSE)
PO Box 60006
Richmond Beach, WA 98160   (206) 546-6410

No, they do not educate seafood; they educate people about seafood. NSE also educates the public about nutrition and promotes the consumption of seafood. The group has published two books: *Light-Hearted Seafood* and *Seafood: A Collection of Heart-Healthy Recipes.* Contact Janis Harsila.

National Society for Prevention of Cruelty to Mushrooms (NSPCM)
1077 S. Airport Road W.
Traverse City, MI 49684   (616) 941-0010

Teachers, students, businesspeople, accountants, landowners, and others united to "prevent cruelty to mushrooms and other neglected or mistreated forms of life, regardless of age, race, sex, religion or other stereotypical attributes." NSPCM sponsors food and clothing drives for the Hannaville Indians of Northern Michigan and hosts an annual Christmas ball. Founded in 1971. 1000 members. Contact Brad Brown, President.

National Society for Shut-Ins (NSFS)
PO Box 1392
Reading, PA 19603   (215) 374-2930

NSFS is a group of concerned individuals united to organize chapters throughout the country in order to educate people to care for and visit shut-ins. The group seeks to promote a sense of emotional and spiritual well-being and self-worth in individuals who are confined to their homes or institutions, due to age, sickness, handicap, or imprisonment (inclusively, "shut-ins"). The Society has designated the third Sunday in October each year as National Shut-In Day, encouraging people to visit the sick, elderly, and imprisoned on that day. Activities include annual Sunshine Day, 24 hours of entertainment and recreation for shut-ins away from the home or institution; National Shut-In Day and Sunshine Week, fostering public recognition of the plight of shut-ins; and Sunshine Productions, producing amateur musical performances for the enjoyment and benefit of shut-ins. It also sponsors Project SUNSHINE, promoting visitation and performance of service by volunteer high school and college students, civic clubs, and church groups to institutionalized and homebound shut-ins. Members receive the quarterly *Sunshine News.* Founded in 1970. Contact Mary Lou Pollock, President.

National Space Club (NSC)
655 15th St. NW, No. 300
Washington, DC 20005

A nontechnical organization of individuals and companies affiliated with the missile and space fields in government, industry, the military, and the press. NSC seeks to establish and maintain U.S. space leadership and stimulate the advancement of peaceful and military applications of space flight and related technologies. The Club sponsors the Robert H. Goddard Historical Essay Competition and holds the annual National Space Outlook Conference. Founded in 1957. 1700 members. Contact Rory Heydon, Executive Director.

National Space Society (NSS)
922 Pennsylvania Ave., SE
Washington, DC 20003   (202) 543-1900

Individuals dedicated "to convincing our nation and its leadership of the critical need for a growing progressive American technology for which a strong space program provides the *thrust and momentum.*" NSS provides a forum for public participation to help insure that the space program is responsive to public priorities. It inspires space enthusiasts to elicit their responses to key issues on the space program and works to promote and create self-sustaining communities, large-scale industrialization, and private enterprise in space. Space news is reported in the monthly *Ad Astra,* a nontechnical magazine covering national and international space exploration and development. The group meets annually on Memorial Day weekend. Founded in 1987. 30,000 members. Contact Lori B. Garver, Executive Director.

National Square Dance Convention (NSDC)
2936 Bella Vista
Midwest City, OK 73110-4199   (405) 732-0566

NSDC is a liaison organization of square dance clubs and dancers whose purpose is to sponsor its convention, which includes square and round dancing, folk dancing, and contra and old-time dancing. That's a whole lot of dancing going on. The group publishes the annual *National Square Dance Convention-Membership Directory,* which lists more than 10,000 square, round, contra, and clogging clubs, and the quarterly journal *National Squares.* Founded in 1952. 25,000 members. Contact Howard B. Thornton, Director of Information.

National Story League (NSL)
52 Stephen F. Austin
Conroe, TX 77302   (409) 273-5100

NSL members are teachers, social workers, librarians, Sunday school teachers, and others interested in children's work. The group strives "to encourage the creation and appreciation of the good and beautiful in life and literature through the art of storytelling." It seeks to discover the "best" stories in the world's literature and tell them to young people with love and sympathy.

Members volunteer to tell and record stories in schools, churches, children's and old persons' homes, hospitals, and playgrounds. The group publishes *Story Art*, a quarterly magazine. Founded in 1903. 15,000 members. Contact Elizabeth Raabe, President.

National Task Force on Prostitution (NTFP)
333 Valencia St., Suite 101
San Francisco, CA 94103   (415) 558-0450

"Call Off Your Old Tired Ethics" (COYOTE) is the alternate name for this collection of prostitutes' rights organizations, whose members include prostitutes, former prostitutes, lawyers, social service providers, and other individuals, as well as women's groups and criminal justice and religious organizations. Their long-range goal is the decriminalization of prostitution and "the removal of the stigmas associated with female sexuality." The task force seeks to protect working prostitutes from arrests for loitering and from entrapment by vice squad policemen.

Activities include referrals to competent lawyers for arrested prostitutes, assistance in obtaining social aid, and coordinating a national campaign. COYOTE has created pressure groups to deal with the criminal justice system and lobby in the state legislature. It maintains a library on sex, women, and prostitution. Founded in 1973. Contact Sharon Kiser, Executive Director.

National Tattoo Association (NTA)
PO Box 2063
New Hyde Park, NY 11040   (516) 747-6953

Organized tattooers who promote tattooing as a viable contemporary art form and seek to upgrade the standards and practices of tattooing. NTA also offers advice on selecting a tattoo artist and studio, and holds seminars for tattoo artists to improve their skills and learn better hygienic practices. The latest in tattoo news and trends is covered in the bimonthly *National Tattoo Association-Newsletter*. Founded in 1974. 1000 members. Contact Florence Makofske, Secretary Treasurer.

National Thanksgiving Commission (NTC)
PO Box 1777
Dallas, TX 75221   (214) 969-1977

These appreciative folks preserve and promote the tradition of Thanksgiving in the United States, with emphasis on the expression of gratitude and praise to God for humankind's blessings. The commission prepares a draft of Presidential Proclamations for the National Day of Prayer as well as Presidential Thanksgiving Proclamations.

National Toothpick Holder Collector's Society (NTHCS)
PO Box 204
Eureka, IL 61530   (309) 467-2535

Members are collectors of antique and recently made toothpick holders who aim to share their information and knowledge about toothpick holders with the rest of the world. The Society invites recognized authorities and researchers of glass and antiques to speak at meetings and has sponsored 12 limited editions of toothpick holders. Holders are covered in depth in the monthly *Toothpick Bulletin* containing information on identification of patterns, reproductions, and trading and selling. It also includes research reports (on toothpick holders). The holders of the holders meet annually on the second full weekend in August. Founded in 1973. 600 members. Contact Audrey Trumbold, Secretary.

National Tractor Pullers Association (NTPA)
6969 Worthington-Galena Road, Suite L
Worthington, OH 43085 (614) 436-1761

NTPA promotes and standardizes the rugged sport of tractor and truck pulling, a competition in which contestants try to pull a weighted sled with a tractor or truck farther than their opponents before its weight overcomes the power of their machines. The association's Pulling Foundation makes available scholarships and the group also maintains a tractor and truck pulling hall of fame. The Pullers publish the *Pull! Program and Yearbook*, a magazine covering all classes of NTPA competition, an overview of the previous year's champions, and stories on safety, sleds, vehicles, and drivers. Other publications include the monthly *Puller Magazine*, the annual *Pulling Rules: Official Rule Book*, and the monthly newsletter *Tire Tracks*. Founded in 1970. 5600 members. Contact David P. Schreier, Executive Director.

National Velthrow Association (NVA)

Velthrow is a game similar to darts, but played by throwing velcro balls at a soft board. This association of individual velthrowers, firms, and groups interested in participating in velthrow competitions promotes velthrow as an ideal office game that fosters unity and goodwill among workers. And if a thrown velthrow accidentally catches one in the head, there is far less damage than would occur with a dart, a disadvantage in some office settings. NVA maintains a velthrow museum and plans to publish a newsletter and directory. Founded in 1985. 80 members.

National Write Your Congressman (NWYC)
12115 Self Plaza
Dallas, TX 75218 (214) 324-5245

NWYC encourages and assists individuals in writing public officials by providing the research and tools needed to correspond with officials. The group offers the public pro and con issue information and voting records of members' legislators. It also conducts monthly polls on timely issues and reports results to Congress and the President. NWYC publishes *Congressmen's Voting Records* annually, and the *Legislative Update, Opinion Ballot*, and *Voters Voice* monthly. Founded in 1958. Contact Roger L. Adamson, President & CEO.

Native Daughters of the Golden West (NDGW)
543 Baker St.
San Francisco, CA 94117 (415) 563-9091

Native-born Californian women who work to promote the history of the State of California, venerate California pioneers, promote child welfare programs, assist in marking and restoring historic landmarks, and participate in civic affairs. NDGW publishes *California Star*, a bimonthly newsletter. Founded in 1886. 13,500 members. Contact Kay Kelly, Executive Secretary.

Native Sons of the Golden West (NSGW)
414 Mason St., Suite 300
San Francisco, CA 94102 (415) 392-1223

A fraternal society of men born in California, NSGW is dedicated to the preservation of the history and landmarks of California and the West. It publishes *The Native Son,* a bimonthly newsletter. Founded in 1875. 13,500 members. Contact Wesley Colgan Jr., Grand Secretary.

The Naturist Society (TNS)
PO Box 132
Oshkosh, WI 54902 (414) 426-5009

The society provides communication and coordination for the clothes-optional recreation movement as a natural solution to many problems of modern living. TNS maintains that "body acceptance is the idea, nude recreation is the way." It sends its message to members and the rest of the interested world through the quarterly *Nude and Natural* and the *World Guide to Nude Beaches and Recreation.* Founded in 1976. Contact Ronald A. Burich, Executive Director.

Naturists and Nudists Opposing Pornographic Exploitation (NOPE)
PO Box 2085
Rancho Cordova, CA 95741-2085 (408) 427-2858

NOPE participants uphold a "clothes-optional ethic" while confronting "pornographic values" in society. NOPE opposes what the group feels is corporate exploitation of human sexuality as seen in advertisements, beauty pageants, pornography, and also the nudist/naturist movement. The group addresses issues of rape, child pornography, and child molestation. NOPE publishes the newsletter *Iconoclast,* covering legal proceedings against pedophiles and other social developments relevant to the demand for pornography, and *CMAG.* Founded in 1987. Contact Nikki Craft, Director.

Negative Population Growth (NPG)
PO Box 1206
210 The Plaza
Teaneck, NJ 07666 (201) 837-3555

Members believe that "a drastic reduction in total population size represents the only viable option consistent with human survival." NPG promotes a 50% reduction in total world population growth over the next 90-100 years. It advocates that the birth rate be lowered by voluntary measures such as national population control programs, financial and tax incentives, and public education. Members receive *Human Survival* three times per year. The group meets annually on the third Wednesday in September in New York City. Founded in 1972. 6000 members. Contact Donald Mann, President.

New Moon Matchbox and Label Club (NMMLC)
Individuals interested in collecting and trading matchboxes and matchbox labels. Other keepers of the flame include the lighter-collectors of On the Lighter Side, cited elsewhere in this book. The

Club publishes the *New Moon Matchbox and Label Club Bulletin* five times per year. Founded in 1980. 125 members.

New Tribes Mission (NTM)
1000 E. First St.
Sanford, FL 32771-1487   (407) 323-3430

Ordained and licensed Protestant missionaries and members of the headquarters and missionary training schools staffs are members of this group, which undertakes evangelical missionary work among primitive tribes in Latin America, the Far East, and Africa. As part of its mission, NTM prints translated literacy materials, primers, and portions of Scripture and complete New Testaments in 20 tribal languages while working with more than 160 tribal languages (translating part or all of the Bible into about one-half these languages). The group publishes *Brown Gold,* a monthly, and *Field Papers,* a quarterly periodical. Founded in 1942. 2836 members. Contact Macon G. Hare, Chairman.

9 to 5, National Association of Working Women
614 Superior Ave. NW, Room 852
Cleveland, OH 44113   (216) 566-9308

The women office workers in 9 to 5 are building a national network of local office worker chapters, each of which strives to gain better pay, proper use of office automation, opportunities for advancement, elimination of sex and race discrimination, and improved working conditions for women office workers. A prime concern is the potential hazards of VDT screens to the office worker. 9 to 5 has introduced legislation or regulations at the state level to protect video display terminal (VDT) operators. It produces studies and research in areas such as reproductive hazards of VDTs, automation's effect on clerical employment, family and medical leaves, and stress, and conducts an annual summer school for working women. The group publishes the *9 to 5 Newsletter* five times per year, as well as *9 to 5: Working Women's Guide to Office Survival* and *Hidden Victims: Clerical Workers, Automations, and the Changing Economy.* Founded in 1973. 13,000 members. Contact Karen Nussbaum, Executive Director.

1904 World's Fair Society
529 Barcia
Rock Hill, MO 63119   (314) 968-2810

The Society seeks to preserve the memory and memorabilia of the 1904 Louisiana Purchase Exhibition, a world's fair held in St. Louis, Missouri, to celebrate the 100th anniversary of the Louisiana Purchase. Members receive word on fair-related activities and collectibles through the monthly *World's Fair Bulletin* and dine annually at a December 1st banquet, commemorating the closing day of the fair. Founded in 1986. 300 members. Contact Max Storm, President.

No Business As Usual (NBAU)
PO Box 2139
New York, NY 10108

Individuals and organizations united to prevent world war and to promote the slogan, "They won't listen to reason, they won't be bound by votes; the governments must be stopped from launching WWIII, no matter what it takes." Catchy. NBAU organizes local and national activities against war with the aim of disrupting and shutting down the daily routine of war preparations as much as possible. NBAU coordinates mass political actions, demonstrations, and teach-in programs. Activists are alerted through the monthly *No Business As Usual Newsletter*. Founded in 1984. Contact Al Binar.

No Kidding! (NK)
Box 76982, Station S
Vancouver, BC, Canada V5R 5S7   (604) 538-7736

A group of married and single individuals who, "for whatever reason," do not have children. The group holds two to six social functions a month, as well as occasional meetings. At the functions, members talk about "careers, studies, travels, interests, sex, politics, and religion . . . but rarely, if ever, about children. It's not that ₉children' is a taboo subject," the group's founder explains, "it's simply not an issue with us." Functions have included wine and cheese parties, water-skiing, sailing, cycling, holiday parties, comedy nights, an almost-annual yard sale and barbecue, and "very softball games (we use a *rubber* ball)." A plus is that no one needs a babysitter. Founded in 1984. Contact Jerry Steinberg, Founder.

North American Bungee Association (NABA)
11593 North Shore Dr., Suite 12C
Reston, VA 22090   (703) 435-0800

Thrill-seeking members of this group periodically perch atop various types of high platforms (bridges, towers, cranes, or hot air balloons), then jump off them. First, though, they carefully harness themselves to the platforms with very long rubber bungee cords, which prevent the brave leapers from actually landing, instead causing them to rebound in spectacular fashion, their blood rushing helter-skelter while they bob up and down like yo-yos of the gods, enabling them to feel that they have just had an acute life experience and necessitating a change of underwear. The association serves as a means of communication among bungee jumpers, educates members on the skills and safety precautions involved in the sport, and plans to offer training and an insurance plan. It publishes the magazine *Bungee Cords* and hosts an annual competition. Founded in 1991. 130 members. Contact Nancy Frase, Founder.

North American Fuzzy Information Processing Society (NAFIPS)
State University of New York
Department of System Sciences
Binghamton, NY 13901   (607) 777-6509

NAFIPS comprises civil and electrical engineers, systems scientists, mathematicians, operations researchers, computer scientists, knowledge engineers, and logicians who promote the scientific study and dissemination of applications and theories of fuzzy sets ("fuzzy" being a technical—not a tactile—term), logic, and measures. NAFIPS publishes the quarterly *International Journal of Approximate Reasoning*. Founded in 1981. 150 members. Contact Prof. George Klir, President.

North American Swing Club Association (NASCA)

PO Box 7128
Buena Park, CA 90622   (714) 821-9953

Individuals, clubs, and organizations interested in the alternative life-style known as swinging (recreational social sex). NASCA presents swinging as a viable life-style to the public. Objectives are to protect members of the swinging community against unfair or harmful business practices; develop a set of standards and etiquette for swinging; present swinging to the communications media in a nonexploitive and factual manner; and encourage participation in swinging. The group acts as a clearinghouse and resource center for the dissemination of social and sexual research data, and maintains archives on swinging since 1969. It publishes the bimonthly *Emerge Playcouple Newsletter,* the quarterly *NASCA Inside Report,* and the annual *NASCA Swing Clubs and Publications Directory.* Founded in 1980. 500 members. Contact Robert L. McGinley Ph.D., President.

North American Tiddlywinks Association (NATwA)

10416 Haywood Dr.
Silver Spring, MD 20902   (301) 681-9345

These serious sportsmen and women promote the growth of the highly competitive but oft-overlooked game of tiddlywinks. They provide a framework for all levels of competition and ensure the availability of regulation sets and mats. In addition to recruiting new players. NATwA sponsors informal and formal matches, including continental and collegiate team championships and pairs and singles matches. The group maintains archives of tiddlywinks publications, media reports, tournament records and statistics, and historical research notes. Yes, historical research notes (this is serious stuff). NATwA also maintains the "Closet of Fame," containing equipment and clothing used by famous players. Membership stays informed about the fascinating world of tiddlywinks by receiving *Newswink* semiannually. Other publications include the *Rules of Tournament Tiddlywinks,* and songbooks for those who like to sing while they tiddly. Founded in 1966. 100 members. Contact Larry Kahn, Secretary General.

North Central Name Society (NCNS)

Waubonsee Community College
Sugar Grove, IL 60554   (708) 466-4811

What's in a name? Why letters of course. Members of NCNS like to compile and study place names, personal names, and names in literature, especially those found in Illinois, Indiana, Iowa, Kentucky, Michigan, Ohio, and Wisconsin (although membership is not restricted to the north central United States). The group annually publishes the aptly titled *Bulletin of the North Central Name Society* and *Journal of the North Central Name Society.* Founded in 1980. 75 members. Contact Laurence E. Seits, Executive Secretary.

Northeast Rat and Mouse Club (NRMC)

506 Merlins Lane
Herndon, VA 22070-3121   (703) 437-7480

Rodent-loving individuals interested in rats and mice as pets or show animals, who gather to promote the enjoyment of rats and mice. To display rats and mice in a better, more affectionate light, NRMC conducts educational programs, holds shows, and publishes the bimonthly *Journal of the NRMC*. Founded in 1989. 200 members. Contact Judith Bertman-Trotter, Vice President.

Northern Cross Society (NCS)
R.R. 1, Box 325
Lecompton, KS 66050

So you're looking for a hobby to add a little extra zest to your life? NCS is calling. Members are backpackers, climbers, hunters, pilots, explorers, mariners, and professional adventurers "dedicated to the preparation for a potential survival experience." Areas of interest include preparing for socioeconomic collapse, natural disasters, and global thermonuclear war (remember the canned goods). NCS educates members in the application of survival techniques and equipment and coordinates private search-and-rescue teams through local chapters. The Northern Cross Register file lists members available for seminars, research, and expeditions, from which membership dossiers can be distributed to scientific, educational, outdoor-oriented organizations, and other potential clients who wish to engage society members for private employment as instructors, guides, consultants, research team members, or professional adventurers. The group presents an annual award for the best nonfiction book in survival literature and the Northern Cross Survivor Award to a person exhibiting outstanding courage and resourcefulness during a survival experience. Founded in 1983. 1400 members. Contact Dennis A. Baranski, Chairman.

Notch
115 Arlington St.
Asheville, NC 28801   (704) 252-7133

This group represents "notch babies," individuals born between 1917-21. It seeks to restore members' social security benefits to their pre-1977 levels. Members' benefits were reduced in 1977 due to fears that the social security system was becoming insolvent. Notch believes that the social security system's financial problems have since been solved. Contact Wilma Rogers, Founder.

Nudist Information Center (NIC)
PO Box 512
Daggett, CA 92327   (619) 254-2500

NIC answers inquiries about the nudist life-style, like "how come no one here is wearing any clothes?" The Center provides information on nudist facilities, conducts public relations activities, and provides lectures for radio and television talk shows. Founded in 1981. Contact Suzy Davis, Owner-Operator.

Occidental Society of Metempiric Analysis (OSMA)
32055 Hwy. 24E
Simla, CO 80835

OSMA investigates all types of metempiric phenomena (unexplained occurrences ignored or discounted by scientists) such as sightings of UFOs, aliens, ghosts, and Bigfoot. The group provides investigative and research services and offers research assistance by providing cassette-recorded answers to research questions (for a fee). It maintains biographical archives and a 1,500-volume library on metempirical, occult, and UFO topics. Members confer annually on October 10 in Simla, Colorado. Founded in 1977. 275 members. Contact Robert J. Everhart, CEO & Founder.

Occupied Japan Club (OJC)
29 Freeborn St.
Newport, RI 02840   (401) 846-9024

Also known as the O.J. Club, OJC is comprised of individual collectors of items manufactured in Japan during the U.S. occupation (1945-52) and stamped "Made in Occupied Japan." Objectives are to exchange information and to increase individual collections through trading and buying. OJC publishes *The Upside Down World of an O.J. Collector,* a monthly newsletter that is printed right side up. Founded in 1979. 283 members. Contact Florence Archambault, Secretary & Editor.

Of a Like Mind (OALM)
PO Box 6021
Madison, WI 53716   (608) 838-8629

Members of the OALM network are women who consider themselves "to be on a positive path to spiritual growth." The network operates a round robin letter exchange for women to "share our knowledge, feelings, dreams, and visions." OALM also publishes a quarterly newspaper that includes spiritual information (about astrology, tarot, dreams, herbs, ethics, politics, herstory, etc.) and individual professional and personal listings. Founded in 1978.

Official Betty Boop Fan Club (OBBFC)
6073 De La Vista
Riverside, CA 92509-5812   (714) 784-1888

The Boop Club includes both individual collectors of Betty Boop memorabilia and businesses that sell Boop collectibles (Betty Boop was a cartoon character who debuted in 1930.) It informs Boop members of broadcasts of their heroine's cartoons and the availability of merchandise. News on Boop and Boop items appears in the quarterly *Official Betty Boop Fan Club Newsletter.* Founded in 1986. 600 members. Contact Barbara West, President.

Official Gumby Fan Club (OGFC)
PO Box 3905
Schaumburg, IL 60168   (708) 893-6214

Fans of the animated character Gumby, who was created in 1956 by Art Clokey and currently appears in a syndicated cartoon series. The Official Club makes available discounts on Gumby-related items and keeps members informed of the little green fella's public and media appearances. Gumby news is discussed in the *Gumby Gram* newsletter. Founded in 1985. 8400 members. Contact A. J. Marsiglia, Director.

Official Rocky Horror Fan Club (ORHFC)
204 W. 20th St.
New York, NY 10011

Fans of the cult film *The Rocky Horror Picture Show.* Need we say more? Contact Bruce Cutter, Representative.

Old Boys Network Turtle Club (OBNTC)
Box 1553
Corinth, MS 38834

Members are "fun-loving folks who are willing to stick their necks out to succeed." The Turtle Club promotes a feeling of fair play, clean thoughts, and a sense of humor. Founded in 1951. 7500 members. Contact Bill Caruth, Chief Turtle Herder.

Old Mine Lamp Collectors Society of America (OMLCSA)
4537 Quitman St.
Denver, CO 80212   (303) 455-3922

Collectors of pre-electric underground illuminating devices. Members see the light via the newsletter, *The Underground Lamp Post.* Founded in 1967. 400 members. Contact Henry Pohs, Editor.

Old Old Timers Club (OOTC)
PO Box 637
Vineyard Haven, MA 02568

Members are men and women active in amateur radio communication forty or more years ago. It seeks to provide contact between members through radio communication and publications, such as the bimonthly *Spark Gap Times* and the *Old Old Timers Blue Book*, with career sketches and photographs of members. The Old Old Timers Club is distinct from the merely Old Timers' Club, whose members have been licensed for at least 20 years. Founded in 1947. 2615 members. Contact Duncan Kreamer, President.

Old Sleepy Eye Collectors' Club of America (OSECCA)
Box 12
Monmouth, IL 61462   (309) 734-4933

Individuals interested in Old Sleepy Eye pottery and mill items. Old Sleepy Eye is a logotype of an Indian head profile which has been imprinted on various stoneware, pottery, and advertising items since the late 19th century. OSECCA fosters interest in and knowledge of Old Sleepy Eye. Founded in 1976. 1000 members. Contact Betty Hallam, Secretary Treasurer.

Old Timers' Club (OTC)
American Radio Relay League
225 Main St.
Newington, CT 06111   (203) 666-1541

OTC is a group of recently licensed radio amateurs who first held a government license (operator or station) at least 20 years ago. The club is organized for certificate recognition of radio amateurs of long standing. Contact Eileen Sapko, Awards Manager.

Oldtime Radio-show Collector's Association (ORCA)
45 Barry St.
Sudbury, ON, Canada P3B 3H6   (705) 560-3095

Members are collectors and traders of old-time radio programs seeking to make available the widest selection of programs of the highest possible sound quality at the lowest possible cost. ORCA provides tape copies of children's stories to blind and handicapped children and tape copies of radio shows to blind and disabled adults. It also sponsors an annual Tape-In. Founded in 1979. 125 members. Contact Reg Hubert, President.

OMB Watch (OMBW)
1731 Connecticut Ave. NW, 4th Floor
Washington, DC 20009-1146   (202) 234-8494

The Watch collects, researches, and disseminates information on the federal Office of Management and Budget (OMB), particularly information affecting nonprofit and community-based organizations. OMBW advocates for more public accountability and increased public knowledge of administrative government issues. The group formed as a reaction to unnamed events that OMB Watch believes have invested the OMB with unprecedented powers and "allow it to remain unaccountable to Congress and the American people." The group is responsible for a flurry of publications discussing its mission, including the bimonthly magazine *Government Information Insider,* the bimonthly newsletter *OMB Watcher, Through the Corridors of Power: A Guide to Federal Rulemaking,* and *Using Community Right-to-Know: A Guide to a New Federal Law.* Founded in 1983. 1000 members. Contact Gary D. Bass Ph.D., Director.

Omega Project (OP)
PO Box 3821
Lihue, HI 96766   (808) 245-5374

Individuals dedicated to the distribution of worthwhile and meaningful writings to assist in the transition "from the Age of Darkness (Old Age) to the Age of Dawn (New Age)." The project sees the New Age as an age of optimism, peace, joy, love, cooperation, and Christ consciousness, changing from what they see as the Old Age consciousness of pessimism, negativity, hatred, and war. OP promotes a positive outlook and view of life. To get the word out on this new world, OP distributes a series of books and cassettes that deal with the unfolding of the New Age. Founded in 1983. Contact Richard Stong, Director.

On the Lighter Side, International Lighter Collectors (OL-SILC)
136 Circle Dr.
Quitman, TX 75783   (903) 763-2795

Members are interested in the history of lighters and lighter manufacturers (as opposed to matchboxes and matchbox labels, which are held dear by members of the New Moon Matchbox and Label Club). OLSILC facilitates the exchange of information and lighter trading among members, lights their fire with the bimonthly newsletter *On the Lighter Side,* and hosts the annual convention swarming with members armed with mucho lighters. Founded in 1984. 300 members. Contact Judith Sanders, Chairman.

1% for Peace
PO Box 658
Ithaca, NY 14851   (607) 273-1919

1% is a nonpartisan volunteer group devoted to creating a

positive peace agenda in the U.S. by mobilizing businesses and citizens. It seeks the passage of federal legislation to redirect one percent of the U.S. defense budget to fund "constructive, people-to-people programs for peace." Contact Neil Schwartzbach, Executive Officer.

One Person's Impact (OPI)
PO Box 751
Westborough, MA 01581   (508) 366-0146

Individuals, organizations, and businesses concerned about the environment and driven to promote individual environmental and social responsibility. The group encourages others "to believe what we are convinced is true—that all life is connected and every person can make a difference." OPI conducts educational programs on incorporating the ideas of social, economic, and environmental responsibility into everyday life. It publishes *One Person's Impact: Practical Actions for Conscious Living,* a bimonthly newsletter, as well as *Environmental Basics for Business, One Kid's Impact,* and *Earth Year Action Guide.* Founded in 1989. 1200 members. Contact Maria Valenti, President.

The One Shoe Crew (TOSC)
86 Clavela Ave.
Sacramento, CA 95828   (916) 682-7655

TOSC is a service organization that finds cost-sharing partners for people who wear only one shoe or those who wear two mismated shoes. Clients include individuals with mismatched feet, amputees, people wearing a brace on one foot, and anyone with a one-sided foot problem who still wears one regular shoe. The Crew matches shoe size and width of clients seeking partners. Clients indicate the general shoe style they prefer and receive pictures of what is available in their size and width. Over 25,000 shoes are available. The shoes are free; clients must pre-pay shipping only. The Crew publishes *The One Shoe Crew News,* a newsletter that includes practical tips and advice. Founded in 1986. 600 members. Contact Georgia M. Hehr R.N., Director.

Open Minded Comics Club (OMCC)
115 Shoreham Way
Merrick, NY 11566

The goal of the OMCC is to help member comic artists and writers develop their skills. A primary activity is the production of the club's monthly newsletter, *Open Minded Comics,* containing stories and art by members. Founded in 1975. 75 members. Contact Aaron M. Deutsch, Founder & President.

Optimist International (OI)
4494 Lindell Blvd.
St. Louis, MO 63108   (314) 371-6000

Ever positive, hopeful, and—yes—optimistic, these business, industrial, and professional service clubs aid and encourage the development of youth and promote active interest in good government and civic affairs. The Optimists' motto is "Friend of Youth." Optimist International publishes two monthlies: *The Optimist Hotline* and *The Optimist Magazine.* Founded in 1919. 160,000 members. Contact Richard Arnold, Executive Secretary.

Organ Clearing House (OCH)

PO Box 104
Harrisville, NH 03450-0104   (603) 827-3055

A group whose motto might be "Organs r us." OCH facilitates the relocation of used pipe organs that might otherwise be discarded and provides interested churches with information about such instruments. According to the group, a used pipe organ can be purchased, moved, renovated, and installed for about the same cost as an electronic substitute and for considerably less than the cost of a new pipe organ. This is important to know if you have an old pipe organ just gathering dust or are out shopping for a new set of pipes. The Clearing House maintains and disseminates list of old organs for sale and recommends organ builders and consultants on request. It supplies historical information about particular organs and their builders through the Organ Historical Society. Founded in 1959. Contact Alan M. Laufman, Executive Director.

Organization for Collectors of Covered Bridge Postcards (OCCBP)

Seven Squantum St.
Milton, MA 02186   (617) 698-9025

Just like the names says: these folks have banded together to organize the collecting of postcards of covered bridges. Their monthly newsletter is called *The Bridge-Covered*, in which they publish poems and articles. Founded in 1977. 346 members. Contact Kay Lloyd, Director.

Original Gilligan's Island Fan Club (OGIFC)

PO Box 25311
Salt Lake City, UT 84125-0311

Not just the Gilligan's Island Fan Club, but the *Original* number. These fans of the television series *Gilligan's Island*, which aired from 1964 to 1967, promote interest in the show and the cast. The pioneering club publishes *Gilligan's Island News*, a quarterly newsletter. Founded in 1972. 600 members. Contact Bob Rankin, Executive Officer.

Ornamental Fish International (OFI)

U.S. Branch Office
102 Charlton St.
New York, NY 10014   (212) 741-1023

There's a world of ornamental fish farmers out there, and they've united to promote the practical and technical development of international aquaculture, especially ornamental fish farming, and to develop and maintain high standards in the industry. The group adheres to international legislation and regulation concerning conservation and the protection of endangered species. Its annual conference location alternates between the U.S. and Germany, and its annual general assembly always takes place in May. Founded in 1979. 145 members. Contact Dino Barbarısı, Vice President.

Our World—Underwater Scholarship Society (OW-UWSS)

PO Box 4428
Chicago, IL 60680   (312) 427-5676

Members of Our World include individuals, organizations, and corporations who promote public education in underwater and water-related activities. The society stresses the responsibilities of sports diving, encourages environmental conservation, hosts "in-depth" (get it?) workshops on related subjects, and bestows scholarships to individuals planning a career in a water-related discipline. Founded in 1970.

Outward Bound (OB)
384 Field Point Road
Greenwich, CT 06830 (203) 661-0797

Outward Bound was founded in Wales in 1941 by Dr. Kurt Hahn to develop both the will and the skill to survive in young seamen who were "outward bound" to the sea and to life. The group currently operates five wilderness schools and six urban centers in the U.S. to help young people and adults discover and extend their own resources and abilities by confronting them with a series of increasingly difficult challenges. Programs operate in 22 states and other areas, including the Rocky Mountains of Colorado, the Superior-Quetico Wilderness area of northern Minnesota, Hurricane Island off the coast of Maine, Oregon's Cascade range, Pisgah National Forest in North Carolina, New York City, Kenya, Nepal, and the Commonwealth of Independent States (that's the U.S.S.R.).

Each school offers courses of four to 90 days' duration, which include physical conditioning, technical training, team training, expeditions, care of the environment, and community service. Technical emphasis is in areas such as camping skills, mountain and rock climbing, canoeing, sailing, river rafting, cycling, kayaking, and orienteering as well as emergency medical aid, evacuation, and search and rescue techniques. Approximately 28,000 hardy people take part in these courses each year, about one-fifth of whom receive financial aid from the group.

Outward Bound also offers substance abuse, mental health, and professional development seminars, and courses for Vietnam veterans and youth at risk. Has assisted in establishing a training program for Peace Corps Volunteers; presently over 250 schools are using Outward Bound methods. Publishes the *OB Newsletter,* the annual *Outward Bound Catalog and Report,* and the book *Outward Bound USA.* Founded in 1962. Contact John F. Raynolds III, President.

Over the Hill Gang, International (OHGI)
13791 E. Rice Pl.
Aurora, CO 80015 (303) 699-6404

The gang includes individuals 50 years of age and older who enjoy the camaraderie of skiing (over hills) and other recreational activities with friends, and share a spirit of adventure. Their goal is to promote active sports, fitness, and the fellowship of those who have seen at least half a century of life. Though the Over the Hill Gang is primarily a ski organization, it has expanded to include other sports such as tennis, sailing, golf, surfing, sail boarding, and ballooning. The group sponsors skiing tours throughout the U.S. and Europe and has sponsored fund-raising projects to support the Colorado Ski Museum, and it publishes *The Legend,* a quarterly newsletter. Founded in 1978. 2000 members. Contact Earl Clark, President.

Overachievers Anonymous (OA)
1777 Union St.
San Francisco, CA 94123   (415) 928-3600

Too busy to budge? Too active to act? Too motivated to move? Join a club! This self-help group for driven but weary overachievers has the motto, "Enough Is Enough." The organization sponsors no meetings or fund-raisers and elects no officers. 10,000 members. Contact Carol Orsborn, Founder.

Overseas Brats (OSB)
PO Box 29805
San Antonio, TX 78229   (512) 349-1394

Overseas Brats are U.S. citizens who have lived or attended school overseas. The group serves as a center of information for overseas high school alumni groups, and as a forum for the brats to share thoughts and experiences gained during their travels. It publishes *Overseas Brats* magazine three times per year. Founded in 1986. 2000 members. Contact Joseph R. Condrill, Publisher & Editor.

P P P P P P P P P

Paddle Steamer Preservation Society (PSPS)
17 Stockfield Close
Hazelmere
High Wycombe, Bucks. HP15 7LA, England   494 812979

Paddlers in seven countries work, through the society, to preserve and stimulate interest in paddle steamers. The society owns two paddle steamers: *Kingswear Castle* on the River Medway in Kent, England, and *Waverley* on the River Clyde in Scotland. Their publication, *Paddle Wheels,* comes out quarterly. Founded in 1959. 2200 members. Contact John Anderson, Hon. Secretary.

Pagan/Occult/Witchcraft Special Interest Group (POW-SIG)
PO Box 9336
San Jose, CA 95157   (415) 856-6911

This special interest group of Mensa comprises individuals sharing a practical or academic interest in witchcraft, nature religions, mythological traditions of various cultures, or related topics. POWSIG studies paganism to foster spiritual exploration and promote a "healthy community on a healthy planet." It also provides consultation to law enforcement and other public officials, sponsors local and regional gatherings, and archives pagan periodicals published worldwide. POWSIG's newsletter *Pagana* is published five to nine times per year. Founded in 1975. 400 members. Contact Valerie Voigt, Coordinator.

Pagans for Peace Network (P4P)
PO Box 86134
North Vancouver, BC, Canada V7L 4J5

Politically active witches and pagans, congregations, and organizations make up the P4P Network, which promotes activities that foster world peace while remaining within the group's religious objectives. The network publishes a bimonthly newsletter, *Pagans for Peace*, that covers theology and upcoming events, and also publishes *Warriors and Soldiers and Cops—Oh, My!* Founded in 1983. 300 members. Contact Samuel Wagar, Coordinator.

Pansophic Institute (PI)
PO Box 2422
Reno, NV 89505

Sponsored by the School of Universal Wisdom, this educational organization functions through its clerical body, the Church of Universal Light. The Pansophic Institute seeks "to assist in the spiritual awakening or unfoldment, as well as the planetization, of humanity." It serves as "a voice for the perennial philosophy or ageless wisdom leading to liberation and enlightenment in the New Age," it "unites Eastern and Western forms of gnosis (spiritual wisdom) and theurgy (techniques of enlightenment) in the light of modern science," and it helps preserve this knowledge and technique.

Courses in meditation, esoteric cosmology, divinations, spiritual healing, superhealth and longevity, ability, thanatology, and empowerment are provided by the institute, where intellectual learning for its own sake is discouraged in favor of learning "that assists one to become enlightened for the sake of all beings." The group also offers courses for ministership in four types of theurgy and theurgic cosmology, and in child education, creativity, and world responsibility. Contact Dr. Simon Grimes, Director General.

Parachute Study Group (PSG)
623 S. Henderson St.
Ft. Worth, TX 76104   (817) 336-0212

Consider the parachute. I mean, *really* consider the parachute. Study the parachute. Study the parachute with a group. Share the experience! That's what the Parachute Study Group does, while collecting parachute-related stamps and organizing parachute mail drops to commemorate special events. The group's newsletter, *Let's Talk Parachutes,* comes out quarterly. Founded in 1974. 80 members. Contact Dr. Charles E. Pugh, President.

Parapsychological Association (PA)
Box 12236
Research Triangle Park, NC 27709   (919) 688-8241

PA spreads the word on scientific findings in parapsychological research and their relationship to other branches of science. It also collaborates with psychical research societies, which differ from parapsychological societies in that their name is slightly shorter. The association's annual *Research in Parapsychology* contains the abstracted proceedings of the group's annual conference (held in August or September) covering current research, theory, and other scholarly treatments of parapsychology. Full members of the society (120) are persons in the U.S. and foreign countries who hold a Ph.D. degree or its equivalent and who are actively engaged in advancing parapsychology as a branch of science. Associates (160) are students or research workers not qualified for full membership, while affiliates are scientists in other fields. Founded in 1957. 280 members. Contact Dr. Richard Broughton, Business Manager.

Parapsychological Services Institute (PSI)

PO Box 217
Carrollton, GA 30117 (404) 836-8696

PSI educates and conducts research about individuals who are experiencing psychical or spiritual events (including dreams that foretell the future, visitations by the deceased, poltergeist manifestations, and hauntings) or who wish to explore the meaning and transformative value such experiences may have on their lives. The institute offers counseling and treatment (psychological, neurological, and parapsychological) to persons who are possessed or are hypersensitive to psychic impressions from their social and physical environments. Publishes *PSI News* and, in conjunction with the Psychical Research Foundation, the quarterly journal *Theta.* Contact Dr. William G. Roll, Executive Officer.

Parapsychology Foundation (PF)

228 E. 71st St.
New York, NY 10021 (212) 628-1550

PF aims to further scientific research in extrasensory perception (telepathy, clairvoyance, and precognition) and psychokinesis, through university groups and individuals, by presenting research grants and scholarships. The foundation publishes *Parapsychological Monographs* and *Guide to Sources of Information on Parapsychology.* Founded in 1951. Contact Robert R. Coly, Administrative Secretary.

Parapsychology Institute of America (PIA)

PO Box 252
Elmhurst, NY 11373 (718) 894-6564

Who you gonna call? The Parapsychology Institute of America investigates ghosts, haunted houses, and other aspects of parapsychology. The group's current obsession is researching digital extrasensory ability—the psychic ability to read information stored in computers. PIA, which includes psychics, psychic researchers, and students of parapsychology, bestows awards for the best and worst practitioners in the field of parapsychology and maintains a hall of fame. The institute publishes *True Tales of the Unknown, We Don't Die, The Uninvited,* and *Amityville Horror Solved.* Founded in 1971. 45 members. Contact Dr. Stephen Kaplan, Executive Director.

Parents' Music Resource Center (PMRC)

1500 Arlington Blvd.
Arlington, VA 22209 (703) 527-9466

PMRC works for "ethical boundaries" in the production of recorded music, specifically to alert parents and children to lyrics describing explicit sex, violence, substance abuse, and the occult. The center has successfully negotiated a consumer information system with the Recording Industry Association of America that encourages record companies to print lyrics on record jackets or label record jackets with the warning, "Explicit Lyrics-Parental Advisory." Believing that warning labels and the display of lyrics on the record covers is a consumer issue, not an infringement of First Amendment rights, PMRC works to publicize this distinction with articles, surveys, and lyric sheets. With advice from psychiatrists, psychologists, and other medical personnel, the center helps parents support children beset with negative messages from the media. The group's Media Watch program encourages parents to monitor radio and television broadcasts and to write letters of complaint or praise to stations, program sponsors, recording companies, and state and national government representatives. Publishes the quarterly journal *Record*. Founded in 1985. Contact Jennifer Norwood, Executive Director.

Patrexes of the Panopticon (POP)
400 Collington Dr.
Ronkonkoma, NY 11779 (516) 737-2171

POP is a collection of fans of British science fiction television series such as *Dr. Who*, *The Hitchhiker's Guide to the Galaxy*, *Red Dwarf*, *The Tomorrow People*, *Blakes 7*, *Star Cops*, and *The Tripods*, as well as the American series *Star Trek: The Next Generation*. In addition to watching sci-fi TV, the Patrexes sponsor competitions and operate a telephone referral service. POP's newsletter, *Black Scrolls*, appears 10 times per year, and its magazine *The Matrix* is published semiannually. Founded in 1987. 400 members. Contact Gregory Jones, Editor.

Peaceful Beginnings (PB)
13020 Homestead Ct.
Anchorage, AK 99516 (907) 345-4813

PB distributes information opposing routine infant circumcision, presenting data stating that there are no valid medical reasons for circumcision of newborns and that the operation is severely traumatic and painful. The group promotes other aspects of childbirth education, including positive birth options, breastfeeding, coping during the first trimester of pregnancy, perinatal loss, and postpartum adjustment. Founded in 1985. Contact Rosemary Romberg, President.

Peanut Pals (PP)
PO Box 4465
Huntsville, AL 35815 (205) 881-9198

A club that unites individuals with a common interest in the study and collection of Planters Peanuts memorabilia. Goal is to exchange information about the history of the Planters Peanut Company and the multitude of items marketed by or associated with the company for the past 80 years. Peanut Pals focuses on interesting people connected with Planters and biographical sketches of members giving accounts of their years in collecting Planters memorabilia. It issues the bimonthly *Peanut Papers* and annually holds a business meeting, swap meet, auction, and banquet. Founded in 1978. 600 members. Contact Judith Walthall, Founder.

Pelican Man's Bird Sanctuary (PMBS)
PO Box 2648
Sarasota, FL 34230 (813) 955-2266

We don't know who the Pelican Man is, but we do know his Bird Sanctuary is a rehabilitation center for injured pelicans, blue herons, sea gulls, and other birds. The sanctuary's association is a group of individuals and corporations who support environmental and wildlife preservation and promote wildlife protection and rescue. Founded in 1985. 3000 members. Contact Dale Shields, President & Founder.

Penny Resistance (PR)
8319 Fulham Ct.
Richmond, VA 23227   (804) 266-7400

The individuals in PR seek to abolish capital punishment by encouraging the use of economic boycotts and tax resistance to resist the death penalty, and by opposing political candidates who support the death penalty. The organization's name is derived from the fact that members withhold one penny from federal and state telephone taxes and one penny from their electric bill to oppose the death penalty. Founded in 1984. Contact Jerome D. Gorman, Secretary.

People Against Telephone Terrorism and Harassment (PATTH)
18159 Village Mart Dr.
Box 239
Olney, MD 20832   (800) 783-5959

PATTH promotes the unrestricted availability of telephone caller identification equipment, which identifies the telephone number of the caller, thus allowing a person to screen his or her telephone calls. The group works for legislation addressing telephone harassment, testifies at public hearings, and provides counseling and support to victims of obscene and threatening phone calls. Contact Stacey Blazer, Founder.

People, Food and Land Foundation (PFLF)
35751 Oak Springs Dr.
Tollhouse, CA 93667   (209) 855-3710

PFLF is an association of small farmers (tillers of small farms, that is, not tiny gardeners), consumers, and individuals concerned with low-water use, arid land crops, organic methods for small farmers and gardeners, and low-tech passive solar models for farm, food processing, and home use. The foundation's Sun Mountain Research Center hosts a "Seminar in Reality" addressing such topics as herbal food preparation, shamanism, self-healing, and floral, medicinal, and culinary uses of native plants. Founded in 1974. 500 members. Contact George Ballis, Coordinator.

People Organized to Stop Rape of Imprisoned Persons (POSRIP)
PO Box 632
Ft. Bragg, CA 95437   (707) 964-0820

United for the protection of prisoners, this group seeks to prevent rape, sexual slavery, forced prostitution, and sexual harassment in U.S. reformatories, jails, and prisons. The organization educates the public about such abuses and seeks correspondents for prison rape victims. Founded in 1979. 25 members. Contact Tom Cahill, Executive Director.

People's Music Network for Songs of Freedom and Struggle (PMN/SFS)
PO Box 26004
Alexandria, VA 22313

Everybody join hands, start swaying, and sing with me now. Music has long been used to foster social change, and the performers, writers, nightclub managers, political organizers, small record label companies, and other optimistic folk in this network honor and encourage that use. They urge political musicians to share their work, advocate the use of music in the progressive community, and publish a semiannual newsletter, *Sassafras*, which profiles political musicians and their music. PMN/SFS also holds a semiannual festival with workshops and exhibits. Founded in 1983. 800 members. Contact Charlie King.

Phenix Society (PS)
PO Box 351
Cheshire, CT 06410   (203) 387-6913

"Cosmic consciousness and planetary stewardship" is the focus of Phenix members. The society encourages personal growth and development through reading, discussion, and meditation, and hopes for an improved quality of life for everyone. Although all activities are conducted by a network of local clubs, information is provided nationwide. The Phenix newsletter, *Mind-Expander*, appears quarterly. Founded in 1973. Contact Virginia Cone, President.

Pia Zadora Fan Club (PZFC)
Zadora Enterprises
Trump Tower
725 Fifth Ave.
New York, NY 10022   (213) 859-7786

Who is Pia Zadora, anyway? Well, she's an American film singer and actress, she was born in 1956, she has appeared in commercials and on *Carson*, and she has a fan club.

Pilgrim Society (PS)
Pilgrim Hall Museum
75 Court St.
Plymouth, MA 02360   (508) 746-1620

The historically minded members of this society collect, preserve, and display artifacts and written and photographic records relating to the pilgrims, Plymouth Colony, and the Town of Plymouth. The society maintains Coles Hill, Forefathers Monument, Pilgrim Hall, and a museum and library of more than 10,000 volumes and 5,000 manuscripts. It publishes the semiannual *Pilgrim Journal* and the quarterly *Pilgrim Society News*, and hosts a conference every December 21 in Plymouth, Massachusetts. Founded in 1820. 900 members. Contact Laurence R. Pizer, Director.

Pilots for Christ International (PCI)
PO Box 9
Parkesburg, PA 19365   (215) 857-1234

Flying for Jesus. This nondenominational association of pilots and aviation enthusiasts in 13 countries are united to foster knowledge of the gospel of Jesus Christ to the aviation community. The group distributes Bibles at airports, provides air transportation for nonprofit organizations and persons in need, participates in air shows, and conducts fly-ins. Their annual conference and air show, where they bestow the Pilot of the Year and Christ the King awards, take place on the third weekend in June. Founded in 1985. 700 members. Contact Bill Starrs, President.

Pinochle Bugs Social and Civic Club
1624 Madison Ave.
Charlotte, NC 28216   (704) 334-4802

The Pinochle Bugs Club is an association of professional African-American women who cultivate social and civic interaction among women of various other organizations. Each member of the club takes the name of an insect, and members' husbands and friends are deemed Pests. Through pinochle tournaments, community projects, the presentation of awards and scholarships, and annual conventions, the club encourages social, economic, educational, and cultural advancement. Their biennial magazine is called *The Beetle*. Founded in 1955. 265 members. Contact Esther Hill, President.

Pipe Collectors Club of America (PCCA)
PO Box 2089
Merrifield, VA 22116-2089   (703) 971-1933

They don't necessarily smoke them, but they do collect them. The club also helps individuals establish local pipe clubs, and it maintains a committee called the Certified Kapnismologists. PCCA's newsletter, *Smoker's Pipeline,* is published eight times per year. Founded in 1983. 1000 members. Contact Robert C. Hamlin, Executive Director.

Placename Survey of the U.S. (PNSUS)

Names of places—that's what interests these surveyors. They're completing a survey of placenames of the United States, including geographical, linguistic, and historical information. The group operates the American Placename Study Center in Thibodaux (that's Thibodaux; there's one for the survey), Louisiana, to gather study materials and act as a clearinghouse, and maintains the American Placename Institute and library. The PNSUS newsletter is published quarterly. Founded in 1969.

Plain Talk (PT)
1301 S. Scott St., No. 620
Arlington, VA 22204   (703) 920-1333

Say it like you see it. Plain Talk, a clearinghouse for information on straight-talking, *plain* English programs, includes firms and individuals in business, government, universities, the media, and other professions. Members volunteer to help state and local governments draft legislation to promote clarity in consumer-oriented documents, especially those affecting individuals and small businesses, such as contracts, warranties, forms, and regulations. The Puns Corps, also listed in this volume, pursues the same goal through a slightly different approach. Founded in 1979. Contact Marian Norby, Secretary.

Planetary Citizens (PC)

PO Box 1509
Mt. Shasta, CA 96067

"Global oneness," or the the interdependence of all peoples regardless of national origin, is the concept that unites Planetary Citizens. The group stresses the "local-global" link by focusing on locally oriented issues of global concern, such as disarmament, energy, international security, a new world economic order, hunger, and population. The Citizens operate a Search for Security Alternatives Program to create change at both the policy and personal level, and they advocate expanding the authority of the United Nations to act on behalf of humanity. Their belief in "One Earth, One Humanity, One Destiny" is reflected in the group's "Planetary Passport" document, its *One Family* quarterly newsletter, the journal *Planet Earth*, and the *Planetary Citizens Catalog*, an extensive mail order list. Founded in 1971. 200,000 members. Contact Donald Keys, President.

Planetary Society (PS)

65 N. Catalina Ave.
Pasadena, CA 91106   (818) 793-5100

"A realistic continuing program of planetary exploration and the search for extraterrestrial life"—the key word being "realistic"—is what motivates the Planetary Society. Through its *Bioastronomy News* and *Mars Underground News*, both quarterly, and its bimonthly journal, *Planetary Report*, the society fosters communication among interested groups and individuals in the U.S. and 70 other countries and distributes information concerning the latest findings and discoveries in the field. The group offers education programs and several annual high school and college scholarships. Founded in 1980. 120,000 members. Contact Dr. Louis Friedman, Executive Director.

Poets for Christ

224 Tennessee Circle
Seymour, TN 37865   (615) 573-4545

Poets for Christ advocate a "Heavenly Revolution." Their intention is to "take the talented writings of Christian poets out of their scrapbooks and closets" and distribute their works to people in all walks of life, "where they can do some good." Founded in 1969. Contact Gene Rickett, President.

Polar Bear Club—U.S.A. (PBC-USA)

376 Naughton Ave.
Staten Island, NY 10305   (718) 979-8370

They swim outdoors in the winter in the north, where it's cold. Well, some of them do; the rest just think about it. The U.S.A. Polar Bear Club, which includes both winter swimmers and potential winter swimmers (and which was known as the Coney Island Polar Bear Club until 1987), meets every Sunday from the end of October through April on Coney Island, at Stillwell Avenue and the Boardwalk, to swim in the ice and snow of the Atlantic Ocean. There, the kind City of New York has provided the Bears with a bath house, where the potential swimmers hang out and imbibe hot soup, coffee, and tea before and after the swim. The group also swims at other sites (as long as the water is cold) if invited, according to 77-year-old Alexander R. Mottola, Polar Bear President. Both men and women belong—mostly senior citizens—with some hailing from areas remote from Coney Island, including Sweden, Norway, Germany, Scotland, Japan, China, and what used to be known as the Soviet Union.

The Polar Bears advocate a program—including exercises such as jogging, ball playing, and other training—to acclimate the body to extreme weather, and believe that swimming in cold winter weather prevents them from catching common winter maladies such as colds and the flu. "People think we're crazy, and we probably are a little flaky to do what we do, but we do it for health, for fitness," explains Mottola. "I never met a person who was angry after going in with us." During the summer, when the water is too warm for swimming, members are concerned with maintaining clean waters and beaches. Founded in 1903. 80 members. Contact Alexander R. Mottola, President.

Police Insignia Collector's Association (PICA)

PO Box 365
Leonia, NJ 07605 (201) 944-6321

PICA members lawfully collect and preserve police memorabilia, such as shoulder patches, badges, hats, and uniforms, keeping in mind that it is generally unlawful and certainly difficult to collect uniforms of the police while they are wearing them. PICA assists collectors in obtaining police items and provides a medium of trading information among members. Founded in 1973. 700 members. Contact James J. Fahy, Secretary.

Polka Lovers Klub of America (Po.L.K.ofA)

15630 62nd St.
Mayer, MN 55360 (612) 657-2374

Ah one and ah two. Po.L.K.ofA. members—aside from creating interesting acronyms—seek to preserve and promote traditional polka music through their annual Polka Fest and their bimonthly journal, *Entertainment Bits.* The group also presents music and dance programs to nursing homes and other such facilities. Founded in 1972. 3547 members. Contact Ruben Schumacher, President.

Popular Culture Association (PCA)

Bowling Green State University
Popular Culture Center
Bowling Green, OH 43403 (419) 372-7861

Pop culture is described by PCA as "the voice and actions of the people in large or small masses, the *vox populi*, ... the people's icons, rituals, heroes, the mass media, including word of mouth and other manifestations of folklore." In other words, it's TV shows, movies, cartoons, pulp fiction, pop and protest music, real and fictional characters, underground culture, art-anything, American or foreign, commercial or artistic, designed for mass consumption. PCA approaches its studies of cultures and subcultures "from a truly international, interdisciplinary and multidisciplinary angle of vision with a time span reaching from the beginning of history to the present."

The official publication of the group is the *Journal of Popular Culture.* Annual membership and subscription to the journal is $25. The group meets annually during March or April in conjunction with its companion association (every group should have a friend), the American Culture Association: 1993 is set for New Orleans, 1994 for Chicago, and 1995 in Philadelphia. Founded in 1969. 2500 members. Contact Ray B. Browne, Secretary Treasurer.

Porlock Society (PS)
Department of English
University of Houston-Downtown
1 Main St.
Houston, TX 77002   (713) 221-8013

The Porlock Society's members, acting out a sort of literary civil disobedience, identify scholarly papers and literary works they deem long and interminable and therefore worthy of interruption. Born out of an academic conference where attendees lamented having to listen to overlong readings, the group formed to seek out and interrupt such readings whenever possible. The Society maintains a hall of fame of authors who have interrupted their own work, and they publish a (presumably concise) newsletter, *Cogito Interruptus.* Founded in 1977. 230 members. Contact Russell J. Meyer, Executive Secretary.

Possum Growers and Breeders Association (PGBA)
PO Box 1166
Clanton, AL 35045   (205) 755-0182

They grow possum and they breed possum; they protect possum and they propogate possum; and they do the same with related species. The group educates the public about the value of possum as a source of "highly nutritious and palatable food and quality fur," it encourages scientific breeding programs and standards, and it provides possum as biomedical models for medical research. On the lighter side, it sponsors an annual Registered Possum Show, a Possum Dog Contest, and a Miss Possum Contest. The association's convention takes place annually on Possum Day, June 29. Founded in 1971. 134,000 members. Contact Frank B. Clark, President.

Potato Eaters (PE)
PO Box 791
Great Falls, VA 22066   (703) 759-6714

Well, they eat potatoes. They also grow, cook, and promote the tubers. The group's Potato Museum is devoted to the history and social significance of the potato and features over 1000 artifacts, a library, an archive, and an audiovisual section. The Eaters sponsor potato cookery competitions and demonstrations, research potato recipes, bestow the Potato Press Prize for potato reporting excellence, and host a monthly feast consisting entirely of (what else?) potato dishes. The group's publication, *Peelings,* appears monthly, and it also publishes recipes, menus, and *The Great Potato Book.* Founded in 1986. 245 members. Contact Tom Hughes, Museum Director.

Praed Street Irregulars (PSI)
Pontine Marshes
17 Mt. Lassen Dr.
San Rafael, CA 94903   (415) 479-6554

Members are interested in the Solar Pons stories of Wisconsin author August Derleth (1909-71). Members also include fans of

Sherlock Holmes and detective and mystery fiction in general. The group is a self-proclaimed "gentle spoof" of the Baker Street Irregulars (Solar Pons is known as the Sherlock Holmes of Praed Street). The Irregulars present the annual Praed Penny Award and publish the *Pontine Dossier* and the quarterly *S'ian Yello Pages*, as well as the monthly *Tide-Waiters Tidings*. Once a year everyone gathers for dinner and occasionally for special luncheons. Founded in 1966. 3500 members. Contact Lt.Col. Theodore G. Schulz, Lord Warden.

Prairie Chicken Foundation (PCF)
1121 Timothy Ave.
Madison, WI 53716 (608) 222-5631

Dedicated to preserving the prairie chicken in Wisconsin, the Prairie Chicken Foundation raises funds and acquires land to develop the prairie chicken habitat in the state. It owns approximately 5000 acres and makes purchases cooperatively with the Society of Tympanuchus Cupido Pinnatus. Founded in 1958. Contact Donald R. Hollatz, President.

Princess Kitty Fan Club (PKFC)
PO Box 430784
Miami, FL 33243-0784 (305) 665-1639

PKFC is a group of individuals and organizations who admire and promote the domestic cat Princess Kitty, a former stray who is now a professional model and actor and billed as the "smartest cat in the world." The first animal member of the International Platform Association, Princess Kitty has a repertoire of more than 70 tricks that include playing a small piano, slam-dunking a basketball, counting, and jumping hurdles. The talented feline performs commercially and for various organizations and children's hospitals, and she has been a featured guest on radio and TV talk shows. Her fan club disseminates information about her life and career and about cat training and pet care in general. It also publishes *Pawprints: Princess Kitty Fan Club Newsletter* quarterly, and it encourages the adoption and rehabilitation of strays. Founded in 1987. 75 members. Contact Moura Wrinkle, President.

Private Citizen, Inc. (PCI)
PO Box 233
Naperville, IL 60566 (312) 393-1555

You've just stepped out of the shower; it's steamy; your hair's dripping in your eyes; you've just located your towel; and the phone rings. And as you soggily contemplate the possibility of electrocution via telephone, someone tries to sell you life insurance or a new telephone service or a coupon book. Can't something be done about these people? Private Citizen, Inc., believes something can.

PCI regulates the intrusion of junk phone calls to allow individuals to preserve their privacy. Subscribers authorize PCI to notify telemarketers not to solicit them; if telemarketers persist in such solicitation, they are levied with a charge for the subscriber's time. The group also lobbies for the regulation of telemarketing. The *PCI Directory*, a list of subscribers, is published semiannually, along with a list of telemarketers receiving the *PCI Directory*. Founded in 1988. Contact Robert Bulmash, President.

Procrastinators' Club of America (PCA)
Box 712
Bryn Athyn, PA 19009 (215) 546-3861

If something's worth doing, it's worth doing later. Individuals in the Procrastinators' Club promote the philosophy of relaxation through putting off until later those things that needn't be done today. Activities include a Christmas party in June and a Fourth of July picnic in January, plus various other lax events that publicize the art of procrastination. The club gives awards to horses that finish last; honors "Be Late for Something Day," Sept. 5; celebrates National Procrastination Week (the first week in March) after the fact; protested against the War of 1812 in 1966, and presents an annual Procrastinator of the Year Award. *Last Month's Newsletter* appears periodically, and every now and then a convention takes place. Founded in 1956. 6800 members. Contact Les Waas, President.

Professional Comedians' Association (PCA)
581 9th Ave., No. 3C
New York, NY 10036 (212) MID-LAFF

The Professional Comedians Association is an association of, well, professional comedians. The group seeks to enhance the professional and economic standing of comedians by providing information on work opportunities, offering group health and dental insurance, and providing discounts on video production facilities and car rentals. PCA also conducts monthly comedy seminars, holds an annual conference, gives awards to outstanding comedians, and publishes a monthly newsletter called *Stand Up*. Founded in 1984. 1200 members. Contact Nick Cosention, Executive Officer.

Professional Psychics United (PPU)
1839 S. Elmwood
Berwyn, IL 60402 (708) 749-4322

Less deductive than Sherlock Holmes but probably more effective than Agent Dale Cooper, these professional psychics are united to assist the police in solving crimes. They provide psychic rescue teams, similar to those in the Psychic Detective Bureau (also listed in this book), to help locate missing persons, offer educational programs on the nature of extrasensory perception, conduct teaching seminars, and sponsor psychic fairs. Founded in 1977. 350 members. Contact Phyllis Allen, President.

Project Blue Book (PBB)
506 N. 2nd St.
Ft. Smith, AR 72901 (501) 782-7077

The military and UFOs: what *is* the connection? Active and retired military or federal investigative personnel who probe into alleged sightings of UFOs comprise Project Blue Book. Now private, this abstrusely named organization was begun in 1949 by the U.S. Air Force but is no longer a government project. Contact Bill Pitts, Director.

Project Starlight International (PSI)
PO Box 599
College Park, MD 20740

These are *serious* documenters of UFOs. Project Starlight

International uses magnetometers, a gravimeter, a spectrometer, a specially equipped mobile laboratory unit, and other electronic and high resolution optical systems to record the physical effects, optical images, and location of UFOs, and the group disseminates this instrumented hard data to the scientific community and the public. Founded in 1964. Contact Ray Stanford, Director.

Project to Research Objects, Theories, Extraterrestrials and Unusual Sightings (PROTEUS)
274 2nd St.
Elizabeth, NJ 07206

The independent investigators in PROTEUS conduct research to determine advanced physics used by extraterrestrial cultures (ordinary physics won't do) and measure the physical, physiological, and psychological effects of extraterrestrial technology on humanity. PROTEUS also holds educational programs on such matters. The group's *Annals of Ufologicial Research Advances* is published quarterly. Founded in 1979. 100 members. Contact Kenneth W. Behrendt, Director.

Project VISIT—Vehicle Internal Systems Investigative Team (VISIT)
PO Box 890327
Houston, TX 77289   (713) 488-2884

Like those in Project Starlight International, the researchers of VISIT include engineers, scientists, analysts, and investigators interested in unidentified flying objects. These universally minded investigators seek to determine whether there is a correlation of engineering systems among UFO cases and to identify and evaluate these systems. They also try to discern just how UFOs fly. They share their research findings with government agencies, public corporations, and the public. VISIT's archives contain 10,000 clippings, reports, and reviews on current UFO cases. The group has two committees: the Advanced Propulsion Concepts Committee and the Human Physiological Effects Committee. Founded in 1976. 50 members. Contact John F. Schuessler, Secretary.

PSI Research
484-B Washington St., No. 317
Monterey, CA 93940   (408) 655-1985

If you belong in this group, you probably won't need to read on. Parapsychological (psi) phenomena such as ESP, telekinesis, nonverbal hypnosis, precognition, and folk healing are the topics of interest in PSI Research. The group promotes research and the international exchange of information on such phenomena, focusing on psi studies in Eastern Europe and China. Founded in 1982. 400 members. Contact Larissa Vilenskaya, Director.

Psychic Detective Bureau (PDB)
Also known as the U.S. Psi Squad, PDB fights crime through the use of mind skills such as psi (the appearance or use of parapsychological events or powers). Like Professional Psychics United (listed elsewhere in this book), PDB assists law enforcement officials in solving mysteries, works to develop psychic power to a level useful to society, and gives the media information on the use of psychic power. The group's newsletter, *The Ultimate Energies: Making*

Your Mind Work for You, appears quarterly. Founded in 1971. 25 members.

Psychic Science International Special Interest Group (PSI-SIG)
7514 Belleplain Dr.
Huber Heights, OH 45424-3229   (513) 236-0361

PSISIG groupies are members and associates of Mensa who scientifically research psychic sciences and arts, such as theories of existence and reality, states of mind, human auras, clairvoyance, telepathy, dowsing, psychometry, healing and defense, multiple personalities and possession, psychokinesis, survival after death, discarnate entities, and extraterrestrial life. The group conducts its research to benefit humanity in mental health, to reduce superstition and fraud, to promote safety, to enhance human relations, and to promote awareness and capabilities in the psychic sciences and arts. PSISIG publishes the *PSI-M* journal five times per year, along with special research reports and videotapes. The group's annual colloquium is held on Columbus Day weekend. Founded in 1976. 310 members. Contact Richard Allen Strong, President.

Psychical Research Foundation (PRF)
PO Box 217
Carrollton, GA 30117   (404) 836-6510

Is there an afterlife? The Psychical Research Foundation scientifically investigates this possibility. The center has conducted research on issues related to the continuation of consciousness after the death of the physical body, such as out-of-body experiences, meditation, hauntings, poltergeist activity, and mediumship. It publishes the quarterly *Theta.* Founded in 1960. Contact Dr. William G. Roll, Research Director.

Psynetics Foundation (PF)
1212 E. Lincoln Ave.
Anaheim, CA 92805   (714) 533-2311

The foundation is a group of men and women "dedicated to a positive, unbiased and unprejudiced mission to discover and recognize valid and scientific principles as proclaimed by existing agencies or individuals and an open-minded search for new and advanced ideas, opinions and methods that may be accepted and used for the betterment of humanity." A mouthful of good intentions. One more time: "Engages in study and research in an atmosphere free from tradition, dogma and doctrine to discover truths that are based on natural law and to discover the methods by which those truths may be used for the advancement and betterment of man in the physical, mental, emotional and spiritual aspects of his life experiences."

To promote their research and findings of principles, ideas, and truths, the group sponsors lectures, demonstrations, workshops, classes, and social and recreational programs. The foundation's Apollo School provides learning programs for students whose learning disabilities, behavior, or age makes them unsuited for public school programs. The group publishes the monthly *Psynetics Newsletter* and conducts an annual congress on the fourth Saturday in April in Anaheim, California. Founded in 1962. 600 members. Contact Richard Kravetz, General Executive Director.

Puns Corps (PC)

3108 Dashiell Road
Box 2364
Falls Church, VA 22042   (703) 533-3668

For fun, the Puns Corps mocks ambiguous and confusing writing (especially that emanating from governmental "burro-cracy"), and for educational purposes, the corps encourages memory enhancement via word play, particularly for nursing home patients.

Using "creative ambiguity and mnemonics," writes chief Puns Corpsperson Robert L. Birch, "triggers the creative imagination and can serve as device for scavenging your mental attic for trivia, or even for divia and monovia. (A monovium is one random fact. Divia are a set of two related facts. A set of trivia are related facts, each a trivium)." Those and other creatively wrought words are defined in the corps's trixionary (tricky dictionary), which lists such artfully defined terms as "brother" as a maker of fine broth, "mother" as a moth specialist, and "resting" defined as "to sting again."

Among the group's many celebrational days is One-Tooth Rhee Day (say it together: "One-Tooth-Rhee, One-Too-Three, one-two-three") January 23 (1-23), to honor "the original landing of the original Americans." Noting (seriously now) that the Guarani language of the Paraguayan Indians is very similar to the Korean language, Birch writes: "According to one entirely apocryphal legend, the Korean ships Profusion and Confusion lost their bearings in the Bering Sea and landed groups of colonists on the Alaskan side of the foggy passage." This expedition, he speculates, "may well have been led by someone called One-Tooth Rhee, who may or may not have had only one tooth."

In 1976 the Puns Corps celebrated the 200th birthday of the legendary Bison Ten Yell (his bicentennial, if you will), an influential Native American who altered his original name (which was Buffalo Chip-Off-the-Old-Block) "when a mission teacher told him that the American buffalo was really supposed to be called a bison."

The group also sponsors Compliment-Your-Mirror Day (to improve mirror morale and get mirrors to smile more often); Memory Day on March 21 (to improve the memory recall capacities of nursing home patients and encourage the recreational uses of the "memory dynamics" system); and Swap Ideas Day, an annual punscoring (PunsCorps-ing, get it?) competition that takes place September 10 in Washington, D.C. The corps regularly grants awards such as the Pedro, a symbol in the form of a little burro, which is presented to the "burro-crat" who has best exemplified the rule: "Never let anyone find the information sought, since it will probably turn out to be irrelevant anyway." Founded in 1977. 850 members. Contact Robert L. Birch, Coordinator.

Puppeteers of America (PA)

5 Cricklewood Path
Pasadena, CA 91107

Puppeteers of America includes amateur and professional puppeteers, educators, recreation directors, youth leaders, therapists, Junior League members, children, and others interested in puppetry. The group presents awards to recognize the use of puppetry in various artistic fields, and it gives the President's Award to a member contributing the most to advance the art of puppetry. The puppeteers hold annual regional festivals and a biennial national Puppetry Festival, with exhibits, workshops, lectures, and professional and amateur productions. The *Puppetry Journal* is published quarterly. Founded in 1937. 2100 members. Contact Gayle G. Schluter, Chairperson.

Puzzle Buffs International (PBI)
1772 State Road
Cuyahoga Falls, OH 44223   (216) 923-2397

Puzzle Buffs share an interest in word puzzles and word games. The association seeks to showcase the puzzle-solving skills of members and to inform the public about the mental exercise and enjoyment of puzzling. The Puzzle Buffs provide puzzles to patients at Veteran's Administration hospitals, nursing homes, and other institutions, sponsor competitions, and grant awards. Their three publications are *GIANTS: The World's Largest Crosswords*, published eight times per year, the quarterly *Puzzle Buffs Newsletter*, and the semiannual *See the USA*, which includes word puzzles, history, geography, industry, and points of interest on every state. Founded in 1978. 39,000 members. Contact Charles R. Elum, President.

Quixote Center (QC)
3311 Chauncey Place, No. 301
Mt. Rainier, MD 20712   (301) 699-0042

Dreaming impossible dreams—and hoping to make them possible-the Quixote Center, a Catholic educational group, attempts to urge the church and society to change their attitudes toward social issues. The center is named for Don Quixote, the character in the novel of the same name by Spanish author Miguel de Cervantes, in recognition of the center's quest after "impossible dreams." The group promotes equality for women and men with a focus on women's ordination and the elimination of sexist language in the church. It advocates lesbian and gay rights, disseminates information about Central America, and supplies medical and educational material aid to Nicaragua. QC explores various expressions of human spirituality and develops new prayer forms adapted to the lives of busy people.

Sister organizations include Priests for Equality and Quest for Peace, which attempts to provide humanitarian aid to Nicaragua to counter Congressional appropriations to the *contras*. The Quixote Center publishes a quarterly newsletter, *Rocinante,* as well as *El Salvador: A Look at the Reality, The Death Penalty in Maryland, Honduras: A Look at Reality, Nicaragua: A Look at Reality, Not Servants, But Friends, A Saga of Shame: Racial Discrimination and the Death Penalty, Set My People Free: Liberation Theology in Practice,* and books concerning the ordination of women. Founded in 1975. Contact Dolores Pomerleau, Co-Director.

R R R R R R R R

Race Track Chaplaincy of America (RTCA)
64 Montgomery Ave.
Long Branch, NJ 07740   (201) 870-0700

RTCA provides religious and social services to persons connected with horse racing tracks (how about a blessing for the guy
who just lost a bundle?). The group sponsors drug and alcohol abuse
programs, holds Bible studies, and conducts an annual chaplains'
seminar. Their *Winners Circle* publication appears five times per
year. Founded in 1971. Contact Rev. Homer Tricules, Executive
Director.

Radical Women (RW)
523-A Valencia St.
San Francisco, CA 94110   (415) 864-1278

Radical Women are those with a socialist-feminist political
orientation who believe that women's leadership is decisive for
basic social change. The group works to reform policies and
attitudes toward reproductive rights, child care, affirmative action,
divorce, police brutality, rape, women of color, lesbians, and
working women. No surprise: RW also opposes the efforts of
conservative anti-feminist groups. Founded in 1967. Contact
Constance Scott, Organizer.

Radio Association Defending Airwave Rights (RADAR)
4949 S. 25A
Tipp City, OH 45371   (513) 667-5472

A group of manufacturers, dealers, and distributors of radar
detectors as well as individual motorists with an interest in the laws
governing use of automotive radar. RADAR works to maintain the
legality of the operation and sale of radar detectors and promotes
the common interests of the radar detection industry. It alerts the
motoring public to potential abuses of police radar and hopes to
foster the proper use of radar for law enforcement purposes. The
group claims that any individual state attempting to pass legislation
declaring radar detectors illegal violates The Communications Act
of 1934, amended in 1982, which places sole responsibility for such
a law on the U.S. Congress. The group also believes that outlawing
radar detectors is a violation of the First Amendment, which
guarantees freedom of speech. RADAR claims that this freedom
includes the right to hear a radar detector. It supports findings of
tests confirming the inadequacy of police radar and believes that
this inadequacy necessitates the use of private radar detection
devices (no, I was not speeding officer, your radar must be on the
blink). The group monitors and communicates with legislatures
regarding legislative action affecting regulation of radar detectors
and police radar. RADAR publishes the monthly *RADAR Reporter*
and a variety of books, including *Beating the Radar Rap* and *The
Safe Motorist's Guide to Speed Traps*. Founded in 1984. 12,500
members. Contact Janice Lee, President.

Rat, Mouse and Hamster Fanciers (RMHF)
1756 14th Ave.
San Francisco, CA 94122 (415) 564-6374

Not to be confused with the American Fancy Rat and Mouse Association and the other rodent-admiring groups described in this book, the Rat, Mouse and Hamster Fanciers includes a whole other rodent in its list of desirable pets. About that particular rodent, the group reminds readers in its bimonthly newsletter: "All domesticated hamsters are descended from a single mother hamster found by an Arab and raised by an Israeli." Not only do these small animal lovers open-mindedly avoid discriminating against single mothers, one may infer, but they raise and nurture the very symbols of Middle-Eastern cooperation. These pets are not only fancy, they're significant social figures.

Many members of RMHF breed their pets carefully to "preserve the outstanding genetic traits developed by devoted fanciers in the past" and to "discover and develop new colors and characteristics." Other members just want to share information or learn how to better care for their pets. For example, RMHF secretary-treasurer John Langdell, M.D., writes that many pet owners have called the group "grieving the loss of their pet rats. Some have accepted our invitation to join the club to learn better care for their pets and to obtain healthier stock from our members. In some cases the pet was over three years old and there was some reassurance on learning that their pet had attained an average life expectancy." So three rat years must be something like 30 human years. Let's hope they pack a lotta living in their little lifetimes.

The club sponsors four competitive shows each year, in January, March, June, and October, in which breeders compete among 10 classes of rats, 15 classes of mice (including satin longhairs, non-satin longhairs, frizzies, satin shorthairs . . .), and 15 classes of hamsters (fifteen classes! And all from a single mother, long ago!). Founded in 1984. Contact John Langdell, Secretary Treasurer.

Rathkamp Matchcover Society (RMS)
1359 Surrey Road, Department Y
Vandalia, OH 45377-1646 (513) 890-8684

The society comprises collectors of match book covers (phillumenists)—not matchboxes and labels, like the collectors in the New Moon Matchbox and Label Club, or lighters, like those in On the Lighter Side—but match book covers. The group names itself after Henry Rathkamp, a collector "who gave the hobby direction." *Voice of the Hobby* is published bimonthly. Founded in 1941. 1500 members. Contact John C. Williams, Secretary.

Re-Geniusing Project (RP)
1432 Spruce St.
Berkeley, CA 94709 (415) 841-4903

Everyone is born with the potential to become a genius and can learn to develop his or her creative skills, according to ReGeniusing Project members. To encourage individuals to utilize and develop their talents and creative abilities, they conduct workshop seminars to develop the "deep crafts" (usually considered "latent" or "inherited qualities") of poets, writers, artists, and other individuals. The association publishes *New Words Project Report* and the book *Waking the Poet.* Founded in 1981. 12 members. Contact Gene Fowler, Coordinator.

Reagan Alumni Association (RAA)
6908 Baylor Dr.
Alexandria, VA 22307   (703) 768-3344

Answers the question, "Whatever became of those Reagan folks?" This association of political appointees involved in former president Ronald Reagan's campaign and administration seeks to advance the "Reagan agenda" and to provide political expertise to President Bush and other future administrations. It also offers a placement service for the former campaign and administration workers (try the Bush administration). The group publishes the *Reagan Alumni Newsletter* periodically and holds occasional Reagan Events. No word on backyard barbecues. Founded in 1987. Contact Louis J. Cordia, Executive Director.

Redeem Our Country (ROC)
1051 S. Lemon St., Suite E
PO Box 333
Fullerton, CA 92632   (714) 871-2952

Save the States with silver. Redeem Our Country seeks to abolish the U.S. Federal Reserve in an effort to promote the return of a monetary system under the silver standard in the U.S. Treasury Department, which ROC considers to be consistent with the U.S. Constitution. The group also attempts to end fractional banking and educates the public on the U.S. monetary system. It publishes the booklet *Redeem Our Country.* Founded in 1981. 73,278 members. Contact Jim Townsend, Chairman.

Redheads International (RI)
PO Box 2000
Corona Del Mar, CA 92625   (714) 832-8883

Redheads in 30 countries have united to promote an attractive image of their kind. According to the group, "being a redhead is a special and lucky blessing!" The group believes redheads, like other minorities, have been unfairly represented in the media as "clowns and characters, never the hero or romantic lead." To promote the respectability of their members, therefore, they host an annual Miss Redheads International Beauty Pageant. The group publishes the *Red Alert Newsletter* and the book *Redhead Dynasty,* and meets every so often. Founded in 1982. 20,000 members. Contact Stephen Douglas, President-Founder.

Remain Intact Organization (RIO)
RR 2, Box 86
Larchwood, IA 51241   (712) 477-2256

Yet another group of people opposed to routine circumcision, the Remain Intact Organization believes circumcision has adverse physical and psychological effects on males. The association distributes literature, audiotapes, and videotapes citing its views on the procedure. Founded in 1980. 1800 members. Contact Rev. Russell Zangger, Director.

Republican Women of Capitol Hill (RWCH)
160B Longworth House Office Building
Washington, DC 20515   (202) 224-3004

Politicians need friends, too. RWCH is a social club for female employees of Republican representatives on Capitol Hill, on the Republican National Committee, or in the administration. Associate members of the club are women who have worked for one of the above. The group provides members with the opportunity to establish contacts and meet influential leaders in Washington, D.C., by holding monthly luncheons featuring speakers such as ambassadors, White House staff members, and congressional representatives. The Republican Women also sponsor an annual fashion show, Christmas bazaar, and embassy parties, and issue the monthly newspaper *Trunk Line*. Founded in 1963. 250 members. Contact Ginny Sandahl, President.

Retired Greyhounds as Pets (REGAP)
PO Box 111
Camby, IN 46113   (317) 996-2154

By promoting retired greyhounds as loving, beautiful pets, REGAP seeks to find homes for retired greyhounds—the racing dogs after which the buses are named—as well as those that have not had successful racing careers. The group points out that greyhound racing is legal in some states and that greyhounds considered too old or too slow are often put to death. Founded in 1988. Contact Sally Allen, Representative.

Rhino Rescue U.S.A.
1150 17th St. NW, Suite 400
Washington, DC 20036   (202) 293-5305

Rhino Rescue supports rhinoceros reserves and research in rhino-rearing and reproduction to save the animal from extinction, and lobbies to prevent the illegal trade of rhino horns. Founded in 1985. Contact Thomas J. Schneider, Chairman.

Richard III Society
PO Box 13786
New Orleans, LA 70185   (504) 827-0161

A group of teachers, historians, students, and others interested in historical research into the life and times of Richard III (1452-85, King of England, 1483-85). The Society seeks "to secure a reassessment of the historical material relating to this period and of the role in English history of this monarch," especially in regard to the fate of the two young "Princes in the Tower" and the character of their uncle, Richard, who was accused of murdering his nephews to claim the throne. The group writes letters and prepares articles to correct "misinformation" about Richard III and publishes an annual memorial in *The New York Times* and *London Times*. In England, the Society maintains several memorials and historic sites and conducts expeditions to places of interest connected with Richard III. The English parent society has erected a life-size sculpture of Richard III by noted British sculptor James Butler in Leicester, the city nearest Bosworth Field, where Richard died in battle. The Society publishes its research in the quarterly *The Ricardian* and hosts an annual conference on the Saturday nearest

October 2nd. Founded in 1924. 750 members. Contact Carole M. Rike, Editor.

Riot Relief Fund (RRF)
25 W. 43rd St., Room 2102
New York, NY 10036   (212) 869-2212

Originally founded to aid families of police officers who were killed during the Civil War draft riots, the fund remains devoted to a strong and dedicated police force for New York City. The group provides aid to the surviving spouses of police officers killed in the line of duty, grants scholarships to officers studying aspects of law enforcement at John Jay College of Criminal Justice, and awards an annual medal to someone who has demonstrated exceptional service to law enforcement. The fund has published *The History of Civil War Draft Riots in New York City* and holds an annual conference in New York City. Founded in 1863. Contact Peter Megargee Brown, President.

Rockette Alumnae Association (RAA)
908 N. Broadway
Yonkers, NY 10701   (914) 423-3636

Live but no longer kicking, these former members of the Radio City Music Hall dance troupe, the Rockettes, are united for social and philanthropic causes. The association awards the Russell Market Dance Scholarship to dance students in the Dance Division of the Juilliard School of Music, publishes an annual journal and a fivetimes-per-year newsletter, and holds a spring charity ball and luncheon. The Rockette alums gather in New York City five times each year, in January, March, May, September, and November. Founded in 1955. 340 members. Contact Fern Weizner, President.

Rocky Mountain Llama and Alpaca Association (RMLA)
593 19 3/4 Road
Grand Junction, CO 81503-9574   (303) 241-7921

An association of owners and breeders of llamas, alpacas, or guanacos and others interested in llamas, alpacas, guanacos, or the people who own and breed them. The group disseminates information on llama health care, reproduction, packing techniques (how to fold a llama into a suitcase), marketing and tax data, herd management, and training. RMLA promotes llama research, education, and ethical business practices. Founded in 1982. 484 members. Contact Judith Sealy, Secretary.

Rodeo Historical Society (RHS)
1700 NE 63rd St.
Oklahoma City, OK 73111   (405) 478-2250

Git along, little dogie. The Rodeo Historical Society, composed of veteran rodeo and "Wild West" show performers, rodeo associations, and rodeo producers and managers, collects and preserves historical rodeo information in its museum and hall of fame and in its semiannual newsletter, *Ketch Pen*. The society's annual Wild Bunch Reunion takes place in Oklahoma City, and its annual induction ceremonies are held in November. Founded in 1968. 1200 members. Contact B. Byron Price, Director.

Role Playing Game Association Network (RPGAN)
PO Box 515
Lake Geneva, WI 53147 (414) 248-3625

Dungeons & Dragons and other role-playing and fantasy games capture the interest of the players, clubs, and retailers that make up this network. In such games, described as improvised, open-ended stories, a referee or gamemaster sets the scene while the players describe the actions of individual characters. The play depends on imagination and group interaction within elaborate rule systems. The network's monthly *Polyhedron Newszine*, features gaming articles, classified ads, and convention listings. Founded in 1980. 9000 members. Contact Jean Rabe, President.

Ronald Reagan Philatelic Society (RRPS)
PO Box 337
Canton, TX 75103 (214) 567-4076

Although this society is not connected in any way with former President Ronald Reagan or his administration, the group consists of stamp and cover collectors interested in the history of the Reagan administration (1980-88) as recorded on topical covers commemorating important events during the period. It issues topical covers relating to Reagan's administration for the collections of members and other collectors. Founded in 1980. 100 members. Contact George H. Goldey, President.

Roo Rat Society (RRS)
Whitman College
Walla Walla, WA 99362 (509) 527-5229

The Roo Rat Society derives its name from the kangaroo rat, a small rodent living in dry, sandy regions of North America, and includes persons dedicated to the study and conservation of wildlife and natural resources on local, national, and international levels. The society supports conservation projects by encouraging members to write to political leaders. Founded in 1963. 256 members. Contact James S. Todd, Scribe.

Route 66 Association
PO Drawer 5323
Oxnard, CA 93031 (805) 485-9923

U.S. Route 66 was commissioned in 1926 as the first highway link from Chicago, Illinois, to Los Angeles, California. Due to its popularity as America's Main Street, it became a national symbol that was glamorized through musical recordings and a television series. The Route 66 Association seeks to recreate the shared sense of adventure, romance, and discovery believed to be epitomized by the highway, in part by its *Route 66 Traveler's Guide and Roadside Companion*. Founded in 1983. 300 members. Contact Dr. Thomas J. Snyder, President.

Royal Association for the Longevity and Preservation of the Honeymooners (RALPH)
C.W. Post
Greenvale, NY 11548 (516) 299-2506

Norton! Individuals in RALPH are interested in preserving and perpetuating *The Honeymooners*, a classic situation comedy series broadcast on CBS from 1955 to 1956. RALPH works to secure the original, unedited prints of the 39 episodes now in syndication. It was involved in the purchase of the bus driver's uniform worn by Jackie Gleason in the series, and also owns original Kramden kitchen furniture used on the program. Founded in 1982. 12,000 members. Contact Bob Columbe, Co-President.

S ^S **S** **S** **S** **S** ^S **S**

Sand Collectors International (SCI)
PO Box 17273
Groenkloof 0027, Republic of South Africa   467562

But it just falls right through your hands. The group fosters cooperation among collectors of sand worldwide and encourages the exchange of samples. It publishes a quarterly newsletter, known appropriately as *The Sands of Time.* Founded in 1985. 55 members. Contact Horst Windisch, Chairman.

Sarcastics Anonymous (SA)
Box 1495
Pleasanton, CA 94566   (415) 462-3470

SA is a quasi-tongue-in-cheek association for individuals who alienate others through the inappropriate use of sarcastic remarks or put-downs. Members also include the unfortunate people who live or work with these individuals. Founder Dr. Virginia Tooper, known as "The Laugh Professor" for her work in helping others improve their laugh lives, is herself a recovered sarcastic. Tooper decided "something had to be done when she was down to her last friend and he wasn't calling. In fact, she lost one perfectly good boyfriend after another through the indiscriminate use of funny remarks."

The group promotes the positive uses of humor and laughter, as opposed to sarcasm, or what the group sees as inappropriately used humor with the aim of getting the laugh "regardless of the results." It provides information on the uses and abuses of humor in personal and professional lives, how to live or work with sarcastic people, and methods for lessening sarcastic tendencies for members wishing to do so. The association hopes to help members avoid the condition known as "sarcastic bottom" (lots of laughs but no friends; or worse, brimming with lots of put-downs but having no one close enough to hear you). It works with sarcastics on how to develop their sense of humor more appropriately by offering workshops in areas such as business, education, and health, with emphasis on stress reduction and communication. The group issues the quarterly *Sarcastics Anonymous and Laugh Lovers News.* Founded in 1984. 320 members. Contact Dr. Virginia O. Tooper, Director of Barbs.

Sasquatch Investigations of Mid-America (SIA)
PO Box 37386
Oklahoma City, OK 73157

They love him and pet him and call his name Sasquatch—also known as Bigfoot—a large, hairy, nocturnal creature sighted in thickly wooded regions throughout the world. Sasquatches are reportedly about eight feet tall, walk upright, and appear to be intelligent and peaceful, though notoriously shy. About 1000 reports of sasquatch sightings have been documented in the U.S., and SIA evaluates this and other data and releases its findings to the public through lectures, radio and television programs, and its annual *Bigfoot News*. It also maintains a library of 300 books and magazines pertaining to Bigfoot, and its members investigate and report sightings in their areas. Founded in 1976. 400 members. Contact Hayden C. Hewes, Director of Research.

Save America's Forests (SAF)
1742 18th St. NW, Room 201
Washington, DC 20009   (202) 667-5150

"Part of the New Conservation Movement," SAF is a support center and voice for the nationwide grassroots forest protection movement in Congress. The coalition of more than 100 groups and lots of individuals is united to pass national laws protecting forest ecosystems. It seeks to prevent clearcutting, bulldozing, slash burning, and pesticide application of public forest land. Members are invited to come lobby in Washington, where the group maintains an office and guest house. Members pledge to phone, write, or visit members of Congress and impart the message of strong and comprehensive forest protection. SAF publishes the quarterly *D.C. Update* newsletter and Action Alerts. Regular membership is $25. Founded in 1990. 235,000 members. Contact Carl Ross, Co-Director.

Save Life On Earth (SLOE)
326 Harvard St.
Cambridge, MA 02139   (617) 491-4948

Participants in SLOE are artists from six continents who created a major touring exhibition against nuclear weapons, which was seen in Europe, Asia, Australia, and North America. SLOE encourages the exchange of artists between Eastern and Western nations and artists of the Third World. It has published *Save Life on Earth* and produces art reproductions and posters. Founded in 1983. Contact Nyna Brael Polumbaum, President.

Save Our Barns Committee (SOBC)
Illinois State Historical Society
Old State Capitol Building
Springfield, IL 62701   (217) 782-4836

Specifically, barns in Illinois, where this state committee of the Illinois State Historical Society is based. The committee collects, disseminates, and documents information on barns in Illinois and makes presentations to historical societies and civic organizations. Additionally, it helps register barns in the National Register of Historic Places. Founded in 1973. Contact H. Wayne Price, Chairman.

Science Fiction Poetry Association (SFPA)
PO Box 1764
Cambridge, MA 02238

Beam me up, Scotty; and don't be snotty. Yes, even amateur poets, or "poetic dabblers," and general readers can join the professional writers in the Science Fiction Poetry Association. SFPA promotes communication among people interested in science fiction and fantasy by sharing marketing news, reviewing current science fiction publications, and publishing the annual *Anthology* and the bimonthly newsletter *Star Line*, which includes award presentations, an annual index, and an anthology of the best poetry of the year. SFPA presents the Rhysling Awards for the best long and short poems. Founded in 1978. 150 members. Contact Elissa Malcohn, Editor.

Science Fiction Research Association (SFRA)
1017 Seal Way
Seal Beach, CA 90740   (213) 985-5341

All sorts of people belong to this sci-fi association: teachers, librarians, students, futurologists, authors, editors, publishers, booksellers, and other science fiction enthusiasts who promote the study and teaching of science fiction, modern fantasy, and their related fields. The group presents the annual Pilgrim Award to a distinguished scholar in the field, and ten times yearly it issues *Book Review Journal* and its newsletter, which lists major works in progress and new publications, surveys science fiction courses and audio-visual aids to teaching, and includes an annotated bibliography of science fiction criticism. The association also holds an annual conference with exhibits. Founded in 1970. 450 members. Contact Peter Lowentrout, President.

Science Frontiers (SF)
2119 College St.
Cedar Falls, IA 50613   (319) 266-8669

Publishers of the quarterly *Science Quest*, Science Frontiers is a special interest group of Mensa interested in scientific anomalies. Founded in 1985. 50 members. Contact Gerald Baker, Executive Director.

Scientific Instrument Society (SIS)
PO Box 15
Pershore, Hereford and Worcester WR10 2RD,
    England   386 861075

Scientific instruments ranging from antiques to early, now obsolete, electronic devices interest these collectors, antique traders, museum staff members, and professional historians. The society publishes information on scientific instruments and sponsors seminars and quarterly symposia. Founded in 1983. 550 members. Contact Howard Dawes, Secretary.

Scientific Marriage Foundation (SMF)
Hopkins Syndicate
802 S. Washington
Bloomington, IN 47401   (812) 331-7752

Sergeant Pepper's Lonely Hearts Club Laboratory, sort of. This interdenominational service organization attempts to find congenial mates for single men and women through science and psychology. The foundation functions as a subdivision of the Compliment Club, directed by psychologist Dr. George W. Crane, and it boasts an advisory board of 2500 clergymen who serve as field counselors. Founded in 1956. Contact S. L. Abram, Executive Officer.

Scripophila Helvetica (SH)
Postfach 163
CH-3000 Bern 15, Switzerland

Everybody loves old money. Scripophila Helvetica members like antique stocks and bonds. The collectors of said historic bonds and securities sponsor exchange markets and lectures, provide documents and expert advice on the theme of financial history, and investigate collections of antique stocks and bonds. The group holds a semiannual auction and issues the *SH Club Bulletin*. Founded in 1979. 100 members. Contact Karl Hafner, President.

SEARCH Foundation
PO Box 43388
Birmingham, AL 35243   (205) 991-9516

It's awfully old, but it *could* still be floating around somewhere. The SEARCH Foundation tries to find and identify the remains of the biblical Noah's Ark through research and field expeditions. SEARCH is an acronym for Scientific Exploratory Archeological Research. Founded in 1969. Contact John M. Bradley Jr., President.

Second Wives Association of North America (SWAN)
58 Walker Ave.
Toronto, ON, Canada M4V 1G2   (416) 961-1337

SWAN, which includes second wives and their husbands (apparently unenumerated), is organized to bring attention to the unique problems of second wives and second marriages in general. SWAN lists such problems as lack of approval from society and financial burdens stemming from child support payments and alimony to the husband's first wife as unique to second marriages. The group seeks to provide support and information and to lobby for changes in laws concerning divorce and child custody. Founded in 1982. 600 members. Contact Glynnis Walker, President.

Seed Savers Exchange (SSE)
RR 3, Box 239
Decorah, IA 52101   (319) 382-5990

Growing, growing, gone. The vegetable gardeners in Seed Savers Exchange are dedicated to finding, multiplying, and spreading heirloom vegetable varieties before they are lost. Members trade seeds through the mail, experiment with vegetable varieties and culturing techniques, and report results through the group's publications. Specifically, the Exchange is interested in locating vegetable varieties that have been in families for many generations or that families have brought to the U.S. from their homeland (such as Burmese carrots) or that have been selectively improved over the years (the new and improved vegetable) or that are no longer available from any seed catalog or that are unusual (such as genetic mutations) or that are extremely disease-resistant, very hardy, of exceptional quality, or have other outstanding characteristics. Super veggies, if you will.

The group's Growers Network allows members to acquire seeds from other members through a plant adoption program. In the summer the exchange holds an annual Camp-Out Convention. Founded in 1975. 780 members. Contact Kent Whealy, Director.

Senior Masters

77 Leland Farm Road
Ashland, MA 01721   (508) 881-8052

Senior citizens who are of retirement age but are "not yet ready to call it quits" remain active after retirement by volunteering or working in an area that interests them. The group provides members inspiration, direction, information, and ideas about activities, and it updates members on discounts available to seniors. The Senior Masters issues a newsletter and a guidebook of post-retirement job opportunities. Founded in 1990. 500 members. Contact Robert S. Farrington, President.

Sensitives of America Club

1718A Northfield Square
Northfield, IL 60093   (708) 501-3519

Sensitives are individuals with extrasensory abilities. The club conducts research and provides information on the criteria for sensitivity, a history of extrasensory perception, and solacing objects for sensitives. It issues the *Solace* newsletter, which includes profiles of famous sensitives, book reviews, and criteria information. Founded in 1991. 10 members. Contact Susan Frissell Ph.D., President.

Sex Addicts Anonymous (SAA)

PO Box 3038
Minneapolis, MN 55403   (612) 339-0217

Sex Addicts Anonymous is a support group for sex addicts that follows a program adapted from the 12-step program of Alcoholics Anonymous World Services. The organization describes sex addicts as people who compulsively repeat sexual behavior that is damaging to their lives. It issues the monthly *Plain Brown Wrapper* newsletter, *Sex Addicts' Anonymous 21 Questions, Abstinence and Boundaries*, and group guides, and it holds an annual conference. Founded in 1977. 3000 members.

Sex and Love Addicts Anonymous (SLAA)

PO Box 119, New Town Branch
Boston, MA 02258   (617) 332-1845

Also known as the Augustine Fellowship, this group includes individuals recovering from a compulsive need for sex, a desperate attachment to one person, or other sexual or emotional obsessive-compulsive behavior. Functioning as a support group to help members achieve comfortable, long-term sexual and emotional sobriety, the group employs the 12 Steps of Alcoholics Anonymous World Services, adapted to the needs of sex addicts. It issues a journal and newsletter and has published the textbook *Sex and Love Addicts Anonymous*. Founded in 1976.

Sexaholics Anonymous (SA)

PO Box 300
Simi Valley, CA 93062   (805) 581-3343

Sexaholics Anonymous is for individuals wishing to stop their sexually self-destructive thinking and behavior such as fantasy, pornography, adultery, masturbation, incest, or criminal sexual activity. The group believes that the sexaholic is addicted to lust and sex as others are to alcohol or drugs; this behavior is often followed by guilt, remorse, and depression, and may damage relationships with family and peers. SA conducts programs based on the 12-step recovery program used in Alcoholics Anonymous to help members achieve "sexual sobriety." The group meets semiannually. Founded in 1979. 8000 members.

Ships-in-Bottles Association of America (SBAA)
PO Box 180550
Coronado, CA 92178-0550   (619) 435-3555

Originally organized as the North American branch of the French group *Bateaux en Bouteilles*, SBAA promotes the art of building ships in bottles and includes members from as far afield as New Zealand, Australia, India, and Japan in addition to the U.S. and Canada. The group exchanges ideas and information among builders throughout the world, primarily through the quarterly journal *The Bottle Shipwright*. The journal introduces ideas of ship bottling submitted by members, news of competitions and exhibits, photos of members' works, and other material related to the art. Dues are $15. Periodically, members gather and discuss the various matters related to ships in bottles. Their motto is not, "A ship in the bottle is worth two in the bath." Founded in 1978. 400 members. Contact Don Hubbard, Membership Chairman.

Shoplifters Anonymous (SA)
380 N. Broadway, Suite 206
Jericho, NY 11753   (516) 932-0165

The group provides referral counseling treatment and rehabilitation for people with shoplifting problems, and applies modern behavioral techniques to terminate stealing habits and convert shoplifters into honest consumers. SA also offers self-help home study courses and conducts research and specialized education programs on causes and prevention of shoplifting. Founded in 1977. Contact Peter D. Berlin, Executive Officer.

Shroud of Turin Research Project (STURP)
PO Box 378
Willimantic, CT 06226   (203) 456-8706

STURP consists of the professionals, logistics support personnel, and physical scientists acting as principal investigators in research work being performed on the Shroud of Turin, a piece of linen that appeared seven centuries ago in the possession of a French knight and is venerated by many as the burial cloth of Christ. The group's purpose is to determine the physics and chemistry of both the cloth and image in order to verify or refute the authenticity of the shroud. To do this, it conducts nondestructive testing and research and attempts to simulate and analyze various images and stains found on the shroud through laboratory tests, including chemical analysis, infrared spectroscopy and thermography, optical and ultraviolet reflectance and fluorescent spectroscopy, photography, x-radiography, and x-ray fluorescence. STURP seeks to coordinate all activities in the field, reviews research proposals, and distributes funding. Founded in 1978. 75 members. Contact Thomas F. D'Muhala, President.

Silent Running Society (SRS)

PO Box 529
Howell, NJ 07731

Named after the science fiction film *Silent Running*, which depicts the care taken by an astrobotanist to save the last of the earth's forests, housed within a spaceship, the society includes businesses, industries, and individuals dedicated to the conservation of trees and reforestation. It attempts to save damaged trees and donates seedlings and trees for tree-planting events and large-scale reforestation on public and private property. The group seeks legislation that will encourage the construction industry to protect trees and to replant where trees are destroyed, and it believes that, with careful planning, new neighborhoods, highways, office parks, and shopping centers can be built without the unnecessary destruction of trees. The society also grants awards to individuals and organizations contributing to the preservation of trees, publishes the annual newsletter *The Log*, and holds an annual tree-planting in October. Founded in 1985. 97 members. Contact Steven Lance Hersh, Founder & Executive Director.

Single Gourmet (SG)

133 E. 58th St.
New York, NY 10022   (212) 980-8788

This social dining club is for individuals who have never married or who are divorced, widowed, or separated from their spouse. The objective is to offer single men and women the opportunity to meet each other over a good meal. It conducts at least four local activities per month, including dinners and trips, all of which are meal-oriented. Restaurants are visited beforehand and are chosen on the basis of their ambience, unusual menu, and food quality. Founded in 1980. Contact Arthur Fischer, Director.

Single Mothers by Choice (SMC)

PO Box 1642, Gracie Square Station
New York, NY 10028   (212) 988-0993

Solitary moms, and proud of it. Single Mothers by Choice offers single women the opportunity to discuss the problems and benefits of being a single parent. The group consists primarily of single professional women in their 30s and 40s who have either decided to have or are considering having children outside of marriage, but it also welcomes women who are considering adoption as single parents. (It does not, however, include mothers who are widowed or divorced.) The group provides support for single mothers, sponsors workshops and play groups for children, and holds an annual summer meeting. Founded in 1981. 1000 members. Contact Jane Mattes, Chairperson.

Single Persons for Tax Equality Association (SPTEA)

2314 Logan Ave. N.
Minneapolis, MN 55411-1938

Economic parity for singles in a couples-only society. This association of unmarried men and women would like to see federal income taxes for individuals based on one tax table. The group issues *SPTEA News* six times per year and holds an annual conference in July. Founded in 1967. 5000 members. Contact E. Foss, President.

Singles in Agriculture (SIA)
Route 2 E. 12820 Highway 33
Baraboo, WI 53913 (608) 356-3483

Through a friendship correspondence program, Singles in Agriculture works to enrich the lives of its members, who are single persons with an agricultural background or who are currently working in a job related to agriculture. The group promotes and conducts educational, recreational, and social activities, including an annual campout. Its quarterly newsletter is called *Over the Back Fence*. Founded in 1986. 1000 members. Contact Franklin Cook, Vice President.

Sinistral Sig (SS)
200 Emmett Ave.
Derby, CT 06418 (203) 735-1759

The word *sinister* stems from the same root as *left;* hence, the group's focus. Sinistral Sig is an association of left-handed people whose IQs are in the top two percent of the population and who are eligible to be members of Mensa; interested individuals are associate members. SS conducts surveys and experiments concerning left-handedness and its relationship to intelligence and brain function, and it publishes such information in its bimonthly publication, *Sinistralian*. Founded in 1977. 100 members. Contact Sharlene McEvoy, Coordinator.

Sleep Research Society (SRS)
Brockton VAMC
Department of Psychiatry 116 A
940 Belmont St.
Brockton, MA 02401 (508) 583-4500

Your eyelids are getting heavy . . . you're very sleepy . . . relax. The Sleep Research Society includes physiologists, psychologists, and physicians with research interests in the study of sleep. The society disseminates scientific papers on the physiological and psychological aspects of sleep and helps researchers in the field communicate with one another, but it does not sponsor research investigations on its own (too tiring). Issues a bimonthly journal, appropriately titled *Sleep*. Founded in 1961. 428 members. Contact Robert W. McCarley M.D., Executive Officer.

Slow Food Foundation
107 Waverly Place, Suite 1R
New York, NY 10011-9172 (212) 254-9408

Welcome to "The Greenpeace of gastronomy," seeking to "recondition our collective gastronomic consciousness." Founded in Italy in response to the opening of a McDonald's in Rome, the foundation counts among its members individuals and corporations in 27 countries committed to traditions that bring family and friends together to share great food and wine in a spirit of conviviality and civility. The foundation, whose logo is a flying snail, questions the "validity of the fast food philosophy, an unconscious credo that erodes our culinary heritage in the guise of efficiency, producing gastronomic distress and littering our landscape."

Slow food is defined as food prepared slowly and lovingly by time-honored methods, using *fresh* ingredients, and consumed at leisure in gracious surroundings. "Civilized eating is vanishing rapidly," says Flavio Accornero, president of the movement. "Real change begins at your own kitchen table." Through "gentle persuasion," the group hopes to motivate the intelligent consumer to investigate the leisurely world of slow food.

Meals should be an opportunity for communication, according to the foundation, which maintains that fast food is "barbaric" and detrimental to health, jeopardizes the gastronomic heritage of regions around the world, is responsible for the eradication of family life, and is an important factor in the deforestation of the Amazon because of the increasing demand for cheap meat. It encourages public education about folklore and local traditions, the health benefits of wholesome foods and beverages, the degradation of quality that comes from excessive processing and packaging of food, and the ecological benefits that come from respecting our lands and waters and by abandoning pesticides and additives. The group works to establish a worldwide reputation for the U.S. as a first-class culinary capital and wine-producing country, not a country of fast food and soft drinks. Issues *Slow Food International Magazine* (in English, Italian, and Spanish) twice a year and holds periodic dinners, wine and food seminars, and tastings. Membership starts at $55 annually. Ban the burger, hold the fries. Founded in 1986. 30,000 members. Contact Flavio Accornero, President.

Smoker's Rights Alliance (SRA)
20 E. Main St., Suite 710
Mesa, AZ 85201   (602) 461-8882

Got a light? Individuals in SRA are interested in preserving the right to smoke without unnecessary interference by government. Their alliance, which provides a means of communication and support for smokers and proponents of smoking, educates and informs members of their rights, the legislative process, and pending anti-smoking legislation. The group also challenges anti-smoking legislation, taxation, litigation, and other discrimination based on smoking habits. Their quarterly newsletter, *Smoke Signals,* includes legislative updates, news, and editorials. Their annual conference includes a smoking section. Founded in 1987. 2500 members. Contact Dave W. Branton, President.

Smurf Collectors' Club International (SCCI)
24 Cabot Road, W., Department E
Massapequa, NY 11758   (516) 799-3221

They're small, they're blue, they're cute, and they're *everywhere.* They're pretty old, too: the lovable little cartoon characters date from 1957. Smurf collectors, dealers, and admirers formed their international club to exchange information about the history of Smurf collectibles, which include one-of-a-kind paint and mold variations, destroyed molds, and both U.S. and European market merchandise. The group publishes the quarterly *Smurf Collectors' Club Newsletter* and *The Smurfs: A Legend in Their Own Time.* Founded in 1988. 800 members. Contact Suzanne Lipschitz, Founder.

Snow Biz (SB)
PO Box 53262
Washington, DC 20008

Individuals interested in collecting snowdome paperweights, of course, make up the membership, which meets annually to discuss the state of said domes. Contact Nancy McMichael, Founder.

Society for Creative Anachronism (SCA)
PO Box 360743
Milpitas, CA 95036-0743   (415) 428-1181

Members of SCA, aside from knowing how to spell "medieval," are interested in learning about the Middle Ages by means of theoretical and practical research into various aspects of its culture. The society's primary activities are Tournaments and Revels, events that provide an opportunity for members to exercise and display skills in medieval music, revelry, dancing, cooking, and martial arts. Members also enjoy showing off the artifacts, such as embroidery, costume, armor, and calligraphy, which have been made or developed privately or in special interest groups. SCA seeks to create a total medieval environment in which everyone can be a participant rather than a spectator. The society publishes the bimonthly *Compleat Anachronist,* the quarterly *Tournaments Illuminated,* and *The Known World Handbook of the Current Middle Ages* and other books. Founded in 1966. 17,000 members. Contact Hilary Powers, President.

Society for Musteline Arts and Literature (SMAL)
13412 Gilbert St.
Garden Grove, CA 92644   (714) 530-1312

Seeking to "loosen the grip of cats and dogs on popular culture by providing an alternative," the artists, writers, and collectors in the Society for Musteline Arts and Literature promote art, sculpture, and literature depicting Mustelidae, a mammalian family that includes badgers, martens, minks, otters, skunks, weasels, and wolverines. The group issues the *SMAL* newsletter. Founded in 1986. 20 members. Contact Mark Merlino, Chairman.

Society for Scientific Exploration (SSE)
Department of Astronomy
PO Box 3818
University of Virginia
Charlottesville, VA 22903   (804) 924-4905

Cryptozoology, parapsychology, unidentified flying objects, geophysical anomalies, and related areas are studied by the scientists and scholars from a wide range of disciplines united in SSE. The society publishes the semiannual newsletter *Explorer* and the semiannual *Journal of Scientific Exploration,* which reports on anomalous phenomena. Founded in 1982. 303 members. Contact Prof. Laurence W. Fredrick, Secretary.

Society for the Application of Free Energy (SAFE)
1315 Apple Ave.
Silver Spring, MD 20910   (301) 587-8686

SAFE's purpose is to apply radiesthesia, or dowsing, in finding water, oil, and other substances, and to research and use natural forms of energy, including solar, wind, metaphysical, and biocybernetic energy. Metaphysical energy is, of course, the energy of the mind, and SAFE deals with the determination and analysis of mind power as a form of electricity. Biocybernetic energy, according to SAFE, is the energy of living things, such as plants, animals, and humans. The group believes that all living things have an electronic force, like the Energizer bunny. Wind and solar energy are the more traditionally understood forms of energy used by the group in its dowsing endeavors. Founded in 1973. 250 members. Contact Dr. Carl Schleicher, Director.

Society for the Eradication of Television (SET)
Box 10491
Oakland, CA 94610-0491   (415) 763-8712

"Watching television is a form of electronic lobotomy!" Members of SET, also known as SET Free, are households that do not have a working television and do not want one. They encourage others to "Just Say No to Television," the viewing habit that amounts to 3.5 billion hours a day globally. "Television is the ultimate product of mindless consumption and greed," says SET spokesperson Pat Brown. SET believes television retards the inner life of human beings, destroys human interaction, squanders time, and draws viewers into abject addiction. "Television brainwashes people. Most programs distort real life. The fantasy images projected through television shows and idiotic commercials confirm American 'middle class' prejudices, biases, heterosexism, and ageism. When anything dramatic happens in the lives of television zombies or if they meet a passionately expressive or non-conforming person with human gusto, they just become terrified!" And furthermore, television "is one long commercial for the patriarchy."

Ironically, the group had an interview filmed for NBC's *Today Show* that did not air, and reports that the television executive who was going to look into it suffered a heart attack and died. So much for real life. To get the word out on the dangers of television, SET issues the quarterly *S.E.T. Free, The Newsletter Against Television* ($5 subscription) and does the occasional radio interview.. It holds an annual conference where everyone grouses about television. Concludes Brown: "Television makes you less an autonomous individual and more prone to being dominated. The only thing to do with a television set is turn it off and throw it out the window." Founded in 1980. 700 members. Contact Steve Wagner, Director.

Society for the Furtherance and Study of Fantasy and Science Fiction (SF3)
Box 1624
Madison, WI 53701   (608) 233-5640

A feminist/humanist perspective of science fiction is the focus of SF3, which conducts a monthly program at the University of Wisconsin consisting of feature movies, discussions, and slide shows. SF3 also sponsors a Book-of-the-Month Discussion Circle meeting and an annual conference during February or March in Madison, Wisconsin. The society maintains an extensive library of amateur publications available to the general public for research and periodically issues *Aurora: Speculative Feminism* as well as the bimonthly *Cube* newsletter. Founded in 1977. 75 members. Contact Diane Martin, Controller.

Society for the Investigation of Recurring Events (SIRE)
Prudential Bache Securities
399 Thornall St.
Edison, NJ 08837   (800) 992-9982

Some things just keep happening over and over and over again.

The society is a group of people interested in the broad field of cycles, rhythms, or periodicities, events recurring in a possibly predictable pattern. Members are also intrigued by links between periodicities and in the laws dictating patterns of recurrence, such as bull and bear patterns of the stock market, the correlation of weather conditions with major crimes, and rhythms in human moods. Membership includes economists, biologists, psychologists, investment counselors, investors, physicians, and educators.

Every month, continuously and without fail, the society publishes *Abstract*, which contains abstracts of monthly meetings and prognostications for financial markets from experts, and *SIRE Newsletter*, which provides information on the finance- and science-related study of cycles affecting the stock market, interest rates, and credit commodities. The group's monthly social hour and dinner, with an address by an authority on cycles, takes place in that macro of a recurring pattern called New York City. Founded in 1957. 300 members. Contact Peter G. Constable, President.

Society for the Investigation of the Unexplained (SITU)
Box 265
Little Silver, NJ 07739   (201) 842-5229

SITU members acquire and investigate reports of all tangible items in the fields of chemistry, astronomy, geology, biology, and anthropology that are not readily explained. The society encourages field work and on-the-spot investigation by offering advice and arranging contacts for members who are planning field trips and expeditions. Field work and research are reviewed by a panel of 15 scientists. Society members have investigated Loch Ness-type creatures in North America, UFOs, Bigfoot, the Bermuda Triangle, cattle mutilations, and ghost and poltergeist manifestations. OK, but what we're really looking for is an explanation of the Reagan years. The group maintains information files of original material, a map collection, and a specialized library, and it issues the quarterly journal *Pursuit*. Founded in 1965. 1500 members. Contact Robert C. Warth, President.

Society for the Philosophy of Sex and Love (SPSL)
University of New Orleans
Philosophy Department
New Orleans, LA 70148   (504) 286-6257

As Sartre never said, "There is no philosophy without sex and love." These philosophy instructors and others affiliated with colleges and universities, privately employed professionals, and students present, distribute, or partake of philosophic papers on the topics of sex and love. The papers are published semiannually, while the group gathers twice a year in conjunction with the American Philosophical Association. Founded in 1977. 70 members. Contact Prof. Alan Soble, President.

Society for the Preservation and Advancement of the Harmonica (SPAH)
PO Box 865
Troy, MI 48099   (313) 647-2706

Harmonica enthusiasts who wish to advance and preserve (that's what the name says) good harmonica music. The society arranges harmonica instruction for hobbyists, and its members regularly perform for service organizations. SPAH publishes a quarterly newsletter called *Harmonica Happenings* and meets annually. Founded in 1963. 3000 members. Contact Gordon M. Mitchell, President.

Society for the Preservation and Appreciation of Antique Motor Fire Apparatus in America (SPAAMFAA)
PO Box 2005
Syracuse, NY 13220   (914) 343-4219

Members of SPAAMFAA are interested in old fire fighting methods and equipment, or who own or wish to own antique (defined as at least 25 years old) fire fighting stuff. The society is chartered by the New York State Education Department as a nonprofit, educational, and historical society dedicated to fire service history and to preserving, restoring, and operating antique fire service apparatus. It sponsors Antique Apparatus Shows and Musters (competitive exhibitions), participates in local Fire Prevention Week activities, and cooperates in public relations efforts of units of the fire service. The group publishes the excitingly named quarterly magazine *Enjine! Enjine!* as well as *The Silver Trumpet,* deftly described as a periodic newsletter. Members and their apparatuses (apparati?) gather annually. Founded in 1958. 2250 members. Contact Marvin H. Cohen, Secretary.

Society for the Preservation and Encouragement of Barber Shop Quartet Singing in America (SPEBSQSA)
6315 Third Ave.
Kenosha, WI 53143-5199   (414) 656-8440

These men interested in barbershop quartet and chorus singing seek to preserve barbershop harmony, a traditional form of American music culture. The society provides an outlet for self-expression in song while serving the community: it created the Harmony Foundation to provide financial support to the Institute of Logopedics in Wichita, Kansas, a residential school for the study and treatment of speech disorders in children. The group selects international barbershop quartet and chorus champions annually, after staging 16 district and 16 international preliminary contests. In addition to publishing barbershop arrangements and songbooks, it maintains a library of 650,000 old songs and issues the bimonthly *Harmonizer.* In 1992 the society's annual show will take place from June 28 to July 5 in New Orleans, Louisiana, and the 1993 gathering is set for June 27 to July 4 in Calgary, Alberta, Canada. Founded in 1938. 37,000 members. Contact Joe Liles, Executive Director.

Society for the Preservation and Enhancement of the Recognition of Millard Fillmore, Last of the Whigs (SPERMFLOW)
PO Box 712
Cascade, CO 80809   (719) 684-2102

"Fillmorons" are dedicated to the celebration of mediocrity in American culture, as epitomized by Millard Fillmore (1800-74), 13th president of the United States and later an unsuccessful Presidential candidate of the Know-Nothing Party. The society considers Fillmore to be the "dullest and unluckiest president we ever had," declaring that his sole accomplishment was "keeping Texas from annexing the state of New Mexico in a fit of pre-football hysteria."

The society bestows the annual Medal of Mediocrity to an individual or event best representing the principles Fillmore "tried to stand for, but usually sat on." A recent event winner was the digging up of President Zachary Taylor to determine whether he was assassinated (poisoned) rather than having died of cholera brought on by heat exhaustion and an overdose of cold milk and cherries. Fillmore, Taylor's Vice President and eventual successor, might have been suspect had Taylor been murdered. Society vice president Phil Arkow notes that this would have spoiled Fillmore's reputation for having done nothing.

SPERMFLOW publishes the *Fillmore Bu(n)gle,* an occasional publication dedicated to the "wonderful, wussful, wistful world of mediocrity." Filled with bad jokes and reports on "admirable bunglers" and losers of all types, the magazine has celebrated such individuals as Pete Rose, Dan Quayle, and Zsa Zsa Gabor. The society also sponsors the annual Dearthday Party, which usually takes place on January 7th. Founded in 1975. 400 members. Contact Phil Arkow, Vice President.

Society for the Preservation of Beers from the Wood (SPBW)
18 Vivian Road
London E3, England   81 9806146

SPBW promotes the production of beer through traditional methods, or, as Merrill Lynch might say (if a company could talk), brew made the old-fashioned way. This may or may not have something to do with wood, although we suspect that the beer the society has in mind may be aged in wood or imbibed from wooden mugs or squeezed from trees. Contact Roger Jacobson.

Society for the Second Self (SSS)
PO Box 4067
Visalia, CA 93278   (209) 688-9246

Second Self members are heterosexual male crossdressers who are not transsexuals, fetishists, or sadomasochists. The society, which is also known as the Tri-Ess Sorority, encourages members to live happy and well-adjusted lives as transvestites and accept their desire to dress in women's clothes. The group conducts public education programs on the true nature of crossdressing and functions as a network for communication among members; local groups conduct regular support group meetings and social gatherings. SSS also plans to operate a couples' auxiliary for members' wives and female friends. The society issues a periodic *Buyer's Guide,* which lists places of business that serve crossdressers without ridicule, and publishes the quarterly *Femme Mirror.* Its annual *Holiday en Femme,* with exhibits, takes place in November. Founded in 1976. 1000 members. Contact Donna Martin, Director.

Society for the Study of Myth and Tradition (SSMT)
656 Broadway
New York, NY 10012   (212) 505-6200

The society's primary purpose is to publish *Parabola Magazine: The Magazine of Myth and Tradition,* which, as its title suggests, is devoted to the study of mythology, comparative religion, and tradition in a cross-cultural perspective. The magazine, which has 26,000 subscribers, promotes an in-depth understanding of the great religious traditions and the meanings they may hold for contemporary life. The society conducts an annual conference and symposium in New York City. Founded in 1976. Contact Joseph Kulin, Executive Publisher.

Society for the Systematic Documentation of Paranormal Experiments (SSDPE)
Box 48862
Niles, IL 60648 (312) 774-5284

Attempting to control the uncontrollable and document the undocumentable, this task force devises and studies paranormal phenomena, using outside observers to provide input into the design of paranormal demonstrations such as levitation and psychokinesis. The society seeks to investigate the paranormal phenomenon of zero-order probability, which the scientific community considers impossible under controlled conditions. The group makes available to the public all their documentation papers. Founded in 1985. Contact Leo Macarow, Coordinator.

Society for Utopian Studies (SUS)
Department of Political Science
University of Missouri at St. Louis
St. Louis, MO 63121 (314) 553-5849

Imagine Walden's Pond, imagine Walden II, imagine there's no heaven. Promoting the study of experimental and literary utopias and utopian thought are academics from a variety of disciplines, architects, futurists, urban planners, environmentalists, and just plain interested individuals. The society issues *Utopus Discovered* three times a year plus the periodic *Utopian Studies,* and it holds a sublime annual conference in October. Founded in 1975. 300 members. Contact Prof. Lyman Tower Sargent, Chair.

Society of American Fight Directors (SAFD)
1834 Camp Ave.
Rockford, IL 61103 (815) 962-6579

You mean it's not real? Actors, stage fight choreographers, and other interested individuals make up the society, which provides training and certification for qualified stage combat performers and instructors. The group also promotes historical accuracy and aesthetic merit in staged fights and seeks to ensure the safety of stage fight participants. SAFD issues the *Cutting Edge* newsletter six times per year, which includes updates on union regulation, society policy, and the activities of members, and the journal *The Fight Master* three times a year, which includes articles related to fight choreography. The annual conference features a stage combat workshop. Founded in 1977. 300 members. Contact Richard Raether, Executive Officer.

Society of California Pioneers (SCP)
456 McAllister St.
San Francisco, CA 94102 (415) 861 5278

They went west, young man. These direct descendants of pioneers who arrived in California before 1850 sponsor cultural and historical programs. The society also maintains a museum of 19th century California art and a library of 15,000 volumes on California, has established biographical archives on pioneers of 1849 or earlier, and maintains the birthplace of Juniperro Serra at Petra on the island of Mallorca in the Mediterranean. Founded in 1850. 1200 members. Contact J. Roger Jobson, Executive Director.

Society of Earthbound Extraterrestrials (SEE)
2140 Shattuck Ave., Suite 2329
Berkeley, CA 94704   (403) 486-3415

"For years people have speculated that the Earth has been visited by creatures from outer space. Well, this is true," asserts the Society of Earthbound Extraterrestrials. They reason: "Haven't you sometimes looked over at the people at the coffee machine and said to yourself, *They're not from here!* Well, you're probably right."

SEE members are interested in extraterrestrial studies and UFO research. They'd like to establish public scientific facilities specifically designated to investigate UFO sightings because, they say, our current public investigative bodies, such as military and police forces, aren't equipped for or interested in UFO research. Explaining the difficulty of UFO investigation, SEE says that 99 percent of all UFO sightings are "stale"; that is, they are over long before anyone capable of checking them on radar (or whatever) hears of them. What we need to do is catch a few "fresh" ones.

The society issues a quarterly newsletter, called *Seescapes,* and holds an annual meeting. Lifetime membership in SEE is $18.95, and members receive "not only a snappy laminated membership card, membership certificate, SEE decals and a membership book, but also the knowledge that they belong to one of the most inexclusive clubs in the Universe." Founded in 1986. 500 members. Contact Otomar Tllak, Director.

Society of Flavor Chemists (SFC)
McCormick and Co.
204 Wight Ave.
Hunt Valley, MD 21031   (301) 771-7491

There's more to life than chocolate, strawberry, and vanilla. The flavor chemists in this society are engaged in flavor creation and development for flavor manufacturing companies. The group fosters and encourages the art and science of flavor technology and promotes professional discourse on the subject. And consumption, too, one hopes, of such favorites as Blue Moon and Tutti Frutti. Founded in 1959. 300 members. Contact Denise McCafferty, Secretary.

Society of Geniuses of Distinction (SGD)
4177 Garrick
Warren, MI 48091   (313) 757-4177

Not just geniuses, but geniuses who have done something. Members are people classified as geniuses whose IQs fall in the 99.999th percentile (according to SGD, one in 100,000) and have distinguished themselves in at least one field. The Society seeks to identify geniuses and provide fellowship, since brilliance oft casts a lonely light. It maintains a hall of fame for those who have proven distinctive in a specialized field. The Society reports on geniuses and their work in the *Journal of Mercury.* Founded in 1985. 21 members. Contact R. Anton Montalban-Anderssen, Secretary.

Society of Inkwell Collectors (SIC)

5136 Thomas Ave. S.
Minneapolis, MN 55410   (612) 922-2792

You guessed it: these collectors are into inkwells. And also pens and accessories. Members of the society research and exchange information about the history, identification, and market prices of inkwells. The society provides a selling and trading area for members, offers professional appraisals, holds an annual convention and show, facilitates networking through a photobank and *Link-Wells*, a direct member contact list, and publishes *The Stained Finger* quarterly. It also maintains small library on inkwells, bottles, and pens, the history of writing, and repair and cleaning techniques, as well as a collection of 500 inkwells and 300 blotters. Founded in 1981. 400 members. Contact Vincent D. McGraw, President.

Society of Limerents (SL)

RR 2, Box 251
Millsboro, DE 19966   (302) 934-7067

Limerents are individuals interested in sharing their experiences of limerence, defined by the group as the state of being in love. Yes, we're talking about *Love*, the condition of extreme affection that one human being may enter due to the inestimable pull of another person, or a suitable inanimate object. The group conducts scholarly research and compiles personal data concerning limerence, and it has published *Love and Limerence* and the *Dark Side of Love*. Founded in 1980. Contact Dorothy Tennov.

Society of Ornamental Turners (SOT)

17 Chichester Dr. E.
Saltdean, W. Sussex BN2 8LD, England

You do the Hokey Pokey and you turn yourself around. That's *not* what ornamental turning is all about. According to the society, the art of ornamental turning uses a lathe that has been converted into a universal shaping machine and is used to produce objects both beautiful and useful. Skilled and semi-skilled amateurs in 14 countries who are interested in ornamental and other turning belong to the society, which promotes the craft and tries to preserve ornamental turning lathes and their operating instructions. The group sponsors an annual museum visit, workshops, and an annual competition for meritorious work. It also meets quarterly in London, England. Founded in 1948. 270 members. Contact Philip Holden, Secretary.

Society of Phantom Friends (SPF)

4100 Cornelia Way
North Highlands, CA 95660   (916) 331-7435

Everyone needs a pal. The Society of Phantom Friends comprises readers, authors, and collectors of popular fiction written for girls between eight and 18 years old. The group's biennial *Girls' Series Companion* is a directory listing girls' series, authors, copyrights, and plot synopses, and its monthly magazine *Whispered Watchword* features book reviews, collecting tips, interviews, short fiction, and book classifieds. The Friends grant an annual Phantom's Choice award for new paperback books and hold an annual convention with exhibits in June or July, with the 1992 meeting on July 10-12 in Mankato, Minnesota, and the 1993 gathering in

Detroit, Michigan. Founded in 1985. 165 members. Contact Kate Emburg, President.

Society of Political Item Enthusiasts (SPIE)
Box 159
Kennedale, TX 76060   (817) 535-6283

People who wear their enthusiasms like a badge. This society for collectors of political memorabilia encourages and promotes the hobby, conducts educational programs in the field, and maintains a museum and 2500-volume library of political biographies and reference works. Six times every year the group issues *Campaign Treasures*, and four to six times per year it publishes *The Local*, listing political memorabilia for sale by members. The society meets annually on the second Saturday in November in Arlington, Texas. Founded in 1980. 400 members. Contact Dr. Robert M. Platt, Executive Officer.

Society of Saunterers, International (SOS, Intl.)
2461 Whitehouse Trail
Gaylord, MI 49735   (517) 732-2547

A group for those who walk that walk. Its mission: to inform dedicated walkers, inspire new walkers, and motivate nonwalkers to walk. Society members believe that walking is the greatest and most lasting activity for physical and mental well-being. Furthermore, they believe that walking most perfectly serves the planet, and vice versa. The group provides information on the creative, ecological, medical, philosophical, and spiritual benefits of walking through its monthly journal, *The Saunterer*. Founded in 1985. 500 members. Contact Anthony J. Morse, President.

Society of Scribes (SOS)
PO Box 933
New York, NY 10150

Calligraphers, bookbinders, lettering artists, and individuals with an interest in book arts are united in the Society of Scribes to promote calligraphy and related lettering arts. The society sponsors the annual Young Calligraphers Student Contest and Exhibition, publishes a carefully crafted journal and a newsletter, and meets annually in February. Founded in 1974. 900 members. Contact J. Kastin, Administrator.

Society of the President Street Fellows (SPSF)
Route 1, Box 296
Hamilton, VA 22068   (703) 882-3021

Librarians, administrators, information professionals, and security personnel promoting library use by nontraditional patrons. The President Street Fellows encourage availability and use of libraries and information centers to persons from all walks of society and examine (and support) patterns of eccentric and unique information-seeking behavior. It regularly presents the Medal of Eccentricity to deserving information seekers. The Street Fellows operate an information clearinghouse and sponsor research into most areas of nontraditional library usage. The group meets annually on Oct. 31 in Savannah, GA. Founded in 1980. 47 members. Contact C. Waldo Grotophorst, Executive Secretary.

Society to Curtail Ridiculous, Outrageous and Ostentatious Gift Exchange (SCROOGE)

1447 Westwood Road
Charlottesville, VA 22901   (804) 977-4645

No, Virginia, there is no longer a Santa Claus. SCROOGE includes persons in the U.S. and overseas united in a lighthearted effort to de-emphasize the commercial aspects of Christmas by supporting those who want to (or must) reduce the exchange of expensive and often useless gifts. Members believe that the "giftgiving frenzy" of Christmas is a stress-inducing and ultimately empty exercise, and they suggest limiting Christmas gift spending to cash; presenting gifts to adults in the form of contributions to their favorite charity; giving personal visits and favors, particularly to the sick and elderly; and exchanging inexpensive gifts that require thought and originality. The society grants a humorous award to the retail store with the earliest Christmas decorations and issues the annual *Scrooge Report*, with commentary on the commercialism of Christmas, hints on reducing expensive gift giving, humorous poetry, and personal experiences of members. SCROOGE does not ever meet as a group. Lifetime membership in the Society is a miserly $2. Founded in 1979. 1145 members. Contact Charles G. Langham, Executive Director.

Society to Preserve and Encourage Radio Drama, Variety and Comedy (SPERDVAC)

PO Box 1587
Hollywood, CA 90078   (213) 947-9800

Dedicated to "old time" radio and quality in contemporary radio programming, SPERDVAC works to preserve programs and research materials beginning with radio of the 1920s. It honors individuals who participated in early radio or who document the history of radio, and offers grants-in-aid to noncommercial radio stations that promote "old time" radio. The group boasts three extensive tape-lending libraries of radio programs, and a library of print materials. SPERDVAC emits the monthly *Radiogram* newsletter, which includes society updates and information on radio personalities, and publishes radio logs, reprints, and scripts. The group's annual convention occurs during November in Los Angeles, California. Founded in 1974. 1500 members. Contact Larry Gassman, President.

Sod House Society (SHS)

1131 Logan
Holdrege, NE 68949

People who love the feeling of having grass overhead and underfoot. No, that's not it. Members are people interested in keeping alive the spirit of the pioneer days. The society seeks to discover and accumulate accurate information and accounts of pioneer families and their activities, and it assists students and researchers interested in the sod house era. The group has published *Sod House Memories*, Volumes I-III, with Volume IV on the way. It meets twice every year on the second Sunday in June and the second Sunday in October. Founded in 1956. 335 members. Contact Mrs. Hal Stevens, President.

Solo War-gamers Association (SWA)
11 Lancaster Dr.
Accrington, Lancs. BB5 5RD, England   254 232898

A group for people who like to play war games by themselves. (Who wins, then?) Members are amateur military historians, military modelers, and other interested individuals. The association promotes war games, including computer-assisted, postal, and solo war gaming, the rules of which escape us. It operates services for data exchange and postal gaming (fighting via first class mail; sounds like a good alternative to scud missiles), and publishes the quarterly *Lone Warrior*. Founded in 1976. 300 members. Contact C. Constable, Secretary.

Somatics Society (SS)
1516 Grant Ave., Suite 220
Novato, CA 94945   (415) 897-0336

Mind over matter. Somatics is a philosophy of behavioral medicine that asserts that humans can enjoy healthy lives and treat and heal their own ailments through mind control techniques like relaxation, concentration, and other mind-over-body practices. Professionals and lay people, including educators, psychologists, researchers, dancers, health clinic personnel, chiropractors, doctors, and physical therapists, make up the Somatics Society, which sponsors classes and workshops and publishes the semiannual *Somatics Magazine: Journal of the Bodily Arts and Sciences*. Founded in 1981. 800 members. Contact Thomas Hanna Ph.D., President.

Son of a Witch (SW)
PO Box 40355
Phoenix, AZ 85067-0355

Members of Son of a Witch have proven their lineal or collateral descent from witches or persons accused, tried, convicted, or executed as witches. The happy-go-lucky group conducts genealogical research and meets annually. Founded in 1975. 150 members. Contact Ralph M. Pabst, President General.

Sons and Daughters of the Soddies (SDS)
Route 1, Box 225
Colby, KS 67701   (913) 462-6787

More people who live in grass houses (see the Sod House Society, listed elsewhere). The Sons and Daughters are persons who have had experience with a sod house, part sod building, dugout, or adobe structure, as well as direct descendants of former sod house dwellers. The soddie kids gather and preserve documents, pictures, history, and items pertaining to the era of prairie settlement in North America, circa 1840-1940, conduct research activities on the use, construction, and location of pioneer sod houses, and conduct the Sod House Survey of former sod dwellers in the United States, Canada, and Mexico. The group is headquartered two miles east of Colby, Kansas, at Sod Town, which consists of several sod buildings and a museum of prairie pioneer weapons, tools, utensils, and vehicles. The soddie association is also known as the Sod House Society of America. Founded in 1955. 25,000 members. Contact Vernon Englehardt, President.

Sons of Confederate Veterans (SCV)
Box 5164, Southern Station
Hattiesburg, MS 39406   (601) 268-6100

Look away, Dixieland. The members of SCV, who are lineal and collateral descendants of Confederate Civil War veterans, engage in historical and benevolent activities and maintain a small library of Confederate materials. The group publishes the bimonthly *Confederate Veteran* and meets annually in August. Founded in 1896. 8500 members. Contact William D. McCain, Adjutant-in-Chief.

Sons of Sherman's March to the Sea (SSMS)
1725 Farmer Ave.
Tempe, AZ 85281   (602) 967-5405

The Sons are persons whose fathers, grandfathers, or great grandfathers were in General William Tecumseh Sherman's army that marched through Georgia in 1864 "from Atlanta to the sea." The group, which also admits auxiliary and nonrelative associate members, provides sources for photocopies of Civil War veterans' records. Founded in 1966. 689 members. Contact Stan Schirmacher, Director.

Sons of the Desert (SOD)
PO Box 8341
Universal City, CA 91608   (818) 985-2713

"Here's another nice mess you've gotten me into." The Sons of the Desert is "an organization with scholarly overtones and heavily social undertones devoted to the loving study of the persons and films of Stan Laurel and Oliver Hardy." Founded in New York City, the Sons encourage the preservation and showing of Laurel (1890-1965) and Hardy (1892-1957) films. Local groups are called Tents and derive their names from Laurel and Hardy films such as *Way Out West* of Los Angeles, California, the *Bacon Grabbers* of Chicago, Illinois, and the *Dancing Cuckoos* in the Detroit, Michigan area. The official publication is the quarterly *Intra-Tent Journal.* The *Way Out West* tent "erratically" issues the journal *Pratfall,* which includes celebrity interviews. More than 20 issues have been published since 1969; the journal's motto is, "Always late—always great!"

The national organization meets biennially, with the 1992 convention in Las Vegas, Nevada. Local clubs meet more frequently. The *Way Out West* tent, for instance, meets every six weeks, holds an annual banquet, and claims Laurel's daughter Lois Laurel Hawes as a member, as were the duo's widows before their deaths. Membership is $25 per year. Founded in 1964. 5000 members. Contact Lori Jones.

Sons of the Whiskey Rebellion (SWR)
PO Box 509
525 N. Woodward
Bloomfield Hills, MI 48013   (313) 646-4300

"Gentlemen and rebels" from all walks and stations of life who have been recommended for and elected to membership. The society seeks to glorify one of mankind's greatest boons—whiskey—and eradicate one of its greatest scourges—taxes. The Sons hold "frequent bivouacs to combat the insidious dangers being posed by creeping taxes and other governmental attempts to minimize the many advantages inherent in the glorification and regular consumption of whiskey." The group issues the *Bivouac Notice*. Founded in 1936. 40 members. Contact John H. Norris, Adjutant.

South African Bird Ringing Unit (SAFRING)
University of Cape Town
Rondebosch 7700, Republic of South Africa   21 6502421

Do birds ring? Like, say, English handbells? No, no—they mean metal leg rings. SAFRING studies bird migration, dispersal patterns, and population dynamics by identifying and tracking individual birds that have been banded with metal leg rings. The unit maintains a data bank of primary banding information for Antarctic Treaty nations that are conducting research on southern ocean and Antarctic birds, and it issues the semiannual *SAFRING News*. Founded in 1972. Contact T. B. Oatley, Coordinator.

Space Settlement Studies Program (SSSP)
Niagara University
Niagara University, NY 14109   (716) 285-1212

There's always another frontier. Members of the Space Settlement Studies Program are interested in the colonization of outer space. The Program functions as a clearinghouse on space habitation, focusing on the social and psychological needs of people living in space, and studies the process of colonizing space and transportation to and from earth. The group also conducts attitudinal studies on space habitation and publishes *Extraterrestrial Society* twice a year, as well as the *Space Journal*. Founded in 1977. 1000 members. Contact Stewart B. Whitney, Director.

Spark Plug Collectors of America (SPCOA)
PO Box 2229
Ann Arbor, MI 48106   (313) 994-3103

This group of people is interested in collecting antique ignition devices. They're primarily interested, as the name implies, in spark plugs, of which 3000 brands have been built since 1890. The society issues the semiannual *Ignitor* and the *Ignitor Hot Sheet* two or three times per year. The collectors meet during August in Portland, Indiana, and during October in Hershey, Pennsylvania. Founded in 1976. 300 members. Contact W.H. Brown, Founder & Director.

Spiritual Counterfeits Project (SCP)
PO Box 4308
Berkeley, CA 94704   (415) 540-0300

This Evangelical Christian group critiques current spiritual trends and movements on the basis of the Bible. It attempts to expose modern cults as they arise, with an emphasis on those resembling or related to ancient Oriental religions. By providing materials on such subjects as transcendental meditation, est, Scientology, the New Age movement, Sun Myung Moon's Unification Church, UFOs, and holistic health, members alert others to what they consider a shift in the cultural trend from Judeo-Christian ethics to occultism, mysticism, and denial of the "personal God of the Bible." The group was successful in bringing suit against transcendental meditation in New Jersey schools. Founded in 1975. 13,000 members. Contact Tal Brooke, Director.

Sports Hall of SHAME (SHS)
PO Box 31867
Palm Beach Gardens, FL 33420

Fans, players, coaches, managers, owners, officials, broadcasters, and others pay a light-hearted tribute to "hilarious bloopers and wacky blunders" in amateur and professional sports. More ominously, the group seeks out reports of "shameful, embarrassing, deplorable, and blundering moments in sports history." The Hall solicits nominations for induction, hoping to "recognize and dishonor boneheaded, futile, and ignoble incidents" in such sports as football, basketball, baseball, hockey, soccer, tennis, golf, boxing, track and field, bowling, auto racing, horse racing, and Olympic events, and it collects memorabilia from "shameful" moments in sports history. The group has published *The Sports Hall of Shame* and other material, and holds an annual induction ceremony to which inductees are invited but seldom attend. It's affiliated with the Football Hall of SHAME and the Baseball Hall of SHAME, both described elsewhere in this book. Founded in 1984. 685 members. Contact Bruce M. Nash, Co-Founder.

Star Trek Welcommittee (STW)
481 Main St.
Hatfield, MA 01038   (413) 247-5339

The Welcommittee (isn't that clever?) is a central information center whose volunteers answer fans' questions about *Star Trek* and provide new fans with complete information about proper trekkie fandom. It encourages a revival of the show and issues the *Directory of Star Trek Organizations.* Founded in 1972. Contact Shirley S. Maiewski, Chairman.

Starfleet Command (SC)
PO Box 26076
Indianapolis, IN 46226

This is another group of trekkies promoting the *Star Trek* philosophy of "infinite diversity in infinite combinations." Members include outer space enthusiasts and individuals interested in science fiction in general. The Command supports the peaceful exploration and use of space and the establishment of a permanent working space station or moon base. It seeks to raise public awareness of the importance of space exploration, encourages youth participation in Space Camp activities, and encourages environmental, conservation, and resource management programs. The quarterly *Starfleet Communications* newsletter reports organization news and activities, science and space related issues, and updates about *Star Trek*. The Command gathers annually, usually in Indianapolis during November. Founded in 1974. 2500 members. Contact Donald H. Dailey, Chief of Staff.

Starships of the Third Fleet
PO Box 710219
Santee, CA 92072-0219   (619) 449-0965

Members of Starships are interested in the factual and fictional studies of space, and they support national space programs. The group maintains the Star Trek Universe Correspondence Club and publishes the quarterly *Space Junk* and the bimonthly *Third*

Dimension. Founded in 1988. 214 members. Contact Kenneth A. Brannon, Fleet Admiral.

Starthrowers
PO Box 192
Franklin, LA 70538   (318) 828-2375

Starthrowers (despite their forceful name) advocate peace, social justice, human rights, improved race relations, and the denouncement of the death penalty. The group organizes boycotts and petition drives to promote legislative support for its causes. It publishes the monthly *Agape Newsletter* and the quarterly *Starthrower Magazine*, as well as books on peace and social justice. Founded in 1965. 50,000 members. Contact Bernard Broussard, Executive Officer.

Still Bank Collectors Club of America (SBCCA)
153 Scott Ave.
Bloomsburg, PA 17815   (717) 784-3946

Still banks are toy banks that have no mechanical parts and do not move, and Still Bank Collectors are organizations, companies, and individuals who encourage the collection of antique and contemporary examples of said items. The group assists members in building their collections, sponsors the Best Find of the Year competition, and meets annually on the first weekend of June. The club's semiannual bulletin is called the *Penny Bank Post*. Founded in 1966. 375 members. Contact Harry A. Ward, President.

Still Waters Foundation (SWF)
615 Stafford Lane
Pensacola, FL 32506-4305   (904) 455-9511

Run deep. Members are students of metaphysics, freethinkers, individual seekers, theosophists, mystics, visionaries, members of the Association for Research and Enlightenment, and animal help groups. The foundation, which does not endorse any one belief system, does its best to raise human consciousness to prepare for the "next age of mankind," to reintroduce cosmic principles, and to obtain and synthesize "those truths which are universally beneficial" from the writings of antiquity, clairvoyant investigators, and religious and philosophical teachings. The group adheres to the philosophy that one may enjoy the best of the spiritual and material worlds through their harmony and balance, and it opposes such practices as vivisection and hunting for sport and works to prevent animal cruelty. The foundation's Still Waters Centre features an auditorium, library, animal sanctuary, nature trails, and astronomical observatory. Founded in 1976. 85 members. Contact John and Carol Pepper, Founders.

Stonehenge Study Group (SSG)
2821 De La Vina St.
Santa Barbara, CA 93105   (805) 687-9350

Participants are individuals interested in astronomy, geology, archaeology, anthropology, meteorology, epigraphy, and related arts and sciences. The study group's activities include expeditions to megalithic sites such as Stonehenge, Avebury, Newgrange, Callanish, and Carnac, where stone circles are available for study. The society also sponsors local lectures and study groups covering archaeoastronomy, druids, legends, biblical interpretations, pre-

Columbian contacts, and Ogham epigraphy, sponsors an annual expedition, and meets annually during February in Santa Barbara, California. The semiannual magazine *Stonehenge Viewpoint* explores myth, ancient religions and legends, earth mysteries, and prehistory through the disciplines including archaeology, epigraphy, astronomy, and geology. Founded in 1970. Contact Donald L. Cyr, Editor.

Stop War Toys Campaign (SWTC)
Box 1093
Norwich, CT 06360   (203) 889-5337

G.I. Joe, beware. The Campaign is a project of the War Resisters League that units individuals and organizations seeking to increase public awareness of what the group considers the damaging long-term behavioral effects of war toys (guns, tanks, and other action toys) and violent television cartoons on children. The group conducts demonstrations targeted at toy manufacturers and cartoon production companies, and develops information packets on protest strategies for grassroots organizations. Founded in 1985. 2500 members. Contact Joanne Sheehan.

Stumpwork Society (SS)
PO Box 122
Bogota, NJ 07603   (201) 224-3622

Stumpwork has nothing to do with trees; it's raised embroidery characterized by movable parts and high dimensions. Stumpwork Society members are embroiderers, needle artists, designers, and teachers working together to instruct, conserve, and restore the art. Originating in the 17th century, stumpwork techniques include ceylon, needlelace, trellis, detached buttonhole, and needleweaving stitches. The society sponsors exhibits of antique and contemporary stumpwork and presents *Threads of Nostalgia: The Ellis Island Connection*, a slide lecture program covering clothing and textiles brought to America by immigrants. The *Stumpwork Society Chronicle* appears quarterly. Founded in 1979. 400 members. Contact Sylvia C. Fishman, President.

Sugar Packet Collectors Club (SPCC)
15601 Burkhardt Road
Orrville, OH 44667   (216) 682-7486

One lump or two? Members of the club collect sugar packets and, through the club, exchange information about the hobby on an international level. The club publishes the quarterly *Sugar Packet* and the *Catalog of Sugar Packets*. Founded in 1976. 100 members. Contact Mitzi Geiser, President.

Survival Research Foundation (SRF)
PO Box 8565
Pembroke Pines, FL 33084   (305) 435-2730

Foundation members are interested in the investigation of postmortem survival, or life after death. The group conducts studies and research on death, near-death experiences, immortality, hauntings, apparitions, poltergeists, reincarnation, mediumship, and out-of-body experiences, and presents the results of their investigations through publications and lectures. The foundation also sponsors programs for the terminally ill and bereaved. The group's Institute for the Interdisciplinary Study of Death conducts a long-range survival research experimental program based on ciphers. Founded in 1971. 100 members. Contact Arthur S. Berger, President.

T ᵀ ᴛ ᵀ ᴛ ᵀ ᴛ ᵀ ᴛ

Tall Clubs International (TCI)
PO Box 1567
Florissant, MO 63031   (314) 921-4873

Paul Bunyon would have liked it here. This international organization unites clubs that represent approximately 4000 women 5'10" or taller and men 6'2" and up. The purpose is to promote "tall awareness" and the happiness and welfare of tall people by encouraging such folk to be undeterred in their perspective on life and in their activities because of their height. It also seeks to educate the public to the needs and problems of tall people, such as obtaining clothes, accommodations, and facilities of suitable size and convenience. The group fosters friendship, companionship, and the exchange of information and ideas among members, and annually honors Miss Tall International, Man of the Year, and Woman of the Year. Founded in 1938. 4000 members. Contact Debbie Rethemeyer, President.

Tara Collectors Club (TCC)
PO Box 1200
Jonesboro, GA 30236

Collectors of memorabilia related to *Gone With the Wind*, who share the sacred purpose of increasing awareness, appreciation, and enjoyment of all aspects of the movie, the books, musicals, video recordings, and other stuff having something to do with *GWTW*. Apparently they are succeeding, because we're all very aware. The club issues the quarterly *Jonesboro Wind*. Founded in 1984. 800 members. Contact Jim Swords, President.

Tattoo-a-Pet (PSU)
1625 Emmons Ave., Suite 1H
Brooklyn, NY 11235   (718) 646-8200

How 'bout a little heart, with, say, "Mom" written inside it? Tattoo-a-Pet provides for the permanent identification of animals via tattoo registration under its trademark (Tattoo-a-Pet), and promotes its use by veterinarians, pet shops, and groomers as a service to pet owners for protection of their pet against loss, theft, and laboratory use. Registration includes a tattoo number (inscribed painlessly on the pet), warning decals for home and car as a deterrent to dognappers, a collar tag, and a permanent computer record of the tattoo number. The group provides services to seeing-eye and working dogs, humane societies, and adoption agencies on a nonprofit basis as a way to prevent the abandonment of adopted animals. It issues the *Directory of Tattoo-a-Pet Agents* and the *Directory of U.S. Tattoo Registration Services*, as well as the quarterly *Tattoo-A-Pet News*. Founded in 1972. Contact Julie S. Moscove, Executive Director.

Tattoo Club of America (TCA)

c/o Spider Webb's Studio
220 Main St.
Derby, CT 06418   (203) 732-4571

Tattoo artists and tattooed folks worldwide make up the Tattoo Club of America, which seeks to promote the art of tattooing and make it more acceptable to the public. It annually awards Mr. and Miss Tattoo honors to the man and woman best representing the world of tattooing, maintains a hall of fame, and holds an annual conference and symposium (with exhibits) during March in New York City. Founded in 1970. 15,000 members. Contact Joe O'Sullivan, Secretary.

Tax Free America (TFA)

11015 Cumpston St.
North Hollywood, CA 91601   (818) 24-UNTAX

No new taxes! The corporation and individual taxpayers in Tax Free America are united to sponsor a national initiative that would replace all federal, state, county, and city taxes and fees with a two percent government service charge on all purchases. The group offers slide shows on tax reform, conducts tax reform seminars, and operates various state political action groups. Founded in 1986. 103,000 members. Contact Boris Isaacson, President.

Terrarium Association (TA)

PO Box 276
Newfane, VT 05345   (802) 365-4721

Remember *Little Shop of Horrors?* Well, this isn't like that. The Terrarium Association includes florists, nursery professionals, garden club members, schools, and others interested in terraria. The association offers instruction on making and maintaining terraria through a series of scintillating publications, including *How to Make a Plant Column, Recipe for a Gallon Garden, How to Plant a Horizontal Five Gallon Terrarium, Soil Formulas for All Phases of Terrarium Gardening,* and *The Terrarium Association Directory of Plant Sources and Bottle Gardening Supplies.* Grab your hoes. Founded in 1974. Contact Robert C. Baur, Director.

Thermometer Collectors Club of America (TCCA)

4555 Auburn Blvd., Suite 11
Sacramento, CA 95841   (916) 487-6964

Big thermometers, little thermometers, antique, decorative, and advertising thermometers, oral thermometers and ... well, you get the idea. Members of the Thermometer Collectors Club of America promote the hobby of thermometer collecting and study scientific, household, and commercial thermometers. The club maintains the Thermometer Showcase Museum and a small library of thermometer catalogs, and it spreads the word on the handy little items through the aptly named *Thermometer News.* The club's annual conference, with thermometer exhibits, occurs during the fall somewhere in the western United States. Founded in 1980. 480 members. Contact Warren D. Harris, President.

Thimble Collectors International (TCI)
6411 Montego Bay Dr.
Louisville, KY 40228

Collectors in 12 countries belong to Thimble Collectors International, which promotes research and study in the field and standardizes names of thimble types and designs. The club educates members in collecting, storing, cataloging, and displaying thimbles, and it encourages members to give presentations on thimble collecting to help noncollectors appreciate the family heirloom thimbles they may already possess or thimbles they may see in the future. In addition to organizing workshops and mall sales, the group maintains a library of magazine articles, bulletins, research papers, and riveting 35mm slides of thimble programs, and publishes a quarterly bulletin and the booklet *Thoughts on Thimbles*. The collectors meet biennially during August. Founded in 1978. 1000 members. Contact Rose Marie Kerchner, President.

Third Generation (TG)
c/o Heritage Foundation
214 Massachusetts Ave. N.E.
Washington, DC 20002   (202) 546-4400

Young conservatives—specifically, conservative individuals and political activists under 35 years of age—make up the Third Generation, which provides a forum for members to discuss current political issues and devise strategies to advance free market economic principles and a strong national defense. The group sponsors biweekly seminars to discuss said issues and showcases speakers who analyze national political trends and defend conservative principles in economic, national defense, and social issues. Founded in 1984. 600 members. Contact Betsy Hart, Executive Officer.

1334 North Beechwood Drive Irregulars
6490 Rosemont
Detroit, MI 48228   (313) 436-8142

Fans of the 1960s pop-rock group the Monkees, whose members included Michael Nesmith (1942-), Davy Jones (1944-), Peter Tork (1944-), and Micky Dolenz (1945-). Purposes are to keep members informed about the careers and projects of the Monkees and to encourage friendship and fun among fans. The group's name refers to the address used by the Monkees on the television series of the same name. The 1334s have sponsored fundraising projects for Ronald McDonald House of Michigan and charities supported by each of the four Monkees. The group sponsors competitions and bestows the "Royal Order of Ta-Da" and "Don't Do That" awards. The Irregulars maintain a museum, biographical archives, and a small library of Monkee business. The group publishes the *Beechwood Banner* and an annual coloring and activity book. Founded in 1985. 1500 members. Contact Sue Roach, President.

Three Stooges Fan Club (TSFC)
710 Collins Ave.
Lansdale, PA 19446   (215) 699-3601

Fans of the Three Stooges, of course *(Oh, a wise guy, eh?)*, a popular slapstick comedy team of film and television, starring brothers Moe Howard (1897-1975), Curly Howard (1903-52),

Shemp Howard (1895-1955), and Larry Fine (1902-75) and, later, Joe Besser (1907-88). To fulfill its purpose of keeping the comedy of the Three Stooges alive, the club keeps members informed of the availability of memorabilia for sale or exchange, conducts research on the Stooges' careers, films, and collectibles, and honors the Stooges with an annual convention. The quarterly *3 Stooges Journal* contains film reviews, interviews, information on collectible items, and rare photographs. Founded in 1974. 2000 members. Contact Gary Lassin, President.

Tippers Anonymous (TA)
PO Box 178
Cochituate, MA 01778 (508) 881-8052

TA supporters dine out with some regularity and are dedicated to "improving service and restoring its reward, tipping, to its rightful status." *TIP*, they hasten to point out, is an acronym for *to insure promptness*. The group does not oppose tipping but does feel that its meaning has been lost in the hectic pace of modern times. Members receive booklets of "report cards" that enable the bearer to rate the performance of servers. Waiters, waitresses, or any other persons involved in direct personal service can be rated excellent, good, fair, or poor, depending upon the service rendered. After the meal, the diner leaves the evaluation slip with the appropriate tip. The server is supposed to then understand that a tip was given as a result of his or her service. Founded in 1960. 15,200 members. Contact Robert S. Farrington, President.

Tippers International (TI)
PO Box 1934
Wausau, WI 54402 (414) 231-5852

Another group of individuals, organizations, and corporations united to help create better communication between customer and service and management people and to restore tipping to its original concept. TI combats high prices and inferior products. Its members receive cards and identifying symbols that can be left with service people (waiters, taxi drivers, chamber maids) to indicate members' satisfaction or dissatisfaction with services received. If the service is good, members leave a card with a gratuity, indicating why the gratuity is given. If the service is poor, members leave a card explaining why no gratuity is being given. Tippers International operates a referral system whereby customers are encouraged to fill out rating cards provided by the management of a business. These are mailed to TI, which acts as a go-between to inform the particular business of practices that displease customers. The group makes available the *Guide for Tipping, Tipping Computer,* and *The Art of Tipping: Customs and Controversies.* Founded in 1972. 30,000 members. Contact John E. Schein, President.

Tonga and Tin Can Mail Study Circle (TTCMSC)
6840 Newtonsville Road
Pleasant Plain, OH 45162 (904) 877-7001

Messages in bottles, sort of. Members of this international organization are stamp collectors interested in tin can philately and the canoe mail delivery system of Niuafoou Island, Tonga, located in the South Pacific. Tin can or barrel mail refers to mail that is placed in a barrel, lowered from a ship, and taken ashore by canoe.

Outbound mail is sealed into a metal can and picked up by a ship. Both operations take place while the ship maintains its forward speed. The group provides free want ad and trading opportunities, sponsors auctions, and offers a new issue service for Tongan stamps. The group issues the bimonthly *Tin Canner* journal, which includes auction news, a membership newsletter, and research reports. Founded in 1981. 200 members. Contact Lawrence Benson, President.

Treasure Hunter Research and Information Center (THRIC)
PO Box 314
Gibson, LA 70356

Treasure hunting, prospecting, exploring, and metal detecting are the passions of THRIC members. The center promotes treasure hunting and metal detecting and opposes restrictions on these hobbies, and it offers a mail-order lending service of books, magazines, and articles on treasure hunting. The *Treasure Hunting Research Bulletin* appears quarterly. Founded in 1986. 250 members. Contact John H. Reed, Director.

Tree-Ring Society (TRS)
University of Arizona
Tree-Ring Research Laboratory
Tucson, AZ 85721   (602) 621-2191

Scientists and research workers in the Tree-Ring Society are interested in dendrochronology, which is the determination of dates and time intervals by studying the sequence of growth rings in trees and aged wood. The society issues the annual *Tree-Ring Bulletin*. Founded in 1934. 320 members. Contact Jeffrey S. Dean, Secretary.

TreePeople (TP)
12601 Mulholland Dr.
Beverly Hills, CA 90210   (818) 753-4600

TreePeople do not live in trees. At least, they don't have to. TreePeople is an environmental problem-solving organization that operates primarily in southern California and promotes community action, global awareness, and an active role in the planting and care of trees. Volunteer tree people plant trees throughout Los Angeles and its surrounding mountain area. The group conducted the Million Tree Campaign in Los Angeles prior to the 1984 Olympic Games, operates the Environmental Leadership Program for elementary school children and the Citizen's Forester Training Program for adults, sponsors the Africa Fruit Tree Project to assist in establishing nurseries for tree propagation in Ethiopia, Tanzania, Kenya, and Cameroun, maintains the 45-acre Wilderness Park, and conducts recycling education exhibits. The group's *Seedling News* is issued bimonthly, then (one hopes) recycled. Founded in 1970. 19,500 members. Contact Andy Lipkis, Executive Director.

Trekville U.S.A. (TUSA)
1021 S. 9th Ave.
Scranton, PA 18504   (717) 343-7806

Fans of the original *Star Trek* science fiction television series, the theatrical movies, and the current television series, *Star Trek: The Next Generation.* Objective is to keep fans informed of events dealing with the U.S.S. Enterprise and its actors, er, crew. Members receive *To Boldly Go,* a publication which includes stories dealing with both the original and next generation crew. TUSA also issues the *Trekville Gazette,* a bimonthly. newsletter with episode reviews, original stories and poems, and book reviews. Founded in 1985. 120 members. Contact Jay S. Hastings, President.

Triplet Connection (TC)
PO Box 99571
Stockton, CA 95209   (209) 474-0885

Members are parents and expectant parents of triplets or larger multiple births. TC works to help families deal with high-risk multiple pregnancy and birth, advises on how to prevent premature birth, and helps them prepare for the aftermath of multiple births (diapers for three or more). The Connection acts as support group for members, helps them network with others, and provides information on breastfeeding, medical sources, clothing and equipment exchanges, and other areas of interest. The group maintains Tender Hearts, a group which offers support to mothers of multiple births who have lost one or more of their babies. Members receive the *The Triplet Connection-Newsletter,* a quarterly which reports on multiple pregnancy and the problems faced by the birth and care of these children. Founded in 1983. 3000 members. Contact Janet Bleyl, President.

Triskaidekaphobia Illuminatus Society (TIS)

Winner of first place in the official *Organized Obsessions* Most Difficult to Pronounce category. Members are individuals who believe the number 13 has the ability to affect the balance of world power and political structures through the Illuminati, who are people claiming to be unusually enlightened, casting their beacon of light throughout the universe. TIS seeks to isolate seemingly unconnected events caused by the numerical forces inherent in the number 13, correlate the meanings of these events, and develop solutions and strategies. It organizes illuminated task forces charged with eliminating triskaidekaphobia (fear of the number 13) from society and plans to develop a think tank. Annually TIS bestows an award for the most significant contribution concerning the power of the number 13. The Society has a collection of newspaper and magazine clippings and videotapes from television shows and operates a hall of fame in support of the number 13. Every so often the group feels moved to issue the editorial report *Thirteen.* Other publications include *The 13th Illuminated Stratum,* a newsletter (appearing up to five times per year) acting as a forum for the exchange of information concerning the TIS, and *Fear to Feel the Illuminated Network of 13 Concealed Phantoms.* The group meets annually on a numerically correct day. Founded in 1984.

True Life Institute (TLI)
1332 N. Lake Ave. at Washington
Pasadena, CA 91104   (818) 797-5527

Also known as the Tax Reformers United Endeavors (TRUE), TLI seeks reform in U.S. monetary and taxation systems through the promotion of national legislation that will uphold the "original intent" of the Constitution and "restore full authority" to the Coinage Act of 1792, which established the gold and silver standards. The group opposes what the Institute views as the Internal Revenue Services's infringement of civil rights and the "unconstitutional" existence of the Federal Reserve System. True Life provides members with paralegal research assistance and advice on tax shelters. It has published the self-help title, *How to Make Legal Pleadings* as well as the *Liberty Album,* a 10-year compilation of *T.R.U.E. News,* which is not published anymore except in retrospect. Other "how to fight the law and maybe win" literature distributed by the Institute includes *Traffic Dismissal* and *Federal Removal Kit.* For those with VCRs, it offers the cassette tape *How to Use a Law Library.* Founded in 1970. Contact Robert W. Lyon, Founder.

20/20 Vision National Project
30 Cottage St.
Amherst, MA 01002   (413) 549-4555

No, not a group promoting optical correctness, but political correctness. 20/20 is a group for concerned but busy people looking for specific, manageable, and constructive public interest lobbying. 20/20 promotes citizen involvement in influencing public policies that endorse protection of the environment, an increase in national and global security, reduction of military spending, and the support of individual economic and social needs. The name is derived from the belief that an individual's contribution of 20 minutes a month and $20 a year can have a significant impact on public policy. The group would obviously clash with the Triskaide-kaphobia Illuminatus Society, which thinks more highly of the number 13.

20/20 members are sent a postcard each month detailing the most effective 20-minute action they can take in concert for the public interest. Every six months they receive a brief report on the results of those efforts. Otherwise, "no meetings; no mountains of mail." 20/20 maintains a network of local lobbying groups which select the monthly action for their local subscribers. According to the group, members complete their monthly action an average 75% of the time. Founded in 1985. 10,000 members. Contact Richard Mark, Executive Officer.

Twins Foundation (TF)
PO Box 6043
Providence, RI 02940-6043   (401) 274-TWIN

The Foundation serves the need for information about twins and provides assistance to twins and other individuals of multiple birth, their parents, and families. Archival and research support is extended to individuals and groups involved in studies on twins. TF enlists professionally successful twins (Schwarzenneger and DeVito?) to serve as role models for adolescent twins. The Foundation maintains the twin hall of fame, twin registry, twin museum, and twin biographical archives. It spreads the word on twins through the quarterly newsletter, *The Twins Letter.* Founded in 1983. 1780 members. Contact Kay Cassill, President.

Twirly Birds (TB)
PO Box 18029
Oxon Hill, MD 20745   (301) 567-4407

Members are pioneering pilots of helicopters and other vertical takeoff aircraft. Folks who have soloed a helicopter or other vertical takeoff aircraft in sustained flight prior to VJ Day are classified as founder members, while individuals who soloed helicopters over 20 years ago are classified as general members. The purpose of the group is to offer members a place to exchange their experience and opinions on the progress of the helicopter and other vertical takeoff aircraft. TB issues the semiannual *Twirly Bird Newsletter* and meets semiannually in conjunction with the American Helicopter Society and Helicopter Association International. Founded in 1944. 250 members. Contact John M. Slattery, Secretary.

U U U U U U U U

UFO Information Retrieval Center (UFOIRC)
3131 W. Cochise Dr., No. 158
Phoenix, AZ 85051-9501   (602) 997-1523

UFOIRC collects, analyzes, publishes, and disseminates information on reports of unidentified flying objects. The Center serves as a referral center and makes available a bibliography of currently available information on the UFO phenomenon. It also conducts research and sponsors photo exhibits while periodically publishing the *Reference for Outstanding UFO Sighting Reports*. Founded in 1966. Contact Thomas M. Olsen, President.

Uglies Unlimited (UU)
3912 St. Michaels Ct.
Sugar Land, TX 77479   (713) 980-9830

UU is a proud group of unattractive individuals who are vexed by discrimination against "uglies." Serving as the guardian of ugly human beings, UU encourages society and employers to accept people for what they are instead of what they look like. It assists members in finding a new self-image (preferably one they like better) and solicits more exposure for uglies in mass media advertising, noting that "uglies can sell products too!" UU pickets and boycotts commercial concerns deemed to be anti-ugly and files complaints with the Equal Employment Opportunity Commission. It conducts a public awareness program on the state of being ugly in society and sponsors the Ugly Stick Competition (prizes are awarded by "a select committee of washed-out judges of past beauty pageants"). The Uglies annually gather during October. Founded in 1973. 150 members. Contact Danny McCoy, Founder.

U.N.C.L.E. HQ
234 Washo Dr.
Lake Zurich, IL 60047   (312) 438-0039

Fans of *The Man from U. N.C.L.E.*, a popular television series of the 1960s that followed the seriocomic adventures of secret agents Napoleon Solo and Illya Kuryakin. Members include fans of *The Girl from U.N.C.L.E.*, the short-lived spinoff. The group lobbies producers and others in the television industry for the airing of U.N.C.L.E. reruns and the creation of new episodes. HQ holds fan gatherings at conventions with themes relating to spy shows and donates materials to the Felton Files at the University of Iowa, in Iowa City. News from HQ is contained in the *Annual Yearbook* and the quarterly *HQ Newsletter*, which offers tips on obtaining memorabilia and lists current activities of the show's cast. In addition to an annual meeting, the group holds bimonthly meetings. Founded in 1976. 500 members. Contact Darlene Kepner, Secretary.

Uncle Remus Museum (URM)
PO Box 184
Eatonton, GA 31024 (404) 485-6856

People interested in Joel Chandler Harris (1848-1908) and his folklore tales of Uncle Remus. The Museum honors the memory of Harris, keeps his works before the public, and distributes the Uncle Remus stories. The Museum is housed in an old slave cabin depicting an antebellum Southern plantation and the imaginary world of Uncle Remus. Founded in 1962. Contact Madeleine Gooch, Secretary.

United Flying Octogenarians (UFOs)
3531 Larga Circle
San Diego, CA 92110 (619) 224-6758

UFOs is a social organization for pilots who have commanded an aircraft in flight (usually with permission) after reaching age 80, a fairly notable accomplishment. The flying octogenarians publish the monthly *UFO News* and meet annually in conjunction with the Aircraft Owners and Pilots Association. Founded in 1982. 88 members. Contact A. R. Boileau, Secretary Treasurer.

United Serpents (US)
PO Box 8915
Columbia, SC 29202 (803) 252-1841

A club for players of the serpent, a wooden, end-blown wind instrument that was first used in France in 1590. Probably at a party. Although it resembles the flute, it is the forerunner of the tuba, proving that instrument evolution is a varied and unpredictable mix. Purpose of the United Serpents (divided they fall or at least play off-key) is to share information and performance techniques with other serpent players and to educate the public about the instrument (although resembling a flute, the serpent is a forerunner of the tuba . . .) The group conducts a biennial workshop at the American Recorder Society early music seminar and annually produces a *Newsletter for US*. Founded in 1984. 150 members. Contact Craig Kridel, President.

United States Amateur Ballroom Dancers Association (USABDA)
8102 Glen Gary Road
Baltimore, MD 21234 (301) 821-9047

Time to buff those patent leathers. Members are individuals interested in competing in or observing amateur ballroom dancing. USABDA promotes ballroom dancing as an amateur social and competitive sport at the local and national levels. It believes that dancing may enhance the development of health, poise, character, and social appearance and seeks to involve young people in dancing. The group issues the bimonthly *Amateur Dancers*, a newsletter containing competition results, letters, financial and developmental reports, a calendar of events, and a junior journal. The group gathers annually for a fall festival and a ballroom dancing championship. Founded in 1965. 4500 members. Contact Constance Townsend, Secretary.

United States Amateur Dancers Association (USADA)
1172 Linda Flora Dr.
Los Angeles, CA 90049   (213) 472-6630

More individuals interested in amateur ballroom dancing. USADA promotes ballroom dancing as a social activity and competitive sport, with special consideration for youth, the elderly, and the disabled. The group, which sponsors the United States Amateur Dance Championship, is attempting to have ballroom dancing accepted as an Olympic event, emphasizing coordination, stamina, and rhythmic intention. USADA meets annually on the second Sunday in December somewhere within the greater metropolitan confines of Los Angeles, CA. Founded in 1968. 250 members. Contact Henrietta Nelson, Secretary.

United States Amateur Tug of War Association (USATO-WA)
PO Box 9626
Madison, WI 53715

Team and individual enthusiasts of tug-of-war seeking to promote the sport of tug-of-war at all age levels, standardize rules, establish competitions, and train new teams. The group encourages the U.S. Olympic Committee to include the sport of tug-of-war as an Olympic game (they'll get to it just as soon as they consider the merits of ballroom dancing). USATOWA annually organizes a national championship. Founded in 1978. 600 members. Contact Joe McDonald, President.

U.S. Boomerang Association (USBA)
PO Box 182
Delaware, OH 43015   (614) 363-8332

More than just simple karma: Everything you do comes back at you, particularly if all you do is throw boomerangs. With clubs and individuals interested in boomerangs as members, the Boomerang Association is dedicated to furthering the knowledge of boomeranging as an art, science, and sport. USBA conducts workshops, clinics, seminars, and educational programs for all ages and maintains listings of manufacturers, local organizations, materials, upcoming events, rules, and rating systems. Members retrieve the latest in boomerang news within the quarterly *Many Happy Returns* newsletter. For boomerang novices, USBA publishes the *Introduction to Boomerangs*. The people with boomerangs meet annually, during which they hold a USBA national tournament. Founded in 1981. 550 members. Contact Chet Snouffer, Director.

U.S. English (USE)
818 Connecticut Ave., NW, Suite 200
Washington, DC 20006   (202) 833-0100

USE promotes and defends the use of the English language in the political, economic, and intellectual life of the United States. The group believes that although the right of individuals and groups to use other languages must be respected, national unity requires a common language that is eroding because of government-funded bilingual education and voting programs, bilingual electronic media, and the tendency to label language assimilation as a betrayal of native cultures. USE calls for adoption of a constitutional amendment making English the official language of the U.S. and repeal of laws mandating multilingual ballots and voter registration materials. The group holds an annual bilingual education conference. Founded in 1983. 250,000 members. Contact Kathryn Bricker, Executive Director.

United States Korfball Federation (USKF)
1330 S. Atlanta Place
Tulsa, OK 74104 (918) 585-2567

Individuals dedicated to the promotion and development of korfball in the U.S. Although little known in the U.S., korfball is a popular Dutch sport comparable to basketball in which eight players, four men and four women, are divided equally into offensive and defensive positions and placed on opposite sides of a half court. The rules of the game do not allow for blocking, dribbling, or running with the ball, which leads us to wonder what you can do with the ball. Seems passing must be more than a fancy. The group seeks to incorporate korfball into physical education and intramural programs in schools throughout the U.S., but did not mention plans to introduce korfball into the Olympics. The group has offered graduate and undergraduate classes in korfball at Portland State University, Portland, OR. Founded in 1979. 70 members. Contact Jan Stukey, Executive Secretary.

United States Othello Association (USOA)
11517 Daffodil Lane
Silver Spring, MD 20902 (301) 649-4378

Persons dedicated to the advancement of the game of Othello, a game played with 64 black and white discs, popular a century ago in England under the name Reversi. The group conducts, sponsors, or sanctions tournaments and maintains a national rating system for active players. USOA helps members learn game strategy and improve their playing skills, primarily through the *Othello Quarterly*, a journal containing reports of tournaments, game analyses, instructional material, and tournament announcements. Founded in 1979. 350 members. Contact Arnold Kling, President.

U.S. Psychotronics Association (USPA)
2141 W. Agatite
Chicago, IL 60625 (312) 275-7055

Members are interested in the study of psychotronics, the science of mind-body-environment relationships concerned with the interactions of matter, energy, and consciousness. USPA is also interested in psychic phenomena, free energy systems, radionics, and alternative health methodologies. The group provides a forum for the exchange of current research developments in psychotronics and is dedicated to maintaining high standards of ethical, humanitarian, and scientific practices in the study and application of psychotronics. Founded in 1975. 800 members. Contact Robert Beutlich, Secretary Treasurer.

U.S. Trivia Association (USTA)
8217 S. Hazelwood Dr.
Lincoln, NE 68510 (402) 489-7604

A group seeking to promote trivia and trivia-related projects, USTA sponsors a syndicated radio program on trivia and maintains the National Trivia Hall of Fame and a library of 8000 volumes of various trivia and reference sources. The group presents the Bogie Award for the best trivia and/or reference book of the year. Founded in 1978. Contact Tom Bowen, Vice President & Treasurer.

The Universal Coterie of Pipe Smokers (TUCOPS)
20-37 120th St.
College Point, NY 11356

An informal group with no dues, no meetings other than an occasional get-together when desired by any number of members, no charter, and no obligations, TUCOPS membership is open to people with a genuine interest in pipe smoking. Through its publication, the Coterie provides members with quotes about pipes and pipe smoking, correspondence on pipe collecting, pipe exchange/"used wood" market, snuff, cigars, and tobacco tins, and tips on where to send for free tobacco, catalogs, and other materials. It also supplies hints on improving the quality of a pipe. Founded in 1964. 7500 members. Contact Tom Dunn, President.

V Fan Club (VFC)
8048 Norwich Ave.
Van Nuys, CA 91402-5616   (818) 901-1466

Fans of the science fiction television show *V*, which was a spin-off of the mini-series of the same name. According to the club, the show was an allegorical sci-fi story which illustrated the methods used in the totalitarian regimes of Germany, Italy, and the Soviet Union in the 1930s and 1940s. And we thought it was about alien critters with a certain reptilian bent. The VFC publishes the quarterly *Hyperlight Cable*. Founded in 1985. 225 members. Contact Kathy R. Pillsbury, Supreme Commander.

Vacation Exchange Club (VEC)
PO Box 820
Haleiwa, HI 96712   (808) 638-8747

Individuals and families interested in exchanging homes (apartments, cottages, or farms) temporarily for holiday and vacation purposes. Members write to each other to make their own exchange or rental arrangements. The club is linked with Homelink International, Cambridge, England; International Home Exchange, Manly, Australia; Sejours, Aix-en-Provence, France; Holiday Service, Memmelsdorf, Germany; LOVW, Groningen, Netherlands; Intercambio de Casas, Madrid, Spain; Taxi-Stop, Gent, Belgium; Casa Vacanza, Padova, Italy; and West World Holiday Exchange, Vancouver, Canada. These groups issue combined directories of U.S. and European home exchange offerings. VEC publicizes these opportunities through the *Exchange Book*, a semiannual directory of some 6000 families in 40 countries seeking home exchange travel and holiday arrangements. Founded in 1960. 10,000 members. Contact Karl & Debbie Costabel, Executive Officers.

Vampire
5116 Mill Race Circle
Richmond, VA 23234   (804) 271-6600

A special interest group of Mensa whose members enjoy vampire literature and lore (non-Mensans are associate members). Vampire aids members in exploring gothic horror writing and acts as a forum for the discussion of books, films, and other horror materials. The group, which encourages members to write and review horror stories, publishes the bimonthly *Vampire* newsletter. Founded in 1984. 80 members. Contact Mrs. Terry Cottrell, Coordinator & Editor.

Vampire Information Exchange (VIE)
PO Box 328
Brooklyn, NY 11229

Members are interested in vampires, including the portrayal of vampires in fiction. VIE distributes information on vampirism and encourages the exchange of information among members. Five times during the year it feels compelled to issue the *Vampire Information Exchange Newsletter*, which provides information on vampirism, including book and movie reviews, news releases, and trading and selling information (wanted: used vampires). The group also issues the annual *VIE Bibliography*, with complete listings and descriptions of vampire-related fiction and non-fiction books. And for those marking their special vampire days, the Exchange produces the annual *VIE Calendar* noting dates in vampire history. Founded in 1977. 150 members. Contact Eric S. Held, Editor.

Vampire Pen Pal Network (VPPN)
29 Washington Square W, Penthouse N
New York, NY 10011   (212) 982-6754

They only come out at night and they're lonely. The Network is a division of the Count Dracula Fan Club, described elsewhere in this book . Members are individuals interested in vampires. Point is to allow vampire lovers to get to know each other. Founded in 1983. 25 members. Contact Ann M. Hart, Director.

Vampire Research Center (VRC)
PO Box 252
Elmhurst, NY 11369

Vampirologists, parapsychologists, sociologists, anthropologists, and hematologists seeking to conduct a demographic study of vampires through social-anthropological research known as vampirology. VRC distributes questionnaires to gather information on individuals who believe that they or acquaintances are vampires. In addition to establishing the Vampirology Hall of Fame, the Center has published the books *Vampires Are, True Tales of the Unknown I, True Tales of the Unknown II: The Uninvited, True Tales of the Unknown III* (looks like there's potential for a series here), and the *Vampire Census*, which we assume provides a head count of vampires, living and dead. The group holds an annual conference with exhibits and every five years or so, vampire time, conducts a symposia, with the next one scheduled during 1995 in New York City followed by a big vampire millennium hoedown in 2000 somewhere in the vicinity of Los Angeles, CA. Founded in 1972. 300 members. Contact Dr. Stephen Kaplan, Founder & Director.

Vegetarian Resource Group (VRG)
PO Box 1463
Baltimore, MD 21203 (301) 366-VEGE

Members are interested in any aspect of vegetarianism and dedicated to working on both the local and national levels to educate the public about vegetarianism and a related code of conduct, veganism, defined as abstinence from using other animal products, such as dairy products, eggs, wool, or leather. The group examines vegetarianism as it relates to issues of health, nutrition, animal rights, ethics, world hunger, and ecology. VRG promotes World Vegetarian Day (October 1), holds cooking demonstrations, and publishes the monthly *Vegetarian Journal* as well as the cookbook, *Vegetarianism for the Working Person* and the children's activity book *I Love Animals and Broccoli.* Founded in 1983. 5000 members. Contact Charles Stahler, Secretary.

Vestigia
56 Brookwood Road
Stanhope, NJ 07874 (201) 347-3638

Vestigia is a group of scientists, engineers, technicians, and other interested individuals established to investigate and conduct research into unexplained scientific phenomena. The group, whose name is the Latin word for investigate (which, in itself, means footprint), trains members in investigative techniques. Founded in 1976. 65 members. Contact Robert E. Jones, President.

Viewers for Quality Television (VQT)
PO Box 195
Fairfax Station, VA 22039 (703) 425-0075

VQT promotes the development and supports the continuation of realistic, illuminating, and intelligent television programs. The group commends the major networks for presenting quality shows and encourages members to petition networks to present quality television. VQT also campaigns to bring cancelled shows with quality back on the air. It endorses shows with its Seal of Quality and conducts television viewer surveys. Quality television (or the lack of it) is discussed in the bimonthly *VQT Newsletter,* with reviews of quality programs, rating analyses, and viewer surveys and results. Founded in 1984. 3500 members. Contact Dorothy Swanson, President & Founder.

Visual Lunacy Society (VLS)
PO Box 5025
Balboa Island, CA 92662-5025 (714) 249-8258

Members like to use rubber stamps as mail art and as an act of rebellion against a bureaucratic society. VLS creates stamps that spoof rubber stamps being more officially used, such as *Returned, Signature of Pope Required,* and *Resubmit in Arabic.* Providing a forum for the exchange of creative ideas and art, the Society publishes *Visual Lunacy News,* a bimonthly newsletter on correspondence art, rubber stamps, and their design and use in a nonconformist, antibureaucratic, and humorous fashion. Founded in 1981. 1500 members. Contact Carl T. Herrman, Namwarki.

Voltaire Society (VS)
PO Box 2077
Lexington, KY 40594

A group of "hedonists and iconoclasts" dedicated to advancing mankind culturally and socially, and to protecting and preserving the ecology and the environment. VS also promotes the eradication of war in all its forms. This group is not related to other organizations using this name, nor are other groups using this name related to this one. Founded in 1945. Contact Robert L. Zimmerman, Director.

Voluntary Census Committee (VCC)
PO Box 26044
Santa Ana, CA 92799   (714) 979-5737

VCC believes that the U.S. Census is an invasion of privacy and an act of coercion since the census must be answered or violators will be fined. The group's goal is to make the U.S. Census voluntary; therefore it encourages citizens to resist the involuntary nature of the census by mailing the questionnaires to the committee or by answering only nonpersonal questions. The group is active only during census years. Founded in 1979. Contact Lawrence Samuels, Executive Director.

Wabash, Frisco and Pacific Association (WF&P)
1569 Ville Angela Lane
Hazelwood, MO 63042-1630   (314) 291-3928

A group for individuals interested in the theory and practice of constructing, maintaining, and operating a ministeam tourist railway. Members participate in all phases of railroading: surveying and grading right-of-way, laying rail, designing and building cars, and maintaining and improving the steam locomotives. WF&P runs a 1.4 mile, 12 1/4-inch gauge miniature railroad along the Meramec River in Glencoe, MO. The system comprises regulation switches and sidings, a machine shop, ticket office, water tower and fuel tanks, a turntable at one end of this point-to-point line and a WYE at the other, an engine-house for locomotives, and a carbarn for equipment. The train runs on Sunday afternoon, 1:00-4:15 p.m. (May through October). The group publishes the quarterly *Whiffenpoof* and meets annually during January in St. Louis, MO. Founded in 1939. 80 members. Contact David J. Neubauer, Vice President.

Wages and Not Tips (WANT)
10044 Princeton Road
Cincinnati, OH 45246   (513) 772-8474

Members believe that tipping waiters is an antiquated ritual that should be abolished, and in its place promotes fair wages for waiters and other restaurant employees. WANT believes that the "restaurant lobby" has imposed the present tipping system, in which consumers leave a gratuity of 15-20% regardless of the quality of service they receive, to enable restaurants to pay their employees subminimum wages. The group encourages consumers to leave waiters, in lieu of tips, cards explaining why WANT members never leave tips. Founded in 1987. 4000 members. Contact Richard Busemeyer, President.

Walden Forever Wild (WFW)
PO Box 275
Concord, MA 01742 (203) 429-2839

WFW is an organization composed of enthusiasts and scholars of Walden Pond, a retreat used by author Henry David Thoreau (1817-62). Its objective is to persuade the Massachusetts state legislature to change Walden Pond Reservation from a recreational park to an educational, historical, and ecological sanctuary. Forever Wild encourages procurement of a professional forester/ecology manager for the reservation and contributes toward the operation of an educational museum and visitor center. The group maintains a repository for letters, newspaper articles, and speeches endorsing the transformation of Walden Pond into an official sanctuary and sponsors the Walden Guardians program for symbolic purchase of Walden parcels of land. Publications include the quarterly *The Voice of Walden* newsletter, the *Report of the Legal Documents Concerning Walden and Walden Abuse, Walden Loon,* and *Walden Facts.* It plans to publish *Voices for Walden,* a book of Walden history. WFW meets every year during September or October in Concord, MA. On the next to last Saturday in May, the group holds the annual Walden Pond Day in Concord. Founded in 1980. 300 members. Contact Mary P. Sherwood, Chairman.

Walking Association (WA)
655 Rancho Catalina Place
Tucson, AZ 85704 (602) 742-9589

We're walking, yes indeed. WA members have a penchant for strolling, desiring to promote walking rights and services. The group works toward the establishment of more walkways and walkway standards. WA provides motivational material to the public to encourage walking as a means of transportation and as a pleasant outdoor experience. The group coordinates small walking clubs with interested groups and participates in conferences and seminars with professional groups to promote and preserve the art of walking. Founded in 1976. Contact Robert B. Sleight Ph.D., Executive Director.

Walter Koenig International
PO Box 15546
North Hollywood, CA 91615-5546 (818) 985-8808

Fans of actor-writer Walter Koenig, best known for his role as Chekov in the original *Star Trek* television series and the subsequent *Star Trek* feature films. The club provides information on the activities and personal appearances of Koenig. It also sponsors charitable programs in support of Red Cloud Indian School. The results of its annual fiction contest are presented within *Innomina,* an annual journal. Founded in 1984. 140 members. Contact Carolyn Atkinson, Chairman.

Watchdogs of the Treasury (WOTT)
4005 Wisconsin Ave.
PO Box 39069
Washington, DC 20016   (301) 251-5879

A conglomeration of corporations, national, state, and local associations, and concerned individuals united to promote public recognition of the importance of fiscal responsibility and prudent government spending. WOTT publicly honors House and Senate members who vote for "meaningful economy in government" with the Golden Bulldog award. Details of Congressional activities are reported in the annual *Economy Voting Record*. Founded in 1981. 39 members. Contact C. Manly Molpus, CEO & President.

We Love Lucy/The International Lucille Ball Fan Club
PO Box 480216
Los Angeles, CA 90048

We Love Lucy is organized to pay tribute to the comedic talents of Lucille Ball (1911-89) and her classic television series, *I Love Lucy* (as well as other productions of Desilu Studios). We Love organizes social gatherings and maintains a biographical archive of files, research data, and photographs related to the Ball's career. The group sponsors an annual auction, with the proceeds donated to a children's charity. The club issues the quarterly newsletter *Lucy* and holds an annual conference. Founded in 1977. 1000 members. Contact Thomas J. Watson.

Welcome to Our Elvis World (WTOEW)
PO Box 501
Lutherville, MD 21093   (301) 296-2958

More fans seeking to perpetuate the memory of rock 'n' roll singer and entertainer Elvis Presley (1935-77). WTOEW issues a bimonthly newsletter and holds a monthly meeting as well as an annual conference. Founded in 1978. 150 members. Contact Ed Allan, President.

Werewolf Research Center (WRC)
Box 252
Elmhurst, NY 11373

Individuals interested in werewolves and other lycanthropic phenomena. WRC is conducting a demographic study of werewolves and interviews individuals who believe themselves to be werewolves. The Center publishes *True Tales of the Unknown* and *Hollywood and the Supernatural*. Members meet at the annual WolfCon. Founded in 1973. 30 members. Contact Dr. Stephen Kaplan, Executive Director.

Whimsical Alternative Political Action Committee (WAC-PAC)
1201 Connecticut Ave. NW, Suite 500
Washington, DC 20036   (202) 328-0199

WACPAC is a nonpartisan organization working to reintroduce humor into the battle for good government. It sponsors commentary on the crucial issues of the day through mailings, press releases, and media interviews. The Committee is currently researching the growing National Humor Deficit to determine why the United States owes more mirth to other countries. Appropriately, on April Fools' Day, WACPAC sponsors annual its Founders' Day event in Washington, DC. Founded in 1982. 823 members. Contact Michael Grant, Treasurer.

Whirly-Girls (International Women Helicopter Pilots)
PO Box 291070
San Antonio, TX 78229   (512) 690-3632

A group of women helicopter pilots working to stimulate interest among women in rotary-wing aircraft. Members serve as standby pilots for search and rescue work. The group awards two scholarships for helicopter flight training. Members receive the *Directory of Whirly-Girls Flight Schools* and a quarterly newsletter. The group sponsors an annual awards dinner. Founded in 1955. 637 members. Contact Sheryl Jones, Executive Director.

Whiskey Painters of America (WPA)
635 Franklin Ave.
Cuyahoga Falls, OH 44221   (216) 929-1765

Professional artists in the fields of commercial, industrial, or fine arts united to promote the fine art of painting in miniature. The group is also dedicated to creating good fellowship among "imbibing artists" in an effort to prove to "fellow bar habitues that bongo drums and free verse are not necessary adjuncts to good art" and "to add interest to an otherwise dull evening." The first artists to become known as "Whiskey Painters" carried little watercolor kits and composed small-sized art works simply to make spontaneous painting workable in cocktail lounges. Whiskey painters apply a lighthearted approach to art which, according to the group, "refreshes the creative spirit." Not to mention exercising the liver. The group maintains a museum of members' paintings and issues the *Handclasp Letter* reporting on activities of the WPA. Founded in 1961. 152 members. Contact L. J. Cross, President.

White House Historical Association (WHHA)
740 Jackson Place NW
Washington, DC 20503   (202) 737-8292

WHHA seeks to enhance appreciation, understanding, and enjoyment of the White House through a publication program, which includes the books, *The First Ladies, The Living White House, The President's House, The Presidents of the United States, White House Glassware: Two Centuries of Presidential Entertaining,* and *The White House: An Historic Guide.* It also makes available slides, prints, and postcards. Founded in 1961. Contact Bernard R. Meyer, Executive Vice President.

Wilderness Leadership International (WLI)
Box 770
North Fork, CA 93643   (209) 683-8295

WLI provides wilderness leadership training to school, church, and other groups. The group conducts research on wild, edible plants and sponsors classes on wild plant nutrition. Upon request, it identifies wild plants. The group maintains a 5000-volume library on wilderness survival and country living and offers correspondence courses on edible wild plants, wilderness survival, herbs for health, and natural remedies. Publications include the *Wild Plants to Eat Workbook* and other books. Once a year WLI conducts a wilderness survival seminar in the Sierra mountain region. Founded in 1974. Contact Jack S. Darnall, President.

Wilhelm Furtwangler Society of America (WFSA)
PO Box 620702
Woodside, CA 94062

Classical music enthusiasts united to promote the music and art of German conductor Wilhelm Furtwangler (1886-1954). The group issues a quarterly newsletter, which includes book reviews and information about newly released recordings as well as reports on association activities. Contact Charles Schlacks Jr., Editor.

William Shatner Connection (WSC)
7059 Atoll Ave.
North Hollywood, CA 91605   (818) 764-5499

Fans and admirers of actor William Shatner (1931-), best known for his portrayal of Capt. James T. Kirk in the original *Star Trek* television series and the six subsequent *Star Trek* feature films. WSC raises funds for charities supported by Shatner and promotes friendship among members. It issues the quarterly *WS Connection Newszine* and meets annually. Founded in 1991. 200 members. Contact Joyce Mason, President.

Windmill Study Unit (WSU)
17060 Jodave St.
Hazelcrest, IL 60429   (708) 335-0508

This study unit of the American Topical Association comprises collectors of philatelic material (that is, stamps) portraying various aspects of windmills and related subjects. The group's *Windmill Whispers* appears bimonthly. Founded in 1974. 155 members. Contact John J. Blocker.

Wine Appreciation Guild (WAG)
155 Connecticut St.
San Francisco, CA 94107   (415) 864-1202

The winery owners and distributors in WAG disseminate information on wine, with emphasis on American wines. The guild conducts wine evaluations and research programs on wine and health, cooking with wine, and consumer wine. WAG offers wine study courses and maintains a big library on wine and food. WAG's annual publications include the *American Wine Directory, Consumer's Guide to Jug Wine, Consumer's Guide to Varietal Wines,* and *Pocket Encyclopedia of California Wines.* The Guild also publishes the *Encyclopedia of American Wine,* the *Wine Cookbook* series, and *Benefits of Moderate Drinking.* Founded in 1974. 873 members. Contact Donna Bottrell, President.

Witches Anti-Discrimination Lobby (WADL)
Hero Press
153 W. 80th St., Suite 1B
New York, NY 10024   (212) 362-1231

They're mad as hell and not gonna take it anymore. Formerly called Witches International Craft Associates, the Lobby consists of persons who practice the religion of witchcraft as defined by the group's director. WADL seeks to educate the public about the religion of witchcraft, obtain paid legal holidays (such as Halloween) for members, and fight discrimination against witches. In 1970, WADL won a discrimination lawsuit against the New York Parks Department when it was refused a permit for its Witch-in. The Lobby also sponsors seminars, conducts research into historic goddess-worshipping cultures, and maintains a library of 20,000 volumes. WADL published the book *Witchcraft: The Old Religion,* and issues the *WICA Newsletter* ten times per year. Founded in 1970. 5000 members. Contact Dr. Leo Louis Martello, Director.

Women in the Wind (WW)
PO Box 8392
Toledo, OH 43605

Women in the Wind members are female motorcyclists and enthusiasts united to promote a positive image of women bikers. WW educates members on motorcycle safety and maintenance. The group's newsletter, *Shootin' the Breeze,* appears nine times during the year. Founded in 1979. 400 members. Contact Becky Brown, Secretary Treasurer.

Women on Wheels (WOW)
PO Box 5147
Topeka, KS 66605   (913) 267-3779

A group "For Today's Female Two-Wheeling Enthusiast." Similar to Women in the Wind (next organization, please), WOW unites women motorcyclists (or female motorcycle passengers) and seeks to gain recognition from the motorcycle industry concerning the needs of female consumers. While promoting motorcycle safety and good riding techniques, WOW works for public acceptance of motorcyclists. The women participate in motorcycle competitions, sponsor charity functions and courses with the Motorcycle Safety Foundation, and organize rallies, interchapter social affairs, and fashion activities. Their magazine, *Women on Wheels,* appears bimonthly and supplies members with stories about being on the road and news of association doings. Every year WOW holds an international "ride-in," a national rally with a bike show, seminars, exhibits, and the like. A year's membership is $25; toll-free number is 1-800-322-1969. Founded in 1982. 2000 members. Contact Patty Mills, National Director.

Wooden Canoe Heritage Association (WCHA)
Box 226
Blue Mountain Lake, NY 12812   (803) 648-7655

Wooden canoes and WCHA too. WCHA is dedicated to the preservation, restoration, study, construction, use, and appreciation of North American wooden and birchbark canoes. The individuals, museums, libraries, and boat and canoe builders in the group seek to stem the destruction of historic examples of wooden and bark canoes and to research and perpetuate the theories and craftsmanship that went into their construction. The association conducts demonstrations, lectures, and workshops, and it collects information about current and historic canoe builders and their craft. WCHA's magazine, *Wooden Canoe,* appears quarterly. Founded in 1979. 1300 members. Contact Phil Willsea, President.

Workshop Library on World Humour (WLWH)
PO Box 23334
Washington, DC 20026   (202) 484-4949

"It's high time that humor be recognized as a civilized force to be reckoned with." Members of the Workshop, who may or may not be funny in their own right, explore the use of humor in the arts, sciences, professions, and everyday life from the earliest societies to the present. Through the group, they aim to contribute to individual enrichment, stimulate creativity, and work toward attaining world peace. With those wacky Eastern Europeans, they have traditionally sponsored a Soviet/American Cultural Exchange of Humorists. Other uproarious activities include publishing a quarterly newsletter, *Humor Events and Possibilities,* an "occasional commentary on cultural turbulence as registered on the Humor Events & Possibilities (HEP) scale." The newsletter reviews books, prints letters, notes special events, and features brief pieces on the ridiculous state of humor in the 1990s. WLWH also hosts an annual International Conference on Humor. Annual membership is $20. Founded in 1975. Contact Barbara Cummings, Secretary Treasurer.

World ArmWrestling Federation (WAWF)
PO Box 132
Scranton, PA 18504   (717) 342-4984

The federation, formed to promote the sport of arm wrestling, includes national arm wrestling organizations from around the world. WAWF publishes *The Armbender* quarterly and hosts an annual world championship tournament. Founded in 1967. 50 members. Contact Bob O'Leary, Founder.

World Championship Cutter and Chariot Racing Association (WCC&CRA)
957 E. 12000 N.
Layton, UT 84041   (801) 771-4991

Shades of Ben Hur. The races promoted by WCC&CRA feature teams of horses harnessed to two-wheel cutters or chariots ridden by one person. Length of the race is 440 yards. The world association consists of local chariot and cutter racing groups, each of which must have 14 teams and run nine association meets to qualify its teams for the national organization. (Most of the local associations happen to be in the western United States.) The world association sponsors annual championship races during the last two weekends in March. *Cutter and Chariot World* appears monthly. Founded in 1964. 36 members. Contact Vick Adams.

World Day for Peace (WDFP)
3570 Williams Pond Lane
Loomis, CA 95650   (916) 624-3333

WDFP, which includes peace group members, teachers, engineers, scientists, and businesspersons, advocates nuclear disarmament through the organization and promotion of a worldwide one-day observance scheduled annually for the fourth Wednesday of October. This day has been designated as the "World Day for Peace," during which participants cease their usual activities to concentrate their efforts on achieving peace. Activities for that day include writing and calling national representatives, vigils, demonstrations, marches, and symposia on nuclear weapons issues. WDFP publishes *A Day for Peace* annually, as well as pamphlets, brochures, and posters. Founded in 1984. Contact Evan Jones, Coordinator.

World Government of the Age of Enlightenment—U.S. (WGAE-US)
5000 14th St. NW
Washington, DC 20011 (202) 723-9111

A nonreligious, nonpolitical—but nonetheless enlightened-organization dedicated to teaching Maharishi Technology of the United Field, which includes techniques for direct experience of the unified field, and Transcendental Meditation (TM) and TM Sidhi, which is based upon the knowledge of the unified field of all laws of nature, as seen through quantum physics and delineated in ancient Vedic science. (Vedic science, you'll recall, was introduced by the Maharishi Mahesh Yogi.) Working with the Maharishi International University in Fairfield, Iowa, and other universities and research institutes, WGAE conducts studies on the growth of natural law at all levels of life, in terms of improved mental performance, health, and behavior of the individual, and increased harmony and coherence in society. The group's semiannual World Peace Assembly takes place around Christmas and during the summer in Fairfield, Iowa, and its semiannual World Parliament of the Age of Enlightenment takes place in the spring and in the fall. Founded in 1965. Contact Thomas A. Headley, President.

World Organization for Modelship Building and Modelship Sport (NAVIGA)
Angererstrasse 8/11
A-1210 Vienna, Austria 1 308575

NAVIGA, which in another language stands for "World Organization for Modelship Building and Modelship Sport," consists of national leagues and federations interested in promoting the building of model ships. The group holds world championships in all classes and conducts courses and seminars on how to judge model ships (not being an instinctive act, judging a model ship must be learned). The group's committees include the Sail, Scale, Speed, and Static committees or as they are popularly known, the 4Ss. *Naviga-Information*, published in English, French, and German, appears quarterly. NAVIGA hold a biennial conference in Vienna. Founded in 1959. 25 members. Contact Hans Kukula, Secretary.

World Organization of China Painters (WOCP)
2641 NW 10th St.
Oklahoma City, OK 73107 (405) 521-1234

WOCP includes teachers, dealers, and other individuals involved or having an interest in porcelain china painting. The world organization sponsors china painting classes and hand-painted china exhibits, and publishes the bimonthly magazine *China Painter*. Founded in 1967. 8000 members. Contact Pauline Salyer, Founder.

World Pumpkin Confederation (WPC)
14050 Gowanda State Road
Collins, NY 14034 (716) 532-5995

The vegetable enthusiasts in this confederation avidly promote and maintain the sport/hobby of growing giant pumpkins, squash, and watermelons. Their leader, Ray Waterman, happens to hold the world record in the Long Gourd category with his 8-foot, 3-inch vegetable. The world pumpkin record, incidentally, stands at over 800 pounds, and the group expects some talented gardener to reach the coveted 1,000-pound mark by the year 2000.

WPC strives to facilitate grower credibility and respect and conducts contests-including the annual World Pumpkin Weigh-Off—that feature cash awards and prizes. WPC's quarterly *World Pumpkin Confederation Newsletter* contains the results of world-wide weigh-off competitions, inspiring photographs of gigantic squash and their proud growers, and association news and activities. Founded in 1983. 1500 members. Contact Ray Waterman, Founder & President.

World Science Fiction Society (WSFS)
Southern California Institute for Fan Interests
PO Box 8442
Van Nuys, CA 91409   (818) 366-3827

United to sustain interest in sci-fi are these professionals and amateurs involved in all aspects of science fiction, including books, magazines, movies, and radio-television. The society presents 12 Hugo Awards annually for achievements in different scifi categories such as Best Novel, Best Short Story, and Best Novella. The annual World Science Fiction Convention usually takes place Labor Day weekend. Founded in 1939. 10,000 members. Contact Carl G. Brandon, Executive Secretary.

World Timecapsule Fund (WTF)
3300 Louisiana Avenue S., Suite 415
Minneapolis, MN 55426   (612) 935-1206

WTF is conducting an international project based on the concept of a time capsule. It will be a "collection of literature, images, and sounds compiled by individuals (mostly students) around the world to portray a personal story about humanity" all stored on compact digital and video disks. According to president Chuck Smith, the project will be completed in 1999 and "appropriately commemorate the turning of the millennium." Several copies of the World Timecapsule will be made, with one copy to be buried and another launched into outer space, creating "a lasting tribute to humankind from the twentieth century, carried as a message in a bottle through space and time."

Smith plans to make copies of the discs available for study at museums and archives. "I think it's intriguing that a child who contributed to the project will be able, 20 or 30 years later as an adult, to look back and see what was important to him then." The World Timecapsule is primarily an educational project for elementary through high school students, permitting them to examine personal and social values in determining what should be preserved and why it is important for future generations. Originally designed to be free to schools through foundation and corporate support, the Fund (due to fundraising difficulties) is currently charging a modest $.50 fee per participating student. Teachers determine what goes into the Timecapsule from their classes. For an annual contribution of $5 to $50, more mature folks can become part of the World Timecapsule Fund and share a bit of immortality. Members have their name recorded in a special category in the actual time capsule.

More expensive membership categories enable the member to record a more extensive message. Members receive the quarterly newsletter *Timecapsule* to keep informed of the project's progress, and the group's annual convention always takes place on the first Sunday in October. Founded in 1986. Contact Charles S. Smith, President.

World Watusi Association (WWA)
Watusi Road
HC77, Box 66
Crawfor, ND 69339   (308) 665-1439

This "Watusi" refers to cattle, not the popular sixties dance. Members, who hail from three countries, include ranchers, enthusiasts of animal novelty breeds, members of the rodeo industry, investors, and cow or bull owners. WWA promotes the Watusi breed of cattle and disseminates information on their uses and value. The Watusi breed, they'll have you know, originated in Africa and is sometimes referred to as the African Longhorn because the cattle possess the largest and longest horns of any cattle in the world. The association conducts periodic cattle shows and sales and registers cattle pedigrees. *Watusi World* appears quarterly. Founded in 1985. 250 members. Contact Maureen Neidhardt, Executive Secretary.

Worldloppet (WL)
PO Box 911
Hayward, WI 54863   (715) 634-5025

Worldloppeteers are cross-country skiers trying desperately to complete a loppet, a series of 12 long-distance cross-country ski marathons held throughout Europe and North America. The races, featuring either the classic or freestyle techniques, total a distance of 632 kilometers and require 20,000 miles of air travel; mercifully, there is no time limit for race completion. The latest race added to the Worldloppet is the Kangaroo Hoppet, running through Australia's Alpine National Park in northeast Victoria. Other courses are located in Austria, Italy, Germany, Japan, Canada, Wisconsin, France, Finland, Sweden, Switzerland, and Norway (each member country is allowed one race). The group, which counts members from 25 countries, strives to give skiers a chance to compete against similar skiers, and to provide international class racers with an alternative to standard international competitions, especially after retirement from national team racing. Each year, WL crowns a Worldloppet champion and holds a general assembly to discuss regulations and problems confronting the sport of crosscountry skiing. Membership fee is $28 per year. Founded in 1979. 3450 members. Contact Linda Edgren, Coordinator.

World's Wrist-wrestling Championship (WWC)
423 E. Washington St.
Petaluma, CA 94952   (707) 778-0210

WWC conducts wrist-wrestling championships—for both men and women—in divisions ranging from bantamweight (under 130 pounds) to heavyweight (unlimited). The annual World's Championship Tournament is held on the second Saturday in October in Petaluma, California, and the annual National Championship Tournament occurs during April or May. Contact Bill Soberanes, Executive Director.

Xerces Society (XS)
10 SW Ash St.
Portland, OR 97204   (503) 222-2788

Named for an extinct San Francisco butterfly (the Xerces Blue), the Society is devoted to the preservation of invertebrates and sponsors an annual international butterfly count on July 4. Members include scientists working in conservation-related fields as well as interested individuals. Xerces identifies and seeks to protect critical invertebrate habitats and their endangered ecosystems. It sponsors the Monarch Project, which protects Monarch butterfly habitats in California. The Society publishes *ATALA: The Journal of Invertebrate Conservation* and the annual *Fourth of July Butterfly Count,* which contains information on migratory habits of butterflies and the discovery of new butterfly species. It also publishes the books, *Butterfly Gardening: Creating Summer Magic In Your Garden* and *The Common Names of North American Butterflies.* Founded in 1975. 1930 members. Contact Melody Allen, Executive Director.

Yarns of Yesteryear Project (YYP)
University of Wisconsin-Madison
Continuing Education in the Arts Department
610 Langdon St., Room 727
Madison, WI 53706   (608) 263-3494

"Are you old enough to remember when you played marbles as a boy with your "lucky shooter" or when dating meant a soda at the drug store fountain? Or when your father shaped horseshoes on a red-hot forge or your mother combed her long hair by kerosene light?" Then take note: YYP is organized for older individuals who wish to write their memoirs. By encouraging older people to take up the leisurely activity of writing about their lives, the group seeks to make a cultural contribution to society. YYP offers writing assistance, including manuscript critiques, workshops, and a home study course in reminiscence writing. Based in Wisconsin, YYP sponsors contests for residents age sixty and up of that state. Founded in 1974. Contact Kathy Berigan, Director.

Zane Grey's West Society (ZGWS)
708 Warwick Ave.
Ft. Wayne, IN 46825   (219) 484-2904

Society members are people interested in American author Zane Grey (1872-1939), who is best known for his adventure stories of the American West. ZGWS publishes the *Zane Grey Reporter* quarterly, the *Zane Grey Review* bimonthly, and *Zane Grey's West* annually. Founded in 1983. 300 members. Contact Carolyn Timmerman, Secretary Treasurer.

Zeppelin Collectors Club (ZCC)
100 E. Chicago St., Suite D
PO Box 1239
Elgin, IL 60121   (312) 742-3328

No, they're not storing full-size zeppelins in the garage. And the group is not in interested in Led Zeppelin, but instead in the history of airships and collectors of airship philatelic (stamp) material and memorabilia. The group serves as a forum for the exchange of information concerning exhibits, special events, awards, and published materials. *The Zeppelin Collector*, published quarterly, is available as a newsletter insert with the *Journal of the Aerophilatelic Federation of the Americas, Jack Knight Air Log,* and *AFA News.* ZCC holds a periodic congress and a quadrennial meeting. Founded in 1968. 300 members. Contact Cheryl Ganz, Editor.

Zimmerman Registry (ZR)
2081 Madelaine Ct.
Los Altos, CA 94024   (415) 967-2908

The Zimmerman Registry seeks, restores, and preserves Zimmerman automobiles (which automobiles? Exactly; hence, the organization), which were produced in Auburn, Indiana, from 1907 to 1915. Founded in 1990. Contact C.A. Zimmerman, Founder.

Zinfandel Club (ZC)
Lamb Building
Temple
London EC4Y 7AS, England   71 3530774

The Zinfandel Club includes wine merchants, authors, and others interested in California wines—rather open-minded for a group based in England. ZC sponsors dinners and wine tastings to promote interest in California wines. Founded in 1976. 211 members. Contact Spenser Hilliard, Hon. Secretary.